D0075675

# ACCIÓN DEMOCRÁTICA

# ACCIÓN DEMOCRÁTICA

## Evolution
## of a Modern Political Party
## in Venezuela

BY JOHN D. MARTZ

PRINCETON UNIVERSITY PRESS
PRINCETON, NEW JERSEY
1966

Copyright © 1966 by Princeton University Press

ALL RIGHTS RESERVED

L.C. Card No. 65-17147

WIDENER UNIVERSITY
WOLFGRAM
LIBRARY
CHESTER PA

DISCARDED

JL
3898
.A25
M3

Printed in the United States of America

by Princeton University Press, Princeton, New Jersey

# Acknowledgments

Only those who have undertaken the writing of an essentially academic work can be fully aware of the importance of outside contributions, both implicit and otherwise. Indeed, many influences may have shaped the author's thinking without his being aware of it. In a study such as the following, personal debts are particularly great, for much of the indispensable material exists only in the memories of those who have experienced certain events. Interviewing can be conducted only with the sufferance and cooperation of those approached by the interviewer; I have been exceedingly fortunate in the cooperation and courtesy of the many figures with whom I spoke.

It is not possible to give a full listing of the many Venezuelans who assisted me in one form or another. Many of those who were directly helpful have been acknowledged in text and footnotes. In other cases, the nature of the information I was given was such as to make footnoting inappropriate. In a few cases I was requested not to reveal my source. I have willingly complied with such stipulations.

The majority of the interviews recognized in such annotations have been with present or former members of the political party Acción Democrática. However, I have also questioned or spoken with leaders of the other major parties, including the two groups that splintered away from Acción Democrática. These comments have been taken into account and weighed in the evaluations contained by this study, although they have not been specifically cited unless there was a matter of information that came directly from that source. It would be possible to list several score of political figures who were helpful to me. It seems most feasible to mention here those who were most generous with their time, their ideas, and assistance.

Foremost is Mercedes Fermín, member of the Chamber of Deputies for Acción Democrática, an educator and feminist who has been a close political confidante of Rómulo Betancourt for many years. Her interest and assistance in my project were constant and unflagging, notwithstanding occasional differences of opinion over political events of the moment. If the aid of any one Venezuelan was indispensable, it was that of Fermín. Mention must also be made of Dr. Luis B. Prieto, who at this writing has become the acting President of Acción Democrática. The present President of the Republic, Raúl Leoni, was helpful on several occasions while serving as AD President.

Among the younger party leaders, AD Representative Octavio Lepage has shown me particular kindness both during trips to Venezuela and at other times. Both of Betancourt's Secretaries to the Presidency have been highly cooperative—first Ramón J. Velásquez and, later, Mariano Picón-Salas. They have been responsible for the publication of a continuing series of valuable political and historical works, copies of which they have kindly provided. Let me also add my thanks to newspaper columnist Guillermo Feo Calcaño, who has shared his views on Venezuelan politics with me at considerable length.

A different form of indebtedness has been incurred through the award of a study grant from the Ford Foundation's Foreign Area Fellowship Program, through which I visited Venezuela in 1962 and 1963. My return to that country in 1964 to collect electoral data and re-interview political leaders was made possible through the complementary assistance of a University Research Council Grant from the University of North Carolina, and also the Institute for the Comparative Study of Political Systems, which subsequently published my monograph on the 1963 Venezuelan elections.

None of the above, of course, is in any way responsible

for the following comments, analyses, or interpretations. I neither can nor do I wish to hold responsible those who contributed both in intellectual and material ways to the over-all project. Among those to be singled out for continual willingness to assist in the project have been Dorothy Soderlund and Maurice Harari of the Foreign Area Fellowship Program; George J. Demetriou of the Institute for the Comparative Study of Political Systems, and several colleagues at the University of North Carolina in Chapel Hill. My particular gratitude goes to these latter men.

Federico G. Gil has provided constant encouragement, willingly giving advice whenever it seemed appropriate. Much the same is true of Harold A. Bierck, whose long study of the Bolivarian states lent insight into a variety of problems. My thanks also go to Frederic N. Cleaveland, Chairman of the Department of Political Science at the University of North Carolina, who made arrangements in my academic duties that permitted my trips to Venezuela at times most convenient for the completion of research.

The greatest credit of all must go to my wife, herself a political scientist, who lent her academic talents at every phase of the preparation of this study. Her patience with the occasional vagaries of Venezuelan life was also a prerequisite to the collection and presentation of necessary information.

Apologies are tendered to the many others who have not been enumerated here. These include political rivals of Acción Democrática who would doubtless disagree with many of my observations. But then, *adecos* are also in disagreement with many of the views presented herein. It can only be added that my findings would have been impossible without the aid of a great many people, but the final evaluation and assessment is necessarily my own.

JOHN D. MARTZ

*Chapel Hill, N.C.*

# Contents

# Figures and Tables

## TEXT

## APPENDICES

# ACCIÓN DEMOCRÁTICA

# Introduction

The rapid increase of popular participation in Latin American political processes has been reflected in the growing importance of the parties.[1] One leading Latin Americanist would "commend the field of Latin American political parties to a whole generation of prospective graduate students in political science."[2] Yet there have been relatively few serious efforts to follow this advice.[3] As another acute student of the area has observed, "Latin American political parties are outstanding in that very little research has been done on them.[4] Thus, the few existing studies have tended to reflect disciplinary deficiencies by emphasizing the legalistic and historical aspects of the situation rather than analyzing the dynamics and inner processes.

[1] The author has developed more fully his views in "Dilemmas in the Study of Latin American Political Parties," *Journal of Politics*, XXVI, no. 3, August 1964.

[2] Russell H. Fitzgibbon, "The Party Potpourri in Latin America," *The Western Political Quarterly*, X, no. 1, March 1957, p. 22.

[3] A very small handful of works has dealt intensively with the parties. Of particular interest are Frank R. Brandenburg, *Partidos Políticos* (México: Problemas Agrícolas e Industriales de México, 1957); Federico G. Gil, *Genesis and Modernization of Political Parties in Chile* (Gainesville: University of Florida Press, 1962); Harry Kantor, *The Ideology and Program of the Peruvian Aprista Movement* (Berkeley: University of California Press, 1953); L. Vincent Padgett, "Mexico's One-Party System: Re-evaluation," *The American Political Science Review*, LI, no. 4, December 1957.

Among the more general discussions are those of Brandenburg, "Political Parties and Elections," in Harold E. Davis (ed.), *Government and Politics in Latin America* (New York: The Ronald Press Company, 1958); Asher N. Christensen, "The General Nature of Political Parties in Latin America," in Christensen (ed.), *The Evolution of Latin American Government* (New York: Henry Holt and Company, 1951), Chapter 12, no. 35; Fitzgibbon, *op.cit.*; and Gil, "Responsible Parties in Latin America," *Journal of Politics*, XV, no. 3, August 1953.

[4] George I. Blanksten, "The Politics of Latin America," in Gabriel A. Almond and James S. Coleman (eds.), *The Politics of the Developing Areas* (Princeton: Princeton University Press, 1960), p. 479.

In some cases the traditional approach to this study has been unavoidable. The personalistic, particularistic nature of Latin American parties historically has tended to render the study of parties difficult for scholarly analysis and precise, meaningful evaluation. In but a few instances has it been possible to examine a party that truly qualified as such in the accepted context of a Western democratic political *milieu*. This condition is currently beginning to change, with the gradual emergence of formally structured national parties having identifiable doctrine and ideology derived from a history of evolution and development.

Before proceeding, it will be useful to set down the general areas to which attention should be given in collecting and evaluating the information concerning a political party. At the outset a study of a party should consider the given polity within which the party operates. The number of national parties and the degree of competition characteristic of the system must be indicated. The first of these two tasks is relatively direct and straightforward, so long as a clear definition of parties is consistently used.[5] As to the matter of competition, such terms as "one-party," "one-party dominant," "two-party," and "multi-party" can be employed. It is probable that such labeling is but a minor means of gaining insight into the parties, but the descriptive value of such facts goes into the broader fabric of the entire party system.

Beyond considerations of a party and its place in the specific polity, one encounters the complementary elements of ideology and organization. As to ideology and program, terminological caution is the byword, for an "ideological" party in one sense would be marxist, communist, or perhaps fascist. More broadly, however, "ideological" implies a formal program or platform. In this

---

[5] The task of defining "party" will be taken up below.

study "programmatic" will be the more common usage; "ideological" will indicate a strong doctrinal current— which, in the Venezuelan context, is essentially marxist. So stated, it becomes the programmatic aspect of party analysis that the late Sigmund Neumann discussed: "Added depth to party analysis may be derived from another approach which has gained momentum in recent years: the study of ideological forces. . . . In order to make the study of ideologies useful for political analysis, we must move beyond doctrinal or formal party program analysis into the area of party behavior. . . . Ideologies are the key to an understanding of the long-range strategy behind the day-to-day tactics of political movements."[6]

The classification of parties through programmatic criteria is feasible and tends to imply some form of a left-right spectrum. An alternative procedure would group the parties as ideological (marxist, etc.), pragmatic, and personalistic;[7] additional possibilities exist. Whether the exercise is justifiable cannot be positively determined until it is undertaken. There is bound to be some distortion if parties are judged purely in terms of program and doctrine, however. In the long run, relevant aspects of organizational as well as programmatic party life must be examined before a sophisticated party typology can increase our knowledge and understanding on the subject.

Interest therefore turns specifically to what might be termed intraparty structure. Thus narrow analysis can be carried out along organizational lines. One must guard, however, against a fascination with the dissection and ordering of organizational data that places exclusive emphasis on formal party organs. Among the specific questions to be explored are such facets of structure as leadership composition and mobility, interest

[6] Sigmund Neumann, "Toward a Theory of Political Parties," *World Politics*, VI, no. 3, July 1954, pp. 554-55.

[7] Almond and Coleman, *op.cit.*, pp. 43-44.

representation, membership recruitment and participation, internal hierarchy, and discipline. These all have some relevance, and one of the problems is that of arranging such data so that a logical sequence and pertinent interrelationships are shown. Obvious but nonetheless practical groupings would be leadership, membership, organization, and articulation.

An examination of both leadership and of membership touches upon composition, class background, and mobility. Leadership as a unit should be analyzed in terms of its mobility and flexibility as well as the representation of relevant sectors of the given society. Unity and disunity also deserve attention. The membership—difficult to grapple with in Latin America—can, at the least, be studied in terms of discipline and internal order. From this it is but a short step to organization itself. The over-all structure, the chain of command and flow of party directives, internal communication, relative degree of centralization, and the operations of basic organizational units must all be scrutinized.

A fourth major area is somewhat blurred but cannot be overlooked: articulation. This embraces party activity in political education, the range of interests effectively represented, and the breadth of popular participation. Political education is becoming an increasingly vital function for parties and interest groups in the emergent nations. A party's articulation of various interests and demands is an important aspect of the political process in such countries, and the degree to which ordinary citizens may be brought into the mainstream of national life, leading to the creation of a national consensus, is particularly crucial.

In brief, then, a party can be examined in terms of the over-all nature of the system in its given polity; beyond this lie questions relating to ideology and to organization. While relatively little attention has been devoted to such matters in the study of Latin American politics, there has been somewhat greater interest in the attempted cataloguing of parties. This task of analytical classification finds students attempting to place all the parties under a set of labels. Robert J. Alexander has employed ten individual rubrics to classify parties: personalist, Conservative, Liberal, Radical, Christian Democrat, Socialist, National Revolutionary, Jacobin Left, Communist, and Fascist.[8] Certainly the programmatic—if not necessarily the ideological—nature of the parties lends itself to some sort of cataloguing. Beyond its relative convenience, however, such an ordering has severe limitations. Students familiar with the subject will learn little that is new, while the layman may be unduly confused.

The apparent contradictions in nomenclature are myriad. In Brazil, Alexander points out, the Social Democratic Party (PSD) is Conservative, the National Democratic Union (UDN) is Liberal, while the Brazilian Socialist Party (PSB) is Socialist and the fragmented Brazilian Workers Party (PTS) belongs to the Jacobin Left. In Uruguay the Blancos (National Party) are Conservatives and the Colorados are Liberal, while in neighboring Paraguay the Colorados are regarded as Conservative. And a nascent party system such as Guatemala's, while in state of rapid flux, offers such titles as the National Democratic Movement (MDN), which is personalist; the Revolutionary Party (PR), which is National Revolutionary; the Authentic Revolutionary Party (PRA), of the Jacobin Left; and the Guatemalan Labor Party (PTG), which is Communist.

The plethora of names and multiple labels is inherently confusing. There is, furthermore, a degree of mobility that makes such typologies somewhat temporary. This is inevitable, especially where party systems are evolving and passing through endless permutations. Without for

[8] Robert J. Alexander, *Today's Latin America* (Garden City: Doubleday and Company, 1962), pp. 147-63.

a moment denying that such classification has some intrinsic value, it must be said that it does not lead the experienced researcher much further. Logic suggests the possibility of grouping these ten categories under a few broad headings that would permit worthwhile generalization.

This kind of classification, importantly, is based upon judgments of an ideological or programmatic nature, with the distinctions often slight. The inclination here is to employ a broader kind of analysis in which programmatic orientation is but one of several different criteria. Furthermore, it is argued that, within a sufficiently general definition, all parties in Latin America can be regarded as either "modern" or "traditional," for want of better terms. Before considering the criteria on which parties might be termed modern or traditional, however, a word regarding definition seems proper.

For those who turn to the literature of stasiology,[9] the diet is largely one of European- or North American-oriented research that yields minimal nourishment. A definition of political parties characteristic of present scholars is that of Neumann, who viewed a party as "the articulate organization of society's active political agents, those who are concerned with the control of governmental power and who compete for popular support with another group or groups holding divergent views.[10] While students of Latin American parties may find little to quibble with in this definition, it sheds too little light on the organizations. And such is the neglect of the Latin American region that the French authority on parties and elections, Maurice Duverger, explicitly excludes reference to Latin America in his book on the grounds that "the frequent and effective interference of the govern-

[9] Duverger provided this term for the science of political parties through use of the Greek *stasis*, meaning faction.
[10] Sigmund Neumann (ed.) *Modern Political Parties; Approaches to Comparative Politics* (Chicago: University of Chicago Press, 1956), p. 396.

ment in both polls and parties denatures the whole system."[11]

In a precise and narrow definition, such as that of Neumann, many of the political fragments of the Latin American political systems would be omitted, consigned to the level of a special interest. For what are sometimes termed parties by Latin Americans would be viewed as factions, pressure groups, or fraternal organizations by North American political scientists. To deal effectively with all such groupings in Latin American politics, therefore, a broad and inclusive definition is necessary. In this context, the following statement has been adopted: a Latin American party is a group of politically motivated individuals who have banded together for the purpose of increasing their influence and effectiveness through electoral means within a given political system.

It is not argued that this definition is necessarily useful in a non-Latin American setting, but its inclusiveness strongly recommends it to those working in the area. To go a step further, those groups qualifying in the preceding definitional terms as parties can themselves be broken down into one of two types: the "modern" and the "traditional" party. Since they coexist in the great majority of Latin American party systems, it is important to make clear the criteria which differentiate them.

The "modern" party in Latin America—which in many particulars parallels what is regarded elsewhere as a true party—has certain major characteristics. Thus the modern party is meant to indicate a group of politically oriented individuals possessing an identifiable common ideology, permanent national organization, popular appeal on a national basis, an existence of at least a decade's duration, and an inner justification based on participation in national policy-making or at least a reasonable prospect

[11] Maurice Duverger, *Political Parties; Their Organization and Activity in the Modern State*, trans. Barbara and Robert North (New York: John Wiley & Sons, Inc., 1963), p. 220.

of capturing power in the foreseeable future. Certainly a
perceivable ideological position and a functioning piece
of political machinery are indispensable, and it is further
maintained that a modern party cannot contribute satisfactorily to a nation's political education and participation unless its appeal is demonstrably national.

Traditional parties may share certain of the above
traits, but not all of them. A party with only regional appeal cannot be termed modern even if its program is
identifiable, its structural organization is national, and
it has existed for over ten years. Or, a party with program, national appeal, a share of political power, and a
decade's existence may nonetheless be personalistic, and
therefore traditional. For a party is not regarded as having a permanent national organization if it is individually
led and cannot survive the removal of the single leader
from its ranks. A splinter or fragment of another, larger
party will have neither the duration nor the permanence
of organization required of a modern party, although it
may indeed have a clear programmatic orientation.

Having said the above, it is appropriate to note that
a number of parties meeting the criteria for modernity
have begun to emerge within the last generation, organizations that along with other traits have proven to be
more than transitory. These have appeared in countries
where the process of modernization has included strong
doses of modern capitalism and technology, reflected by
the creation of an industrial proletariat and an incipient
middle class. The need has arisen—as in Venezuela—for
a modern political party, dedicated to the broad objectives of political education, to a search for a genuine
popular feeling of nationality and identification with
objectives on which a consensus might be formed. The
first party to fill this role in Venezuela was Acción Democrática.

Acción Democrática as well as several similar parties
in Latin America have become known commonly as

*aprista* organizations, a term which derives from the apparent prototype of all such organizations, the Alianza Popular Revolucionaria Americana (APRA) of Peru. Such parties have variously been termed "modern,"[12] "social democratic,"[13] and "indigenous nationalistic,"[14] to mention a few. They have shared the over-all objective of directing the energies of their people toward emergence from the traditional social, economic, and political customs. At least two broad distinguishing characteristics have been attributed to them. First, they have sought sweeping social and economic change, with attention centered on land reform and the integration of the lower classes into the political process. Second, they have represented a movement indigenous to the area; international connections are few, and these are entirely within Latin America.[15]

In the concluding chapter of this book, it will be contended that what are often called *aprista* parties in Latin America—including the AD of Venezuela—are more appropriately termed "national revolutionary." For the present, it must be added that both *aprista* or the preferred "national revolutionary" apply primarily to ideological or programmatic doctrine. Thus, a national revolutionary party is a modern party, but is also a *particular kind* of modern party. Those with different programmatic bases might be modern and yet, say, christian democratic or even communist.

Thus it will be argued that the programmatic designa-

---

[12] William Whatley Pierson and Federico Guillermo Gil, *Governments of Latin America* (New York: McGraw-Hill Book Company, Inc., 1957), pp. 318-20.

[13] Kalman H. Silvert, *The Conflict Society: Reaction and Revolution in Latin America* (New Orleans: Hauser, 1961), pp. 256-57.

[14] Asher N. Christensen, "The General Nature of Political Parties in Latin America," in Christensen (ed.), *The Evolution of Latin American Government* (New York: Henry Holt, 1951), p. 508.

[15] Blanksten, from Almond and Coleman, *op.cit.*, pp. 485-86.

tion for Acción Democrática is "national revolutionary."
Beyond this, it will be argued that, in fulfilling the other
standards set forth, the AD is equally a modern party.
In the pages to follow, efforts will be made to cast light
on the criteria already posited. Following a relatively
brief chronological narrative which traces the outlines of
the party's evolution, two parts will deal in the first
instance with organization and structure, with leadership
and membership, and with program and doctrine and in
the second with the party's relationships with such elements of Venezuelan politics as organized labor, non-
partisan groups, the military, and rival parties, ending
with a detailed look at the events and the significance
of national elections in 1958 and 1963.

The concluding chapter will summarize and discuss the
elements of a "modern" Latin American party as defined
above. Brief attention will also be given to the nature of
the Venezuelan polity in recent years and the kind of
inter-party relationships characteristic of the system.
It is hoped that additional studies along the general lines
of the present research may shed further light on the
state of knowledge and disciplinary investigation of Latin
American parties. Only a substantial number of careful
party studies can render possible the kind of hypothesiza-
tion or conceptualization that has tentatively been prof-
fered here.

What follows is an examination in some depth of a
particular political party—one of the great parties in
contemporary Latin America. It is not a comparative
study, notwithstanding the low-level generalizations employed in the simple task of classification. Let it be repeated that this kind of classification is by no means a
guarantee of flashes of new insight; however, it is one
more of the relatively small steps which will lead in time
to the necessary refinement of disciplinary tools and the
sharpening of concepts. There is also a conviction that the
present primitive condition of our knowledge of Latin

American parties makes it difficult to hypothesize about the relationships between such areas of interest as leadership and unity, membership and disciplinary sanctions.

To summarize, it must be repeated that fully developed, carefully refined hypotheses cannot yet be presented. It is suggested only that certain basic kinds of classification are possible; moreover, the areas already outlined will, when filled with accurate information, make it possible to continue the search for a theory of Latin American political parties at a higher level. The very process whereby the AD eventually acquired status as a modern party is not without significance; and brief attention will be given to the success or failure of rival parties which, later than the AD, also attempted to achieve political modernity. Although conclusions will necessarily be tentative and preliminary, they will hopefully have some value *beyond* the mere description of a political party. Without for a moment denying the problem of comparability from one Latin American political system to another, it is far too early to give up hopes that by learning about a given political institution or dynamic process in one country, we learn a little more about similar forces and processes elsewhere in the region.

# PART ONE

# The Party: A Descriptive History

# CHAPTER I

# Antecedents of a Party System

## 1928-1941

Following the broad pattern of the nineteenth century, Venezuelan government in the early 1900's continued to serve as the personal preserve of *caudillista* domination. A significant shift in regional emphasis had been registered in 1899, when Cipriano Castro descended from the Andean southwest and marched to Caracas and the presidency. Less than a decade later, afflicted with collapsing health induced by extreme moral dissolution and victimized by the shrewdly calculating ambitions of his principal lieutenant, Castro left Venezuela. His purported health cure in Europe lasted until his death there sixteen years later, while Venezuela was ruled by his former revolutionary colleague from mountainous Táchira, Juan Vicente Gómez.

A cunning *mestizo* who spent his first forty years within a few miles of his birthplace, the seemingly indestructible Gómez lived a story of political durability and acumen that has been recorded at length elsewhere.[1] Substituting for Castro's "Revolución Restauradora" the equally meaningless "Rehabilitación Nacional," Gómez combined his political insight with new economic resources accruing from the driving expansion of the national petroleum industry. Retaining power for twenty-seven years, the tyrant's career ended with his peaceful death in bed as a septuagenarian in December 1935.

The land over which Gómez ruled, lying on the northern coast of South America, embraces 352,142 square

---

[1] Cf. Thomas Rourke, *Gómez; Tyrant of the Andes* (Garden City: Halcyon House, 1936); John Lavin, *A Halo for Gómez* (New York: Pageant Press, Inc., 1954); Laureano Vallenilla Lanz, *Cesarismo Democrático* (Caracas: Imprenta Garrido, 3d ed., 1952).

miles that make it Latin America's seventh largest country. The name was derived from "Little Venice," as early explorers of the Lake Maracaibo region called it. Bounded by Colombia, Brazil, and British Guiana, it is divided by geographers into four basic regions. The nation's backbone includes the Andean highlands and adjacent coastal areas, running from San Cristóbal in the southwest toward the coast. The Andes divide, with the spur to the right turning east and continuing parallel to the Caribbean. The other branch, the Sierra de Perijá, continues north.

The coastal highlands contain Caracas, the capital, as well as the population centers of Valencia, Barquisimeto, and Maracay. Major ports are La Guaira and Puerto Cabello. The Andean chain to the southwest is distinguished by higher altitudes, somewhat differing agricultural pursuits, and a dissimilar ethnic composition of the people. The Sierra Nevada de Mérida has numerous peaks rising above 15,000 feet. Trujillo, Mérida, and San Cristóbal are major cities.

Toward the country's northwest lies the Maracaibo Basin with its series of hot lowlands where the nation's major source of petroleum is located. The two remaining geographic regions are of lesser importance. The *llanos* and the Guayana highlands contain nearly three-fourths of the national territory but no more than 10 percent of the people. The *llanos* are sloping plains and valleys extending from the Andes toward the Orinoco River; the region is partially flooded from April to October and stands parched and dry the remaining months. The highlands of Guayana, lying to the south of the Orinoco and extending to the Brazilian border, are geologically older than the Andes, with elevations rising no higher than some 9,000 feet.

Venezuela is currently in the midst of a population explosion that is estimated at no less than a 3.7 percent increase annually. After numbering 2.4 million in 1900 and only 3.8 million in 1941, the population has grown so that in the early 1960's, the total has passed the 8 million mark. Rising birth rates, improved health and living conditions, declining mortality figures, and new immigration have all contributed to the increase. Population density is regarded as low by hemispheric standards. Presently some 80 percent is found in the northwestern quarter of the country, running from the Andes across the Maracaibo Basin and east to the thickly settled central highlands.

Tremendous urbanization also characterizes contemporary Venezuela. At the time of Gómez's death, twothirds of the population was rural. Yet today the situation is nearly reversed. The recent mission from the International Bank for Reconstruction and Development estimated that, in 1959, some 70 percent of the population lived in localities with 2,500 inhabitants or more.[2] Internal migration, moreover, is not merely a farm-to-city shift, but is essentially a change from regions of minimal economic activity to those of greater prosperity. Many have been drawn from the Andean states to the several centers of petroleum and industrial production. When General Gómez died, 11 percent of the population lived outside its native state; by 1950, the figure had exactly doubled.[3] The trend remained strong as Venezuela moved into the decade of the 1960's.

The nation has stood out from its neighbors, among other reasons, by dint of its natural resources and wealth. The petroleum era dawned in the 1920's, while vast iron ore deposits were found later and have developed significantly in the years since World War II. Income from the two—primarily the former—has contributed to

[2] Mission of the International Bank for Reconstruction and Development, *The Economic Development of Venezuela* (Baltimore: The Johns Hopkins Press, 1961), p. 4.

[3] Arturo Uslar Pietri, *Sumario de Economía Venezolana* (Caracas: Editorial Arte, 2d ed., 1961).

the highest per capita income in Latin America, now in the neighborhood of $600-$650. Yet few Venezuelans have earned their living directly from the petroleum industry, and at least half the population lives close to subsistence levels. Not without reason is the nation regarded, paradoxically, as a highly prosperous "underdeveloped" country.[4]

The enormous petroleum income has not only provided a dynamic impulse to the economy but has contributed to a sorely unbalanced occupational and economic condition. Spots of prosperity have developed while the nation has shifted from an agricultural to an industrial, urbanized economy. Domestic industry is still in its formative stage, but moves forward steadily. The agricultural sector still lags far behind. Over 20 percent of the population labors in the fields, although contributing no more than 3 to 4 percent of the national product. Low productivity and low per capita income remain the usual standard in the countryside.

Problems of the *latifundia* and the large landowner were ignored until recent years, and one of the characteristic elements in Venezuelan agriculture is still the *conuquero*, a migrant peasant who tills the land of another, repaying the owner either by rent, part of the crop, or his own labor. Once the soil is depleted, he and his family move. Under the Gómez tyranny and after it, the Venezuelan economy and society has reflected basic ills. The landed aristocracy continues efforts to direct the lives of landless rural peasants; in urban areas, the wealthy oligarchy maintains its position although a salaried middle class is gradually beginning to take hold. The 1950 census of the government claimed some 15 percent of the economic population as belonging to this nascent group.[5]

The various forms of social, economic, and political

---

[4] Mission of the IBRD, *op.cit.*, p. 3.

[5] Venezuela, Ministerio de Fomento, *Octavo Censo General de Población* (Caracas: Imprenta Nacional, 1957), p. 48.

*malaise* have led to an inevitable reaction in the form of a dedicated drive for basic reform. The conviction has grown that progress can and must be achieved across a broad spectrum of problems and issues. The continuing effort has drawn attention from like-minded Latin Americans elsewhere, for the natural endowments of Venezuela provide a potential for reform that in many ways is unequalled elsewhere in the hemisphere. Among the earliest evidence of a movement to better conditions was a series of protests against Juan Vicente Gómez. Given the tyranny of his regime, initial demonstrations necessarily followed political lines.

## The Generation of '28

During the long *gomecista* era, political activity was held to a minimum. Legal opposition was impossible, and open displays of dissatisfaction met with sharp physical repression. Although the Partido Comunista de Venezuela was founded in 1931—thus asserting its claim as the country's first real party—its activities were clandestine and limited.[6] Full party activity and the creation of a democratic opposition awaited the death of Gómez. Among the leaders of 1936 and 1937 were a small band of young men who had already ventured into political life some years earlier. These—members of the Generation of '28—in a very real fashion made possible the coming of a party system through disorganized, ineffectual, yet politically significant outbursts against dictatorship.[7]

The *gomecista* era was not devoid of open opposition,

[6] For the party's clandestine organizational manifesto, see Venezuela, Presidencia de la República, *Documentos que Hicieron Historia; Siglo y Medio de Vida Republicana, 1810-1961* (Caracas: Ediciones Conmemorativas del Sesquicentenario de la Independencia, Vol. II, 1962), pp. 166-76.

[7] For a more detailed narrative, see Martz, "Venezuela's 'Generation of '28,'" *Journal of Inter-American Studies*, VI, no. 1, January 1964, pp. 17-33.

and university students were in the forefront. As early as 1912 Caracas students cried out their defiance publicly, and the Universidad Central was closed from 1912-1923. The reopening of university gates failed to stem student opposition, and soon "cultural meetings" were organized at which national politics were debated. Although the passing of years has dulled somewhat the memories of surviving participants, they agree that discussions, while imbued with an idealism verging on youthful romanticism, at the same time often revolved about concrete problems of national development.[8] Among the participants were many who later became prominent in the struggle for freedom and democracy: Jóvito Villalba, Rómulo Betancourt, Raúl Leoni, Gonzalo Carnevali, and Joaquín Gabaldón Márquez.

The Federación de Estudiantes de Venezuela (FEV) had reorganized in 1927 after two previous dissolutions. It was tolerated by a confident Gómez, who boasted that revolutionary opposition had become an anachronism under his rule. On January 26, 1928, FEV president Raúl Leoni announced the scheduling of a students' week. From February 6-12, the "Semana del Estudiante" was to be celebrated by social events, the crowning of a queen, and cultural discussions. Student plans, however, included activities that were far from the presumed innocence of juvenile festivities. Leoni had delegated major roles to a pair of second-year law students named Villalba and Betancourt; the former was to speak at the National Pantheon, the latter at the Capitol theater.

On February 6 at 11 A.M. during the laying of a floral offering to Simón Bolívar at the Pantheon, Villalba delivered a fiery address that sharply denounced the government. Referring to bolivarian ideals of freedom and unity, he called for a vast reform of national life. The

---

[8] Interview with Raúl Leoni, December 6, 1962; with Gonzalo Barrios, November 27, 1962; with Carlos D'Ascoli, January 17, 1963.

concluding invocation of Bolívar declared that "only in the University, where the true Venezuela has been in hiding for years, can the rebel cries of freedom be heard again. . . ."[9] That same evening the young poet Pío Tamayo echoed similar sentiments in verses read at the coronation of the student queen, and on Wednesday Betancourt declared that, thanks to the government, "our poor people seem forgotten by God and crucified in republican anguish."[10]

By the end of the week the government had jailed Villalba, Betancourt, Tamayo, and Guillermo Prince Lara in the Cuartel del Cuño on charges of subversion, thus setting off a chain reaction of protest as hundreds of students demonstrated in the streets. Delegations from the FEV appeared before municipal authorities and later sent an open telegram to Gómez. They roamed Caracas wearing blue caps with initialed "FEV" buttons, and the angered dictator gave the direct order for the jailing of 220 members. Citizens joined protesting students in Maracaibo as well as Caracas, where sections of town were barricaded. Faced by such pressure the government unexpectedly relented and freed most of the students. But the flames of discontent were fanned anew by a group of young officers and cadets at the Military College.

There was dissatisfaction over the widespread assignment of soldiers as overseers of cane-cutting laborers and cattle herders on the numerous Gómez holdings; plotting between junior officers and their university colleagues culminated in a major onslaught against the dictatorship on April 7, 1928. A military uprising began at dawn, and the vacant presidential palace, Miraflores, fell to the insurgents. The tide was narrowly turned by the failure of the rebels to seize the barracks of San Carlos, a major arsenal in Caracas. The officer most re-

[9] The complete text is in Venezuela, Presidencia de la República, *op.cit.*, p. 143.
[10] *A.D.*, no. 19, September 13, 1958, p. 9.

sponsible for the successful loyalist defense was an alert
General Eleazar López Contreras, soon to be rewarded
by Gómez with appointment as Minister of War and
Navy.

That these events were regarded as a distinct threat
to the regime is revealed in a letter of April 26, 1928, by
Eustoquio Gómez. "You cannot imagine the activity of
the People of Caracas any more than I could. . . . The
Government would have been overthrown had it not been
for the energetic measures we took. . . ."[11] And later the
Minister of Interior Relations characterized the uprising
officially as communist; repression was sharp. Offending
officers were imprisoned indefinitely, while students were
sent to the interior as laborers on road construction crews.
Gómez was quoted in the official organ *Nuevo Diario* to
the effect that he was dealing with his children as a
severe parent should. "I have opened the doors of the
University to the students and secured and paid fine pro-
fessors that they might learn honorable professions; . . .
since they do not wish to study, they can learn to work."

The flight into exile by those who escaped official repression marked the end of the first major expression of
democratic sentiment in the face of the regime. But the
seeds planted by the youthful members of the Generation
of '28, barely out of adolescence, survived despite the
inhospitable climate of *gomecismo*. For these revolutionaries themselves, the experience had been profound. Fifteen years later Rómulo Betancourt told a Colombian
newsman of his own response. "I had the first concrete
revelation that the popular mass was beginning to intervene in Venezuelan history as a new factor. The student
movement had initially been wrapped within its own

[11] Rafael Gallegos Ortiz, *La Historia Política de Venezuela; de
Cipriano Castro a Peréz Jiménez* (Caracas: Imprenta Universitaria,
1960), p. 149. This historical narrative contains several interesting
excerpts from relevant letters or personal documents bearing on
the period under discussion.

pride. We students considered ourselves . . . as chosen to transform the country. Then our people suddenly made known their presence; and without leaders, without labor and political organizations, without action committees or strike funds, the people organized a massive demonstration in Caracas. . . ."[12]

In the immediate aftermath of Gómez' crackdown, the exiled students toyed with dreams of violent insurrection before turning to more intellectual plans of change and reform. The leaders of the Generation of '28, however, were scattered across the hemisphere and beyond. Not until 1935 were the youthful insurgents able to return home. An account of these years in exile is found in Chapter IV. For the moment it need merely be noted that only a few individuals were politically active while abroad. Although intellectually curious about Venezuelan and Latin American problems, there was little of a systematic attempt to prepare the majority for their return home.

### Birth of a Democratic Opposition

With the passing of the aged Gómez on December 17, 1935, a breath of fresh but turbulent air crossed Venezuela. Public outbursts against vestigial reminders of the long tyranny included such acts as the destruction of the offices of *Nuevo Diario*, and many of the tyrant's sycophants fled the country. General Eleazar López Contreras moved rapidly to quell demonstrations, yet exercised due caution in efforts to control an incendiary situation. Less timid *gomecistas* lingered in an effort to retain their illegitimate patrimony. Into this situation stepped returning members of the Generation of '28, determined to establish a rule of law under which democratic reforms could be effected.

[12] Luis Enrique Osorio, *Democracia en Venezuela* (Bogotá: Editorial Litografía Colombia, 1943), p. 157. Interviews with other prominent politicians by Osorio were also reproduced in this volume.

Agitation following Gómez' death brought violence and bloodshed in early February of 1936. The suspension of several constitutional guarantees was announced on the 10th by the Minister of Interior Affairs, provoking an open letter of protest from the Federación de Estudiantes de Venezuela three days later. FEV president Jóvito Villalba demanded a restoration of guarantees, persecution of remaining *gomecistas*, and the deliverance of all imprisoned political figures awaiting trial. Félix Galavis, Governor of the Federal District, reacted strongly to the circulating letter. Prohibiting the publication of articles attacking public officials or inflaming the citizenry with "communistic" principles, he ordered all editors to submit material for pre-publication approval. On Friday the local newspapers suspended publication in protest, the FEV called for a general strike, and the newly organized Asociación Nacional de Empleados (ANDE) led Caracas unions in supporting the stoppage.

An estimated 25,000 people gathered in Plaza Bolívar to protest, and at 10:30 A.M. without warning, soldiers appeared on the balcony of the Casa Amarilla and fired down indiscriminately into the crowd. Some 200 were wounded in the incident and eight died. At 3 P.M. an angry procession marched upon Miraflores Palace, headed by Villalba, the rector of the Universidad Central, and several labor leaders. López Contreras confronted the crowd and submitted to demands at once, lifting press censorship while deposing Galavis and arresting him on a charge of murder. The crowd was mollified, and the General survived without further concession.[13]

He continued, however, to walk a tightrope between the two warring elements in Caracas. With neo-*gomecistas* gradually coming under control, López Contreras

[13] *Ahora*, February 16, 1936, p. 1. Charges against Galavis were later dropped. The reasons are outlined in Rodolfo Luzardo, *Notas Historico-Económicas, 1928-1963* (Caracas: Editorial Sucre, 1963), pp. 46-47.

showed signs of fearing pressure from more democratic forces. He prepared for the April convocation of Congress by announcing what became known as the February Program on the 21st of the month. Reforms in a number of areas were suggested, including public health and social assistance, fiscal and commercial policy, education, immigration and colonization. With the critical transitional period nearly past, the General argued, it was time to attack the more pressing problems of the nation. "I believe that the moment to formulate guidelines for a political and administrative program has arrived; such a program would respond to the present needs of the Republic, as I see them. . . . [Here] I must limit myself to sketching a few urgent matters whose solution must no longer be postponed."[14]

The February Program provided the acting chief executive with a basis for seeking broad support, and a byproduct was temporary encouragement of democratic forces. While López Contreras was solidifying his position, the Venezuelan party system began to take form. In the months to follow, four political organizations emerged: the Unión Nacional Republicana (UNR), the Partido Republicano Progresista (PRP), the Movimiento de Organización Venezolana (ORVE), and the Bloque Nacional Democrático (BND). The first to be organized was the UNR.

Constituted primarily by young entrepreneurs, the Unión Nacional Republicana included many prominent caraqueños who had quietly opposed Gómez. Heterogeneous in doctrine, it claimed in its initial public statement to seek "modern solutions to the social and economic problems of Venezuela."[15] Its formal platform was

[14] Venezuela, Presidencia de la República, *op.cit.*, pp. 184-85.
[15] Manuel Vicente Magallanes, *Partidos Políticos Venezolanos* (Caracas: Tip. Vargas, 1960), p. 79. This is one of the best non-journalistic sources of information on the budding parties of 1936-37.

proclaimed on July 9, 1936, favoring "the conversion of Venezuela into a modern State with the application of methods of constructive socialism. . . . The UNR proclaims the fundamental right of individuals to the free expression of their opinions, the duty of submitting to the opinion of the majority expressed in the vote, and to universal suffrage. . . ."[16]

The UNR was an early supporter of the February Program as the way to bring progress to Venezuela. Declaring the impatience of the left and the intolerance of the right equally perilous to the national democratic movement, the UNR was generally favorable to López Contreras' continuation in office as a guarantee of moderation. Assuming the role of a liberal bourgeoisie, the UNR reflected basically the more enlightened opinion of upper-class *caraqueños*. Never officially outlawed, it was to survive the rightist reaction of late 1936 and 1937, then gradually fading away into oblivion. Its leaders drifted into other parties or became avowed independents. Venezuelan businessmen, after years' involvement financially and socially with leaders of the old regime, were without the political vocation required by the circumstances of the time.

The UNR was followed into existence by the Partido Republicano Progresista, the first legal organizational effort of the communists. Directed by Miguel Acosta Saignes, Carlos Irazábal, and Rodolfo Quintero, the PRP at first included non-communists who later joined other groups. The most radical organization at the time, its economic measures included a demand for immediate parcelation of lands, the removal of capitalistic controls on infant industries, and detailed protective guarantees for the workers. Despite its militant tone, the PRP was nonetheless willing to cooperate with other groups. As its Manifesto declared, "The Party, conscious of the urgency in uniting forces in the struggle for the triumph

[16] *UNR*, no. 4, October 29, 1936, p. 1.

of democracy and for the complete destruction of *gome-cismo* . . . will not haggle over efforts to cooperate with the rest of the existing political organizations that may be pursuing parallel or similar goals. As a consequence, the Party will work to celebrate pacts for action to facilitate the united struggle against absolutism, be it on a national or a local scale."[17]

The Bloque Nacional Democrático stood apart in the sense that it was largely regional, founded in Zulia by the journalist and labor activist Valmore Rodríguez. Among its early leadership were Juan Bautista Fuenmayor and Olga Luzardo, both later prominent communists. The BND found its sense of political democracy almost identical with that of the Movimiento de Organización Venezolana. The BND program called itself a result "of one of the most forgotten and most exploited regions of the Republic. . . ." Its list of reforms, shaped to a degree by regional needs, urged a general promotion of the economy, a systematic use of the land, a career civil service, judicial autonomy, and comparable measures.[18]

Of the greatest contemporary significance was the Movimiento de Organización Venezolana (ORVE), which first emerged less a political party than a broad-based electoral front. It was founded with the primordial purpose of uniting all anti-dictatorial sectors into a broad popular front. So it was that one of its founders, the intellectual Mariano Picón-Salas, coined the motto and promise "to look for what unites us and to avoid what divides us." Generally regarded as the direct ancestor of today's Acción Democrática, ORVE quaffed deeply of the heady wine of free discussion and political activity. The group teemed with ideas, and Picón Salas later recalled how "in youthful meetings, over much coffee and many cigarettes, our words overflowed with fervor

[17] Venezuela, Presidencia de la República, *op.cit.*, p. 233.
[18] *Ibid.* Text of the declaration on pp. 236-39.

as we sought to define our economic problem . . . a general inventory of Venezuelan needs."[19] Formally constituted on March 1, 1936, at a gathering in Caracas' Nuevo Circo, ORVE came into being in the presence of spokesmen from the FEV and ANDE as well as General Elbano Mibelli, the new Governor of the Federal District.

Rhetorical flourishes and a call to action came from Rómulo Betancourt, who declared that ORVE intended to direct public opinion toward the solution of its problems while collaborating with authorities to prevent any recrudescence of despotism. The audience also heard ORVE's official statement of purpose, which demanded the transformation of Venezuela into a modern state. There was a call for political democracy and social justice. "We want to organize a country in which each man contributes to society and where the State unifies and conciliates collective discord. . . . We want to unite and not to divide Venezuelans. We want to make of politics—previously the affair of small oligarchic circles— a national spirit . . . revealing permanently the creativity of the Venezuelan soul."[20]

Self-characterized as a *policlasista* or multi-class organization, ORVE aspired to a reorganization of society. Members were reminded of deep personal responsibility, through which inertia and disorder were to be opposed. Despite its refusal to call itself a party, ORVE increasingly resembled one, and its directorate included many names that would later reappear in Venezuelan politics. Besides Picón-Salas and Betancourt, these included Leoni, D'Ascoli, Alberto Adriani, Alberto Ravell, and Guillermo López Gallegos. By the autumn of 1936, Luis B. Prieto, Gonzalo Barrios, and Andrés Eloy Blanco, subsequently

[19] Mariano Picón Salas, *1941; Cinco Discursos sobre Pasado y Presente de la Nación Venezolana* (Caracas: Editorial La Torre, 1941), p. 5.
[20] *Ahora,* March 2, 1936, pp. 3-4.

founders of Acción Democrática, joined this group of leaders. The leadership temporarily followed a cautious course, and public pronouncements were limited, although study commissions were preparing papers on various problem areas.

Congress was scheduled to meet in April, and the organizing parties awaited the event with some optimism. On March 31, 1936, three groups announced the formation of the Bloque de Abril. In this so-called April Bloc, the UNR, the PRP, and ORVE joined together in a call for broader public liberties and economic reforms. In its public declaration—the Plataforma de Lucha—the Bloque called upon Congress to elect a constitutional president, amend the document to permit new congressional elections promptly, and further revise the charter by creating a pair of national vice-presidents. A new electoral law and census were recommended, as well as a demand for state and municipal elections. Signers of the proclamation included Raúl Leoni for ORVE, Carlos Irazábal for the PRP, and Esteban Palacios Blanco for the UNR.[21]

Congress met as scheduled on April 19, 1936, its membership still composed of *gomecistas* whose presence dramatized the indirect electoral system then falling under attack. López Contreras was named constitutional president, but reforms were not forthcoming. The session lengthened as the growing force of oligarchic reaction showed in an official stiffening of attitudes toward the democratic opposition. Preparatory drafts for a new constitution embraced none of the proposals of the Bloque de Abril. It was also announced that Congress would remain in session throughout 1936 rather than disbanding preparatory to new elections.

The next point of conflict came over a law allegedly guaranteeing public order and individual rights. Known

[21] Gonzalo Barrios, *Bloque de Abril* (Caracas: Lit. y Tip. Vargas, 1936), pp. 7-8.

as the Ley Lara because of its introduction by the government's Dr. Alejandro Lara, the law has been generally regarded as restrictive in spirit and repressive in intent.[22] López Contreras attempted to justify it during the course of a June 4 broadcast reporting on congressional activity, but the opposition was unconvinced. The response was a joint statement, issued by the Bloque de Abril and subscribed to by ANDE, FEV, and the BND. Four demands were outlined: dissolution of Congress and general elections by year's end; withdrawal of the Ley Lara; a rehauling of security forces and police in Caracas; and finally the confiscation of all remaining wealth of the Gómez family, funds being applied instead toward the solution of labor disputes.[23]

There was no official response, and the opposition then created a Comité de Defensa Democrática, composed of representatives of the organizations that had signed the earlier manifesto. The Committee called for a general protest strike, limited to metropolitan Caracas and planned for twenty-four hours' duration. Unexpectedly, a surge of popular feeling broke open, and the enthused strike leaders chose to extend the strike. Almost without planning the protest spread from the capital to Maracaibo, Valencia, Barquisimeto, and several important oil fields. The stoppage ran from June 9 to 13, when the demonstrations collapsed largely of their own weight. Significant concessions from the government were not forthcoming, and the prestige of the opposition was damaged. Gonzalo Barrios, a prominent *orvista* participant, has cited the unwise extension of the strike as characteristic of the opposition's tendency to shape intelligent over-

[22] For a dissenting view, however, see Luzardo, *op.cit.*, pp. 49-54.

[23] Luis Troconis Guerrero, *La Cuestión Agraria en la Historia Nacional* (Caracas: Editorial Arte, 1962), p. 170. This posthumous publication contains information based on several documents and manifestoes that have since been lost.

all strategy and then mar its impact through poor tactical implementation.[24]

Betancourt was also to comment retrospectively upon the error. "Impressed by the ascendent wave in the streets, we prolonged the duration of the strike beyond the just limit that had been fixed. And as we did not point out . . . any insurrectional or revolutionary conclusion to the strike, it ended by falling back and dissolving. . . ."[25] The opposition was nonetheless heartened by the response, and therefore viewed the episode as one additional step in the hesitant progress toward democracy and public participation. Another postscript to the strike was the loss of prestige of the UNR, whose leadership had uncertainly held back from the strike call at the outset, lending but minimal support. In the aftermath of the strike, ORVE picked up groups of defectors from the ranks of the UNR.[26]

The strike of June 1936 marked an important turning point in the course of post-Gómez developments. The democratic opposition had not made use of public opinion when the government might have granted substantial concessions. The moment was a fleeting one, and was soon lost. The response of the right—including moderate conservatives as well as reactionary remnants of *gomecismo*—grew increasingly sharp. The activities of the opposition came to be restricted with greater firmness as 1936 moved toward its conclusion.

## Inexperience and the Rightist Reaction

The opposition, exuberant over its apparent appeal to the masses, soon chose to capitalize on it. For ORVE in particular, a second stage was entered with the announcement of a detailed program on July 11, 1936. The

[24] Interview with Gonzalo Barrios, November 27, 1962.
[25] Rómulo Betancourt, *Venezuela: Política y Petróleo* (Mexico: Fondo de Cultura Económica, 1956), pp. 85-86.
[26] Interview with Raúl Leoni, December 6, 1962.

several study commissions presented their final reports and the complete program—published only in mimeographed form—appeared in fragments in the weekly *ORVE*. The organization declared that only the rising generation might comprehend demands for new solutions to national problems. Particular emphasis was placed on political and electoral democracy, constitutional revision, socio-economic reform, revised policies on petroleum concessions, and education.[27]

*Orvista* leadership was also undergoing revision. Secretary-General Picón-Salas had resigned in June, dissatisfied with direction of the strike. His position was soon filled by Betancourt, and by August a new Comité Central Directivo was operating, including Gonzalo Barrios as Secretary of the Youth Movement, Juan Oropeza as Secretary of International Policy, Inocente Palacios as Secretary of Propaganda, and Carlos D'Ascoli as Secretary of Coordination.[28] Denials by the leadership failed to conceal the fact that ORVE was becoming a political party. Talks were also undertaken with like-minded political groups in an effort to bring about a fusion of the opposition. On Wednesday night, October 28, 1936, a number of young politicians met in the Caracas headquarters of ORVE to announce the founding of the Partido Democrático Nacional (PDN). Six organizations signed the proclamation: ORVE, the PRP, the FEV, the BND, and two labor groups, the Frente Obrero and the Frente Nacional de Trabajadores. Of all the organized opposition groups, only the UNR was left out.

The group's general orientation was underlined by repeated use of the phrase "Partido Unico de la Izquierda," the single party of the left. PDN founders hoped to present an effective and coordinated organization that might offer a broadly representative alternative to the government. FEV leader Jóvito Villalba was

[27] *ORVE*, nos. 11 and 12, July 12 and 19, 1936.
[28] *El Popular*, no. 17, August 8, 1936, p. 1.

named Secretary-General, while Rómulo Betancourt assumed the post of Secretary of Organization. Four more *orvistas* sat on the executive committee: Secretary of International Relations D'Ascoli, Press Secretary Juan Oropeza, Secretary of Feminine Affairs Mercedes Fermín, and Peasant Movement Secretary Francisco Olivo. Beneath this Comité Central Ejecutivo was a 43-member Comité Central, on which several subsequent leaders of Acción Democrática were placed, such as Manuel Martínez, Luis Lander, Raúl Leoni, Valmore Rodríguez, Augusto Malavé Villalba, and Ramón Quijada.[29]

The PDN program of 1936 was never published in full, although excerpts appeared in *ORVE, El Popular,* and *Ahora.* The PRP weekly, *El Popular,* printed relevant passages on October 31, 1936. In the preamble the PDN promised to be ". . . the political organization that will unify all Venezuelans interested in the implanting of an authentically democratic regime guaranteeing the independence and liberty of our people. . . .

"We condemn all absolutist or autocratic regimes, whatever be their names or the ends with which they are justified. We will fight for the restitution to our people of their sovereignty by means of the election of their representatives through universal suffrage and, as an immediate thing, the effective liquidation of *gomecismo. . . .*"[30]

The desire for meaningful unity of democratic forces was made clear then and on subsequent occasions. Carlos D'Ascoli wrote that the PDN proposed "to carry to reality . . . reforms and institutions *strictly adapted to the possibilities of our environment* and at the same time reflecting the will of the immense majority of Venezuelans."[31]

Member organizations of the fledgling PDN gave

[29] *El Popular,* no. 29, October 31, 1936, p. 2.
[30] *Ibid.*
[31] *Ahora,* November 4, 1936, pp. 1, 6. The emphasis is D'Ascoli's.

warm support. An *ORVE* editorial saw the need of a
single party, which might constitute "an effective solid
bloc, national in scope and representation. . . ."[32] The
PRP weekly gave fulsome praise for the new organization, and even the UNR, although not a charter member,
promised through its Director-General Martín Pérez
Guevara an early reply to a PDN letter calling for a
common front.[33] PDN organizers were in the midst of
plans for coming elections when their hopes were suddenly drenched by a governmental denial of legality to
the group. López Contreras, having emerged victorious
from his quietly fierce battle with recalcitrant *gomecistas*,
had decided to turn against the nascent parties.

Both by temperament and by choice the President opposed a widening of political participation, a position in
which he was buttressed by powerful oligarchic elements.
The conservative daily *La Esfera* had been leading the
campaign with a series of articles charging all leftists
with being surreptitious communists. Social and economic
groups became apprehensive before the rising tide of
popular activity, and a series of miscalculations by the
opposition increased their fears. First of these was the
disorganized mob which marched on Miraflores in February demanding satisfaction for the killings in Plaza
Bolívar. Major concessions might have been extracted,
but opposition leadership settled for relatively little.

Conservative elements were further alarmed when
Jóvito Villalba, then the most popular and prestigious of
opposition leaders, was overwhelmed by the fervor of a
large audience and uttered the unfortunate phrase, "the
law is the refuge of the rheumatics." Scandalized repercussions were scarcely mollified when the opposition neglected to disavow the sentiment. An obvious implica-
tion was a belief in subverting public order through vio-

[32] *ORVE*, no. 18, August 30, 1936, p. 1.
[33] *Ahora*, November 13, 1936, p. 1.

lence.[34] A final error was the four-day strike in June, where the outpouring of public sentiment could not but startle the interests against which it seemed directed. Combined with earlier events, this created an unfavorable impression on the President and his supporters. The direction in which the opposition was moving appeared inimical to the traditional wielders of political and economic power. Thus the eventual confrontation was inevitable.

Transitory events made the issue of legalizing the PDN the chosen battlefield. The government seized the initiative by denying legality to the Partido Democrática Nacional. Governor Mibelli of the Federal District rejected the official application for legal status on November 2, 1936, and the battle was joined. The Law of Public Order (Ley Lara) specified that an applying organization would present its documents and "concrete program" for judgment by federal authorities, who might withhold approval if the program was adjudged irresponsible.

Party organizers—who had not been confronted with a comparable problem in the first months of 1936—appealed to the courts. On November 25 the PDN directors published the text of their appeal to the Corte Federal y de Casación, including a forthright denial of communist agitation. The government was challenged to prove any involvement with communist plotting or propagandizing. The signatories, rather, summarized their immediate goals as electoral reform, progressive agrarian revision, new petroleum policies, and unrestricted constitutional guarantees. Governor Mibelli, who had abstained from rendering a judgment rather than officially rejecting the application, insisted upon his authority in so abstaining. In mid-December the Corte Federal y de Casación upheld him by a vote of 5-3, thus preventing the formal organization of the Partido Democrático Nacional.

[34] Troconis Guerrero, *op.cit.*, pp. 167-68.

The denial of legality to a unified leftist opposition, then, was a major step in the rightist reaction. It was followed closely by unilateral intervention in a labor strike that broke out in December. The basis of the dispute was the labor law of 1936; drafted with a sympathetic eye toward the petroleum workers, whose 25,000 members numbered less than 2 percent of the working population, the law permitted the organization of petroleum unions at the major camps in the Maracaibo Basin. These groups presented a list of demands on November 30, 1936, calling for improved housing and work facilities. The workers also demanded a salary of ten *bolivares* daily (then slightly over three dollars).

Failing to gain satisfaction, union leaders called a general strike on December 14. One labor historian has called it the result of just demands by the workers in the face of a refusal by private organizations to discuss fully and fairly existing labor conditions.[35] More than 20,000 workers left their jobs, and feeling on both sides was rapidly exacerbated. López Contreras called for conciliation from both labor and management, but his pleas went unheard, and the stoppage dragged through the holidays and into 1937. Finally despairing of voluntary agreement, the President imposed his own solution on January 22, 1937. Citing article 178 of the labor law, he decreed a compulsory return to work. Petroleum workers received an increase of up to one *bolívar* (roughly 30 cents), but other demands were ignored. The regime also dissolved the first Congreso de los Trabajadores Venezolanos, which, at the close of December, had become the first national trade-union organization in Venezuela.[36]

By early 1937, having rejected the activities of organ-

[35] Jesús Prieto Soto, *El Chorro; Gracia o Maldición* (Madrid: Industrias Gráficas España, 1960), p. 61.

[36] For an informed account, see Edwin Lieuwen, *Petroleum in Venezuela; A History* (Berkeley: University of California Press, 1954), pp. 81-82.

ized labor as well as those of a united political opposition, the regime paused briefly in its shift to the right. While the PDN was non-existent, its erstwhile parent groups remained operative, and preparations were made for January congressional and municipal elections. The vote was the first to be conducted under the Constitution of 1936, which had perpetuated the indirect electoral system while further restricting suffrage.

From 1858 until 1936, all males of 21 or over had been permitted to vote for municipal councilmen and for members of state legislative assemblies. The voter was twice-removed from a direct presidential vote, as municipal and state officials elected national congressmen who in turn chose the constitutional chief executive. The charter adopted in July of 1936, however, further narrowed suffrage to literate men of 21 or over. In a country with over 70 percent illiteracy, this shrank the electorate tremendously.

January elections involved the partial renewal of Congress by the appropriate state bodies, as well as many municipal races. The latter were important in Caracas, where most of the anti-government strength and organization was located. ORVE was seemingly the most active of the opposition groups; after working diligently to encourage and facilitate a heavy electoral census, its organizers feverishly promoted propaganda activities. "In every district ORVE will initiate and introduce signed petitions and demands before the [Electoral] Councils. From the districts where ORVE is organized, action must be spread to remaining districts of each state."[37]

Elections on January 28, 1937, saw government candidates win as expected in most races, but a handful of opposition figures were named congressmen despite the indirect method of selection. Notable among these were Barrios (Senator, Portuguesa), Prieto (Senator, Nueva

[37] *ORVE*, no. 37, January 23, 1937, p. 1.

Esparta), Oropeza (Deputy, Lara), Leoni (Deputy, Bolívar), and Felipe Hernández (Deputy, Zulia). Other winners from opposition ranks, although not *orvistas*, were Villalba (Deputy, Nueva Esparta), and from the Federal District, Senator Andrés Eloy Blanco and Deputies P. B. Pérez Salinas, Martín Pérez Guevara, Juan Pablo Pérez Alfonzo, and Rómulo Gallegos.[38]

The government reacted swiftly; less than a week later, on February 3, several politicians were jailed for unannounced reasons. The next day Caracas authorities ordered a total cessation of activity by all five groups which had created the abortive PDN. Governor Mibelli called them "factors of disturbance to social tranquility," and squelched the organizations with ease. Hostile congressmen were then dealt with as the Corte Federal y de Casación nullified the elections of Barrios, Leoni, Oropeza, and Villalba. The only remaining congressman whose ties with ORVE had been close was the esteemed poet and intellectual Andrés Eloy Blanco, who retained his senatorial seat throughout the 1937-1941 term.[39] Once the election returns had in these cases been annulled, the final step was total removal of opposition leaders.

After a brief interim, a presidential decree appeared in the *Gaceta Oficial* on March 13, 1937, by which forty-seven opposition politicians were expelled "for a term of one year for being affiliated with communist doctrine and for being considered prejudicial to public order. . . ."[40] Among the forty-seven were several men affiliated either then or later with the Venezuelan communist movement, as well as most democratic opposition figures. Communists on the list included Salvador de la Plaza, Gustavo Machado, Rodolfo Quintero, and Juan Bautista Fuenmayor. Non-communists to be expelled included Betancourt, Villalba, D'Ascoli, Rodríguez, Barrios, Leoni, Qui-

---

[38] *Ahora*, February 4, 1937, p. 1.
[39] Interview with Raúl Leoni, December 6, 1962.
[40] *Gaceta Oficial*, March 13, 1937, p. 1.

jada, Troconis Guerrero, Malavé Villalba, and Alejandro Oropeza Castillo. Authorities efficiently rounded up and expelled all but two of those named; Rómulo Betancourt and Alejandro Oropeza Castillo eluded officials and went into hiding.[41]

Aside from Andrés Eloy Blanco, the only nationally known figure who remained to voice public criticism was the widely honored novelist Rómulo Gallegos. Formerly the teacher of many youths of the Generation of '28, later a leader of Acción Democrática, Gallegos had been unaffiliated, and had differed with *orvista* tactics more than once. With the passing of active organized legal opposition to the government, Gallegos' judgment regarding the brief 1936-1937 period is a fitting one.

"A national transformation could be realized only . . . through the leadership of our uncontaminated youth in the ranks of the opposition. . . . Perhaps immoderate at times, they did [what seemed] fully justified by the necessity of uncovering the profoundly deep roots of old ills. . . .

"I believe that, notwithstanding inevitable errors . . . these young people have fulfilled their mission during the activity of a year of democratic experience. I know intimately most of those belonging to those ranks, and I repeat my conviction that without them, work could not have been undertaken that might truly help to project Venezuela toward a prosperous future."[42]

## Return to Legality

The emergence of truly national, effective political parties still lay well in the future. The years following López Contreras' expulsion of the opposition leadership saw the continuation of efforts that in time led to the creation of Acción Democrática. For four years its leader-

41 Interview with Alejandro Oropeza Castillo, November 7, 1962.
42 *ORVE*, no. 33, December 17, 1936, p. 1.

ship labored clandestinely—still using the old name of the PDN—while erecting a structure on which a permanent organization might be set up. Until 1941 efforts were hemmed in by official harassment and legal restrictions (the details of which are analyzed in Chapter IV). In the meantime, national affairs continued to revolve about the President, who was proving a strangely consummate politician.

Born in 1883, Eleazar López Contreras had been one of the youngest *andinos* to fall upon Caracas under the leadership of Cipriano Castro in 1899. He moved through the military hierarchy slowly, achieving public notice for the first time with his quelling of the 1928 uprising. Soon advanced to the leadership of the military as Minister of War and Navy, he shone during the latter years under Gómez as a financially honest figure amid a grossly corrupt regime. His careful maneuvering against the most atavistic elements of *gomecismo* in 1936 proved adept.

Crafty, cunning, popularly referred to as *el socarrón*—the sly one—López Contreras controlled a delicate political balance. Elections were restored to Venezuela, but the outcome was prearranged. A progressive labor law was written in 1936 and then consistently ignored. Political criticism was suffered in moderation after 1937, yet prominent democratic leaders had been shipped abroad. Continually shifting his position, the President willingly bent with the force of circumstances but never yielded entirely. On the death of Gómez he lamented "the immense national misfortune at the death of General Juan Vicente Gómez, illustrious *caudillo* who knew how to guide Venezuela to achieve the heights of its present majesty. . . ."[43] Yet days later he avoided punitive action when busts of the expired dictator were torn down and smashed.

[43] Venezuela, Presidencia de la República, *op.cit.*, p. 176.

A fair judgment is difficult even today. López Contreras' political skill and sense of timing was clearly superior. Perhaps a valid interim assessment is that of Gallegos Ortiz, who has written that the President was neither a symbol of democracy nor a defender of the dark methods of *gomecismo*. His period was largely by way of a transition.[44] A part of that transition was the organizing in public form of his own political forces, "cultural" groups known as Sociedades Cívicas Bolivarianas. Later they came to be known collectively as the Agrupaciones Cívicas Bolivarianas (ACB), thus attempting to enfold the President in the sacrosanct cloak of Bolívar. The name alone made it possible for progressive forces opposing the President to be criticized as anti-bolivarian, although to be truly bolivarian in this sense meant to qualify as staunchly conservative, if not reactionary.

López Contreras took public pride in his handling of the opposition. Even twenty years after the fact, he wrote of the events of 1936-1937 thusly:

"My government continued being tolerant of the leftist group, although it was trying to bring about a revolt. . . .

"The leftists prepared a general strike that might well have led the country into a state of civil war, with repercussions of an international order that would have included the suspension of oil exploitation. It was only then, at the beginning of 1937, that my government chose to decree, in accord with the Constitution, the expulsion of forty-seven political leaders of the left. . . ."[45]

Despite the expulsion, one final effort was made to construct a legal opposition organization. Directed by José Rafael Gabaldón, the attempt was intended "to organize a party capable of gathering to its ranks all the

[44] Gallegos Ortiz, *op.cit.*, p. 186.
[45] Pedro Luis Blanco Peñalver, *López Contreras ante la Historia* (Caracas: Tipografía Garrido, 1957), p. 72. Included are a number of recollections by López Contreras himself.

truly and incontrovertibly democratic forces of the country." An organizing committee was created; two days after Christmas of 1937, a constituent meeting was held where a basic program was laid down and presented in the name of the Partido Demócrata Venezolano (PDV).[46] Several former orvistas who had escaped the expulsion order were involved, including Andrés Eloy Blanco, Luis B. Prieto, and Juan Pablo Pérez Alfonzo. A lengthy elaboration of party principles concluded with a call for "an act of patriotic devotion . . . an oath to struggle for the abolition of personalism . . . and for the triumph of an integral democratic system."[47] Detailed organizational plans were also announced. The PDV, however, swiftly followed the road of the PDN in being denied the right to public existence. Governor Mibelli announced that the list of PDV partisans included several men who had belonged to the dissolved parties, therefore legality could not be extended. The disappointed organizers carried a protest to the Corte Federal y de Casación, where on March 29, 1938, their appeal was denied.

Despite the harassment of the opposition through this period, a gradual relaxation set in. By 1940 and 1941 the clandestine Partido Democrático Nacional enjoyed increasing leniency, during which time it took definite measures to build organizational strength. In the spring of 1941 the outgoing government decided to pass the reins of power into new hands, and López Contreras chose as his successor a fellow tachirense, Minister of War Isaías Medina Angarita.[48] The PDN itself decided

[46] Magallanes, op.cit., p. 107. This party is not to be confused with the Partido Democrático Venezolano (PDV) later created by the Medina regime.

[47] Partido Demócrata Venezolano, El "Partido Demócrata Venezolano" y su Proceso (Documentos) (Caracas: Editorial Elite, 1938), p. 3.

[48] Isaías Medina Angarita, Cuatro Años de Democracia (Caracas: Pensamiento Vivo, 1963). The recently published posthumous

to participate in elections if possible, and supported a symbolic candidacy of Rómulo Gallegos.

Famed as a teacher, an internationally renowned author whose *Doña Bárbara* was a beloved Venezuelan classic, Gallegos had served in Congress for several years, and had been for a few weeks López Contreras' Minister of Education. His role had been essentially that of an interested, dedicated citizen rather than that of a practicing politician. Interviewed early in 1941 by a group that included Betancourt, Blanco, Prieto, Barrios, and Leoni, Gallegos accepted the invitation to become their candidate.

There was no expectation of winning the election. As Betancourt told an interviewer the following year, he and his colleagues "knew it was not going to be a triumphant campaign, but a simple affirmation of our civic spirit; for the government candidate had a sweeping majority in the legislative chambers. But we wanted to combat the continuist thesis, we wanted public debate over the candidates, we wanted to conquer the very streets through a popular movement, one which had long been entombed in the catacombs of clandestinity."[49] In short, they intended to focus public interest with a vastly popular figure, and at the same time improve the prospects for subsequent legalization of the party.

Gallegos accepted the adverse conditions and, once committed to the campaign, traveled and spoke widely. Although temperamentally foreign to political strife, he proved a more effective campaigner than his opponent, stirring provincial emotions as had few Venezuelans before. The novelist closed his campaign with a speech

---

memoir of Medina Angarita, modest in length and in content, nonetheless contains valuable statements of his views on several yet-controversial matters.

[49] Osorio, *op.cit.*, p. 164.

in Valencia on April 12, 1941, reiterating the belief that "the greater part of our public ills stem from political abstentionism imposed upon us by long dictatorships exercising tremendous repression."[50]

Electoral formalities took place in Congress on April 28, and the certain result was spelled out with 130 votes for Medina and 13 for Gallegos. The official candidate succeeded to Miraflores supported by the same forces that had been long dominant. Within a few months, however, the symbolic presidential campaign bore fruit in the legal founding of Acción Democrática. Leaders of the PDN met in private assembly in Caracas a month after elections, and agreed that the Medina government was disposed to permit legal organization of the party. Thus, on May 13, 1941, an application for legalization was handed to the government.

Care was taken to avoid concrete or detailed statements that might cause a delay in winning recognition from authorities. Thus the program as presented to officials in the Federal District was deliberately vague. Permission was finally granted on July 29, 1941, and efforts to form a national party were immediately stepped up. In August the party constituted a sectional directorate in the Federal District, including such men as Manuel Martínez, P. B. Pérez Salinas, Alberto López Gallegos, and Raúl Leoni.[51] Organizers were also sent out to establish state sectionals after that of the Federal District was created. By the close of August units had been formed in Zulia, Guárico, and Falcón, while organizing commissions were activated in other states. Local and municipal sectionals also grew.

On Saturday, September 13, 1941, Acción Democrática was officially born before an estimated 10,000 people in

[50] Rómulo Gallegos, *Una Posición en la Vida* (Mexico: Ediciones Humanismo, 1954), p. 200. This is a collection of major public statements by Gallegos.
[51] *Ahora*, August 9, 1941, p. 1.

Caracas' Nuevo Circo. Party President Rómulo Gallegos opened with a brief address, in which he observed that barely six months earlier he had stood on the same spot to explain that his presidential campaign was aimed at "initiating the incorporation of a sector of the Venezuelan citizenry into an attitude of political responsibility, in exercise of their rights and in fulfillment of their duty." He declared that the AD was the logical expression of growing popular participation and that it intended to open the doors to democratic exchange. In phrases reminiscent of ORVE, he said the new party came not to divide the country but "to work, without stridency, without tumultuous flag-waving, without class rancors or hunger for reprisal. . . . We trust in progressive work, the result of the absorption and penetration of advanced ideas. . . ."[52]

Gallegos' address was followed by several others. Andrés Eloy Blanco discoursed on "Cultural Offensive of the Party," Luis B. Prieto on "Party and the Problems of Education," Mario García Arocha on "Party and the Electoral Question," Ricardo Montilla on "Party and the Province," and Betancourt on "Party and Venezuelan Economic Reality." Betancourt's concluding remarks referred back to the events of 1936 and 1937. "We said and we promised, in those turbulent days of 1936, that we were resolved to maintain popular ties. . . . And now, having returned from recent hard experiences . . . we bear the proud satisfaction of having been worthy of the faith deposited in us. . . ."[53]

The AD leadership immediately proceeded with organizational efforts, building upon the framework created during four years of clandestineness. The result was the construction of a truly national, revolutionary party.

[52] *Ahora*, September 14, 1941, pp. 2, 9. See other articles for more detailed accounts of the speeches and activities at Nuevo Circo.

[53] Venezuela, Presidencia de la República, *op.cit.*, p. 304.

Yet when Acción Democrática unexpectedly leapt to power in 1945, organizational tasks were yet incomplete. The experience prior to 1941 had been a mere preliminary to the formidable challenge of creating an effective, modern political party.

# CHAPTER II

## Constructing a Modern Party

### 1941-1948

From 1941 on, Acción Democrática attempted to make good the motto of "not a single district nor single municipality without a party organization." It was a demanding task, and AD leaders criss-crossed Venezuela ceaselessly during the next four years. The impact was as strong on *adecos* as upon the citizenry. The spirit of this unending campaign has been eloquently expressed by Rómulo Betancourt for the entire AD directorate.

"1941-45 was a four-year period that left an indelible impression. In my youthful exile I had always wanted to know the immensity of Venezuela, town by town, hamlet by hamlet; to look within and to live with its problems; to discuss its destiny with men and women of the mountains and of the plains, of the Oriente and of Guayana. I achieved that secret desire in years that taught me much more of my country than I would have learned through book study. I navigated the Orinoco in a shaky, native-built launch; and I traveled by *curiara* on Lake Maracaibo and by boat on the Tuy River. I slept in *ranchos* on the plains of Guárico, on the Upper and Lower Apure River, listening to details of life and work from the lips of peons . . .

"[This] resulted in capturing the widespread feeling of frustration and discontent, the product of coexistence on the same land of two separate countries: the minoritarian with substantial well-being and the other, infinitely more numerous, situated barely on the edge of civilization."[1]

[1] Rómulo Betancourt, *Venezuela: Política y Petróleo* (México: Fondo de Cultura Económica, 1956), pp. 135-36.

## Reorganizing an Opposition

Recruitment through a general expansion of the framework of the old PDN continued unceasingly. Two basic factors made revision imperative: the rapid growth of the new AD, and the need for an organizational system more conducive to free and public activity. As is spelled out in Chapter IV during the study of 1937-1941 underground activities, the PDN suffered under restrictions imposed by clandestineness. After 1941 it remained for Acción Democrática to broaden and open the entire structure.

Executive organs were amplified, as two vice-presidencies were added while the former Secretariat of Press and Propaganda was divided into separate bodies on the national level. A Feminine Secretariat was reestablished, while a Youth Secretariat appeared for the first time since the early months of ORVE. An innovation of major significance was the establishment of a Comité Directivo Nacional (CDN) in addition to the older Comité Ejecutivo Nacional (CEN). While the latter was composed of major national officers, the CDN extended its representation through the inclusion of delegates from regional party organizations as well as scattered delegates from professional and occupational sectors. As will be seen later, refinement of the CDN brought it to primacy within the entire party structure.

Regional executive bodies were set up as Comités Ejecutivos Seccionales (CES), and the Disciplinary Tribunal, formerly a national body, extended branches down to the Sectionals. On the lowest level, the diffuse and dissimilar cells of PDN days were replaced by units known as Juntas de Barrios or as Juntas Locales. A full set of legislative or deliberative organs was created in state capitals as well as other important population centers. A continuing series of open meetings was initiated, at which thousands of citizens for the first time were touched in some measure with a feeling for political participation. Regional conventions were held annually.[2]

The first elections to be contested by Acción Democrática came in Caracas municipal contests in January 1942. The Party presented ten candidates as *principales* and three as *suplentes*.[3] In opposition were members of the Agrupación Cívica Bolivariana, at that time still the official party. The choice before Caracas voters, argued the AD, fell between democratic forces and the government, which represented a minority. Four of the ten AD *principales* won: Barrios, López Gallegos, Alberto Ravell, and Cirilo J. Brea. Among the losers were Leoni and Oropeza. All three of the *suplentes* were elected: Manuel Martínez, Valmore Rodríguez, and Aníbal Mestre Fuenmayor. Only 9,000 votes were cast in a city whose population was then estimated at 400,000; the fact was duly noted in AD post-mortems, and the party declared its determination to work harder in the future simply to get out the vote.

The party held its first National Convention on June 6-8, 1942, at which party officers and national executives were elected. The first set of AD officers—which had been functioning since the previous fall—was formally invested. The Comité Ejecutivo Nacional comprised nine men: President Rómulo Gallegos, First Vice-President Andrés Eloy Blanco, Second Vice-President Luis B. Prieto, Director of Organization Rómulo Betancourt, Director of Press Juan Oropeza, Director of Finance Valmore Rodríguez, Director of Labor and Agriculture P. B. Pérez Salinas, Director of Correspondence Gonzalo Barrios, and Juridical Director Inocente Palacios. A forty-

[2] Acción Democrática, *Tesis Organizativa y Estatutos* (Caracas: Editorial "Antonio Pinto Salinas," 1958), pp. 4-5. This party publication is an invaluable record of organizational plans in the early years. Although it comments little on the matter of effectiveness, the broad outlines of AD organization are presented.

[3] *Suplentes* act as alternates or substitutes in the event that the *principal* cannot exercise his official duties.

five-member Comité Directivo Nacional was also named,[4] while the three-member Disciplinary Tribunal was constituted by Juan Pablo Pérez Alfonzo, Ricardo Montilla, and Anibal Mestre Fuenmayor.[5]

Acción Democrática was already looking forward to contesting the 1943 congressional elections, as was the Medina administration. Continuing reliance on indirect electoral processes left to state officials the final selections. The government's determined effort in 1942 had resulted in the election of 286 of its 302 candidates for legislative assemblies, while 981 of its 1,405 candidates became municipal councilmen. The government was therefore assured of victory in January 1943.

Recognizing the hopelessness of its cause, the AD through its Comité Directivo Nacional suddenly announced a policy of abstention. Party supporters were reminded that with candidates twice-removed from popular participation, official government candidates could not be effectively opposed. The official declaration in November conceded that official arrogance had diminished with the departure of *lopecismo*, but added that the Medina authorities were still active in arranging appropriately pliable state and municipal bodies. Abstention was offered as a realistic alternative to electoral combat. Party members were urged to spread the message that Acción Democrática remained determined to achieve constitutional reform permitting an electoral system of universal suffrage and direct voting.

Renewal of half the Congress in January 1943, therefore, occurred without organized competition from the

[4] The order is of retrospective interest for the relative position of currently prominent party members. The first ten were, successively, Gallegos, Blanco, Betancourt, Prieto, Palacios, Rodríguez, Leoni, Oropeza, Barrios, and D'Ascoli. Others included Pérez Alfonzo (12), Lander (13), Eligio Anzola Anzola (21), Leonardo Ruiz Pineda (31), Pérez Salinas (36), Malavé Villalba (37), Quijada (39), and Dubuc (40).

[5] *Acción Democrática*, no. 22, June 13, 1942, pp. 1, 8.

AD. Individual exceptions were the candidacies of Andrés Eloy Blanco from the Federal District and Rómulo Betancourt from Miranda. Both were granted permission by the party to campaign individually; it was hoped that their personal stature might carry them into office. Blanco won in Caracas, as he had done some years before, while Betancourt lost in Miranda by a 36-32 margin.[6] The government won an emphatic victory in the Senate but somewhat surprisingly gained only two-thirds of the seats in the Chamber of Deputies, where several independents succeeded in being elected.

Motivated at least in part by the outcome of elections to the Chamber, as well as a desire to rid the official machine of remaining *lopecistas*, President Medina initiated the organization of an official government party. López Contreras' old ACB had shriveled into obscurity by this time, and on April 15, 1943, the President sent a circular telegram to executive authorities in the respective states. The almost immediate result was formation of the Partidarios de la Política del Gobierno (PPG), a singularly appropriate name for the "partisans of government policy." This *medinista* creation was subsequently rechristened the Partido Democrático Venezolano (PDV), and for the remainder of his term it represented official interests in the traditional Venezuelan fashion. Despite the support of a small number of intellectuals and professionals—called the "luminous wing of the PDV" by Andrés Eloy Blanco—the party never became more than an extension of the administration.

In September of 1943 the AD celebrated its second anniversary. Rómulo Gallegos enthusiastically if somewhat unrealistically declared that the party was truly national, with sectional organizations throughout Venezuela. "I am convinced that our party is undertaking a transcendental function in the political history of Vene-

[6] *Acción Democrática*, no. 53, January 23, 1943, p. 1.

zuela, because it is not an organization to serve personal ambitions . . . but a concert of wills . . . put at the service of Venezuela, in an effort to elevate the dignity of our citizenry. . . ."[7]

As organizational activity continued, attention turned rather heavily to the labor movement, where the competition between democratic leftists and communists had been raging for years. Strife became more fierce as Medina's attitude, a blend of personal tolerance and temperamental laxness, permitted labor a greater degree of freedom than it had previously experienced. While Acción Democrática continued to attack Medina's labor policy sharply, the communists gradually were drawn closer to the regime. Details of the clash between the AD and the communists over control of organized labor are set forth in Chapter IX. The outcome, however, was the establishment of *adeco* domination over the developing labor movement by 1945.

The advent of presidential elections that same year brought a rising tempo of activity that was further nourished by a basically uncertain situation regarding the succession. The issue was the center of attention when the III National Convention of the AD met in Caracas May 25-27, 1945. Some 300 delegates gathered to consider a carefully prepared program. Both the party representation and the agenda itself were better arranged than at previous conclaves. Each sectional sent a delegation of at least five and no more than twenty-five members, both men and women. Representatives of labor, of youth, and of the peasant movement were in attendance. The composition of delegations had been decided through local assemblies and regional conventions prior to the National Convention.[8]

Several broad resolutions were framed and adopted. These included statements on the international situation

[7] *Acción Democrática*, no. 84, September 18, 1943, pp. 1, 4.
[8] *Acción Democrática*, no. 159, May 22, 1945, pp. 1, 3.

and on feminine suffrage. The former urged the tightening of hemispheric ties and self-determination for all peoples, the end of colonial status and a repudiation of unrepresentative or unconstitutional regimes. The declaration on women's rights called for an intensified campaign by feminine party members in favor of suffrage, and a Comité Femenino Nacional was created to strengthen the drive. Of greater interest, however, were measures dealing directly with the impending political crisis.

The critical decisions dealt with the elections and a presidential succession. Acción Democrática was reluctant to select a candidate, referring to the continued electoral system and the existence of a government-financed official party. Recalling Gallegos' symbolic candidacy in 1941, the AD observed that there was little to be gained; the repetition of a tactic appropriate to 1941 conditions would in 1945 have been little more than an exercise in futility. The anticipated candidacy of López Contreras for a second term was sharply condemned, and a public statement was released which included the text of a letter to the PDV charging it with responsibility for growing political tension.

A call was issued for nationwide party activity in favor of universal suffrage, reforms in the electoral census, and a general democratization of laws of public order. The Comité Ejecutivo Nacional, finally, was authorized to convene an extraordinary National Convention before elections if a change in circumstances seemed to warrant it. Barring some unexpected eventuality, however, the AD declared itself as abstaining from presidential elections.

Party leaders were not sanguine about presidential prospects at the time, but circumstances led to the calling of the IV National Convention less than six months later. Yet it was not ultimately a decisive factor, for the question of the presidential succession was settled by a confluence of forces and circumstances that could scarcely be foreseen as early as May.

## The Rise to Power

Notwithstanding Isaías Medina Angarita's ability to choose his successor, the situation was fraught with cross-currents that complicated matters inordinately. At the heart of the matter was the very nature of the out-going administration. While the President was himself a product of the Táchira military, he had not been fully representative of its traditions and general mentality. The tenor of his government proved far more moderate and easy-going than that of its immediate predecessor. To be sure, as López Contreras' chosen successor, Medina on inauguration day had taken an "Oath of Bolivarian Faith" before the Liberator's tomb in the National Pantheon: "I swear to be faithful to Bolivarian Doctrine and to the republican principle of alternation in Public Power."[9] Aside from the lack of substance to such a vow, however, Medina's attitude was flexible. The complete return of political exiles and the legalization of opposition parties gave an early indication of this relaxation of controls. Press freedom was reestablished, and political freedoms were extended noticeably.

The President's loosening of official controls was influenced to some extent by the coming of World War II. The coincidence of his tenure with the international contest between democratic and fascistic forces cannot be forgotten. As one scholar has observed, "Once Caracas broke diplomatic relations with the Axis, on the last day of 1941, and associated itself with the Allied cause, the continued restrictions on civil liberties in Venezuela became more and more anachronistic."[10] Medina's judg-

[9] Eduardo Picón Lares, *Ideología Bolivariana* (Caracas: Editorial Crisol, c. a., 1944), p. 158.

[10] Edwin Lieuwen, *Venezuela* (London: Oxford University Press, 1961), p. 60.

ment was astute to the point of riding the prevailing winds. In his favor must be added the observation that a number of Latin American dictators pursued repressive policies throughout the war, notwithstanding supposed partnership and cooperation with the democracies.

The economic boom during the war years had produced a further aura of well-being, at least in Caracas itself. An increase in petroleum revenues played a major part in financing a four-year plan that emphasized construction projects. The Petroleum Law of 1943 also provided for a more enlightened attitude. Although sharply attacked by Acción Democrática, it eliminated untold contradictions and repetitions in the existing statutes of 1910, 1918, 1920, 1921, 1922, 1925, 1928, 1935, 1936, and 1938. Domestic refining was promoted, governmental technical and administrative powers were broadened, and the Venezuelan share in profits was greatly increased, with minimum royalties set at 16⅔ percent.[11]

With the approach of elections, the *medinista* forces, led by the PDV and supported by leaders of the communist movement, found themselves opposed not only by the AD to the left but by rightist forces which were regrouping about Eleazar López Contreras. As early as 1944 the ex-president had publicly indicated a growing itch for a return to public life by releasing a "clarification" that left him clearly available. Alluding to his long military career, López Contreras claimed to have governed in a "liberal and humane spirit" while remaining aloof from party politics. Thus, he continued, past experience showed his motives to be patriotic rather than personal. Such being the case, he could scarcely reject the demands of his countrymen.

This statement, largely unsolicited, provoked a mild

[11] For details of the legislation, see Edwin Lieuwen, *Petroleum in Venezuela; A History* (Berkeley: University of California Press, 1954), pp. 93-97.

furor among *medinistas* that was amplified by Acción Democrática. A party editorial, belittling López's allegedly apolitical career while taunting his refusal to discuss the issues of the day, regarded as "highly dangerous" the possibility that the General might return to the presidential chair.[12] Concern grew even greater as the struggle between *medinistas* and *lopecistas* assumed greater proportions. Betancourt in later years referred to it as a tropical version of the ancient rivalry between Guelphs and Ghibelines.[13] The AD became apprehensive over the increasingly ominous confrontation in the halls of Congress and in the ruling classes between followers of the two *andinos*. Acción Democrática was anxious to capitalize on the split between the two generals, but a way of doing so was not immediately clear.

As the AD wrestled with the problem, General Medina attempted to impose a solution when, in midsummer, his Partido Democrático Venezolano met in convention and, ignoring the *lopecista* campaign, nominated Venezuelan Ambassador to Washington Diógenes Escalante. A respected moderate and also a civilian, Escalante seemed a promising nominee; he would be the first non-military president of Venezuela in a half-century. Acción Democrática seized upon the nomination as a possible solution and dispatched Rómulo Betancourt and Raúl Leoni to Washington for a conference with the Ambassador.

Betancourt has since written of the interview with Escalante in the lobby of the Hotel Statler.[14] While his visitors perched on suitcases, the Ambassador agreed to the need for broad reform, beginning with constitutional changes permitting direct elections and universal suf-

---

[12] *Acción Democrática*, no. 100, January 22, 1944, pp. 1, 4.

[13] Betancourt, *op.cit.*, p. 185.

[14] His version appears in Betancourt, *ibid.*, p. 192. His interpretation of events during the summer of 1945 continues in the pages which follow.

frage. The result of the interview was an AD decision to support Escalante as a national unity candidate. It was further stated that the AD anticipated a new set of national elections following the constitutional and electoral reforms to which it believed Escalante was committed. This resolution of conditions also appeared to minimize the trouble-making potentialities of López Contreras.

Circumstances soon proved unfortunate. Betancourt had noted during the Washington meeting that Escalante would remain silent for long minutes before replying to oral queries, and his countenance was that of a man whose nervous system was somehow afflicted. Only a few weeks later the Ambassador suffered a nervous collapse; this lessened the possibility of collaboration between General Medina and the organized opposition. López Contreras immediately renewed his drive for a second term, organizing his supporters into a "Grupo Pro-Candidatura de López Contreras."

Still searching for a solution, Acción Democrática adopted as its electoral formula the selection of an independent unity candidate for a one-year term, during which time constitutional reforms might be adopted and freely contested elections held through universal suffrage. Rómulo Gallegos held a personal interview with Medina in early September to advance the proposal. The AD was hopeful—as Gallegos explained four years later during a speech in Mexico—that, without betraying military conspirators with whom the party was dealing, the party might "make one last possible effort to avoid a commotion disturbing to normality, while also giving an opportunity to President Medina to pass honorably into history, with the initiative of my proposal appearing to be his."[15]

Medina himself was in a difficult position, and the

---

[15] Speech delivered in Mexico on September 13, 1949.

pressures were great. Mario Briceño-Iragorri, a prominent intellectual who as President of Congress was closely affiliated with the enlightened wing of the PDV, later wrote of the crisis within the party at the time. A substantial group of *lopecistas* urged López's return; however, Medina recognized the degree to which this would resemble simple *continuismo*.[16] In the view of several, the struggle to balance warring political passions was simply too great. In any event, Medina deliberated for several days, emerging from seclusion on September 12 with the announcement that the nominee would be Angel Biaggini, the Minister of Agriculture. The decision was duly ratified by the PDV on October 1st.

Although Biaggini was not a political unknown, he had relatively little political authority of his own, and was not temperamentally colorful or magnetic. Moreover, as a civilian, he had few if any useful ties with the military leadership, except indirectly through the influence of Medina. The selection of Biaggini brought to an end the search by Acción Democrática for a non-violent solution to the problem. The IV National Convention was called into special session to consider the nomination, but the rejection of the Minister of Agriculture as a unity candidate was a foregone conclusion. The AD saw no peaceful path before it, and therefore the leadership opted in favor of violent means.

As early as June of 1945 the AD leadership had discussed with military dissidents the possibility of an unconstitutional change of government. Dr. Edmundo Fernández, an old friend of Betancourt, had brought the unexpected news that certain junior officers were anxious to confer on the possibility of a *golpe de estado*. The details of the conspiracy and the evolving relationship

---

[16] Mario Briceño-Iragorri, *Ideario Político* (Caracas: Editorial "Las Novedades," 1958), p. 210. This provides an interesting narrative of recent Venezuelan political affairs by an enlightened intellectual who was firmly opposed to Acción Democrática.

between AD directors and the military officers are recounted in Chapter X. In the weeks ahead the politicians
came to believe that the rebels were likely to make their
move even without civilian support. At the same time,
the AD's effort to reach agreement with Medina within
constitutional boundaries went on.

The choice concerning involvement in the conspiracy
was a difficult one for *adecos*, particularly in view of
strongly enunciated principles decrying unconstitutional
changes of government. Furthermore, Acción Democrática had long been a champion of purely civilian government and had consistently maintained that military
interference in political affairs was inappropriate, indeed inimical to the nation's best interests. For a time
it seemed to Betancourt and his companions that the
hard choice might be unnecessary; certainly the possibility of an Escalante candidacy promised to free the
*adecos* from confronting the choice. With the events that
brought about the Biaggini candidacy, however, evasion
by Acción Democrática was no longer possible. The conspirators were in daily contact, and the decisive meeting
was held the night of October 16, at which time the insurrection was tentatively scheduled for December.

On the night of the 17th Acción Democrática held a
rally in Nuevo Circo, where Betancourt hinted at the
possibility of violence if the impasse over a candidate
continued unresolved. "We admit that we want a pacific
change of regime," he declared, "that is, an evolutionary
solution to the complex political situation in the country.
But this evolutionary aspiration will be frustrated if
those who govern continue in their attitude of singular
disdain for public opinion."[17] Partial discovery of the
plot later that night forced the hand of the conspirators,
and early the morning of the 18th, military insurgents
captured the Escuela Militar and moved on to occupy

[17] *El País*, January 6, 1946, pp. 1, 4.

Miraflores and the palace barracks. At the same time the AD mobilized its supporters where possible, engaging in sporadic battle through the afternoon.

By day's end the revolutionaries had won control; both Medina and López Contreras, along with their major supporters, were exiled. So it was that the night of October 18, in a presidential palace lit by gaslight due to the temporary absence of electricity, a seven-man junta took an oath to the Venezuelan people. Two men were leaders of the military rebels: Major Carlos Delgado Chalbaud and Captain Mario Vargas. An independent civilian was Edmundo Fernández. The remaining four members of the Junta Revolucionaria were civilians from the leadership of the AD: provisional president Betancourt, Raúl Leoni, Luis B. Prieto, and Gonzalo Barrios. Thus, by force of arms, Acción Democrática was in control.

## Electoral Democracy

If the decision by the AD to join the military insurgents was momentous, the three years to follow were no less memorable in the stream of Venezuelan history. It was a period of activity and accomplishment on a scale never before experienced. Mistakes and miscalculations were made, as the AD itself is prompt to admit. At the same time, the 1945-1948 *trienio* marked a structural transformation that has provided the basis for future national development. Not even the retrogressive policies of a ten-year dictatorship succeeded in eradicating the effects of this turbulent period.

These years were highly significant in the over-all evolution of Acción Democrática. Luis B. Prieto notes that, from a purely party point of view, the AD learned lessons which are still being applied.[18] By 1945 the *adecos* had become skilled political organizers and activists. Nonetheless, they had never exercised the responsibilities of

[18] Interview with Luis B. Prieto, December 11, 1962.

power, and the change from opposition to national leadership was taxing. Moreover, the experience of dealing with rival democratic parties—which was by no means handled well during the *trienio*—at least made possible a modified set of attitudes toward legal opponents in the post-1958 era.

The immediate task before the AD-dominated Junta Revolucionaria was a restructuring of the electoral system so that the long-advocated method of direct elections and universal suffrage might be instituted. Free elections were promised at the earliest possible date, with the resultant Constituent Assembly empowered to draft a new constitution under which further elections might regularize the political regime. In the meantime, with the military having restored internal tranquility, the civilians set about their tasks.

With the military taking little part in the formulation of policy outside the area of security, Acción Democrática found itself responsible for the operation of government. The Junta named a twelve-man cabinet in which the AD predominated. Prieto served as Secretary of the Junta, Barrios as Governor of the Federal District, Leoni as one of two Ministers of National Defense and Minister of Labor, while Betancourt presided. Prominent *adecos* who fleshed out the cabinet were Minister of Communications Valmore Rodríguez, Minister of the Treasury Carlos D'Ascoli, and Minister of Development Pérez Alfonzo. A few independents were included; Vargas and Delgado Chalbaud of the military served respectively as Minister of Interior Relations and as second Minister of National Defense.[19]

The first weeks were especially hectic, and Miraflores

[19] Venezuela, Junta Revolucionaria de Gobierno, *El Gobierno Revolucionario de Venezuela ante su Pueblo* (Caracas: Imprenta Nacional, 1946), pp. iii-v. This is one of a large number of Junta publications which provide an excellent record of official actions and views during the *trienio*.

Palace became known as "the decree-machine" because of the stream of executive directives. Junta members virtually lived in Miraflores, and visitors tramped unannounced through their offices at all hours, adding to the maelstrom of confusion and noise. As things were gradually put in reasonable order, the drive for electoral and constitutional reform gathered momentum. As early as October 30 Rómulo Betancourt had broadcast that the Junta was concerned with the establishment of legislation permitting unfettered participation by the citizenry; even sooner the Junta had declared that its members would be forbidden from becoming candidates for the presidency at the next election. Betancourt himself drafted the statement, and he was the individual most obviously affected.

Recalling the event several years later, Betancourt wrote that his action was neither a sign of unwillingness to face responsibility nor a maneuver to block the ambitions of fellow Junta members. However, he felt it improper that a ruling member of such an admittedly unconstitutional government should reflect upon its motives by becoming a candidate. Furthermore, although convinced that the next president would be a representative of the AD, he believed the appropriate man was Rómulo Gallegos.

Groundwork for a revision of electoral prescriptions was laid when, on November 17, the old Consejo Electoral was dissolved and a special committee was designated to write a new statute. Its membership drew on some of the finest talent available, and was by no means the exclusive preserve of Acción Democrática. Included were Lorenzo Fernández and Luis Hernández, respective delegates of the newly-organized COPEI and URD groups. Others were independents Jesús Enrique Losada, Nicomedes Zuloaga, Germán Suárez Flamerich, Ambrosio Oropesa, Luis Eduardo Monsanto, Martín Pérez

Guevara, and the AD's Andrés Eloy Blanco. They were, without exception, widely esteemed public figures.

Deliberations were lengthy, but results became public on March 15, 1946, when the Junta Revolucionaria de Gobierno issued Decree No. 216, which laid down the electoral system for a constituent assembly. In Article 2 it granted suffrage "to all Venezuelans from 18 years up, without distinction as to sex and without exception other than prohibitions on persons under indictment by a sentence that has declared them without such political rights." Since illiterates were receiving the vote, there were provisions for citizens to be handed an envelope with party *tarjetas* or cards bearing both party symbols and colors. A new Consejo Supremo Electoral was decreed, composed of representatives of all parties. Any party could nominate candidates to elective office, while legislative representation on both national and regional levels was based on percentage of the total vote. Minority representation was buttressed by an article stipulating that, when a party failed to elect either senators or deputies, it would be assigned congressmen by dividing its total votes by the national electoral quotient.[20]

An additional step toward the creation of a representative electoral system came with the restoration of constitutional freedoms which had been suspended in October. The result was an electoral campaign without precedent in Venezuelan history. A sudden proliferation of parties and political fractions led to the legalization of thirteen different groups. All directed their activities toward elections to the Asamblea Nacional Constituyente

[20] Venezuela, Leyes y Estatutos, *Compilación Legislativa de Venezuela, 1946* (Caracas: Imprenta Nacional, 1947), pp. 9-35.

Details of the electoral prescriptions are found in Venezuela, Leyes y Estatutos, *Estatuto para la Elección de Representantes a la Asamblea Nacional Constituyente y Garantías Ciudadanas, Acordadas por el Gobierno Revolucionario* (Caracas: Imprenta Nacional, 1946).

(ANC) or Constituent Assembly scheduled to meet on October 27, 1946. Most of these were essentially *ad hoc* interest groups which exerted little impact and soon fell by the wayside. Besides the AD, however, three parties aspired to true national stature, and the experience of the *trienio* laid the foundations for permanent organizations.

The three competing organizations were the Comité de Organización Política Electoral Independiente (COPEI), the Unión Republicana Democrática (URD), and the Partido Comunista de Venezuela (PCV). Each was to increase in strength and influence over the following years, and the first two are presently important factors in Venezuelan political life. The history and development of the parties are sketched in Chapter XI in the course of analyzing AD relations with its competitors. Only a brief outline is needed here.

Perhaps the most bitter and unrelenting critic of the AD was the catholic COPEI, whose origins went back into the mid-1930's. Begun in effect as a group of university students opposed to the Federación de Estudiantes de Venezuela (FEV) during the period of Villalba's dominance, it coalesced under the direction of Rafael Caldera, Lorenzo Fernández, Víctor Giménez Landínez, and others. They had adopted at least a moderately favorable position toward the presidency of López Contreras, and the formation of COPEI following the October Revolution of 1945 reflected an evident strain of political conservatism. Rafael Caldera served the Junta briefly but soon withdrew, becoming perhaps the single most prominent leader of COPEI.

The party was imprecise in its programmatic position, beyond a broad dedication to christian democratic thought. There was explicit approval of the Revolution, however. "We are with the Revolution, with its ideals and promises. . . . But we are . . . against the tendency

that may make of the revolution a sewer of hatred. . . ."[21]
Beyond this, COPEI spoke broadly of fighting for social
justice and the rights of the underprivileged. Yet the
conservatism of many supporters was marked, and the
sheer fact that the party's major source of strength was
located in the Andean chain to the southwest, gave testimony to the presence of such political thought. COPEI
was to a considerable degree regional during the *trienio*,
and the Andean isolation from Venezuelan affairs and
national government had been historically pronounced.
As *tachirense* Ramón J. Velásquez recently recalled, ties
were stronger with Colombia than with Venezuela;
Bogotá's *El Tiempo* was received in this area almost daily,
while days and even weeks might pass without a Caracas
paper.[22]

The URD was nationally based but generally weaker
than COPEI. Another offshoot of the October Revolution, it soon became a personal vehicle for the ever-
embattled Jóvito Villalba. Having broken with the leadership of the old PDN during the clandestine period, Villalba had become an unaffiliated senator during the
Medina regime. One of the most skilled parliamentarians of the day, he seemed drawing close to Medina's PDV
when the October Revolution broke out. Finding himself alone, with personal prestige but neither party nor
organization, he became a member of and soon took over
leadership of the URD.

Where COPEI tended to draw into its ranks remaining
*lopecistas*, the URD in its turn was influenced by *medinista* forces, including several former members of the Partido Democrático Venezolana. Beyond this, the URD
became best known for its proclivity for oratory, with

[21] The text of COPEI's Manifesto in 1946 is found in Venezuela,
Presidencia de la República, *Documentos que Hicieron Historia*;
*Siglo y Medio de Vida Republicana, 1810-1961* ( Caracas: Ediciones
Conmemorativas del Sesquicentenario de la Independencia, Vol.
II, 1962), pp. 385-403.
[22] Interview with Ramón J. Velásquez, January 18, 1963,

Villalba excelling. Party doctrine was nebulous throughout the *trienio*, and programmatic statements were occasional rather than systematic. There was a call by Villalba for a government of "national concentration"
including representation from all parties; the AD greeted
it with derision, and its leadership mentioned publicly
that Jóvito had left the old PDN of his own accord when
there had been dirty political work to be done.

With Villalba himself differing little from the *adecos*
in his views, the URD had difficulty in staking out a
clear position for itself, and the tradition of party uncertainty and ambiguity on doctrinal matters began at
this time. The *urredista* statement of intent was a characteristic piece of relatively meaningless rhetoric. "In
social matters we are revolutionaries. We have declared
and accepted the necessity of social revolution in Venezuela. . . . In politics we are liberals, because we conceive
that the transformation of the country will have to come
from the efforts of all Venezuelans. Since our founding
we have predicated our existence as a party on the
struggle for unity of all political forces in a government
of National Integration."[23]

The third source of significant opposition to Acción
Democrática was its old adversary within the labor
movement, the communist party. Ever since the split with
the AD during clandestine activity in the late 1930's
the communists had been clashing with them, and the
struggle for the domination of organized labor had exacerbated relations between the two. An intraparty clash
between the competing leadership of Juan Bautista
Fuenmayor and Gustavo Machado had led to a temporary division into two factions, both of which initially
opposed the October Revolution. Subsequently they
patched up differences in order to present a list of candidates for the Constituent Assembly. Only later were

[23] "La Convención de U. R. D. Marcará el Fin de la Jefatura
Unica," *Momento*, no. 111, August 29, 1958, pp. 33-34.

the factions to divide again into so-called "Red" and "Black" groups.

The electoral campaign centered on the activities of four organizations, then. Certain minor party agreements were arranged: the Unión Federal Republicana (UFR), a state organization in Mérida, and the Frente Independiente (FI), from Trujillo, both joined with COPEI; the URD was tied together for electoral purposes with the tiny Partido Liberal. On October 27, 1946, Venezuela went to the polls for the most democratic and representative national election it had experienced. An estimated 36 percent of the population voted, a sharp contrast with the customary 5 percent under earlier election laws. Furthermore, 92 percent of those enrolled in the new census participated. In all, a total of 1,395,200 votes were cast. The overwhelming winner was Acción Democrática.

The AD polled 1,099,691 votes, or 78.8 percent of the total, thus winning 137 of the 160 seats to the Constituent Assembly. COPEI was a distant second with 13.2 percent and 19 seats. The URD won 2 seats, as did the communists (leaders of their two warring factions, Machado and Fuenmayor). Acción Democrática carried every state but Táchira, which went to COPEI. URD strength, such as it was, came from the northeast and along the Caribbean, while communist votes came primarily from Caracas and the Maracaibo area. The order of the also-rans, after the PCV, was the Organización Democrática Electoral, the Partido Socialista Venezolano, the Frente Popular Independiente de Portuguesa, and Unión Barinensa Independiente.

Political reconstitution of the nation moved forward as the Asamblea Nacional Constituyente convened on December 17, 1946. Controlling as it did 137 of 160 seats, Acción Democrática dominated the writing of a new constitution. Its leadership in the Assembly was provided by the legislative President, Andrés Eloy Blanco,

Second Vice-President Augusto Malavé Villalba, and the AD parliamentary leader Luis Lander.[24] Debates were heated and sometimes bitter, but Blanco's wit, diplomacy, and brilliance contributed mightily to the calming of tempers, and the final record of debates is not unimpressive in its level of discussion.

The final document was signed into law on July 5, 1947, Venezuelan Independence Day. Although counts differ slightly, it was at least the twenty-second constitution to be adopted since independence. The preamble is a useful indication of AD thought in the mid-1940's, setting forth three broad areas of interest:

1. The harmony, the well-being, and the social and individual security of Venezuela and of all who live in its territory and under its law.

2. The affirmation of appropriate nationality, supported in accordance with fraternal cooperation in the concert of Nations, in projects of peace and of progress, and with mutual respect of sovereignty.

3. The support of democracy as the only and irrenounceable system of governing internal conduct and pacific collaboration in the design of promoting that same system in the governments of all peoples of the earth.[25]

The document's social and economic passages far surpassed anything previously included in a Venezuelan constitution. Articles 53-57 committed the state to an extensive system of social security, including state construction of low-cost housing for workers, and responsibility for the protection of their health by means of

[24] Mercedes Fermín pointed out in an interview on October 4, 1962, that this trio was characteristic of AD multiclass representation. Thus Blanco was a poet and teacher, Malavé Villalba a labor organizer, and Lander a youth recently emerged from student ranks.

[25] Cf. Venezuela, *Constitución de 5 julio de 1947* (Caracas: Imprenta Nacional, 1947).

services such as the prevention and eradication of disease. Articles 61-63 set down in part the role of labor; work was declared a right and a duty to be fulfilled by every citizen as his contribution to society. Furthermore, workers were guaranteed the right to organize and to strike—excepting essential public services—as well as pensions, sick pay, severance pay, paid vacations, and assurance of profit-sharing plans.

Purely political matters were discussed succinctly. The electoral system of direct, universal suffrage was enshrined in the national charter, while the presidential term was set at four years, with an outgoing executive ineligible for reelection for eight years. The Supreme Court was empowered to vote on the constitutionality of laws, and a direct vote was also to provide for the membership of a two-house congress. This commitment to a bicameral legislature was not universally applauded by *adecos*, and its passage related to one of the matters over which the greatest controversy centered.

The 1947 Constitution reflected in broad strokes an incongruity between the political centralism and administrative decentralization for which the party had long appealed. While the extent of state duties and obligations favored a strengthening of centralized government, there was a bow toward decentralization through the vestigial remnants of federalism that were seen in the two-house legislature. Acción Democrática itself had long pondered the matter without reaching any satisfactory resolution. As Betancourt had written, it was felt that federalism had been "a cause of disintegration, and in each of the States an insular and provincial performance of legal duties has been the result."[26] Yet the eradication of all traces of federalism was somehow unsavory to the AD, and so the Constitution of 1947 left the matter unclear.

An additional dispute of some gravity arose during

[26] Rómulo Betancourt, *Trayectoria Democrática de una Revolución* (Caracas: Imprenta Nacional, 1948), p. 167.

debates over the proposed authorization of the chief
executive to order preventive detention of all those
believed to be conspiring to subvert the government.
After discussing such steps with the Council of Ministers,
the President was to have ten days in which to send the
decree to Congress for legislative consideration. If not approved, the emergency measure would be withdrawn. If
adopted, the Corte Suprema de Justicia still had to study
the decree within seventy days; the Court could either
sustain or reverse it.

The measure was ultimately embodied in Article 77,
despite the small but vocal opposition by COPEI, the
URD, and the PCV. Members of the Junta declared that,
repeatedly threatened with revolutionary outbursts of
violence, they saw a real need for such powers, so long
as adequate safeguards could be built in. The military,
including the counter-revolutionaries of 1948 who were
soon to deride the 1947 document mercilessly, agreed to
the measure, as they assured AD leaders at a private
meeting while the Assembly was debating the matter.[27]

## Legalization of Power

Following elections to the Constituent Assembly,
Acción Democrática had convened its VI National Con-
vention on November 30, 1946. Chosen as President and
First and Second Vice-Presidents, respectively, were
Gallegos, Blanco, and female leader Cecilia Núñez Sucre.
Alterations in certain of the important posts reflected the
absence of several leaders due to governmental responsi-
bilities. Thus, a number of new officers were elected,
among them Secretary-General Alberto Carnevali, Secre-
tary of Organization Luis Augusto Dubuc, Secretary of
Finances Manuel Martínez, Secretary of Culture Luis
Manuel Peñalver, Feminine Secretary Mercedes Fermín,
Secretary of Propaganda Luis Troconis Guerrero, and
Juvenile Secretary José María Machín. A new position

[27] Betancourt, *Política y Petróleo*, p. 802, note 8.

was the Secretary of International Relations, to which Luis Lander was named.

During the months of the Constituent Assembly the leadership posts in AD continued along these lines, but with the nearing of presidential elections in late 1947 the party called its VII National Convention in order to nominate Rómulo Gallegos. He was released from the AD presidency, a post assumed by Blanco, while a special electoral committee was formed by Blanco, Rodríguez, Fermín, Vicente Gamboa Marcano, Raúl Ramos Giménez, and Elpidio La Riva Mata. A week after the Convention, on the sixth anniversary of the party's founding, Gallegos formally accepted the nomination before a Caracas crowd of 30,000. Calling for a program of national concord, justice and public welfare, he delivered one of the most eloquent addresses of his career.[28] In it he called for the concrete goals of industrial development, public works and construction, improved health and education, and agrarian reform.

Gallegos stressed the importance of party responsibility in the campaign that was to follow. Speaking more as the pedagogue than as a partisan candidate, he asked for the observance of high civic standards, and his repeated plea for moderation was also voiced by the party's Comité Ejecutivo Nacional. The CEN called for respect and tolerance from all supporters. Loyal *adecos* were urged to help fellow citizens in the full enjoyment of freedom and impartiality in the election. The party, said the CEN, saw the campaign as an electoral debate that was to go down in history as a model of irreproachable civic behavior.

The campaign was nonetheless immoderate, due in no small measure to the overexuberance and intolerance of the AD rank and file. The announcement by COPEI on

[28] Rómulo Gallegos, *Una posición en la Vida* (México: Ediciones Humanismo, 1954), pp. 256-94. For a detailed commentary on the address, cf. *El País*, September 13, 1947, pp. 1, 5, 11.

October 13 of the presidential candidacy of Rafael Caldera was met with scathing criticism from many *adecos*; it was returned in kind by *copeyanos*. The URD after long consideration rejected the idea of a Villalba nomination in favor of a slate of congressional candidates. There was an unspoken recognition of the impossibility of running a strong race, and Villalba himself saw the likelihood of finishing behind Caldera in third place. The communists, divided once again, were unable to agree on tactics. Gustavo Machado was nominated by his wing of the party, while the faction headed by Rodolfo Quintero stood aloof from the presidential struggle, offering only a short and partial list of candidates.

Venezuelans went to the polls for the second time in fourteen months on December 14, 1947 (see Figure 1). Again the victory went to the AD. Rómulo Gallegos won the first presidential election based on direct democracy and universal suffrage, polling 871,752 votes, virtually 75 percent. Caldera received 262,204 votes, a fairly strong showing under the impossible conditions facing him; Machado was last with 36,514. The AD won its legislative races with a slightly smaller margin than that of Gallegos, as its 838,526 votes represented 71 percent of the 1,183,-764 congressional ballots. COPEI received 20 percent, while the URD and the Machado communists failed to win a seat. After minor adjustments had been made in compliance with the electoral quotient, Acción Democrática controlled 38 of 46 Senate seats and 83 of 110 in the Chamber.[29]

[29] The 1946 electoral statute established the use of a quotient system in the case of minority parties failing to elect congressmen through the direct vote. As illustrated through the December 1947 elections, the total number of legislative votes (1,183,764) was divided by the number of seats in each house. Thus, the 44-seat Senate had a quotient of 26,903; the 103-seat Chamber had a quotient of 11,492.

These quotients were then applied to parties failing to win a seat through direct elections. The URD's 51,427 votes was divided

FIGURE 1*

TRIENIO ELECTIONS

| Date and Offices | AD | COPEI | URD | PCV | Misc. |
|---|---|---|---|---|---|
| 27 October 1946 (Constituent Assembly) | | | | | |
| Total: 1,395,200 | 1,099,601 | 185,347 | 53,875 | 50,837 | 5,540 |
| Percentage: 100 | 78.8 | 13.2 | 3.8 | 3.6 | 0.6 |
| Seats: 160 | 137 | 19 | 2 | 2 | 0 |
| 14 December 1947 (Congress) | | | | | |
| Total: 1,183,764 | 838,526 | 240,186[a] | 51,427 | 43,190 | 10,435 |
| Percentage: 100 | 70.8 | 20.5 | 4.3 | 3.7 | 0.7 |
| Senators 46 (44)[b] | 38 | 6 | 1 | 1 | 0 |
| Deputies: 110 (103)[c] | 83 | 19 | 4 | 3 | 1[d] |
| 14 December 1947 (President) | | | | | |
| Total: 1,170,470 | 871,752 | 262,204 | | 36,514 | |
| Percentage: 100 | 74.4 | 22.4 | | 3.2 | |
| 9 May 1948 (Municipal Councilmen) | | | | | |
| Total: 693,154 | 491,762 | 146,197 | 27,007 | 23,524 | 4,664 |
| Percentage: 100 | 70.1 | 21.1 | 3.9 | 3.4 | 0.5 |

* Official returns as announced by the national Consejo Supremo Electoral.

[a] This total represents the addition of 200,695 COPEI votes and 39,491 from the Unión Federal Republicana, which represented COPEI in Mérida.

[b] 44 Senate seats were contested; application of the electoral quotient awarded an additional seat to both the URD and the PCV.

[c] 103 Chamber seats were contested; the application of the electoral quotient awarded four seats to the URD and three to the PCV.

[d] The Partido Liberal Progresista was a regional party that named one deputy from Amazonas through direct means.

NOTE: In legislative races of December 14, 1947, the Senate quotient was calculated at 26,903; that of the Chamber was 11,492.

The state-by-state breakdown revealed that Gallegos carried all but two states—Andean Mérida and Táchira—both of which went to Rafael Caldera. In the legislative

by the Senate quotient, resulting in 1 seat; division by the Chamber quotient brought 4 seats there. This procedure was also applied to the PCV, adding one Senator and 3 Deputies. In December of 1947, therefore, 2 additional Senate seats and 7 Chamber seats were added to the Congress through the quotient.

race AD defeated COPEI in Táchira by some 6,000 out
of 50,000 votes, however; only in Mérida were AD legislative candidates outpolled (by the COPEI-affiliated
Unión Federal Republicana). A final oddity was the
single seat in the Chamber of Deputies won by a member
of the Partido Liberal Progresista (PLP), a semi-faction
organized for a one-man candidacy in the sparsely populated federal territory of Amazonas. Thus, while the URD
with over 50,000 votes nationally was unable to elect a
congressman directly, the PLP sent to Caracas a man
who polled a grand total of 860 votes.

On Thursday the 12th of February, 1948, Junta President Betancourt delivered his final message to Congress.
He recalled that the AD had formulated three basic objectives when it joined with the military rebels in 1945:
restoration of popular sovereignty, depersonalization of
public power, and the establishment of administrative
morality. Claiming that all three had been fulfilled, he
concluded the Junta report amid cheers from the audience. Three days later Rómulo Gallegos took the oath of
office before a distinguished gathering that included intellectual figures from across the hemisphere. Devoting
his address to a call for a policy of concord, he noted
that the partisan struggle had been vehement, but that
the conclusion of the campaign would hopefully usher
in a new era. "My party won the right to govern with
its program by winning in the electoral field. We have
thereby contracted an obligation to constitute the government with men of Acción Democrática, but we have also
promised to choose collaborators who, without belonging
to our party, agree with us on various social, political
and administrative problems, sharing our determination
to solve them. . . ."[30]

There was, however, no moratorium on political strife.
The AD itself remained vocally active. Its next efforts

[30] Gallegos, *op.cit.*, p. 299.

centered on municipal elections held May 9, 1948. For the Venezuelan voter, participating in his third vote in eighteen months, it may well have seemed almost too much of a good thing. This was one explanation for the reduction in the number of voters, and it is probably the most convincing. Where 1,395,200 had voted in October 1946 and 1,183,470 in December 1947, only 693,154 cast their ballots in May 1948.

Acción Democrática had worked hard to avoid the anticipated drop in voter participation. Less than a week before elections, Secretary-General Alberto Carnevali declared in a broadcast that the AD regarded municipal elections in the interior as critically important. But the citizenry proved impossible to arouse once again. Thus the turnout was substantially smaller, although the AD percentage of 70.09 was comparable to previous elections. COPEI again polled just over one-fifth of the vote with 146,197, while the URD and PCV trailed far behind. Once again COPEI won in Táchira, while its UFR affiliate defeated the AD in Mérida. There were, in short, no real surprises. Both the AD and COPEI received roughly the same percentage as in previous votes, while the URD and PCV were woefully weak. There was no indication that Acción Democrática had been seriously damaged by members defecting to other parties, although the leadership in the wake of the municipal contests recognized a danger that public attention in general was waning.

Party affairs for the remainder of 1948 were centered largely on planning through congressional sessions; the rest of the work was organizational. The AD held its VIII National Convention at the end of May—the last such for a full decade, as events were to prove. The leadership recognized that the party had serious organizational problems, notwithstanding the chain of electoral victories. Foremost were the difficulties brought about through sheer numbers. From an estimated 75-80,000 in 1941, party inscriptions had reached nearly 400,000 during the *trienio*, and it was bidding to pass the half-million mark.[31] This dizzying increase not only caused problems in operation and direction but, as party documents later conceded, the attractions of power brought a number of new recruits more concerned with personal gain than party advantage. In states where the party organization had been small, the regional leadership was virtually inundated by the weight of numbers.

Furthermore, party leadership had been confronted with the demands of national government ever since the October Revolution. Rómulo Betancourt, the party's organizational genius, had been swamped with the tasks of the provisional presidency, while pressures had also been hectic and unremitting on his colleagues. The top-drawer leadership of the AD—Barrios, Leoni, Prieto, Rodríguez, D'Ascoli, and others—had no choice but to thrust greater party responsibility on younger and less experienced men. Added to this was the further problem that there were still areas of national life in which the AD had not yet formulated positive and detailed programs. Yet the years after 1945 had provided scarce opportunities for the contemplative study and analysis of fundamental national problems. The traditional existence of standing study commissions was interrupted by the press of directing the country, and by mid-1948 it was apparent that the party needed to reformulate policies and generally streamline the machinery.

At the VIII National Convention Rómulo Betancourt was installed as party President, with Valmore Rodríguez and Luis Lander becoming First and Second Vice-Presidents. The rising young Luis Augusto Dubuc was named Secretary-General. Other new names included Labor Secretary Luis Hurtado, Cultural Secretary Domingo Alberto Rangel, Public Relations Secretary Braulio Jatar Dotti, and Youth Secretary Jorge Dager. More familiar names were Press Secretary Troconis Guerrero, Propa-

[31] Interview with Raúl Leoni, December 6, 1962.

ganda Secretary Martínez, Feminine Secretary Núñez Sucre, and Agrarian Secretary Quijada. A revised list of the Comité Directivo Nacional was also announced, composed of seventy-four names.[32] The major address was delivered by President of the Republic Gallegos, who reflected the refusal of opposition parties to heed his call for concord by increasing partisan reliance on his own organization.

The party leadership left the Convention determined to implement more fully the programs dictated by government policy, while daily organizational tasks continued. Yet the burdens of responsibility remained heavy. The attempt to thrust Venezuela bodily into the twentieth century was causing understandable turbulence, and sharp political opposition was coming from interests adversely affected by AD policy. As the Gallegos administration seemed to drift aimlessly in the summer of 1948, the party rank-and-file responded by maintaining and indeed increasing the tone of partisanship. The dialogue between the Acción Democrática and the opposition parties, such as it was, broke down. An exchange of views became increasingly difficult, and both COPEI and the URD still encountered occasional problems when party rallies were disrupted or local leaders were jailed for brief periods on questionable charges.

The party was still a young and sprawling organization by no means sufficiently equipped or experienced to

[32] The listed order of the CDN membership ran Gallegos, Betancourt, Blanco, Prieto, Pérez Alfonzo, Leoni, Barrios, Rodríguez, D'Ascoli, Lander, Núñez Sucre, Carnevali, López Gallegos, Troconis Guerrero, Peñalver, Fermín, and Dubuc. Others of later prominence and their 1948 positions were Ruiz Pineda (19), Malavé Villalba (26), Quijada (27), Pérez Salinas (32), Siso Martínez (41), Rangel (56), Ramos Giménez (69), and Paz Galarraga (71).

It should be emphasized that numbered listings are not common, and there is a substantial amount of imprecision involved. Nonetheless, the order of CDN members at any given time is not meaningless, and can be instructive to close students of the party.

operate and institute the far-reaching national revolution envisioned by its leadership. In many ways it was clearly in a state of adolescence, with maturity well into the future. Given a different set of circumstances, the AD might have weathered the years ahead, as did Mexico's revolutionary PRI after years of turmoil and bloodshed. However, the Venezuelan political environment proved too much for the ardent young revolutionaries. The result was the November 1948 counter-revolution which swept Acción Democrática from power, relegating it to a decade of exile while bringing to the Venezuelan people a superficial prosperity that failed to hide a politically corrupt, socially unenlightened despotism under military direction.

# CHAPTER III

# Vicissitudes of Political Leadership

## 1948-1964

The inauguration of the Gallegos government in the spring of 1948 was hailed across the continent as a shining victory for reformist democratic forces, and the intellectual stature of the new chief executive only added to the favorable view abroad. Yet barely nine months later Gallegos was overthrown, his ministers dispersed, and the seemingly invincible apparatus of Acción Democrática smashed to bits. The simple explanation—that a dissatisfied military, with a tradition of political intervention, overturned a government supported by the majority of the people—is perhaps the best one. Yet it is by no means the whole answer. Much of the pressure that created a situation in which the military felt free to operate originated from sources other than the armed forces. The shortcomings of Acción Democrática in terms of political leadership cannot be minimized.

## *The Process of Alienation*

The policies of the AD during the *trienio* had first been directed at essentially political goals. These were embraced by the electoral law as well as relevant passages of the Constitution of 1947. The subsequent political activism of ardent *adecos*, however, led the opposition to question their dedication to principles of political competition and the toleration of dissenting views. As described later, the inter-party relations were mutually irritating, to understate the case. However, with the gradual constitutional reorganization of the country came the increasing impetus generated by social and economic policies. These played a major part in the process of alienation.

The major thrust of party doctrine, then, moved away from the political sphere following the establishment of conditions and regulations under which Acción Democrática felt confident of its place. Luis Lander, later writing from exile for *Cuadernos Americanos*, pointed out the overriding importance of providing better living conditions. The AD argued that the masses had to be prepared for economic advances, in a sense, only after experiencing the unfettered play of political democracy. Thus they had to be shown that it was possible to participate by means of democratic elections in the winning of a better life. Venezuelans could then "see in practice how the causes of their misery can be eradicated, and how to solve their problems by democratic means. They see the denial of liberty, systems of dictatorial government, and the effect of economic methods of exploitation as being . . . cultivated by the spread and growth of communist ideology."[1]

The provisional Junta which assumed power in October 1945 quickly stated its determination to raise living conditions; before the close of the year a Ministry of Labor had been created, through which the development of trade unionism was actively promoted. Both ideological conviction and political realism led the AD to place its fundamental reliance for popular strength on the worker. In 1946 alone over 500 unions were organized, more than doubling the number of the previous year, and the establishment of thirteen federations led in 1947 to the founding of the Confederación de Trabajadores de Venezuela (CTV), then as now a major economic and political force.

During this period a number of work contracts were negotiated, the majority of which were shepherded along benevolently by the government. Characteristic was an eighteen-month collective contract for the entire oil

[1] Luis Lander, "La Doctrina Venezolana de Acción Democrática," *Cuadernos Americanos*, IX, julio-agosto 1950, p. 23.

industry signed on June 14, 1946, which provided a variety of fringe benefits in addition to a basic wage raise. The dominant union in the CTV, the FEDEPETROL oil workers, strongly supported the government in turn, and was further rewarded with a new three-year collective contract in late 1947, again highly beneficial to the workers. Such pro-labor policies made a powerful impact on the nation, and entrepreneurial circles were less than elated. Although petroleum workers were the elite of the labor movement, workers in other areas also benefited substantially. During the *trienio,* according to figures from the Banco Central, real wages rose by 65 percent in Venezuela.[2]

Over-all economic development led to the creation of a central economic agency in May of 1946, the Corporación Venezolana de Fomento (CVF). Aiming at increased agricultural production and the establishment of new industries, the CVF relied upon generous injections of petroleum income in extending credits to private business. A variety of state corporations were also set up to boost productivity in different areas. Other autonomous agencies important to the economy were the Banco Obrero and the Banco Agrícola y Pecuario (BAP). The latter proved the major credit instrument in increasing and diversifying production. By 1948 the infusion of large sums of money led to an enlargement in credit activities of 81 percent over the preceding year, and the number of small farmers who received credits rose from 46,000 to 81,000.

The extensive agricultural program began on an *ad hoc* basis, and the presumably long-range reform law was passed by the Gallegos government less than a month before the November counter-revolution.[3] But such meas-

[2] As cited in Edwin Lieuwen, *Venezuela* (London: Oxford University Press, 1961), p. 79.

[3] A somewhat partisan book that nonetheless gives an excellent survey of land conditions and of the proposed goals of the AD

ures as the importation of machinery and the establishment of technical instruction were introduced for the first time, and pilot projects for extensive irrigation were also set up. The historic problem of land redistribution and the presence of *latifundismo* helped dictate the final form of agrarian reform. Although the AD deliberately tried to avoid any appearance of punitive or expropriatory measures toward the large landowners, there were, nonetheless, indications of strong opposition that had not fully come into the open when the government fell.

Social welfare and education were also included in the AD's *trienio* activities. The most famed accomplishment, perhaps, was the remarkable eradication of malaria in the short space of two years—thus eliminating a disease previously contracted annually by nearly one-fifth of the population. Hospital construction and medical training were expanded, and the assault on undernourishment and disease was reflected by a tripling of the Ministry of Health's budget. As for education, appropriations were also tripled, a program of adult education was initiated, and illiteracy was combatted by a campaign mounted on both adult and childhood levels. The *adeco* attention to previously ignored needs of the middle and lower classes in Venezuela left a heritage that exists today in a general political and social commitment to aid the underprivileged. Such was not the case in the 1940's, however.

The attempted implantation of such far-ranging reforms was a harsh and drastic wrench from the past. With so many unorthodox measures violently championed and just as violently opposed, the *trienio* was inevitably hectic. Aside from organized opposition from COPEI, the URD, and the PCV, large landowners joined with the urban aristocracy to oppose the Revolution and its broader implications. They believed that their interests

program in 1948 is Luis Troconis Guerrero, *La Cuestión Agraria en la Historia Nacional* (Caracas: Editorial Arte, 1962).

could not be maintained unless reforms were brought to a swift halt under a regime of a different nature.

The displeasure of the traditional forces in society was augmented by the government's vigorous prosecution of those who had allegedly profited during the two preceding governments. A special Tribunal of Civil and Administrative Responsibility was created soon after the *golpe de estado*, and 168 former officials were charged with embezzlement and self-enrichment in office. The measure was justified by the strangely puritanical AD as necessary to create a tradition and consciousness of public morality. It was, nonetheless, a drastic policy that was in contradiction to historic practice, and one that stiffened the backbone of the opposition. The major trials in these proceedings resulted in confiscations of an estimated $120 million in property.[4] The AD has always claimed that justice was done, but the opponents of the party understandably viewed it as political vengeance for past wrongs suffered by Acción Democrática. Notwithstanding genuine AD conviction that an example of past corruption had to be made, an equally strong argument can be presented concerning the party's lack of pragmatic political wisdom.

A final area in which opposition was created was the AD approach to the Catholic Church. The clergy was seriously concerned about the issue of religion and private education. The AD, back as far as the days of ORVE and the PDN, included a handful of leaders whose views were strongly anti-clerical. However, never in the majority on this matter, they failed to sway the organization from a relatively mild position. Thus it was held that religious freedom and individual choice in observance

[4] Betancourt discusses the matter at some length in *Política y Petróleo*, pp. 225-27. A dissenting view that injustices were involved is found in Rodolfo Luzardo, *Notas Histórico-Económicas, 1928-1963* (Caracas: Editorial Sucre, 1963), pp. 158-59. Also see the criticism of a *medinista* cabinet minister in Julio Diez, *Historia y Política* (Caracas: Pensamiento Vivo, 2d ed., 1963), pp. 30-33.

were inviolable and, furthermore, that religious involvement in politics was inadmissible. A realistic awareness that most Venezuelans were Catholic, led to recognition of the validity of existing Church-State agreements, some of them over a century old. But the AD also maintained that the Church had no right to attempt any ideological tutelage in public schools. Moreover, private educational institutions should come under national jurisdiction to the extent of receiving official sanction from the Ministry of Education.

The clergy was highly suspicious of the AD from its inception, and general political immoderation increased the mistrust. The implied supervision of private education, as the Church viewed AD policy, appeared to be a clear threat. Furthermore, the inclusion of new educational methods and the application of government propaganda materials heightened their suspicion. Thus yet another sector of the society was to a large extent alienated from the party at the head of government.

The groups antagonized by the AD include the following: landowners fearing agrarian reform; manufacturers pressed by rising labor costs; clergy fearful of the AD educational practices and the party's general outlook toward religion; former high officials from *medinista*, *lopecista*, and even late *gomecista* days now deprived of office and sometimes of property; the traditional social elite that feared the potential threat from a rise in the political power of the masses; foreign investors who dreaded the alleged "radical" direction of party policies;[5]

[5] There have been a variety of reports and rumors to the effect that foreign oil interests took a major part in the overthrow of the Gallegos government, through indirect but influential means. Rómulo Gallegos himself charged such interference from Cuban exile shortly after being deposed. Betancourt makes little reference to the matter in *Política y Petróleo*. It is impossible to state categorically that the oil interests were totally removed from the events of November 1948. While in all probability there was quiet satisfaction at the change of regimes, no solid evidence exists that would substantiate charges of improprieties by the oil interests.

and growing party opposition by rival organizations that both resented and mistrusted the rather brassy, even arrogant AD apparatus.

Even with the alienation of these sectors, Acción Democrática might still have survived, although the presence of a less-than-skilled political leader in the presidency was a further handicap. However, the Venezuelan armed forces were also on the scene. It is ironic that although the AD uncompromisingly attacked many groups that which it most carefully courted was the one to bring down the government. There can be no question but that the military benefited far more from an *adeco* regime than it had from the preceding administrations of Andean general-presidents. This is further borne out in the discussion in Chapter X.

As it was, the military intervention in November of 1948 was inevitable, with the only question being one of time and circumstance. Even for those who argue that mishandling of an incendiary situation by President Gallegos proved fatal, there is little to suggest that the counter-revolution could have been avoided. At best, a more astute president would merely have delayed the final blow. Gonzalo Barrios, who was at the side of Gallegos through the final critical hours, has since observed that there had been so many threats and unsuccessful conspiracies during the *trienio* that the climactic confrontation with the military was not immediately recognized as something of real gravity.[6]

When the critical moment arrived, Gallegos was informed of the military's demands: inclusion of more officers in the cabinet, ministerial representation for COPEI, and the exiling of Rómulo Betancourt. Gallegos gave no immediate response, but in a short time replied

[6] Interview with Gonzalo Barrios, November 27, 1962. A useful compendium of newspaper articles and editorials bearing on the overthrow is contained in José Rodríguez (ed.), *Quién derrocó a Gallegos?* (Caracas: Tip. Garrido, 2d ed., 1961).

to the ultimatum in the negative. On November 24, 1948, he was placed under arrest by the newly emergent military triumvirate. The cabinet was taken into custody and jailed, as were virtually all congressmen of Acción Democrática. Some were exiled swiftly, while others remained for months until freed in response to foreign pressure.

An eloquent message of protest by Rómulo Gallegos, written in his Caracas home, was not permitted to circulate; it later appeared in Mexico.

"I have just received the news that the Presidential Palace of Miraflores has been occupied by military forces. . . . I know that . . . they are already coming to take me into custody. Thus culminates an insurrectional process by the forces of the Caracas garrison and of the high military command, initiated ten days ago with the intent of exerting pressure in order to impose certain political conduct on me. . . . To such pretensions I have energetically fought in defense of the dignity of civil power, against which this blow has been directed in order to establish a military dictatorship."[7]

There was no real alternative left to the AD. Talk of arming party supporters and especially organized workers, then sending them into the streets to man the barricades against regular military forces, was at no point feasible. The arms were lacking, in the first place, and the only result would have been a bloodbath that the armed forces could not have lost. AD leaders feared that the resultant civil war would have been tragic.[8] As it

[7] Venezuela, Presidencia de la República, *Documentos que Hicieron Historia; Siglo y Medio de Vida Republicana, 1810-1961* (Caracas: Ediciones Conmemorativas del Sesquicentenario de la Independencia, Vol. 2, 1962), p. 415.

[8] Views expressed to the author in the following interviews: Raúl Leoni on October 29, 1962; Mercedes Fermín on October 18, 1962; Gonzalo Barrios on November 27, 1962; José González Navarro on November 21, 1962; and Andrés Hernández on November 21, 1962.

was, unapprehended party activists went into hiding and took up the fight from underground. It was to be a long and bloody struggle. Acción Democrática went into deep eclipse, and the travail of the years ahead was to be a sore test for the courage and resiliency of the leadership.

## Dictatorial Domination

The overthrow of Rómulo Gallegos drove Acción Democrática into hiding once again, and the repression of the decade from 1948-1958 was far greater than the sometimes cavalier persecution of the old PDN years before. The incoming military regime regarded the AD as the major threat to its power, and therefore undertook a concerted effort to eradicate the party completely. For a full decade the AD went into eclipse, although its survival despite the problems of an exile existence was a significant chapter in party history, as is described in more detail elsewhere.

The Junta that replaced Gallegos was at the outset directed by Lt. Col. Carlos Delgado Chalbaud, son of a former anti-Gómez military leader and himself a major figure during the *trienio*. As will be seen in Chapter X, Delgado's personal role in the *golpe de estado* has been debated lengthily, and his untimely death made impossible any final resolution. Certainly he was to all intents and appearances the dominant figure of a three-man junta that also included Major Marcos Pérez Jiménez and Major Felipe Llovera Páez.

Delgado Chalbaud claimed to desire a return to democratic forms and representative government; the point is debatable. In all likelihood he hoped to assume the presidency himself, presumably after an election in which Acción Democrática would be banned. This eventuality was canceled when he was gunned down on November 19, 1950, under circumstances that suggested possible collusion by rivals within the government.

Lip service continued to be paid to democratic forms, but all pretense was dropped after the public repudiation of the regime in 1952 elections. Pérez Jiménez' efforts to win office at the ballot box were rejected by the electorate on that occasion, and only by annulling the vote and creating an illegal and unrepresentative national assembly was he able to assume the presidency under the guise of electoral procedures. And from that time forward the regime grew openly dictatorial, corrupt, and devoid of respect for private rights and individual liberties. All parties—not merely the AD—were driven underground, the number of political prisoners mounted, and the government's reputation became increasingly unsavory.

Economically the decade was plush. The postwar boom, rising petroleum prices on the international market, plus a temporarily remunerative policy of oil concessions in 1956 and 1957, contributed to a period of good times and high living upon which the regime capitalized.[9] Construction and public works were of the spectacular nature, many of them of questionable utility. Caracas' Centro Bolívar was erected as a mid-city kind of Rockefeller Center; the Humboldt Hotel was built atop Mount Avila, a spectacular white elephant ever since its completion; an expensive cable-car was built in two stages to reach the Hotel; and the world's costliest officers' club was built in a Caracas suburb. Somewhat less ostentatious building included a major extension of transportation arteries and a number of public dams and industrial complexes.

Substantial sums were also devoted to securing support from the military. In addition to the officers' club, expensive modern weapons, jet airplanes, and new navy ships were provided to them. At the same time, education

[9] For perhaps the best account in English of the *perezjimenista* dictatorship—somewhat lurid but accurate in its essentials—see Tad Szulc, *Twilight of the Tyrants* (New York: Henry Holt and Co., 1959).

—which had received great impetus during the *trienio*—fell into neglect. The 5 percent of the budgetary appropriations which education customarily received under Pérez Jiménez was for several years the lowest in the hemisphere. Technical and vocational schools were ignored, literacy campaigns forgotten, teacher education slighted, and attendance decline overlooked. The regime similarly ignored the need for agrarian reform, reduced the commitment to public health and to hospital construction, and neglected the importance of economic diversification.

The continuing economic prosperity of the nation—although grossly maldistributed—made possible the wave of expenditures. Production of oil was particularly responsible; international demands increased substantially, first during the Korean fighting and later at the time of the Suez crisis. Prices rose and income did likewise; and if this were not enough, the regime in 1956 and 1957 sold new concessions. These, which were nearly as extensive as all those previously owned, drew an estimated $1.25 billion into Venezuela.

Dark as was the record, it must also be noted that it was under Pérez Jiménez in the 1950's that iron ore came to the fore as a significant contributor to the national economy, and this was to play an increasingly important part in the years ahead. Foreign investment, which had been somewhat leery of massive commitments during the *trienio*, returned in large sums. Tax policy was highly favorable, while the administration's anti-labor policy held down production costs. Not only were wages kept in check but there was nearly a 25 percent shrinkage of the labor force in petroleum alone.

Strongly implicit in the Pérez Jiménez economic policy was a lack of concern in the "human resources" previously encouraged by Acción Democrática. Material accomplishments aside, the lot of the average Venezuelan was no better. The social ills that all the democratic parties had recognized during the *trienio* became aggravated with the passing of time. Slum and unemployment conditions multiplied in Caracas, which had tripled in population to more than 1 million inhabitants during the dictatorial decade. A large influx of immigrants, largely Italian, settled in the city rather than proceeding to the provinces, as had been intended, therefore exacerbating still more the inequalities of life in the metropolitan center. In the countryside it was believed that the concern of the regime was limited strictly to the citizens of Caracas; both the rural and urban lower-income groups, then, came to feel for different reasons that the government was indifferent to their welfare.

Tales of graft and corruption are inevitable in a regime such as that of Pérez Jiménez, and figures are difficult to come by. Edwin Lieuwen estimated on the basis of assorted reports and sources that the dictator himself amassed $250 million during his tenure, while untold millions were accumulated by his cronies.[10] There can be little serious doubt that the level of administrative immorality was high, and the examples of public graft contributed to the deep skepticism with which today's average Venezuelan views the bureaucracy.

Political oppression was centered on open opponents to the regime, and the membership of AD, COPEI, and the URD suffered most directly. At the same time, it became unwise to voice open criticism of the regime. Press censorship was established immediately after the 1948 counterrevolution, and true freedom of the press did not return for ten years. Unfavorable foreign publications were seized upon arrival in the country, while official propaganda flooded the newsstands. The lack of political liberty and of constitutional guarantees became increasingly arbitrary in application, and contributed to growing dissatisfaction on the part of urban middle groups which

[10] Edwin Lieuwen, *Venezuela* (London: Oxford University Press, 1961), p. 98.

at one time had seen the administration as a stabilizing influence on the country.

In 1957 Pérez Jiménez suffered a serious blow from the pastoral letter of Venezuelan Archbishop Rafael Arias Blanco of Caracas. The silence of the Church during preceding years was broken in a sharp attack on the misuse of the nation's funds. Arias charged that social problems were multiplying rapidly, seemingly without concern in official circles; living conditions for the majority of Venezuelans were increasingly wretched. He also deplored the condition of the labor movement. Furthermore, in the Archbishop's words, ". . . an immense mass of our people is living in conditions that cannot be regarded as human. Unemployment leads many Venezuelans to despair . . . the excessively low salaries on which a large number of our workers must survive is inexcusable . . . and the situation is worsening."[11]

National elections were due by the close of 1957, and the regime set about the task of somehow legitimatizing its continuance in power. In July it was announced that a vote would be held in December, but no details were furnished. Not until November was the matter elaborated. In what proved to be a final miscalculation by the government, its Consejo Electoral announced a vote to be held December 15, 1957. Instead of an ordinary election, however, a plebiscite was to be held, giving the voter the opportunity to indicate whether or not he wanted the President to remain in office.

The voter, it was explained, would receive a blue and a red card, the former representing an affirmative vote and the latter a negative one. A provision for blind voters permitted the use of a round card for a pro-government vote and a square one for a negative response. A curious item—reflecting the flood of immigrants—was the granting of a vote to all foreigners of at least 18 years' age

[11] The text is found in Venezuela, Presidencia de la República, *op.cit.*, pp. 420-30.

who had been in Venezuela two years or more.[12] Under this arrangement, some 2,700,000 votes were reportedly on December 15, with 85 percent approving the dictator's continuation in office. In fact, however, this proved one of the final errors in judgment that helped to precipitate the revolution.

By the end of 1957 opposition to the regime had grown within all three military branches, while the university students were in the vanguard of what became known as the Junta Patriótica. On New Year's Day of 1958 an uprising began in Maracay with a brief bombing of Caracas by a group of air force rebels. Army and navy units also rose up, but the timing was bad and coordination poor. The regime managed to survive after sending loyal troops to march on Maracay. Pressure led to the reshuffling of Pérez Jiménez' advisers, including the dismissal of both the Minister of Interior Relations and the Chief of Seguridad Nacional, key figures and close cronies of the dictator.[13]

The non-military opposition had been building up its own strength. Through the efforts of exile organizations as well as revolutionaries in the country itself, the Junta Patriótica began to take shape as early as summer of 1957. In an effort to mount a united front against the regime, the communists were also included, while many participating university students were of decidedly leftist leanings, including their leading figure, Fabricio Ojeda. The smuggling of arms and material into the country had been growing, and the abortive military rebellion

[12] Venezuela, Consejo Supremo Electoral, *Procedimiento para Efectuar la Votación el 15 de diciembre de 1957* (Caracas: Imprenta Nacional, 1957).

[13] The former, Laureano Vallenilla Lanz, was the son of Gómez' apologist of the same name who wrote of "democratic caesarism." The younger provided Pérez Jiménez with the rationale of the "new national ideal," arguing that Venezuela was not yet ready for democracy and representative government. The head of security forces, Pedro Estrada, was among the most hated representatives of the regime.

on January 1, 1958, added impetus to the revolutionary movement. Disturbances broke out with increasing frequency, while a new wave of clandestine pamphlets and leaflets were passed around Caracas.

The Junta Patriótica issued a "Manifiesto de Liberación" soon after the first rebellion. Claiming that the military was now uniting with the people against the usurpers, the Junta called for a pacific solution to the problems of succession, also demanding an electoral law without restrictions or qualifications.[14] When the government ignored the message, civic resistance mounted. With the final moments for the dictatorship at hand, Acción Democrática formally proposed in writing a united effort with COPEI and the URD; this embraced, among other things, the selection of a single, unopposed presidential candidate in the next free elections. Difficulties in delivering the message to Rafael Caldera in Venezuela rendered a formal agreement impossible, but by this time the final uprising against the usurper had come.

The arrest of five priests had turned the Church completely against the government while outraging the people; Pérez Jiménez, no longer the hard-willed ambitious young officer of earlier years, wavered after the loss of his two close advisers; new members of the government included an unsympathetic navy commander, Rear Admiral Wolfgang Larrazábal. A general strike was called by the Junta Patriótica on January 21, and all business activities in Caracas came to a standstill. Security forces lashed out one final time against the populace, street fighting spread, and the toll of dead and wounded mounted. Other cities joined in the revolt, and on January 22, 1958, concerted military pressure forced the resignation of Marcos Pérez Jiménez. The following day he gathered up suitcases of money and a few close friends, fleeing from Caracas' military airport to seek refuge in the Dominican Republic of Generalissimo Rafael Leóni-

[14] Venezuela, Presidencia de la República, *op.cit.*, pp. 433-43.

das Trujillo. Final casualty lists included at least 300 killed and over 1,000 wounded.

A military junta took command under the leadership of Wolfgang Larrazábal, the Junta Patriótica assumed an influential if unofficial place in affairs during the early days of freedom, while party leaders and apolitical exiles—estimated to be as many as 10,000—began to stream back into the country. For Acción Democrática as for the other parties, national reconstruction as well as party reorganization lay ahead. If the latter task was greater for the AD than for its rivals, this was a result of longer and more determined persecution by the military regime. In 1948 Acción Democrática had been the only significant, well-organized political party in Venezuela. The decade of repression having passed, it remained to be seen if there were more than vestigial remnants of loyalty to the party inside Venezuela.

### Reconstituting Democratic Government

Returning from ten years' exile, Acción Democrática pursued the same general program with which it had long been identified. Its convictions undimmed by the long hiatus, the party renewed its activities with the restoration of public freedoms by the provisional government. Faced with a task of reconstruction of nearly staggering magnitude, the party and its leaders acted with restraint and inter-party cooperation that contrasted sharply with the experience of the *trienio*.

Early in 1958 the Larrazábal provisional government began to move toward the restoration of representative government. On January 24, 1958, it began the dismantling of repressive forces with the removal of the leadership of the Seguridad Nacional, and this was followed by a dissolution of Congress, state legislatures, and municipal councils. The treasury was nearly empty, and the financial situation was aggravated by a controversial decision to honor immediately foreign debt obligations estimated at nearly $1.5 billion. At the same time a Plan de Emergencia committed the regime to a highly extravagant kind of relief program that temporarily alleviated lower-class miseries in Caracas but contributed nothing to the improvement of conditions. Spending in other areas was also erratic and somewhat wasteful, but the state of affairs internally was gradually stabilized.

Larrazábal's year in office was sometimes turbulent; several attempts at counter-revolution kept the capital in a state of alarm. The Admiral's personal coolness under fire and his growing popularity with the *caraqueños* aided in his fight for stability, although civilian critics tended to remain suspicious of his motives as well as those of other high-ranking military leaders.[15] The provisional government remained firm in moving Venezuela toward elections, and Larrazábal repeatedly assured skeptics that the return to democracy would be full and complete.

Interviewers were told that the government's orientation was of a "frankly democratic character," and the Admiral believed that the Junta's most important measures were the series of steps designed to permit a restoration of representative government. On February 3, 1958, the government had issued Decree Number 20 to void the December plebiscite and dissolve political bodies constituted by *perezjimenismo*. An electoral commission was named to write a new law on February 22, and it was issued on May 24 in Decree Number 234.[16]

[15] One public indication of concern was the May resignation from the provisional cabinet of two prominent civilians, Eugenio Mendoza and Blas Lamberti. Both were scrupulous in keeping private their complaints, but it later became known that both questioned Larrazábal's intentions regarding his political future.

[16] Documents and commentaries on the events of 1958 are brought together in José Umaña Bernal, *Testimonios de la Revolución en Venezuela* (Caracas: Tip. Vargas, 1958). For Decree Number 234, see p. 253.

Political leaders had flocked back to Venezuela after the flight of the deposed dictator, and reorganization led to the preparation of campaign plans. For Acción Democrática, the task was that of fitting its existing clandestine organization and underground leaders into the new democratic environment, while rebuilding the leadership following losses accrued over the preceding decade. Furthermore, an enlarged citizenry that had spent ten years without direct knowledge of or frequent contact with the AD had to be reached.

Acción Democrática faced the necessity of reestablishing a national apparatus that would be comparable in extent and comprehensiveness to that of the mid-1940's, and its goals were set high, as always. Leadership had not been stripped of all talent, but losses since 1948 were substantial. Between death by natural cause and political assassination in Venezuela, such men as Blanco, Rodríguez, Ruiz Pineda, Carnevali, Troconis Guerrero, and Hurtado had been lost. Early reorganizational efforts centered about the reconstituting of long-suspended democratic organs.

On January 26, 1958, the clandestine Comité Ejecutivo Nacional met with returning members of the exiled Comité Coordinador Exterior and worked out a temporary arrangement whereby they met jointly to direct party affairs.[17] Since command organs existed only in Caracas and a few of the larger cities, the AD set about the reconstitution of these bodies. A special executive body was created to facilitate the process, the Comisión Nacional de Organización. Headed by the party Secretary of Organization, it also included his *Adjunto* (assistant or deputy) and two staff members. A rotating schedule was drawn up whereby at least one of the four remained at the Casa Central (party headquarters) in Caracas while the others traveled. Later it was agreed

[17] The relationship of exile and underground leadership is described in Chapter IV.

that each member of the Comisión would be roughly responsible for a given geographic zone.

The Secretary of Organization, in normal times responsible for communications and coordination between party sectionals and the national executive, now devoted himself in large part to the regional organs. At the same time party leaders gathered for a May meeting where a number of decisions were reached, all of which were communicated to party members as instructions pending the holding of a convention in August. Six points were announced, and the main theme was national unity in support of the government. The political truce with other parties was reiterated, partisan competition renounced for the time, while the membership was urged to hold itself constantly alert to dangers of a possible counter-revolution.[18]

Preparations for a national convention in August were necessarily hasty. As Luis B. Prieto later observed, the time was exceedingly short. During January and February most leaders were returning to the country, locating a home, and reestablishing their families and occupations after ten years' absence. The sheer physical matter of seeking and locating one's friends was a delaying factor.[19] Not until late spring were the first regional conventions scheduled, and the last ones only came in late July. The first mass gathering of Acción Democrática in nearly eleven years was held on July 4 at Nuevo Circo before an estimated 20,000. Rómulo Betancourt delivered an eloquent history of the party antagonism to international communism.

The IX National Convention met in Caracas' Teatro Apolo under the presidency of Dr. Prieto on Sunday, August 10, 1958. It was a momentous gathering for the

[18] Further details are found in running issues of the party weekly, *A.D.* Of particular interest are the articles in no. 9, July 5, 1958, p. 7, and no. 16, August 23, 1958, pp. 14-15.

[19] Interview with Luis B. Prieto, December 11, 1962.

party, and major organizational revisions were made. Structural and programmatic resolutions as adopted at the 1958 Convention have since remained constant, and will be detailed later. Among the more evident developments, however, was the revelation of clearly identifiable divergent currents within the party.

This factionalism, which is discussed in Chapter VI, did not have all its origins in the 1958 Convention, but indications of coming intraparty competition were evident then. To summarize for purposes of the present context, the first and most prominent was the group regarded as the Guardia Vieja (GV) or Old Guard. Comprising a majority of the party leadership, it included members of the Generation of '28 and of '36-'37. Betancourt, Leoni, Barrios, Prieto, D'Ascoli, Martínez, and other veterans of ORVE and the PDN were the most prominent. As builders of Acción Democrática and initiators of the movement even before its formal creation in 1941, they were held in almost reverential awe by most of the party rank-and-file, especially in the interior. Betancourt himself was easily the dominant figure; his opinion was sought by all, while GV colleagues regarded him with messianic faith.

Next came a group largely comprised of the generation after the Guardia Vieja—university graduates of the 1940's who had earned their spurs in the service of the *trienio* government at middle levels. This group also included several younger men who were pressed into national party leadership when members of the Guardia Vieja were occupied with ruling the republic. Its major figures at this time were Raúl Ramos Giménez and Jesús Angel Paz Galarraga, while others included José Manzo González, José Angel Ciliberto, and César Rondón Lovera. Originally nameless, this faction become identified in the late 1940's by the initials ARS, which referred to a leading Venezuelan advertising agency that had, during the mid-1940's, used the slogan "let us think for you." The name had been applied half-critically, half-humorously to this group and particularly to Ramos Giménez. By 1958 it entered popular usage.

While the ARS sector was by no means clearly identifiable on programmatic grounds, the same was not true of a disenchanted group of Young Turks known as the Muchachos, or Boys. Dissatisfied with veteran leadership, these immoderate young radicals were in most cases fresh from university training and barely into their thirties. Characterized at the time as followers of an ultra-revolutionary line, the Muchachos followed the ideological and organizational direction of Domingo Alberto Rangel, a brilliant, opinionated, and vociferous controversialist who spewed forth an unending stream of words, both written and spoken. Another leading activist was Simón Sáez Mérida, a stubborn partisan of radical solutions, a reader of Marxism, and already a dogmatic admirer of a Cuban guerrilla fighter named Fidel Castro.

The Convention atmosphere was mildly strained, although the three elements shared a concern for reorganization and the direction of a successful campaign. The age difference between the Guardia Vieja and the Muchachos underlined the beginning of an internal problem of generations, and the position of the former might have been less dominant but for the immense skill, prestige, and political capital accruing to Betancourt from his extraordinary thirty-year career. He and his senior colleagues maintained control of the party machinery while younger members were merely vocal.[20]

The 300-odd delegates were not treated to fireworks, despite heat and humidity that wilted tempers rapidly. The election of officers to the new Comité Ejecutivo Nacional was calm, although hinting at the presence of

[20] It is nonetheless illuminating to observe that the moderate weekly *Momento* discussed the AD's "five key men," of whom only Betancourt was of the Guardia Vieja. The others were Ramos Giménez and Paz Galarraga of ARS, and Rangel and Sáez Mérida from the young radicals.

divergencies within the leadership. The aging Gallegos was acclaimed as Honorary President and Betancourt as active President. The competition over lesser posts is described below. In the end, however, Raúl Leoni and Gonzalo Barrios were named First and Second Vice-Presidents, after which Luis B. Prieto was elected Secretary-General. *Arsista* José Manzo González was chosen to the important post of Secretary of Organization. Of the nineteen-person CEN which emerged, the Guardia Vieja dominated, while five *arsistas* were chosen and only two Muchachos.

Before and during the Convention a number of special commissions had been meeting, and they produced a set of doctrinal papers that were accepted with minor variations as party theses and programs. Once these programs had been approved, the single remaining item was the presidential candidacy. Not until a few weeks before December elections was the matter finally resolved. All of the parties by the summer of 1958 were conferring in the search for a single unity candidate, and negotiations were still going on at the time of the AD gathering.

The only choice at the Convention was therefore an equivocal statement leaving several alternatives. The possibility of a collegiate executive was viewed by Betancourt himself as interesting, but there was little enthusiasm from the party. Ultimately the party adopted a statement setting forth three possibilities. The first proposed a unity candidacy, the second a single party nominee, and the third a five-member collegiate executive. In the event of the latter, the executive would include three representatives of the non-communist parties, a military man, and a representative of the business sector.

In the weeks after the Convention, interparty conversations continued. Gonzalo Barrios for the AD, Lorenzo Fernández for COPEI, and Ignacio Luis Arcaya for the URD met frequently to exchange views. Firm agreement on a solution proved elusive, however. Barrios has re-

called that the plural executive plan was never formulated in concrete terms, and COPEI in particular was
cool to the possibility.[21] Eventually the impossibility of
choosing an unopposed unity candidate was conceded,
and the parties turned to the nomination of separate
men. Time was short, and each of the parties had to make
their decision quickly.

Acción Democrática held its decisive meeting on Saturday, October 11, when the Comité Directivo Nacional
and a group of special delegates came together in Caracas. Prieto reported in detail the breakdown of inter-
party efforts to select one national candidate, and Betancourt followed by underlining the impossibility of any
further multiparty agreement under existing circumstances. The following day they voted either to adopt a
plan for a collegiate executive or, if the other parties
named their candidates, to nominate Betancourt.[22] The
latter course was shortly adopted.

COPEI had easily made the choice of Rafael Caldera,
at the time its only leader of true national stature. In
the case of the URD the nomination was less certain
than had been expected. Jóvito Villalba had been campaigning for his party in the interior, but the possibility
of his nomination was menaced by the specter of the
candidacy of Junta President Wolfgang Larrazábal. The
first impetus to the Admiral's candidacy came from a
newly organized party, the Movimiento Electoral Nacional Independiente (MENI), born in June of 1958 in
Miranda. Organized by a group of non-politicians headed
by Dr. Vicente Emilio Oropeza, MENI publicized the
possibility of a Larrazábal candidacy at a time when
there was little real support for it. In the face of the
Admiral's disclaimers, his candidacy was postulated

[21] Interview with Gonzalo Barrios, November 27, 1962.
[22] *Momento* (Caracas), no. 118, October 17, 1958, pp. 28-30,
32-33.

widely, and enthusiasm began to grow in some areas, notably Caracas.

Despite his original refusal, Larrazábal finally consented to run. Less than a month before election day and a good three weeks after Betancourt and Caldera had begun to comb the country for votes, the Admiral resigned from the government and joined the race. He was formally nominated by the Unión Republicana Democrática with the personal support of Villalba, and the URD soon usurped the position of MENI in taking over major responsibilities for the Larrazábal race.

The general desire for moderation and tolerance was soon reflected in a tri-party agreement. Known as the Pact of Punto Fijo, the agreement promised party cooperation in defense of the democratic system. "The sincere definition . . . of the rights that are held by the parties as representatives of . . . the lasting interests of the Nation . . . are the guarantee that deliberations have recognized . . . presentday urgencies in Venezuela." Six general principles were agreed upon, including a defense of the Constitution and a commitment to honor election returns. A government of national unity was to be formed, with the winning candidate staffing his cabinet with members of all three parties. A common minimal program was also accepted, details of which were appended.[23] As a further safeguard against violations of the agreement, a tribunal known as the Comisión Interpartidista de Unidad was set up, composed of representatives of the three parties. Signers of the Pact of Punto Fijo were Betancourt, Leoni, and Barrios for Acción Democrática; Caldera, Fernández, and Pedro del Corral for COPEI; and Villalba, Arcaya, and Manuel López Rivas for the URD. Later, on the day before elections,

[23] Acción Democrática, *Pacto Suscrito el 31 de Octubre de 1958 y Declaración de Principios y Programa Mínimo de Gobierno de los Candidatos a la Presidencia de la República en la Elección del Día 7 de Diciembre de 1958* (Caracas: La Nación, 1958).

the three presidential nominees signed the appended Declaration of Principles.

The campaign was a hectic one, with all three nominees relying on such innovations for Venezuela as helicopter travel. The AD campaign was the best organized of the three. A fourteen-man Comando Electoral directed by Luis Lander operated out of party headquarters in Caracas, and coordination of the massive party effort was centered there. Betancourt himself centered his effort on the interior; in the course of a forty-five day campaign he delivered 132 speeches and held nearly two dozen press conferences. Visiting every state while missing only two remote federal territories, he spoke on a wider range of topics and problems than either of his opponents. At the same time his party created a special task force for the campaign in Caracas, where AD weakness and Larrazábal's popularity were recognized.[24]

The campaigns concluded at midnight on Friday, December 5. Saturday the candidates signed the Declaration of Principles before Dr. Fidel Rotondaro of the Consejo Supremo Electoral. All three voted early Sunday, then awaited the decision as returns began to trickle in. Caracas reports mounted swiftly to give Larrazábal a strong lead, but the traditional *adeco* appeal in the interior gradually asserted itself. Labor-strong oil centers fell into the Betancourt column, and COPEI lagged except in its customary Andean strongholds. By Monday morning the victory of Acción Democrática was clear.

Returns can be summarized briefly.[25] Rómulo Betancourt received 1,284,092 votes, just short of 50 percent. Larrazábal, who had accepted unsolicited support from the communists in addition to URD backing, polled 885,167 votes; 84,451 came from the communists. Caldera's 396,293 amounted to a bit less than 15 percent.

---

[24] The party's "Caracas problem" is discussed in the chapter on elections.

[25] See a full account in the chapter on elections.

In the legislative races both the AD and COPEI figures were similar to those of their presidential candidates. The notable discrepancy appeared in URD totals, for its legislative candidates polled more than 100,000 fewer votes than did Wolfgang Larrazábal, giving some measure of the extent to which they rode on his coat tails. The capital, which gave Larrazábal a clear vote of confidence while Betancourt ran a distant fourth, was sorely disappointed by the national defeat of its momentary hero, and there were several violent outbursts on the day following elections. The government moved quickly to restore order, however, and the Admiral took to television and radio in a prompt appeal for compliance with the results. By the end of the month Caracas was resigned to the verdict, and the divorce of opinion between the capital and interior seemed less irreconcilable. Betancourt, anxious for a policy of unity, told interviewers: "The task is not easy, but is realizable where the will and desire clearly exist. I will form a coalition, not a single-party government . . . Acción Democrática, the party to which I belong, has aided me in this task by relieving me of party obligations in the selection of collaborators in the government. . . . I do not for a moment doubt the loyal cooperation that I will have from all parties and from the other collective sectors [of Venezuelan politics]."[26]

## Problems of Maturity

Having thus set forth his position, Betancourt proceeded to name a cabinet including representatives of the three parties, as well as political independents. A communist appeal for inclusion was turned down. The AD victory gave them a Senate majority of 32 of 51, while their margin in the Chamber was 73 of 133. In state assemblies Acción Democrática had elected 193 of 307

[26] *Visión* (Mexico), January 2, 1959, pp. 7-8.

members, resulting in an outright majority in 15 of 20 legislatures. The party had survived the long exile and overcome organization problems to reestablish its primacy. But the performance of both COPEI and the URD showed that they were ready to assume positions of virtual equality in a competitive multi-party system. Thus the AD was confronted with the challenge of significant party rivals at the same time it was ultimately responsible for the functioning of a tri-party national coalition government. The dangers of internal factionalism within the AD itself added to the tests lying ahead for the party. The problems of a relative maturity were clearly substantial.

One of the major challenges confronting Rómulo Betancourt as he assumed office had to do with political questions. Even granting his known political sorcery, the perils seemed insurmountable. When freed from formal obligations to the party in 1959, he was regarded as an ardent partisan, and at least a few questioned his promise to rule a tri-party coalition. Yet he first gave the lie to such doubts with the naming of his cabinet on February 11, 1959. The thirteen-man body, expanded by two with the inclusion of the Governor of the Federal District and the Secretary to the Presidency, included only three outright *adecos*. There were also three from COPEI, three from the URD, and six independents.

Two *adecos* held key posts: Minister of Interior Relations Luis Augusto Dubuc and Minister of Mines and Hydrocarbons Juan Pablo Pérez Alfonzo. The former, one of the more powerful young men in the party, had been active during the clandestine activities under Pérez Jiménez, and was a major contributor to the 1958 reconstruction. The latter was somewhat older, his affiliation dating back to the days of the PDN. Recognized as the party's leading authority on petroleum matters, he was perhaps the one man who had contributed as much to the formulation of AD petroleum policies as Betancourt.

Even before the cabinet had been named, acting AD President Raúl Leoni attempted to lay the basis for a modicum of party amity, promising that Acción Democrática would "not try to break the climate of unity and coexistence that has characterized the development of the Venezuelan historical process."[27] With minor exceptions, this remained the party's position throughout the five years to follow. The AD continued to provide a substantial number of state governors and directors of semi-autonomous organs, with cabinet membership holding stable at three or four. The major change came with the May 1962 shift in the Ministry of Interior Relations, when Dubuc was replaced by Carlos Andrés Pérez, a highly competent young man in his late thirties. Dubuc returned to the Chamber and resumed a major role within the parliamentary wing of the party.

Acción Democrática also performed yeoman duty in legislating measures for the executive. While the party held a majority in both chambers, it adhered to the spirit of the Pact of Punto Fijo. Under the determined Betancourt and a completely loyal Raúl Leoni, executive and legislative authorities worked together with considerable cooperative smoothness. Leoni served as President of the Senate and therefore of Congress, while COPEI's Rafael Caldera presided over the Chamber of Deputies as well as being Vice-President of Congress. This arrangement continued for two years, during which time the URD left the coalition and entered the opposition,[28] while AD radicals broke away to form the marxist-oriented MIR. These two alterations still left the AD, in mid-1960, with a majority of 31 of 51 in the Senate. In the Chamber, the loss of 17 deputies to the MIR reduced the AD to 56 of 133 seats. The government co-

27 *El Nacional*, January 12, 1959, p. 1.
28 Details of the URD withdrawal are given in Chapter XI.

alition of AD and COPEI continued to enjoy a com-
fortable total of 75.

With the convening of Congress in 1962, replacements
were needed for Leoni and Caldera, both of whom
stepped down in order to intensify personal activity
within their respective parties. Their successors were not
certain, for the *arsista* rebellion had recently led to the
second internal rift in Acción Democrática, and the
government coalition saw its legislative seats reduced
yet again. When the dust from the *arsista* schism finally
settled, the government barely retained control of the
Senate by 27-24; in the Chamber it was outvoted by the
URD-MIR-ARS-PCV opposition, 78-55. The new head
of the Senate and President of Congress became Dr.
Prieto, who merely replaced his friend Leoni. In the
lower house, however, *arsista* Manuel Vicente Ledezma
was named President; the URD's Enrique Betancourt y
Galíndez was named First Vice-President and the MIR's
Jesús María Casal the Second Vice-President.

Loss of control of the Chamber became a major source
of congressional obstructionism to the government after
1962. That it was little more than a nagging irritant was
a result of the President's earlier success in passing reform legislation promptly. While there were few major
changes from traditional *adeco* policy, the President
relied to a large extent on the cooperation of the other
parties in the formulation of major decisions. After the
defection of the URD, he worked closely with COPEI
during the remainder of his term; given the general
consensus between the parties on major issues, it proved
possible to establish a reasonably effective working relation. Betancourt himself, while ever the combative and
determined leader, showed himself more amenable in
personal dealings than he had been during the *trienio*,
and friction of this nature was kept to a minimum.

In the early months of his administration the President devoted efforts in the economic field toward a

rejuvenation of the sagging financial condition of the country. By July of 1960 he began the implementation of a comprehensive four-year economic development plan. Although the plan was delayed some months due to a political crisis, its over-all framework remained. Based on lengthy consultation with political and economic leaders from all sectors of national life, it outlined a three-pronged drive that, among other goals, aimed at a 25 percent increase in gross national product. Industrial diversification and the encouragement of a domestic industry was to provide adequate housing and clothing for national needs; the communications network was to be improved and extended; and lastly, agriculture was to received renewed impetus, with particular attention given to an increase in agricultural production as well as land redistribution. The estimated expenditure was to be some $8 billion.

In connection with the last item, the government had already passed an agrarian reform law in March of 1960. Legislation established the Instituto Nacional de Reforma Agraria as the organ responsible for administering the program. In what Betancourt referred to as an "integrated" program of land reform, a series of steps were outlined, beginning with a detailed survey of the land problem, gaining early momentum through the granting of unoccupied government lands to the landless, and proceeding through a number of additional steps. Expropriation, although not the sole mechanism involved, played a part in the program. Government appraisers were to make a fair judgment as to the value of any land to be seized. Progress was slow at the outset, and only toward the end of Betancourt's administration did the program begin to make inroads into the traditional Venezuelan land problem. By the end of his administration, previously landless *campesinos* had settled roughly four million acres, one-third of which had come from privately owned estates. Nearly 60,000 families were settled on lands of their own.

Labor-management relations changed as freedom returned to the Venezuelan worker. Collective bargaining assumed importance once again, and Venezuelan management proved far more tractable than before. Foreign capitalists also came to be satisfied by Betancourt's moderation as his administration passed its early stages, and it was recognized that the avoidance of radical revolution rested on Betancourt, his labor support, and the continuing *rapport* between the President and the military. A characteristic development was a joint request in August 1960 from organized labor in conjunction with numerous industrialists and businessmen to solicit government assistance. Another straw in the wind was the signing of long-term contracts in February 1960 between the oil workers of FEDEPETROL and the oil industry. The result was a shortening of the work week from 48 to 44 hours, a wage increase, broader fringe benefits, and a reassertion of the rights of collective bargaining.

The Betancourt policies in this area generally reflected a continued commitment to the development of Venezuela's human resources. The degree to which success was achieved was due not only to the President and his party, however. For COPEI and URD had also evolved beyond the rank immaturity of the *trienio*, and the general agreement of all three parties on a broad range of issues was striking. As the 1963 election campaign was to prove, the major differences were over the implementation of proposed reforms.

Domestic policies, then, were fairly well set and initiated before the government lost its legislative majority. External affairs, however, almost overthrew the regime and interrupted national development on several occasions. The President extended the traditional *adeco* policy of non-recognition of unconstitutional and unrepresentative regimes in the hemisphere. His diplomats also pressed for collective action in the Organization of American States against such anachronistic regimes as that of Trujillo in the Dominican Republic. As a result of this effort, the Byzantine workings of Dominican leaders led to a projected assassination of Betancourt that narrowly failed. An explosion in his car killed one of the passengers, and Betancourt's hands are badly scarred as a result. In the aftermath of this abortive event, the Trujillo regime was sharply censored, and punitive action was taken by the OAS at the Sixth Conference of Foreign Ministers in San José, August 1960.

The stability of the regime was also potentially endangered by the position of Venezuela's armed forces. This will be discussed in detail below; for the present, let it merely be said that Betancourt bent over backward to maintain satisfactory relations with the military leadership. There were several outbursts that threatened civilian government, including an attempted invasion from Colombia in April 1960 under the direction of a former Minister of Defense. A pair of military uprisings by individual units in 1962, one in Carúpano, the other in Barcelona, were further complicated by the involvement of leftists. The national military leadership remained firm in its support of constitutional government, however, and stood by proudly in March 1964 when Betancourt transferred the presidential sash to his freely elected civilian successor.

The most dramatic source of instability came with the growing opposition to the Betancourt government by Fidel Castro and the revolutionary Cuban regime. The advent of communism had led the Cubans to attempt the exportation of revolution. The failure of standard tactics by Venezuelan communists made it clear that, lacking an appropriate domestic market for radical revolution, the Cubans would have no easy task. The determined democratic orientation of the Venezuelan government stood as a challenge to Cuban prestige. It also threatened to repel the dynamics of the Cuban Revolution, which fed upon continual expansion. The competition between communism and democratic reformism was suggestive to all of Latin America concerning the best road of achieving socio-economic progress and a better life for the common man. A fundamental and relentless combat therefore ensued.

In time the confrontation between the governments of Betancourt and Castro was being waged on the streets of Caracas; by 1962 the communists had decided upon a campaign of unlimited political and terrorist attacks. The republic was plagued by the violence of the self-styled Fuerzas Armadas de Liberación Nacional (FALN). The loyalty of the peasantry to the government and to Betancourt personally contradicted theoretical claims by the extreme left that the coming revolution would be won in the interior. Thus the peasants joined regular military forces in putting down the abortive uprisings in Carúpano and Barcelona, and some months later captured and turned over to authorities Fabricio Ojeda, the presumed leader of leftist guerrillas. At the same time, the pace of irresponsibility was stepped up in metropolitan areas, with Caracas in particular subjected to a series of nocturnal bombings, warehouse fires, and bank holdups.

The terrorist campaign envisaged twin goals: withdrawal of foreign investment and military intervention in politics. The burning of the Sears warehouse and a North American tire factory indicated the effort to drive out foreign enterprise; the explosion of a bomb in a nightclub rest room at the plush Hotel Tamanaco typified efforts to frighten away foreigners. The continual round of violence and lawlessness was also intended to bring about a military *golpe*, after which the leftist extremists might pose as national liberators fighting in the vanguard of an anti-military "peoples' revolution." In

1963 the pace of terrorism was stepped up yet again. Communist and *mirista* deputies lashed the government verbally, enjoying congressional immunity although their official party activities had been suspended. Among the more important events of 1963 was to be, in addition to the party electoral competition, the fight between the government and the extreme left over the scheduled participation of the citizenry in choosing a new government.[29] As electoral maneuvering unfolded in 1963, there remained an omnipresent threat that the actual balloting would never be held.

Perhaps the most important as well as most dramatic test of the extent to which Acción Democrática and indeed the entire party system had matured was the holding of national elections in December of 1963. In addition to countless partisan issues that are outlined elsewhere, the major parties saw the contest as the first opportunity in a full five years to test their relative strength with the electorate. At the same time, the handling of the campaign and the dialogue over proposed policies was interrupted repeatedly by the incursions of terrorism and violence from extremists of the left. The continuing relationship of civil-military authorities also assumed a major significance as 1963 slipped past.

The battle between the government and extremists continued down to election day.[30] Revulsion swept the populace with the attack by terrorists on September 29 against an excursion train halted on a Sunday afternoon between Los Teques and El Encanto; five national

---

[29] A persuasive if partisan speech in March 1962 by the Secretary-General of Acción Democrática later appeared in printed form: Jesús Angel Paz Galarraga, *Violencia y Suspensión de Garantías* (Caracas: "Pueblo y Parlamento," 1963).

[30] A detailed discussion of various clashes is found in the government's *Gobierno y Nación Defienden en Venezuela el Régimen Democrático; Actos contra el Terrorismo Comunista* (Caracas: Publicaciones de la Secretaría de la Presidencia de la República, 1964).

guardsmen were murdered while several others were wounded.[31] Nonetheless, the attacks continued unremittingly. Toward late November the leftists tried desperately to force a military seizure of power. On Tuesday the 19th a strike call was ignored, but intermittent exchanges of gunfire in the workers' districts of Caracas led to the death of 21 and the injury of at least 100. Sniping the following day led to further clashes. There was at least one attempt at mass assassination of the presidential contestants. On November 27 four terrorists kidnapped a North American officer assigned to the Caracas military mission, and a day later a two-engined Avensa airliner was highjacked during a flight from Ciudad Bolívar to Caracas.

The next day the government announced the discovery of Cuban arms in Venezuela and called for investigation by the OAS. Charging Cuba with aggression after revealing a three-ton cache of arms uncovered on Paraguana Peninsula, Venezuela initiated a process that ultimately led to the convening of the Ninth Conference of Foreign Ministers in the summer of 1964. November 29 the terrorists called for a curfew, threatening to kill anyone on city streets after midnight. The restriction was to continue until the following Monday, after elections.

Caracas was bustling and noisy on Friday, but on Saturday uncommonly quiet. On election eve, there was serious question whether the populace would defy threats of FALN terrorism. As election day dawned sunny and mild, lines began to form at polling places as early as five o'clock. Before mid-morning lines throughout the city were long. Despite occasional outbursts of shooting, the day's toll reached only 12 wounded and 1 killed. The turnout in Caracas was obviously large, and, as re-

---

[31] The grisly details, documented with photographs and photostated newspaper excerpts, were presented by the government in a booklet, Ministerio de la Defensa, *La Agresión a Mansalva* (Caracas, 1963).

ports trickled in from the interior later in the day, it was
clear that the rural response was much the same.

By noon the pattern was clear; the president of the
electoral council called the outcome a "smashing success," and President Betancourt denied any surprise but
added that he was "highly impressed . . . by the manner
in which the people voted." Beyond all doubt the democratic response had been tremendous.[32] The pride with
which the electorate voted was the highest possible expression of responsible civic participation. Final figures
revealed that 91.33 percent of the registered electorate
took part. Given the presence of an extraordinary combination of factors both internal and external, election
day went down as historic in Venezuela, and perhaps
in all of Latin America.

So it was made possible for the Venezuelans to continue their search for full political maturity under the
aegis of an effective party system. On March 11, 1964,
before a distinguished group of diplomats and official
guests in the congressional chambers, the presidential
sash was removed from the shoulders of one man and
lowered upon those of another. In a brief but impressive
ceremony that included the transfer of the key to the
tomb of Simón Bolívar, Rómulo Betancourt concluded
his five-year constitutional term and passed on the authority of office to his duly elected successor, lifetime
associate, and fellow organizer of Acción Democrática.
Thus Raúl Leoni, clearly the victor although a minority
president, assumed responsibility for his republic. His
party, notwithstanding grave problems and future un-
certainties, remained the leading political organization
in Venezuela.

[32] A collection of newspaper editorial and accounts from the
press of the world was brought together and published by Venezuela, Presidencia de la República, *Victoria Democrática en
Venezuela; Editoriales de la Prensa Mundial* (Caracas: Secretaría
de la Presidencia, 1964).

# PART TWO

# The Party: Organization and Structure

# CHAPTER IV

# The Party and Exile Operations

As of 1964, fully ten of the AD's twenty-three years of existence had been spent in exile. And for the party founders whose political activism dated back to 1928, twenty-one of the thirty-six years to follow were lived in political exile, almost all of it outside Venezuela proper. The importance of the collective exile experience therefore assumes a large role in the evolution of Acción Democrática. Exile politics under the best of circumstances is an erratic and highly abnormal kind of existence. In the Venezuelan democratic movement which led to the founding and development of today's party system, three distinct periods are identifiable.

These may be conveniently labeled chronologically: the first extended from 1928 to 1935, the second from 1937 to 1941, and the third from 1948 to 1958. Yet in each case the accompanying circumstances were different; therefore the nature of clandestine activities during the period was individual. In the first instance, a small number of young revolutionaries spent much of their time in ideological inquiry, in an extended intellectual exercise through which the search for relevant Venezuelan programs might be carried out. Organizational activity was relatively minor and informal in the extreme.

The second period of exile was one of substantial political activism. Because it came at a time when the leadership had at least determined certain broad areas of policy, the major emphasis was given to organizational work. Convinced that the proper programmatic paths lay before them, the exiles bent their efforts toward the prolongation of *ad hoc* structures, that they might be strengthened for the ultimate legalization that was to come. Less attention was given to the amassing of public support than to the problem of recruiting new party organizers.

The final and most extended period of exile activity was marked by yet another kind of operation. This time the major concern was that of sheer survival. Acción Democrática faced the difficulty of retaining a nucleus of organized leadership although persecuted by the regime at home and troubled by the struggle for daily existence abroad. The morale problems incumbent upon the leadership of an exile organization that passes a full decade away from home are substantial. And by no means of least importance is the effort to keep alive the name and image of the party in the hearts of the population at home.

These, then, were among the differing problems and concerns during the separate exile experiences. Of these, the first can be dealt with in the briefest fashion.

## The Search for Ideology

The outbursts of the Generation of '28 in the student demonstrations of that year constituted a rather amorphous, undirected protest against the tyranny and backwardness of the Gómez regime. There was little if any true understanding of national problems on the part of the youthful rebels; as a consequence, much of the seven-year exile was to be an intellectual search for an ideology. The concern and the curiosity of the exiles drove them in an effort to understand Venezuelan life, to identify national problems, and to seek solutions within an internally consistent programmatic or ideological framework.

When first exiled by the regime, the revolutionaries thought in terms of overthrowing the government, and efforts were guided in this direction. In 1929 a military invasion was attempted by General Ramón Delgado Chalbaud, a disaffected military man who had long opposed the regime. As a part of this attack, a small ship was launched toward the mainland from Santo Domingo, carrying nearly a dozen young Venezuelans including Rómulo Betancourt, Raúl Leoni, Simón Betancourt,[1] and Hernando Castro. Following their departure on the coastal vessel *La Gisela*, the opening of sealed orders directed their attack to a small islet on the eastern shore, several days' sailing distance. *La Gisela* proved unequal to the task, and the bedraggled group of revolutionaries landed at Barahona, on the eastern Dominican shore.[2]

Following this ill-fated effort, the young exiles concentrated on a continuing dialogue—both verbal and written—that centered about Venezuela and its problems. Of the subsequent founders of Acción Democrática, a number settled in Colombia, notably Raúl Leoni, Valmore Rodríguez, and Ricardo Montilla. Rómulo Betancourt was in Costa Rica, while Gonzalo Barrios had crossed the ocean to Spain. It was during these years that the inquiry into marxism took place, an episode which was to haunt the party periodically in later years.

The most common charges of marxism or communism have revolved about the activities of Betancourt in Costa Rica. Betancourt himself has never denied his affiliation with communism at that time, and indeed he was one of the leading organizers of the Communist Party of Costa Rica. Urging an emphasis of national problems and solutions rather than servile obedience to the Comintern, he insisted upon the primacy of local conditions. Increasingly disassociating himself from more pliable party members, he resigned from the party in 1935 to mark the close of his connection with the movement. In 1944 he made one of the explanations that became periodically necessary.

"I joined a small Communist group in Costa Rica in 1930. I came with high hopes of an armed invasion

---

[1] No relation to Rómulo.

[2] The first-hand account of this adventure is told in Rómulo Betancourt, *Venezuela: Política y Petróleo* (México: Fondo de Cultura Económica, 1956), p. 786.

against the tyranny of Gómez. Desperation over our inability to overthrow the hated tyrant, as well as igno-
rance of the socio-economic realities of the American
people . . . all provided fertile terrain for the messianic
hope of a revolution 'a la rusa.' . . . During this transitory
stage within the Communist Party, I was never one of
the drawing-room bolsheviks who discoursed on social
revolution while hoping that there might be a *golpe*. . . .
I was seeking a truly American doctrine or ideology or
set of answers."[3]

While his disillusionment with communism grew until
he severed all connections with the party, Betancourt
maintained a steady flow of correspondence on the subject, with his colleagues in Colombia. This too led to
later charges of communism, generally discussed within
the context of the initials ARDI and a mysterious Plan
of Barranquilla. ARDI—the Agrupación Revolucionaria
de la Izquierda—was an informal group numbering no
more than a dozen participants. Most of these became
located in Colombia, including Leoni, Rodríguez, Montilla, Carnevali, Mariano Picón-Salas, Carlos D'Ascoli,
and Simón Betancourt. Even the initialed name was
rarely used, and activities consisted of discussions for
the exchange of ideas.

These discussions constituted a form of ideological
apprenticeship. According to Raúl Leoni, ARDI dealt
with essentially theoretical arguments, and meetings
usually took place in either Bogotá or Barranquilla; efforts were made to find a set of principles within which
genuinely Venezuelan solutions might be provided for
a range of problems.[4] The revolutionaries' adult experience in Venezuela had been negligible, and so they were
confronted with the necessity of developing a theoretical
basis that would permit specifically Venezuelan applications.

[3] *El País*, February 15, 1944, p. 11.
[4] Interview with Raúl Leoni, December 6, 1962.

Beyond question there was a passing flirtation with marxism during this period on the part of later founders of Acción Democrática. The exiled Generation of '28 had some familiarity with the Mexican Revolution and with the Peruvian *aprista* movement, but these were secondary influences. The astute Gonzalo Barrios today declares that marxism for a time provided a convenient peg on which to hang proposed solutions.[5] Thus, the existence of a marxist tinge in the early search for answers to partially formulated questions is not startling. Barrios' statement is echoed and elaborated upon by Betancourt's own writings on the intellectual climate of the exiles during these years.

"We [of the Generation of '28] shared a phenomenon common with the majority of students exiled in the thirties. . . . We began to dream of a bolshevik revolution, with the 'czar of Maracay' shot at dawn. Nevertheless, none of those who later would found Acción Democrática became members during this first exile of political groups subordinated to the Third International. . . . The small group of our countrymen, already embryonically organized at that time, which later would become the Communist Party of Venezuela, proceeded to deepen the abyss between their group and ours, unleashing an abusive compaign against us in which they still persist. . . ."[6]

The so-called Plan of Barranquilla, which helped to provide opponents with ammunition at the time, became publicly known in the late summer of 1936 as the result of a proclamation by the government of Eleazar López Contreras. Embroiled in a campaign to discredit the democratic opposition, the regime issued a *Libro Rojo* or Red Book alleging to be a collection of correspondence from Betancourt in Costa Rica to Leoni and others in Colombia. Entitled *La Verdad de las Actividades Comu-*

---

[5] Interview with Gonzalo Barrios, November 27, 1962.

[6] Betancourt, *op.cit.*, pp. 69-70.

*nistas en Venezuela* (The Truth About Communist Activities in Venezuela) it claimed to have "proved" the group's communist affiliation. The document was also republished in excerpts during the close of 1936 and early 1937 under the running title, "Hay o no Hay Comunistas en Venezuela?" (Are There or Are There Not Communists in Venezuela?)[7]

Among the younger anti-government leaders attacked in the book were several who in 1936 belonged to the PRP and later formed the Communist Party of Venezuela. Thus some degree of credence was given to the charges. However, as a piece of propaganda the *Libro Rojo* convinced only those who needed little real convincing. The correspondence between Betancourt and others contained true excerpts of cited letters, carefully intermingled with spurious passages from genuine communist literature. The very phrase "Plan de Barranquilla" was but infrequently used. An interesting footnote to the incident was recorded in 1945 when Raúl Leoni examined archives in Miraflores following the October Revolution. He unearthed his own letters, carefully edited with frequent deletions and including penciled excerpts from attached communist literature.[8]

During their first exile experience, in short, the men who were to found Acción Democrática acquired some familiarity with marxist formulas; only Betancourt was briefly active in the Communist Party. However, the imported slogans of Soviet communism soon fell on deaf ears. As these men came to a broad understanding of Venezuelan problems, the illogic of foreign direction and an essentially alien ideology impressed itself. While

[7] Articles appeared in the pro-regime *La Esfera*. The actual document was Estados Unidos de Venezuela, Servicio Secreto de Investigación, *La Verdad de las Actividades Comunistas en Venezula; Relación y Parte de la Numerosa Documentación que Posee el Servicio Secreto de Investigación Acerca de la Realidad de la Propaganda Comunista Dentro del País* (Caracas, 1936).

[8] Interview with Raúl Leoni, December 6, 1962.

the eager young exiles were politically immature, they recognized the need for exclusively Venezuelan programs. Beyond the additional fundamental experience of learning to support themselves abroad—often a traumatic affair when first undergone—these men acquired sufficient knowledge to create a basis on which future planning and policy would be based. Throughout, the basic political tone was to be democratic rather than totalitarian. To quote Betancourt once more, "We defined and proclaimed ourselves defenders of economic nationalism, agrarian democracy and social justice, ardently debating possible means whereby the country could recover and strengthen a regime of public liberties. That was the step which we logically considered as a top priority if we were to place our national revolutionary message before the people."[9]

## *Organizing a Nucleus*

Following the death of Juan Vicente Gómez at the end of 1935, the period during which legal opposition could be enjoyed was brief. By the beginning of 1937 the annulment of elections, the disbanding of political parties, and the expulsion of forty-seven political leaders forced a renewed period of clandestine activity. Notwithstanding the brevity of legal party opposition, it was generally felt that the groundwork had been laid for future operations. The major task during the forthcoming return to illegality lay in the formation of a well-ordered, trained party nucleus, one which might assume the leadership of the movement when it eventually was permitted to exist once again. Organizational emphases were strong, and for the AD-to-be, the key figure was Rómulo Betancourt.

Engaged in an organizing trip through the interior at the time of the government decree in 1937, Betancourt succeeded in escaping the net spread by authorities in

[9] Betancourt, *loc.cit.*

Caracas. For nearly three years he mocked police pursuers while laying the groundwork for future organizational development. The illegal Partido Democrática Nacional, under his guidance, moved to assume the leadership of progressive democratic forces in Venezuela. Dedicated to the construction of a fully national organization, Betancourt and a small handful of colleagues centered their attention on the struggle for political liberty, the defense of social justice, and, perhaps most importantly, the formation of a broad labor movement including both urban workers and rural peasants.

Leonardo Ruiz Pineda, a younger party activist, later wrote that during the 1937-1939 underground preparations, Betancourt "formalized the ideology and philosophical course of the PDN as the organization of the left, making it an instrument of the democratic, anti-imperialist revolution."[10] Yet almost before the bases for a viable underground organization could be laid, the PDN was torn by an ideological clash between communists and non-communists. While it seemed somewhat in the nature of an internecine feud at the time, this conflict was to be a major event in the evolution of today's Acción Democrática. Certainly it was the single most important issue during this period of clandestine organization.

The attempted legalization of the PDN in 1936 had been based upon the inclusion of all opposition forces, and the communist Partido Republicano Progresista placed a number of its members in influential positions. With the events of 1937, communist and democratic forces battled to gain ascendancy of the movement. The communists initially exerted a powerful influence, and their members fought hard for control of the PDN's directing *cuadros*.[11] This ended in a division that tem-

---

[10] *A.D.*, no. 9, July 5, 1958, as cited on p. 12.

[11] No satisfactory translation of this word exists; regarding party organization, it is intended as a small directing group—not necessarily composing a specific party organ—that in practical terms holds responsibility for decisions.

porarily weakened the forces of the democratic left, while simultaneously concluding the only instance of cooperation between the two.

Veteran leaders of the AD universally regard even the brief period of collaboration as a grave mistake. Leoni believes that the effort was a reflection of youthful naïveté and political inexperience. The communists were, at that time, generally older and more experienced politically. Non-communist members of the PDN, he feels, were politically "romantic," and this romanticism took the form of a blind faith that doctrinal differences could be overcome through a common cause, such as the restoration of unfettered party activity.[12]

Non-communist PDN members were also handicapped in 1937 by the absence of the great majority of their leaders, and communist activity within the party was generally more active in its early months. Red organizers fought to gain total control while insisting that the "Partido Unico de la Izquierda" should focus its economic programs almost entirely on Venezuelan labor, to the exclusion of other groups. Democratic members objected that the role of the PDN was necessarily that of a *policlasista* party, with national roots and a democratic program, serving as the vanguard in the struggle for political liberty, social justice, and the triumph of nationalism over imperialism.

The split became irrevocable when the communists published the clandestine *El Martillo* with a strong attack on non-communist members. The final rupture followed almost immediately. On February 14, 1938, a PDN manifesto was circulated with the declaration that the party was "revolutionary, democratic, anti-imperialist and *policlasista*." The manifesto further warned that forthcoming communist propaganda would place a different light on the split, and urged all those with democratic beliefs to unite in the inevitable battle with the

[12] Interview with Raúl Leoni, October 29, 1962.

Reds. The statement was candid in admitting the serious loss of strength entailed as a result of the rupture.[13]

The rivalry led to competition throughout the country, centering on the students and organized workers. The diminished PDN, with its communist membership removed, reiterated the belief that Venezuela, economically a semi-colonial country with development dependent on foreign capital, could only progress through the winning of political democracy by a party of more than one class. Communists were taunted for ignoring many sectors of the nation in their preoccupation with labor. Furthermore, the purified PDN embraced in its ranks, as Betancourt claimed, "workers and peasants; students, professional people and intellectuals; farmers, merchants and small industrialists, . . . a belligerent and disciplined Party that daily marched into struggle against the anti-historic forces opposed to national progress."

The debate over the question of a one-class party, hotly waged on both theoretical and practical terms, was an eventual source of strength for the PDN. Once again Betancourt's subsequent account merits attention. ". . . The thesis advanced by the communists was hardly realistic . . . [for] urban middle classes, the students and professionals, the varied body of small farmers . . . would not join in workers' parties, but rather would join those of full and comprehensive national revolutionary plans. In 1937 this debate was in large part theoretical, . . . In later years, visible and concrete facts cleared away the doctrinaire dispute, showing who was right."[14] The PDN continued to pursue the objective of a broad party into which members of all classes were recruited and welcomed. Workers and peasants in particular were viewed as the most revolutionary and cohesive forces, but

[13] One of the few accounts in writing by a participant is found in Luis Troconis Guerrero, *La Cuestión Agraria en la Historia Nacional* (Caracas: Editorial Arte, 1962).

[14] Betancourt, *op.cit.*, p. 787, note 7.

everyone who subscribed to party doctrine was welcomed.

Doctrinal matters during this period of clandestineness centered on the conflict with the communists; otherwise, attention was given primarily to organizational tasks. The anti-communist manifesto of February 1938 and the resultant numerical weakening of the PDN left it a veritable "pocket organization," as its leaders conceded. Its enemies derided it as being so small that party meetings could be held in an automobile, and this was not a great exaggeration. Betancourt's most notable colleagues during the first year of clandestine operations were largely the rising student leaders who had been excluded from the 1937 deportation order. Such names as Luis Lander, Luis Augusto Dubuc, and Leonardo Ruiz Pineda began to be heard. Prieto and Pérez Alfonzo, who remained at large in Venezuela, were also increasingly active.

The Partido Democrática Nacional developed organizationally along cellular lines. Used as the party base, cells first developed in Caracas, then spread to state capitals. Small committees of five members were the basic nucleus, meeting for weekly discussions and reports. Individuals entered appropriate professional or trade organizations, such as labor or the peasant movement. The directing Comité Ejecutivo Nacional (CEN) operated from the capital, and soon a series of regional units, the Comités Ejecutivos Regionales (CER) also took shape. The size of organs and the number of members grew in spite of official harassment. Leaders traveled constantly, both to avoid apprehension and to strengthen ties between often-isolated groups of supporters.

National and regional executives further developed secretariats such as Organization, Press and Propaganda, Finance, Labor, and a Disciplinary Tribunal. In certain instances political bureaus were also formed, composed of members of the relevant executive board and empowered to make all political decisions. The party vocabulary made common usage of "cell," "bureau," and *"frac"* (organizational fractions),[15] and these were retained throughout the exile period. Secretariats proliferated on the national level, while varying from one regional organization to another. Regional secretariats rarely numbered more than three or, at the very most, five.[16]

Following the termination of the one-year exile ordered by López Contreras, several leaders returned to Venezuela. From Colombia came Villalba, Rodríguez, Troconis Guerrero, and Inocente Palacios. Villalba soon returned once again to Colombia, having left the PDN permanently. The other three, however, assumed posts of regional leadership in Zulia, Táchira, and the Federal District. Activities continued under intermittent persecution that only infrequently brought physical danger.[17]

Underground opposition held its perils, to be sure. Betancourt's wife and young daughter were kept under surveillance. On one occasion he made a spectacularly melodramatic automobile escape amid a fusillade of bullets, until Elbano Mibelli finally suggested through a mutual acquaintance that Betancourt should leave Venezuela since it was not capable of guaranteeing his life. Nonetheless, repression was far less rigorous than, by contrast, that under Pérez Jiménez. It is not unusual for senior members of today's Acción Democrática to recall the days of the PDN with something verging on nostalgia. During much of this four-year period, PDN member-

---

[15] The term *"frac"* or the more common usage today, *fracción*, has come to be used in applying to a fairly large number of party members with a particular concern, such as the labor *fracción* or wing, the parliamentary "party," and so forth.

[16] The best single source for this material, although far from complete, is Acción Democrática, *Tesis Organizativa y Estatutos* (Caracas: Editorial "Antonio Pinto Salinas," 1958), pp. 3-6.

[17] Gonzalo Barrios, for example, recalls the practice of permitting jailed university students to leave custody for a day in order to attend examinations (interview with Barrios on November 27, 1962).

ship was an estimated 600-800. It was generally a closely knit organization; its functioning was far from flawless, yet it fit the situation well enough. A notable accomplishment—one of the highmarks of the period—was the convocation of the I National Conference in September 1939. Between forty-five and fifty delegates came together in the *quinta* "La Hermanita," located in Catia, Caracas. Regional leaders attended the meeting, notwithstanding warrants for the arrest of several. Four main points were on the agenda: political thesis, agrarian thesis, party program, and organizational statutes. Conclusions were reproduced in mimeographed form; more recently they have appeared in the volume by Troconis Guerrero.

The *pedenista* declarations fit into the ideological evolution of what became Acción Democrática, although they were drafted without a great deal of specificity. There was nothing inconsistent with the programmatic and doctrinal statements that followed the subsequent founding of the AD in 1941. As it was, the holding of the meeting gave encouragement to the supporters of the party. Soon after the conclusion of the Conference, police restrictions began to show greater laxity, and PDN leadership began to soften the anger of its attacks on the government while increasing quiet efforts to extend party organization. The leadership was also revised, with newly arrived men relieving those who had been laboring for some time under the pressures of clandestinity.

Betancourt had by this time decided to leave Venezuela for a time. During roughly two-and-a-half years he had purged the organization of communists, strengthened the commitment to political democracy, and reshaped the organization. As a propagandist he had also contributed more than 600 columns which appeared in *Ahora* under the heading "Economy and Finance." Following the conclusion of the Conference, he was literally in the process of writing a letter to López Contreras, asking for an audience after which he would leave the country, when the long-frustrated police captured him. He went into exile in Chile—without meeting López Contreras.

The mark of Betancourt's organizational accomplishments was the continued existence and even strengthening of the party structure while he was absent. Not until some time later did he return to the country, as presidential elections were nearing and the symbolic candidacy of Rómulo Gallegos was privately decided upon. The organizational tasks of 1941-1945 of the legalized Acción Democrática were arduous, as is pointed out elsewhere. However, it was the spadework accomplished by just a handful of men in the late 1930's that made possible the rapid growth of the party in the years to follow.

## Fight for Survival

With the ousting of Gallegos in November 1948, Acción Democrática was driven from the country with a vengeance; in the decade to follow, the regime did everything possible to erase the party from existence and from memory. And so the battle was joined on two fronts: in Venezuela, a brutalized underground organization labored ceaselessly to survive, all the while attempting to keep vivid the image of the party with the Venezuelan people. Abroad, the leadership undertook to revitalize itself without losing the unity of purpose and discipline that had characterized the party. Morale had to be maintained among the party rank-and-file without unduly jeopardizing the membership. Acción Democrática was to show that the party *mystique* had a powerful and enduring quality. The poet Andrés Eloy Blanco expressed it in lyrical terms. Reflecting the most admirable spirit of the party, he declared that the AD was not merely a group of individuals interested in politics but was, rather, a conscience. "To dissolve Acción Democrática is to say that faith is dissolved, conscience is dissolved. . . . The *mystique* does not recognize decrees."

The decade of exile under a military regime can be divided conveniently into two segments separated by the 1952 election, a highwater mark for these years. Before the election the AD had been reconstituted inside Venezuela in skeletal form; afterwards, increasing official repression tested the party's capacity for survival even more. In the pre-1952 period, the party demonstrated considerable resilience and unlimited determination. Barely a day after the junta in December 1948 announced the dissolution of Acción Democrática, a clandestine manifesto circulated in the streets of Caracas. It represented the beginning of the long underground struggle, in which illegal publications were to be important. ". . . from this very date the Party begins its political task of a clandestine nature. . . . The Party enters a period of sacrifices and of organized resistance, an undertaking for which our movement counts on imperishable sources of fervor. . . . We do not hide the magnitude of the effort before us, nor do we pretend to conceal the prospects for combat which are offered us. . . . Acción Democrática begins today its clandestine resistance, which will continue until it wins for Venezuela a rule of freedom, political dignity, administrative honesty and public decency."[18]

Precipitously thrown from power, the AD faced two immediate tasks. As Betancourt told the party in a retrospective analysis in 1958, the first necessity was for the broadest possible denunciation of the *golpe* and its significance as a direct attack upon fundamental liberties by the military usurpers. Second was the restructuring of a clandestine apparatus, "a difficult task for a Party that had operated seven years as a legalized organization and

[18] Much of the information and many of the quotations here are taken from clandestine documents, many of them scarce. The majority were examined through the courtesy of various members of the party.

had forgotten the systems of struggle . . . as learned and applied in the years from 1937 to 1941."[19]

The first goal was achieved to a striking degree. The hemispheric press had from the outset condemned the military seizure of power, and later denials of basic political freedoms were widely attacked throughout following years. Democratic leaders throughout Latin America were drawn into sympathy for the Venezuelan—and the AD—cause. The greatest benefit to the party from this campaign was less the winning of widespread sympathy than the establishment of strong fraternal ties with Latin American parties and movements of similar orientation. Friendships with figures of the democratic left in Costa Rica, in Bolivia, and in Cuba, were of later importance in hemispheric relations.

In attacking the problem of organization, Acción Democrática was initially handicapped by the absence of its top leaders. In the early months and even beyond, daily tasks fell in large part to young party activists and university students who enjoyed temporary immunity from the authorities through relative political anonymity. At the same time they had no real knowledge of necessary activities, and none could draw upon direct experience from the PDN. The uneven nature of the organization from one state or district to another, was at the outset a reflection of such inexperience and lack of guidance.[20]

Several structural readjustments were adopted. The Comité Directivo Nacional was suspended indefinitely, as were all conventions and deliberative assemblies. Sheer numbers made such meetings impossible. The supreme

[19] Rómulo Betancourt, *Posición y Doctrina* (Caracas: Editorial Cordillera, 1958), pp. 170-71. Several pertinent speeches and declarations from 1957 and 1958 are included in this volume.

[20] Much of this information comes from participants in various stages of the clandestine opposition. The author is indebted to many, especially Octavio Lepage, Evelyn Trujillo, and Enrique Tejera París, for the details of the following paragraphs.

authority inside Venezuela became the Comité Ejecutivo Nacional. The CEN in turn created a special Political Commission that was responsible for basic political decisions. Thus it was more feasible to gather together a small number of leaders for covert discussions. Once decisions were reached, all lower party units were to follow the CEN directive without debate or discussion.

The basic cellular unit, the *Grupo de Base*,[21] was invigorated wherever possible. *Grupos* were often assigned strictly professional functions, since the regular "fractions" of labor, student, and peasant organs could not be effectively maintained. In a few instances even jail units, or *Grupos de Cárceles*, were established. A special secretariat, the so-called Vigilancia Interna, was created with over-all responsibility for passwords, codes, contacts, and other necessary underground paraphernalia. Security measures dictated an essentially horizontal rather than vertical flow of party decisions. Discipline was strengthened by the dogged perseverance of security forces, and members often worked virtually alongside one another for years without knowing that both were participants in the apparatus.

The exiled leadership after a time asserted itself in the organizational pattern. Following early months of semi-stunned search for sanctuary and then for employment, the exiles re-formed. Major centers were established in five cities: Buenos Aires, Argentina; Santiago, Chile; San José, Costa Rica; Mexico City; and New York City. Habana, Cuba, served as a focal point of activity until the government of Prío Socarrás was ousted in 1952 by Fulgencio Batista. Rómulo Betancourt had been in Cuba until that time, after which his travels included stays of some length in both Puerto Rico and Costa Rica.

---

[21] The *Grupo de Base*—literally the "base group"—became comparable to the small cell or unit at the very bottom of the structure. During the resistance its duties and responsibilities varied widely, according to the circumstance of the moment.

Committees were established in each of these cities, with over-all direction coming from the Comité Coordinador del Exterior, which tried with varying degrees of success to oversee all activities. Based much of the time in Costa Rica, this committee not only directed exile activities but maintained all possible contact with leaders inside Venezuela. The Comité Coordinador Exterior was, for example, responsible for the convening of the Conferencia de Exilados in 1956. Communications between the clandestine CEN in Caracas and the Comité Coordinador Exterior were naturally erratic, with radio messages as well as private emissaries used. Organizational purity required that the exiles exercise supremacy, but practical considerations led the leaders inside Venezuela to have the final judgment on matters directly affecting them.

In November 1948, direction of the underground movement fell to acting Secretary-General Luis Augusto Dubuc, but he was captured in a few weeks and imprisoned. Leadership then devolved on a few young supporters and activists, among whom Octavio Lepage was prominent. Later Leonardo Ruiz Pineda, himself a young man but already a veteran of party struggles in Táchira, also a Minister of Communications under Gallegos, assumed the post of Secretary-General. As he wrote in 1952, the early problem of the party revolved about the possible rapid decovery of power. Many *adecos* inside the country were more anxious to launch disorganized violence than to work for the restructuring of the party. Thus discipline was sometimes maintained with great difficulty.

In mid-1952 the AD's *Libro Negro* circulated clandestinely, calling upon party members to fulfill their duty by working as directed, disciplining themselves to directives from above; it set forth the over-all goal of the party as that of orienting the people politically and "creating the consciousness of its democratic destiny."[22] Problems of party discipline nonetheless loomed large, and such directives did not dispose of the controversy over tactics. Party members were urging that an all-out attack be launched against the regime; yet the leadership was interested in pursuing the possibility of contact with democratically oriented members of the military, hoping to plant seeds of dissension. Such contact could not be effectively rendered if the AD did not give assurances that it was not embarked upon a campaign of terrorism. The disciplinary problem was gradually brought under control, although the party leadership in time was forced to abandon as impractical the idea of communicating with receptive military men.

Organizational changes and revisions did not come overnight, but were in part the result of trial and error, evolving over a period of time. In the meantime the AD continued an active publicity campaign throughout the hemisphere. It took many facets, all of which were intended to achieve both international sympathy and growing support inside Venezuela. An illustration of the former came with a series of public letters calling attention to political prisoners in Venezuela. Betancourt wrote to United Nations Secretary-General Trygve Lie in November of 1950 to report on a worsening of conditions. "It is no exaggeration to expect and hope that the UN . . . [might] try to raise the iron curtain of martial law and rigid censorship of information in my country, demanding of its government some loyalty to the promise to respect liberty and freedom. . . ."[23]

---

[22] The original text is virtually impossible to locate; important excerpts and a discussion are included in a posthumous work: Leonardo Ruiz Pineda, *Ventanas al Mundo* (Caracas: Editorial Arte, 1961).

[23] The text of this and the Gallegos letter to Mrs. Roosevelt appear in Acción Democrática, *Cartas de los Presos Políticos y Otros Documentos* (Caracas: 1951).

Rómulo Gallegos addressed a message of similar content to Eleanor Roosevelt from Mexico City in May 1951. Mrs. Roosevelt, serving as President of the United Nations Commission on Human Rights, was told that "the fortunes of hundreds of imprisoned countrymen worries me particularly." Some had been jailed over a year without appearing before a judge, and, he claimed, many were "exposed to daily mistreatment by their jailers, while some have suffered physical tortures. . . . I write in hope that I might receive some echo to this just demand for human rights and individual freedoms."

Propagandizing was also increasingly common on the home front. By the time of Delgado Chalbaud's assassination in late 1950, the underground presses of the AD had increased their effectiveness. On September 13, 1951, the tenth anniversary of the party's founding was marked by a pair of statements by the Comité Ejecutivo Nacional. In the first, the faith of loyal members was cheered. "The vitality of the Party has been proved in three years of persecution. Its 10,000 prisoners, its 600 exiles, its 20,000 persecuted families, . . . have not been able to quench the fighting *mystique*. . . ." The party then reaffirmed its struggle against the military dictatorship.[24]

The second leaflet on that date attacked a recent move by the regime to obtain a large loan from foreign oil enterprises.[25] The government had undertaken a loan to be repaid from future taxes. This, claimed the party, was fresh evidence that the government's economic policy was faltering. The AD argued that no future Venezuelan government, if representative of the will of the people, could recognize "loans granted to the present Junta government and will be, on the contrary, in the unavoidable

[24] Acción Democrática, *A.D. y la Lucha por Libertad* (one-page leaflet signed by Comité Ejecutivo Nacional, 1951).

[25] Acción Democrática, *Acción Democrática contra Maniobra Anti-Nacional Monstrua* (one-page leaflet signed by party Comité Ejecutivo Nacional, 1951).

moral position of being bound to invalidate the concessions. . . ."

With the passing of time the anti-government attitude
hardened increasingly. Not only did the possibility of
approaching the dissidents within the government lessen
but the persecution of security forces demanded an
equally tough-minded and unyielding response. The
slaying of Delgado Chalbaud also seemed to remove all
semblance of restraint by the government; increasingly
the official attitude treated the AD as a mere band of
violent conspirators. The stridency of Seguridad Nacional
was demonstrated by an official communiqué on April
14, 1952, singling out Secretary-General Ruiz Pineda and
his associate Alberto Carnevali as leaders of a conspiracy
against the life of Pérez Jiménez and his collaborators.

The following day Acción Democrática responded with
a three-page, typewritten manifesto which appeared in
the streets of Caracas, signed by Ruiz Pineda. Titled
"Declaración del Comité Ejecutivo Nacional," the document denied the charges pointedly. The Seguridad Nacional was, according to the Secretary-General, trying to
destroy the party's international reputation, creating confusion within AD ranks while distracting attention of
apolitical citizens from governmental shortcomings.

Referring to the evolving official political organization
that was preparing for fall 1952 elections, the manifesto
charged Pérez Jiménez with intentions of perpetuating
himself in power. His pretensions had led to the organization of the Frente Electoral Independiente, financed by
national funds, to further Pérez Jiménez' maintenance in
power. The AD, wrote Ruiz Pineda, intended to unite
anti-*perezjimenista* sentiment. All partisan organizations
and representatives of public opinion were to be drawn
together as fully as possible in order to install a government that would "reestablish public liberties, put an end
to administrative immorality, and convoke free and sover-

eign elections to which all Venezuelan democratic forces are firmly committed."[26]

By the coming of 1952, Acción Democrática had revised its organization, hammered out fundamental positions, and formalized its opposition to the regime. External sympathy had been evoked, friendship with like-minded leaders of neighbor countries strengthened, and contacts with other opposition parties initiated. Marcos Pérez Jiménez had in the meantime been gradually moving toward the convoking of national elections. Inside the country both COPEI and the URD prepared for the contest with a mixture of hope and concern. Electoral dilemmas and decisions lay ahead for all the anti-government elements. These are analyzed at length in Chapter XI. For the present it need merely be recalled that the AD quietly threw its support in the 1952 contest to the URD nominee, Jóvito Villalba. Although the extent of the AD contribution is controversial, Villalba clearly won the elections notwithstanding official involvement on behalf of Pérez Jiménez. The regime therefore intervened, reversed election returns, and instituted the rule of the military under "constitutional" terms.

Regardless of the role of the parties in the 1952 election, the vote was an overwhelming indictment of the regime by the Venezuelan people. As one participant later wrote, the campaign "served to create a clear conscience of civil rebellion. All the forces of the country were brought together in that rebellious attitude."[27] For Acción Democrática in particular, the question posed by the governmental defiance of public opinion was that of finding an outlet for effective opposition in the months and years ahead.

A wave of disbelief followed the electoral farce, but

[26] Acción Democrática, *Declaración del Comité Ejecutivo Nacional* (three-page leaflet signed by Leonardo Ruiz Pineda, 1952).

[27] Mario Briceño-Iragorri, *Ideario Político* (Caracas: Editorial "Las Novedades," 1958), p. 227.

no means of effective protest could be found. There were proposals of a general strike, but *adecos* in Venezuela recognized that the organization was not capable of handling such a massive logistical task. The AD's Alberto Carnevali charged that the military was being used by Pérez Jiménez as a tool to defraud rather than to defend the institutions. Thus he proclaimed for the AD a state of permanent rebellion against the dictatorship. Acting as Secretary-General, he proposed in the name of the party an offensive against the regime and its agents, one in which all anti-government groups would be fully active.

Yet the sharpening controls of the regime had begun to take an increasingly heavy toll. On October 21, 1952, Leonardo Ruiz Pineda had been deliberately murdered by the police in the heart of Caracas. The next day authorities announced the death as if they had apprehended the lowest common criminal; later the dead man's widow was imprisoned when she visited the Ministry of Interior Relations to claim the body. In a ceremony conducted by party exiles in Mexico, ex-president Gallegos lamented the loss of a friend and patriot, while denouncing the murder. "A new kind of dictatorial brutality has been initiated in Venezuela; a political adversary has been assassinated. . . . Venezuela has always repudiated homicide as a kind of political struggle, and while it has been guilty of forgetting some of the insults and unpardonable grievances, it will not be able to forget the truth of this deed."[28]

Barely three months after Alberto Carnevali had replaced his slain friend as covert Secretary-General, he was himself fired upon by government agents on January 18, 1953. The Caracas home in which he was lodged fell under attack, and several party members perished in the battle. Carnevali was taken into custody and held

[28] Rómulo Gallegos, *Una Posición en la Vida* (México: Ediciones Humanismo, 1954), p. 514.

incommunicado. Ailing at the time of his capture, an exploratory operation revealed the appearance of generalized cancer of the digestive tract. Pleas from friends and family failed to move authorities, who denied permission to move him to a clinic. He soon expired in jail. Not long after, on April 24, 1953, Carnevali's own replacement, Eligio Anzola Anzola, was taken captive by security forces following an exchange of gunfire in suburban El Paraíso. Lawyer, jurist, and former Minister of Interior Relations, Anzola Anzola was seriously mistreated before being shipped from Venezuela.

As repression grew more brutal, the number of victims mounted. In June 1953 the young writer and economist Antonio Pinto Salinas was attacked on a highway leading toward the *llanos*. Like other members of the underground he periodically moved from Caracas to the interior, both for recuperative and for security purposes. He was ambushed while attempting such a move. And during the same year other members of the AD, especially those of its younger generation, were imprisoned and victimized. Rigoberto Henríquez Vera and José Angel Ciliberto, major figures in the party in 1958 and after, were cruelly mishandled. *Campesino* leaders Ramón Quijada and Tomás Alberti were also imprisoned and held under inhumane circumstances.

The toll on the AD leadership was heavy, and extended beyond those who died under fire in Venezuela. Among those who died in exile were Andrés Eloy Blanco and Valmore Rodríguez, both members of the very highest party command. Blanco passed away in Mexico, Rodríguez in Chile. Luis Troconis Guerrero had died from extended illness in 1951, another serious loss to the party. In spite of such depredations, however, the tempo of activity continued. So rigorous was the repression in Venezuela that underground activities lessened, but party publications continued. *Resistencia* circulated within the country; while sharply curbed, it was never totally restricted. Leaflets and overt messages from the party CEN were never completely stemmed.

At the same time, a plethora of exile publications existed. *Información Venezolana* was edited in Habana from 1950-1952 and then, with the return of Batista, was moved to Costa Rica. *CTV* was issued periodically in Mexico by former leaders of the labor confederation, and other occasional organs included a multigraphed *Mensaje* that from time to time showed up in Spain. Most important of all was *Venezuela Democrática,* the self-proclaimed "voice of national-revolutionary principles." Appearing in early 1955 under the joint editorship of Gonzalo Barrios, Ricardo Montilla, and Juan Pablo Pérez Alfonzo, it appeared fairly regularly until terminating in late 1957.

In September 1955 it printed an anniversary message by Rómulo Betancourt titled "Reaffirmation of Faith." Conceding the solidity of the dictatorship, he promised that the fight would go on with unflagging determination. The AD, as a mass movement, would continue to fight as the representative of the Venezuelan people. And to this sentiment was added an article by Barrios that had been read to a large group of *adecos* marking the party anniversary in Mexico. Barrios enjoined younger party members not to lose faith in party programs and ideas, for the AD would continue to be a part of the revolution for progress and well-being. Venezuela, he insisted, would be liberated. This meant not merely a freeing of the country from imperialistic control and economic dependence, but also a responsible nationalism, agrarian democracy, and a representative government dedicated to total social justice.[29]

With the passage of time, party leaders pursued myriad personal activities. Supporting themselves through various means of employment, a number served with the United Nations. The prospect of an eventual return to

[29] *Venezuela Democrática,* no. 5, September 1955, p. 7.

Venezuela was never forgotten, however. Easily the most important event for the AD exile organization was the Conferencia de Exilados held in Puerto Rico in early 1956. Two major items were set before the assembled exiles: adoption of a new policy, referred to as La Nueva Táctica, and preparatory adjustments with a view to electoral manipulations which the government might undertake in 1957.

The Nueva Táctica, as Betancourt later recalled, foresaw an "inevitable governmental crisis" as the five-year mandate of Pérez Jiménez drew to a close. The lack of international prestige was coupled with growing internal discontent, and the regime could scarcely afford too fraudulent proceedings. A wave of hemispheric events which had recently swept away dictatorships in Argentina, Colombia, and Peru also increased the moral pressure on the regime. Acción Democrática concluded lengthy and heated debates by adopting a policy of full and active cooperation with all other parties. This was intended to be meaningful, and represented a step beyond the nominal collaboration of earlier years. From the Conferencia de Exilados was born the cooperation that later bore fruit in the unitary movement which participated in the revolution of January 1958.

The assemblage of *adecos* also discussed basic party theses. In addition to the tactical decision about a united front, the party adopted programmatic statements on a wide range of subjects. Many of these reiterated former positions on anti-imperialism, agrarian reform, and national industrialization. Administrative honesty was stressed, the ornamental nature of the regime's public works program was condemned, and the usual stand on the religious question was restated.

Acción Democrática, declared the exiles, remained essentially an organic front of the historically exploited classes—workers, *campesinos*, technicians, small producers, and merchants. "This organic front of the non-parasitical classes embraces the nation's most numerous groups, which share coincident political, economic and social interests, with fortunes and destinies linked to those of the Democratic Revolution. There are no insoluble clashes of interest that would open a chasm between the vast front of classes and of sectors of Venezuelan national industry." The official declaration concluded with a renewed insistence upon internal discipline. With messianic *caudillismo* removed from the party years earlier, it was less a federation of classes than a single front. All members were equally obligated to organizational obedience. "After a collective course of political conduct has been established by the appropriate organs . . . that course becomes a duty for all party members."[30]

The gathering of exiles was the last major event to take place during the 1948-1958 period. Resistance inside the country continued, and contacts with the URD and COPEI were gradually improved and strengthened. The 1957 publication of Archbishop Arias' criticism of the regime cheered the exiles, and the government's problem of forthcoming elections gave renewed hope that a return home might be forthcoming. By June 1957 *Venezuela Democrática* was editorializing that all democratic parties were joined together in an informal but nonetheless effective union. Indeed, with tri-party unity a fact, there was "no fear of its being put in danger by narrow particularistic attitudes."

Two months later the party collaboration was reflected in the next issue of the exile paper; Betancourt, Gallegos, and Villalba all wrote of the determination to maintain a united front against Pérez Jiménez. Betancourt wrote that "The three parties are identical in the purpose of refraining from waving party banners or individual

[30] Acción Democrática, *Ratificación de Principios Teóricos y de Orientación Programática Normativos de Acción Democrática* (Caracas: Secretaría Nacional de Prensa y Propaganda, 1958), pp. 21-23.

ambitions. . . . We are identified in the irrevocable purpose of obtaining a climate of coexistence and of collective harmony in Venezuela under a responsible government that respects human rights."[31]

The events of December 1957 and January 1958 have already been narrated. The exile collaboration of the parties played a secondary role in the overthrow of Marcos Pérez Jiménez, but its spirit was reflected in the cooperation within Venezuela through the Junta Patriótica. The pattern of cooperation between the AD, COPEI, and the URD was to a considerable extent influenced by the collaborative spirit that came to the fore in the latter part of 1957.

Thus Acción Democrática finally emerged from ten years' exile, the deadliest and most demanding experience of its history. Its essential goals were achieved: the survival of the party, the continuation of a skeletal organization, the unity of its exile leadership, and the winning of at least moral support for its cause from across the hemisphere. But the price was costly. As later events were to reveal, the party had suffered seriously during this period of exile—far more than ever before. While the viability and permanence of the party was underlined by the 1948-1958 period, it inevitably created stresses within the organization, some of which threatened to shatter the party. These can only be treated after examination of the internal workings of the party machinery. Only in the light of certain post-1958 developments can the strains of the lengthy exile be illustrated.

[31] *Venezuela Democrática*, see Año III, nos. 13 and 14, June and August 1957, pp. 1, 6, and 8.

# CHAPTER V

# The Party Organization: Structural Framework

Basic to the rationale of this entire study is the contention that much of the importance of Acción Democrática among the parties of Latin America is its reliance upon organization. Furthermore, it has been this, the machinery of the AD, that more than any other single factor has been responsible for the succession of electoral victories through the years. Organization has been a hallmark of the movement from the early stages of ORVE, and has always remained important. The original leaders of the movement that became the AD recognized the need for a truly national party, with organs and representatives extending to the most remote parts of the Republic. For years the watchword was to expand the party until not a village or hamlet was without some small local outpost.

Venezuela's evolution toward modern nationhood, with all the political and administrative trappings thereof, further heightened the party's concern with matters of structure. Its record of virtually unbroken electoral successes stems from an apparatus that is constant in its activities and unremitting in the recruitment of new members. Leaders of the party today are especially proud of the fact that the party rather than the person is placed first. All are firm in their insistence that the element of *caudillismo* has been kept to a minimum.

Certainly the leadership of Rómulo Betancourt, despite his own best efforts, has inevitably assumed some appearance of personalism. Yet it can be argued that the degree of *caudillismo* in the AD is, by Latin American standards, slight. Subsequent remarks will note Betancourt's quiet but determined preferences at the 1963 convention which the assembly overrode. This is but one suggestion of the minimal effect of personalism within the party.

Interviews with party leaders have revealed a common expression of faith in the fundamental role of the machinery, the *aparato*. An interesting sign of the party's success in this area has been the extent to which younger Venezuelan parties have copied it. Despite variations in detail, the skeletal forms of the other parties are consonant with the AD model.

The party organization, then, is a key to the effective operation of Acción Democrática, whether in power or out, whether legally active or temporarily driven underground. The dynamics of the system do not inevitably follow the guidelines of statutory requirements, although outright deviation from specified organizational patterns is not common. For the sake of thoroughness and clarity, the following discussion will set forth the structural framework of Acción Democrática as expressed in official publications. The succeeding chapter will analyze the actual operations of the organization, paying particular attention to matters of party unity and factionalism.

## National Organs

Basic structural purposes are set forth in the opening article of the party statutes. "The Party . . . will act in the national political field to organize, educate and lead the people of Venezuela to the full realization of a social and economic structure based on liberty and justice. . . ." Article 2 goes on to declare that the party "is of a democratic and revolutionary character, and is formed by base and by directing organs. The latter will emanate from the former by means of majority vote. . . ."[1] Such is the basic statement preceding the structural details.

---

[1] The bulk of this material, although organized differently, is taken from Acción Democrática, *Estatutos* (Caracas: Ediciones de la Secretaría Nacional de Propaganda, 1962). Footnoting is

The party organization is susceptible to analysis from two angles. The first is a functional division based upon legislative, executive, and judicial bodies. This provides one convenient means of differentiating activities and responsibilities. The second envisages a basically politico-geographical approach, beginning with national organs and working down to regional, district, and local ones. The latter will be used in this discussion for purposes of convenience, as well to stress the fact that the AD structure is essentially pyramidal. Except during times of clandestinity, the flow of decisions and directives has been vertical rather than horizontal (see Figure 2).

Four national organs head the party: the Convención Nacional, the Comité Directivo Nacional (CDN), the Comité Ejecutivo Nacional (CEN), and the Tribunal Disciplinario Nacional (TDN). Statutorily their relative importance follows the same order although, in terms of practical politics, it differs somewhat. The Convención Nacional[2] is the supreme authority in the party, and its decisions are not subject to appeal. All other organs and all party members are bound by Convention decisions. A resolution can be overridden or reversed only by another Convention, and the basic party program and statutes can be modified or adapted by this body and no other.

As the supreme organ, the National Convention sets the political line that all others must accept and execute. It is an expression of the party's internal democracy that all important decisions must ultimately be taken by the party base, as voiced at such a national gathering. Ordinarily convened annually, the Convention may be held on whatever date is fixed by the Comité Ejecutivo

---

minimized by the use of pertinent chapters and articles in the statutes. Practical variations to written regulations were discussed in personal interviews, most notably a pair with Political Secretary Said Moanack on November 19 and November 27, 1962.

[2] *Estatutos*, Chapter IV, Articles 18-27.

FIGURE 2*

AD ORGANIZATIONAL CHART

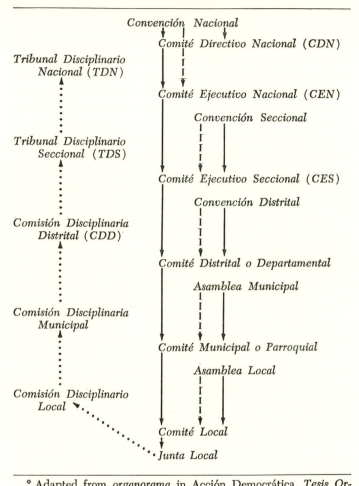

* Adapted from *organorama* in Acción Democrática, *Tesis Organizativa y Estatutos* (Caracas: Editorial "Antonio Pinto Salinas," 1958), p. 64.

line of authority ——————
line of elections —— —— ——
line of disciplinary
     appeal · · · · · · · ·

Nacional. Extraordinary meetings may also be called, either by resolution of the previous Convention or by petition from the CEN, the CDN, or a majority of the Sectionals. In 1945, to illustrate, two National Conventions were held within the space of a few months, owing to the turbulence of an uncertain presidential succession. In the long haul, regularity has been the rule, however. At the close of 1963, the AD had enjoyed thirteen years of legality while celebrating the same number of Conventions.

The National Convention is charged with the study of "all economic, social and political problems of the country, and of everything relative to the Party; it will deal with all problems brought to it by its members and will discuss the Reports of the directing organs, national as well as sectional."[3] It is also empowered to set the political line and programmatic orientation of the party, as well as naming the Comité Ejecutivo Nacional and the Tribunal Disciplinario Nacional.

Convention delegates are chosen from five categories. Members of the CDN are included, ordinarily numbering some 120. The TDN members—five *principales* and five *suplentes*—are also included. The third group comprises all Secretary-Generals, Labor Secretaries, and Agrarian Secretaries from the Comités Ejecutivos Seccionales. Thus some sixty members are added. The great bulk of the delegates, however, come as representatives of the twenty-five Sectional Conventions that precede each National Convention. Representation is based on one for each 2,000 party members and one more for fractions over 1,000. Finally, other affiliated organs may under certain unusual circumstances name a small number of delegates.

The result is an assemblage of some 700 delegates, the majority of whom come as representatives of Sectional

[3] *Estatutos*, Chapter IV, Article 24.

Conventions. Voting is individual; state delegations are not required to cast a bloc vote, although frequently they are unanimous during Convention votes. Procedural rules are approved in a preparatory session before the official opening of the Convention. This session also names a twelve-man group to conduct the actual meetings. It includes a President, two Vice-Presidents, a Secretary-General, four Auxiliary Secretaries and four Directors of Debates. The Convention is traditionally opened by the President of the Party, after which the special directing group takes charge.

Second in statutory power is the Comité Directivo Nacional.[4] As described in Article 31, the CDN is "the maximum authority of the Party in the period between the meetings of the National Convention and, as a consequence, is empowered to fix or to modify the *tactical* [my emphasis] lines of the Party and to realize . . . the readjustments and changes that are considered necessary for the forward progress of the organization." In an effort to sharpen CDN powers, the statutes also grant it the authority to issue directives aimed at the enforcement of any Convention resolutions or decisions that, in the judgment of the CDN, have not been fully or properly implemented.

Ordinarily the CDN meets every six months, although it may be convened at any time by resolution of the CEN or upon the written request of either fifteen members of the CDN or of three or more Sectionals. Regular procedure requires the CEN to call the CDN within fifteen days, although this can be waived in the event of urgency. This latter procedure was at the heart of the struggle between party regulars and the *arsistas* in December 1961 (see Chapter VI). The ARS-controlled CEN on that occasion attempted to delay the meeting of the CDN, which had been requested by more than fifteen members of the latter.

[4] *Estatutos*, Chapter V, Articles 28-34.

The Comité Directivo Nacional comprises some 120 individuals. Its membership is constituted by the Comité Ejecutivo Nacional—around twenty-two—by the President of the Tribunal Disciplinario Nacional, and by the two party labor and youth groups—the Comité Sindical y Agrario Nacional and the Comité Juvenil Nacional. Once again, as with the Convention, the greatest number of members comes from the states. Each sends two members to the CDN: one is the Secretary-General of the Sectional, the other a permanent delegate elected by the Sectional. Ex-Presidents and ex-Secretary-Generals (national) were added to the CDN in 1962 and, finally, an additional ten national party leaders may be invited, who have the right to speak but not to vote. Honorary Party President Gallegos also attends; his presence is also justified by his position as a former Party President.

The size of the group permits the holding of meetings without elaborate internal rules, although preparations are worked out by the CEN in some detail. A series of reports or *informes* will be read and debated; the President will usually comment on the over-all position of the party, and the Secretary-General reports on electoral matters. At the CDN meeting in December 1962, President of the Republic Rómulo Betancourt appeared to give a lengthy summary of the national political picture. It was not known at this writing whether or not his successor might do the same.

Just as the Comité Directivo Nacional is responsible for party decisions between Conventions, so is the Comité Ejecutivo Nacional[5] responsible between meetings of the CDN. Elected by the National Convention and lasting until the next one, the CEN, as stated in Article 35, "is the maximum organ of permanent action for the Party." Of these three, only the CEN is effectively in continuous session. Its powers are multiple, certain of which are

[5] *Estatutos*, Chapter VI, Articles 35-61.

FIGURE 3*

NATIONAL PARTY ORGANS—COMPOSITION

I. *Convención Nacional*
   CDN
   TDN
   Sectional Sec of Org
   Sectional Sec of Ag
   Sectional Sec of Labor
   Sectional delegates
   (1 per 2000 party members)

II. *Comité Directivo Nacional*
   CEN
   Pres of TDN
   Party ex-Pres
   ex-Sec Gens (natl)
   Comité Sindical Nacional
   Comité Agrario Nacional
   Comité Juvenil Nacional
   Sectional Sec Gens
   One Delegate per Sectional

III. *Comité Ejecutivo Nacional* (22)
   Pres; 2 VPs; Sec-Gen; Sub
   Sec-Gen; 4 Pol Secs; 12
   Admin Secs; Sec-Gen of
   Distrito Fed. Seccional

   A. *Comité Político Nacional* (11)
   Pres; 2 VPs; Sec-Gen; Sec
   of Org; Sec of Ag; Sec of
   Labor; 4 Pol Secs

III. *continued*

   B. *Secretariado Nacional* (14)
   Sec-Gen; Sub Sec-Gen;
   12 Admin Secs

   C. *Comité Sindical Nacional* (16)
   Sec of Labor; Adjunto of
   Labor; Lab Sec of Libertador Seccional; Pol Sec;
   12 labor ldrs

   D. *Comité Agrario Nacional* (9)
   Sec of Ag; Adjunto of Ag;
   Ag Sec of Miranda; Pol
   Sec; 5 ag ldrs

   E. *Comité Juvenil Nacional* (11)
   Sec of Yth; Adjunto of
   Yth; Yth Sec of Libertador;
   Pol Sec; 7 yth ldrs

   F. *National Admin. Secretaries* (12)
   Organization; Labor; Youth;
   Agriculture; Relations; Education and Culture; International Affairs; Press; Propaganda; Finance; Parliamentary and Municipal Affairs;
   Studies and Indoctrination

---

* Information compiled from Acción Democrática, *Tesis Organizativa y Esta-tutos* (*Caracas*: Editorial "Antonio Pinto Salinas," 1958).

essentially administrative. Thus the CEN is responsible for calling the Convention and the CDN into session, for overseeing the implementation of resolutions passed by those bodies, and for presenting reports on the continuing activities of the CEN at meetings of the other two organs.

The CEN is also responsible for the publication of the party press organ, for the distribution of informational material to all levels of the party, and for the submission to all Comités Ejecutivos Seccionales of any matters that should be brought to their attention. The Comité Ejecutivo Nacional is therefore something of a clearing house for the dissemination of information. Yet it is far more; all continuing efforts to strengthen and expand the organization fall under this body. It is authorized to fix the tactical line of the party when necessary and to issue necessary directives to that end.

Furthermore, the CEN is empowered "to fix the position of the Party on national, international or local occurrences in which the Party has an interest, adjusting said position to the resolutions of higher organs." More detailed powers are spelled out during an enumeration of the CEN membership. The body meets twice monthly, and is capable of coming together on a few hours' notice. The Comité Ejecutivo Nacional customarily has some twenty voting members; in early 1963 there were twenty-two including a President, two Vice-Presidents, a Secretary-General, a Sub-Secretary-General, four Political Secretaries, twelve administrative Secretaries,[6] and the Secretary-General of the Comité Ejecutivo Seccional for the Federal District and Libertador.[7] Each of the twelve administrative Secretaries have an assistant or Adjunto. Adjuntos generally attend CEN meetings with the right to speak but not to vote.[8]

[6] Secretary of Organization; Secretary of Labor; Secretary of Agriculture; Secretary of the Youth Movement; Secretary of Relations; Secretary of Finance; Secretary of International Affairs; Secretary of Parliamentary and Municipal Affairs; Secretary of Studies; Secretary of Press; Secretary of Propaganda; and Secretary of Education and Culture.

[7] Libertador department of the Federal District traditionally is of great importance to the AD organization and is therefore represented in this fashion on the national level.

[8] In late 1963 the party added two new posts to the CEN: the Secretary for Economy and Technical Affairs; and the Secretary

Within the Comité Ejecutivo Nacional there is a further breakdown into two sub-units: the Comité Político Nacional and the Secretariado Nacional. The former, often called the Buró Político, is regarded as the very heart of AD leadership on a national, day-to-day basis. It has eleven voting members: the party President, both Vice-Presidents, the Secretary-General, the four Political Secretaries, and the respective Secretaries of Organization, Labor, and Agriculture. Prior to the XII National Convention in 1962, the Vice-Presidents, the Agrarian Secretary, and a fourth Political Secretary were not included. Meeting weekly—currently at 4 p.m. Tuesday— it is subject to the call of either the President or the Secretary-General, and any three members may also request a session.

The Secretariado Nacional, a fourteen-member body, is essentially administrative rather than policy-making. Composed of the Secretary-General, the Sub-Secretary-General, and the twelve administrative Secretaries, it is the center of the AD bureaucratic structure. Responsible for the execution of the continuing tasks of organization and routine activity, it meets regularly every fifteen days. It may also be called into special session by the Secretary-General or by three of its members. The Comité Ejecutivo Nacional is thus broken down into a policy-making unit and an administrative secretariat. Each of the two groups makes decisions whenever possible without referring them to the entire CEN. As Article 40 adds, *"decisions of extreme importance in both* [political and administrative] *fields must be taken by the full CEN."*

The CEN includes three functional bureaus, commonly termed *clasista* or "class" bureaus by the *policlasista* or "multi-class" AD. These are the labor, agrarian, and youth bureaus—the Comité Sindical Nacional, Comité

---

of Community Development. Thus the CEN rose in number to twenty-four.

Agrario Nacional, and Comité Juvenil Nacional. The first is composed of sixteen members, headed by the Labor Secretary and his Adjunto, also including the Labor Secretary of Libertador department, one of the Political Secretaries, and twelve national labor leaders named by the party labor assembly, the Pleno Sindical Nacional. The smaller Comité Agrario Nacional, at least nominally separate, is directed by the Agrarian Secretary and his Adjunto, with a Political Secretary, the Agrarian Secretary of Miranda state, and five agricultural leaders chosen by the party agrarian convention, the Pleno Agrario Nacional.

The labor and agrarian committees meet every fifteen days. They also combine to form a twenty-five-member Comité Sindical y Agrario Nacional that attempts to coordinate labor and agrarian policy. These meetings are ordinarily monthly. Long-established party organs, they provided a model that was followed when the 1958 Convention created the Comité Juvenil Nacional for the party youth. Directed by the Youth Secretary and his Adjunto, its eleven members include the Youth Secretary of Libertador department, a Political Secretary, and seven youth leaders named by the party youth convention, the Pleno Juvenil Nacional.

In actual practice, the heads of the three *clasista* bureaus are selected by the *pleno* directly involved. Thus the Pleno Sindical Nacional normally elects the twelve labor leaders to sit on the Comité Sindical Nacional, as well as the AD Labor Secretary. Technically, the AD Labor, Agrarian, and Youth Secretaries are chosen at the National Convention, but rarely is there any divergence. AD leaders recall only two cases in the history of the party where the Convention rejected the choice of the occupational *pleno*—both from the Pleno Juvenil Nacional.

Individual duties of the full members of the Comité Ejecutivo Nacional are in many cases obvious. The responsibilities of the President are what might be expected, as is the case with the two Vice-Presidents. Party statutes make no distinction between the Vice-Presidents, although the First nominally outranks the Second. The Secretary-General is in many ways second only to the party President in *statutory* power.[9] Responsibility for over-all coordination of the CEN is his, and twice monthly he receives written reports from administrative secretaries. He is responsible for the operation and coordination of the various party wings or *fracciones*, while working with the President in the maintenance and enforcement of internal discipline. In past times the post has occasionally been the most powerful within the party. A prime example was the Secretary-Generalship of Rómulo Betancourt.

Of lesser but substantial importance is the Secretary of Organization, who works closely with the Secretary-General. Enumerated duties include the registration and control of the party membership on a national scale. Local party units are to be developed where none exist. The Secretary of Organization must also coordinate the work of the CEN with Sectionals, usually sending instructions in the form of a general circular. Specific instructions to a given unit are sent in an individual letter. In normal times the Secretary of Organization will devote the bulk of his attention to matters of communication.[10]

The four Political Secretaries are key men in the leadership, and their talents are ideally versatile. Statutory duties are but two, according to Article 44: to act "in the study and resolution of political problems," and to

[9] This is not to suggest that the Secretary-General is second only to the President in prestige. In 1963, for example, it would be difficult for any individual, acting as Secretary-General, to enjoy greater prestige within the party than Vice-Presidents Barrios and Prieto.

[10] Octavio Lepage, "La Secretaría Nacional de Organización," *A.D.*, no. 9, July 5, 1958, p. 7.

"assist the President and the Secretary-General" in all necessary ways. Frequently acting as trouble-shooters for the leadership, these men are limited in their operations only by their capacities. Participation on the labor, agrarian, and youth bureaus has been mentioned above.

The responsibilities of the Secretaries of Propaganda and of Press are parallel if not identical. The former is occupied with the diffusion of party doctrine and related efforts to increase the familiarity of party members with basic AD beliefs. In the process he edits books, pamphlets, and assorted material intended to spread the doctrine widely. He is also responsible for the weekly appearance of *Combate*, a highly partisan view of the week's political and economic developments in Venezuela. The Press Secretary deals with the national press, providing news handouts, arranging press conferences, and presiding over the party's Comité de Escritores, or Committee of Writers. He is the editor and publisher of the weekly *A.D.*, which reports on party activities. And his informal duties in the publication of the pro-AD Caracas daily *La República* are substantial, although he is not officially its editor nor can he direct it personally. Significantly, *República's* Managing Editor Luis Esteban Rey also serves as the Adjunto to the party Press Secretary.

Another pair of officers with related but separate tasks are the Secretary of Studies and the Secretary of Education and Culture. The former is charged with the centralization of all matters of orientation and indoctrination. Conferences, lectures, courses of instruction, and the issuing of pamphlets and books are all a part of his duties. The Secretary of Education and Culture must plan AD educational policy, lead the educational *fracción*, establish party libraries and social centers, and stimulate intellectual, artistic, and sports activities within the party.

The Secretary of Relations directs his attention not toward purely internal matters but, rather, toward relations beyond the confines of the party itself. He is authorized to develop and promote activities of peripheral party organizations, notably professional ones. Furthermore, he is responsible for party relations with the national government at intermediate as well as higher echelons. Finally, his interest extends to party contacts with any and all organizations, factions, and institutions.

The CEN thus provides the sum total of executive direction at the national level.[11] Its activities are as diverse and complex as those of the fourth national organ—the Tribunal Disciplinario Nacional—are uncomplicated. The TDN stands at the head of all judicial organs and, but for the National Convention itself, is the final arbiter. The over-all effect of the disciplinary system and its sanctions is considered in the chapter on membership and leadership. For the moment it need merely be explained that all judicial matters may be appealed to the TDN. Any and all members of the party may be brought before it on charges of disloyalty or violation of party discipline.

Article 115 provides five different forms of sanctions, depending upon the severity of the violation. The mildest form is a mere declaration of censure and a general admonition. This is followed by a temporary suspension, and then by permanent removal from posts of leadership. The ultimate penalties are temporary or final and definitive expulsion from the party. All decisions may be carried beyond the TDN to the CDN or the National Convention. Membership in the Tribunal Disciplinario Nacional consists of five *principales* and five *suplentes*, all named by the Convention. In the event of a vacancy, the CEN may name an interim member.

[11] Regarding the two new posts created in late 1963, that of Secretary of Economy and Technical Affairs is presently a recognition of technological progress and its impact on the nation; the Secretary is to bring together experts on given problems. The Secretary of Community Development is to redirect party attention toward local problems, which many *adecos* believe have been slighted in recent years.

An additional party organ at the national level is not mentioned in the party statutes; this is the special election team set up in both 1958 and 1963 to direct the campaign. The so-called Comando Electoral has been operated both times under the direction of Luis Lander. In 1958 it was composed of fourteen members, while a smaller group of five was known as "los cinco grandes," the five big ones. In addition to Luis Lander, who supervised and integrated the work of the others, they included J. A. Sánchez Vegas, whose staff was responsible for the raising of money, and Press Secretary Héctor Strédel, whose dozen aides provided copy, sent out propaganda, prepared radio commercials, and issued four or five bulletins daily. The 1963 team headed by Lander was more extensive in the regions but maintained a small, tightly knit directorate in Caracas. While basic policy decisions were not made, the Comando frequently dictated steps that coordinated the activities of the party in specific regions with the campaign of the presidential candidate. In both 1958 and 1963 the party relied heavily upon the Comando. Its duties were not only those of managing a campaign, but also the training and preparation of local party members who were to represent the party as observers at all the voting booths. The task of political education in such circumstances was crucial.

## Regional and Local Organs

The existence of national offices and organs is relatively meaningless without a broad following for the men placed in posts of regional and local authority. Venezuela has some 650 municipalities, 150 districts, 20 states, 2 federal territories, and a federal district. Acción Democrática has followed these lines of the political organization of the Republic. Article 12 sets forth the nature of the commitment. "In each one of the States of the Republic, in the Federal District and in the Federal Territories, a Sectional of Acción Democrática will be organized, whose structure and functioning will be determined by these Statutes."

Party organs on the state level consist of the Convención Seccional, the Comité Ejecutivo Seccional (CES), and the Tribunal Disciplinario Seccional (TDS). The Convención Seccional[12] is supreme on the state level; all its decisions are binding on members and on other state organs. Powers of the Sectional Convention include the election of the Comité Ejecutivo Seccional, the Tribunal Disciplinario Seccional, and the delegate to the Comité Directivo Nacional. It also fixes the party line on regional matters, in accord with decisions and directives issued by national bodies. Reports from the Comité Ejecutivo Seccional are heard and discussed, while inquiries from the national level are also expedited.

The Sectional Convention customarily meets annually on being convoked by the CES, and is scheduled two or three months prior to a National Convention. It may also be called into extraordinary session by the CEN, the CES, or upon petition of the majority of the Juntas Distritales. Conventions are attended by two delegates from the Comité Ejecutivo Nacional, by the entire Comité Ejecutivo Seccional, the President of the Tribunal Disciplinario Seccional, and the Labor, Agrarian, and Youth committees of the Seccional. Secretaries of Organization from the Comités Distritales are also present.

The bulk of the delegates come as representatives elected by the next lower level of conventions, the Convenciones Distritales or Departamentales.[13] The total number is dependent upon the population; each District is permitted a three-man delegation, in addition to which it will have an additional representative for each 1,000 party members or fraction over 500. Even the least populous area will have a minimum of three delegates. The

---

[12] *Estatutos*, Chapter VIII, Articles 64-70.
[13] The sole exception is that of the Federal District, where delegates come from Asambleas Zonales or Parroquiales.

Comité Ejecutivo Seccional also has the right to invite observers—with neither vote nor voice—up to 10 percent of the elected delegates. These may be drawn from national and regional congressmen, ex-Secretary-Generals of the CES, and members of the state executive (Governor, Secretary-General, and Directors).

The state-level executive organ is the Comité Ejecutivo Seccional.[14] The CES is charged with control of the party organization in the state during the interim between Sectional Conventions. Its enumerated powers include the calling of the Convention into session, the fulfillment of directives from the national level, the distribution of all informational material to other organs on the sectional level, and the obligation to respond with appropriate action on its own initiative in the absence of orders from above. The CEN is to be informed monthly on economic, political, and social problems in the region, as well as of all party activities during the preceding month. A final requirement for the Comité Ejecutivo Seccional is the presentation of a list of instructions to the Comités Ejecutivos Distritales.

The CES is chosen for a year's duration—or for the time elapsing between one Sectional Convention and the next—and generally meets on a weekly or bi-weekly basis. In organization and membership the CES is analogous to the CEN, although having freedom of choice on the formation and internal structure of its secretariats. The average-sized CES will have eleven members, although this may vary slightly. The ranking official is the Secretary-General; his colleagues ordinarily include Secretaries of Organization, Labor, Agriculture, Finance, Propaganda, Press, Youth, Parliamentary, and Municipal Affairs, plus three Political Secretaries. In less populous areas, such as Apure, local authorities may combine the Secretariats of Press and Propaganda; one of the other posts may be eliminated entirely. In sharp contrast, a

[14] *Estatutos*, Chapter IX, Articles 71-78.

state like Zulia, with over 100,000 registered party members, has an organizational specialization nearly as precise as that of the Comité Ejecutivo Nacional.

Again following the pattern of the national organ, the Comité Ejecutivo Seccional includes a Comité Político Seccional or Buró Político Seccional. Responsible for decision-making on political matters, it is composed of seven men: the Secretary-General, Secretary of Organization, Labor Secretary, Agrarian Secretary, and three Political Secretaries. Specialized groups within the CES are the Comité Sindical Seccional, the Comité Agrario Seccional, and the Comité Juvenil Seccional. All three are five-man groups, headed by the appropriate Secretary, his Adjunto, a Political Secretary, and two leaders elected by the Pleno Sindical Seccional or the Pleno Agrario Seccional. The Labor and Agrarian Committees may also meet jointly as the Comité Agrario y Sindical Seccional. Each of the Secretaries is responsible for his staff's budget and reports regularly on its activities. Article 73 gives the Sectional Convention the authority to create new posts if necessary.

The judicial body at the regional level is the Tribunal Disciplinario Seccional (TDS) integrated like the national organ by five *principales* and their five *suplentes*. The TDS is expected to be alert for and aware of any individual deviations from party programs or statutes and is empowered to apply sanctions carrying the same severity as those of the Tribunal Disciplinario Nacional, while its decisions may be appealed to the TDN, the CDN, or the National Convention.

Moving down the pyramid to the district level, the party retains the usual legislative, executive, and judicial bodies.[15] As always, the assembly is supreme. Thus the Convención Distrital or Departamental, is the ultimate authority within the district. As Article 84 states, "the attributes of the District or Departmental Convention

[15] *Estatutos*, Chapter IX, Articles 79-84.

will be the same as the Sectional Convention, adjusted to the limits and the matters that correspond to the former." Convention representation comes from two delegates of the CES, members of the Comité Distrital or Departamental, the President of the Comisión Disciplinaria Distrital or Departamental, and Secretaries of Organization from the Comités Municipales or Parroquiales. Delegates from the lower level are elected by Asambleas Municipales or Parroquiales. Each such local assembly may name a basic three-member delegation.

The Comité Distrital or Departamental is the corresponding executive organ at this level, with the responsibility of calling into session the Convención Distrital or Departamental. It is also charged with the supply and distribution of information regarding district affairs to higher authorities, while likewise passing along directives and information from higher levels. Ordinarily the CED will have seven members, although the statutes are unclear on the matter. Judicial activities are carried out by a Comisión Disciplinaria Distrital or Departamental of three members, elected by the District Convention.

Two levels of party organization remain—the municipal and the local.[16] On both, the existence of organs depends upon the nature and size of the population, the number of party members, and the geographic expanse over which the membership may be scattered. The Asamblea Municipal provides legislative discussion and debate, while executive functions are handled by the Comité Municipal or Parroquial. The latter must have at least three officers: Secretaries of Organization and Propaganda, of Labor and Agriculture, and of Finance. Usually it will have five members, however, and additional posts may be created with the authorization of the appropriate Comité Ejecutivo Seccional. A Comisión Disciplinaria Municipal is also present, formed by three members elected by the Asamblea Municipal.

[16] *Estatutos*, Chapter X, Articles 86-98.

At the foot of the pyramidal structure are the all-important base units, known individually as *grupos de base*. The general pattern includes an Asamblea Local, Comité Local, and Junta Local. The first is supreme authority in the given locality, which may be either a *barrio* (ward) or a *caserío* (hamlet). Given the nature of local party activities, the Asamblea Local meets from two to four times monthly, and may be convened even more frequently. It is called into session by the Comité Local, although the appropriate CES or CED may also do so if the situation warrants. Its prime task is the usual "fixing of the political line of the party" in the locality as appropriate to directives from above. It also discusses reports or queries sent down to them, after which recommendations and resolutions are transmitted back up the pyramid.

The executive organ is the Comité Local, with authority over the *barrio* or *caserío* when the Asamblea is not meeting. Besides calling the Asamblea into session, it is responsible for the strengthening of the party in the locality, for distributing information and propaganda. A close check is kept on internal party discipline, and monthly reports are sent to the next higher executive body. The Comité Local is the base organ for the distribution of party publications. Its membership is at least three, composed of Secretaries of Organization and Propaganda, of Labor and Agriculture, and of Finance.

The "fundamental base of the party is the Junta Local," in the words of Article 86. Constituted by all party members in a *barrio* or *caserío*, its maximum membership is 100 recognized "Active Members." When there are more than 100 members, a new Junta Local is organized. If a minimum of five Juntas Locales have come into being in a given geographic region, the party may also organize an Asamblea Secundaria, which is interposed between the Junta Local and the Asamblea Local. Such Asambleas Secundarias are infrequent, and generally are found only in large urban centers. The final possible breakdown comes through division of the Junta Local into twenty-member Secciones, with each one assigned a specific responsibility by the Comité Local. Article 89 explains that these Sections are "for purposes of the fulfillment of tasks of study and indoctrination, of meetings, of finance and of propaganda, and for the greatest efficiency in the fulfillment of partisan tasks. . . ." Sections have no deliberative functions.

The system does not inevitably function as party statutes suggest; a few matters of common practice have already been suggested. It thus behooves us to take a closer look at the realities of the organizational system, noting in particular the degree of cohesion and unity, of factionalism and disunity that has characterized Acción Democrática through the years.

# CHAPTER VI

# The Party Organization: Unity and Factionalism

A study of the party's organizational system necessitates a two-pronged approach. To begin with, it is useful to reassess the major organs within the over-all *aparato*, noting deviations from or exceptions to the statutory requirements. Secondly, the intrusion of individual ambition and of personal programmatic orientation demands a consideration of unity and factionalism. To be sure, problems of factionalism come out in the study of the AD leadership. Nonetheless, the impact of serious defection on the entire machinery makes appropriate a treatment of the matter in the present context.

## Realities of Party Operations

The national level in particular must be scrutinized carefully for an understanding of the party in operation. It is customary for party leaders to speak of Acción Democrática as being a "régimen de asamblea," ruled by the workings of internal democracy. Although the commitment to participation and free expression is important, this should not lead to a misunderstanding of the nature of party legislative assemblies. While they are uniformly supreme for their given level, this supremacy is often not effectively exercised. The phrase "régimen de asamblea" in reality tends to imply the collective judgment of ranking executive officers after due exchange of ideas, rather than that of full-blown assemblies.

The National Convention does not in any real sense lead the party, nor is it possible to say that national leadership is directly responsive to the Convention in more than a general way. At the National Convention as well as other legislative levels, the act of participation and of political education on the part of the elected delegates is of major importance. The political education of its membership is a principal aspect of the AD's goals, and it is furthered substantially by the almost continual round of legislative assemblies that culminates in the National Convention. Certainly national leadership is provided essentially by executive officials, and thus the CDN and CEN are in a policy-making sense more important than the Convention.

Party leaders agree that the Comité Directivo Nacional is both the most interesting and the most important party organ. Whereas the Convention is occupied in large part with tiresome speeches and long reports, most of which are approved unanimously by the assemblage, the CDN is able to grapple effectively with current problems. The 120-odd members in attendance permit far less chaos and confusion than the Conventions, while a carefully constructed agenda can be followed or altered, as appropriate, without undue difficulty. The representation of party views and opinions is, if anything, more complete than at the CEN.

Over a period of years some of the most vital party decisions have originated with meetings of the Comité Directivo Nacional. Virtually all significant party leaders are present—something not always the case with the Comité Ejecutivo Nacional—and there is usually an accurate reflection of majority sentiment within the party. Discussions can be and are held in a spirit of give and take, with individual equality the rule while even the most prestigious leader may be subjected to close questioning. An interesting AD characteristic is that, while its veteran founders are greatly respected by younger leaders, this does not mute all criticism or willingness to debate at length.[1] Even a casual observation of party congressmen in the *adeco* caucus room off the halls of the Senate and the Chamber indicates the exchange of

[1] Interview with Víctor Mazzei González, November 20, 1962.

views and ideas. Furthermore, national leaders are consistently present and available to the rank-and-file.

The lengthy rhetoric and phraseology that often mark Convention speeches are absent in the knowledgeable and ordinarily sophisticated exchanges of the CDN.[2] There is no concern with arousing the enthusiasm of hundreds of delegates in search of oratory and flag-waving; neither is there any necessity for the discretion demanded at Conventions covered by the press. As a consequence, the airing of all points of view is possible before a final decision is reached. Thus the exchange in the CDN has become the arena at which Acción Democrática has found itself most successful in balancing the needs of a national cross-section of informed opinion with the convenience of debate by a restricted number of individuals.

Another practical consideration in the importance of the CDN is the party's traditional preference to defer major decisions from the CEN to the CDN. Easily the majority of the AD's most important political and tactical decisions have been taken by the CDN. Even the factional struggles of the post-Pérez Jiménez period were ultimately resolved at sessions of the CDN. The Convention also is accustomed to delegating major decisions to the CDN. Even the choice of a presidential nominee has been taken beyond the halls of the Convention. During the problems of succession in 1945 the delegates outlined a set of alternatives, leaving the final choice to the executive leadership. Then in 1958 the question of a nominee was very much in doubt. Again the Convention ended by adopting a series of alternatives and empowering the CDN to make the final judgment after lengthy interparty conversations in which the CDN was intimately involved.

That the influence of the Convention may be growing is suggested by the experience of 1963. Whether or not

[2] Interview with Said Moanack, November 19, 1962.

this comes to represent a significant trend within Acción Democrática cannot yet be determined. At the XIII Convention in July 1963 the party nominated Raúl Leoni as its candidate for the presidency of the Republic, and the clear preference of the delegates for Leoni was a decisive factor. The preference of certain AD leaders, including Betancourt himself, for a set of alternatives from which the CDN might later choose, was voted down by a Convention that knew its own mind and would not be dissuaded. This may well reflect a growing political awareness of the average *adeco* supporter. Certainly he will remember in the future the impact of his decision in 1963.

The Comité Ejecutivo Nacional, meeting as it does almost continually, is in a position to usurp unto itself nearly all the significant policy-making powers, but has chosen not to do so. As indicated above, it tends to defer to the CDN where possible, while restricting its activities within two categories: short-run political tactics and administrative work. The latter speaks for itself, and is conducted by the Secretariado Nacional. As for the former, the Buró Político is dominant within the CEN. Only occasionally will it draw up formal resolutions or drafts to be presented before the CDN. This does not, of course, prevent individual party leaders from preparing detailed reports on certain problems for CDN consideration.

The inclusion of the deputies or Adjuntos in CEN meetings brings the number of *adecos* in attendance to more than thirty. When these people must hear reports of technical or administrative matters, the form of meetings seems a luxury of inefficiency that the party cannot afford. For instance, the necessity of the Secretary of Parliamentary and Municipal Affairs listening to a report on the organization of the agrarian *pleno* by the Secretary of Agriculture, is minimal. Likewise, the Secretary of Finance may be wasting his time by listening to others discuss matters of detailed international relations.

As one of the Political Secretaries has commented, the requirement of full attendance at regular CEN meetings is an anachronism that has no place in a modern political party.[3] Reformers are now proposing that CEN meetings requiring full attendance be sharply minimized. The CDN meeting at the close of 1962 passed along the problem to a study group that was to present recommendations at the XIII Convention in 1963. The press of electoral problems forced the proposed reform to be tabled. However, there are still those who feel strongly that a revision is in order.

Reformers have been talking of a revision that would parallel the present system in both COPEI and the Partido Comunista. Something resembling the present Buró Político would be organized as the day-to-day authority on most policy-making decisions. All the other secretaries would continue with their individual staffs as a part of a national administrative secretariat. This would streamline CEN decision-making, improve administrative efficiency, and free the party officers from attending meetings at which their participation was superfluous.

The relationship of legislative and executive organs on the national level is paralleled on a lower plane. The assembly is the supreme authority, yet the daily routine, the regular activities and continuing duties fall into the hands of the executive bodies. It is worth underlining again the importance of legislative bodies in providing political education to the participants. Observation of a regional or other party assembly is impressive as a barometer of enthusiasm and spirit elicited from the delegates. This arousing of partisan interests should not be minimized as a party function.

Virtually every gathering will have at least one national AD leader present; more often than not, several

[3] Interview with Said Moanack, November 27, 1962.

will attend, giving a greeting of exhortation that is warmly received, later mingling on the floor of the meeting or at a social event afterwards. The singing of the AD anthem, the waving of white handkerchiefs or banners, and the frequent outbursts of the chanted party initials, "A.D., A.D., A.D.," all lend a festive spirit, a sense of participation and of belonging that are invaluable to Acción Democrática.

The party has taken due care to institute a careful set of legislative regulations that are embodied in Chapter XI, Articles 99-107 of the statutes. Decisions are taken by an absolute majority of those members present at the assembly or convention. All votes are cast individually, rather than by bloc. The leader of a state, district, or municipal delegation may announce all the votes from the given region, but will declare the number of individual votes being cast. All propositions are voted on in inverse order of their presentation, and, in the hypothetical event of a tie vote on three consecutive ballots, the proposal is considered rejected. Any member objecting to a decision can put his negative vote in the form of a written protest that will be duly read to the assemblage at its next gathering.

Legislative bodies are regarded as validly constituted when 60 percent of the delegates are in attendance. This requirement is reduced to 30 percent in the case of local assemblies. All decisions are valid and binding on party members, whether or not they have attended. Such assemblies are generally open to the public, including the balloting on policy matters. Elections for party officers are never public, however. Furthermore, portions of the National Conventions are closed to the public, although news of their major occurrences invariably leaks to the press long before the release of official statements.

Party officers are elected singly and are nominated individually, not according to a slate or prearranged list. The voting for delegates to the various legislative bodies is usually conducted through the presentation of an indeterminate number of lists of candidates. The balloting is then held with eligible members voting separately for each delegate to be named. The candidate who receives an absolute majority is elected. If the leading candidate lacks the absolute majority, then a new vote will be held, with the process continuing as long as necessary. *Suplentes* are chosen in the same fashion, once *principales* have been named.

In addition to the organs discussed above, Acción Democrática has affiliated and professional *fracciones* that play a role in party life.[4] These are several in number, including doctors, engineers, lawyers, teachers, and so forth. Party members of national and state assemblies are organized into parliamentary wings or *fracciones*, and representatives on municipal councils are also so formed. There are an additional series of ties with labor and *campesino* movements that are considered here in a later chapter. These are peripheral to the basic core of the party's structural framework, however, whatever their contributions to the over-all strength.

## Ideological Factionalism

The unity of Acción Democrática and its predecessors has traditionally been outstanding. Even in the chaos and inexperience of early years there were no significant exceptions. Jóvito Villalba withdrew from the old PDN after a short time, but this was a personal action that had little organizational significance. It was also during the underground period of the PDN that a struggle was waged between the democratically inclined members and the communists. With the failure of the latter to control the organization, they withdrew, taking with them those who preferred one-class, totalitarian solutions to Venezuelan problems.

With the founding of Acción Democrática in 1941, a

[4] *Estatutos*, Chapter XI, Articles 99-109.

history of unity and discipline began to evolve. With the passing of time, those outside the party came to take for granted its monolithic nature. Behind the façade, however, were the glimmerings of disunity. They were nurtured by the experience of 1948-1958, which tended to emphasize the difference in age between veteran exile leaders and young student revolutionaries braving the Seguridad Nacional in Venezuela. The desire for a swift and immediate revision of the entire nation and society also grew among younger party members during the dictatorial decade. But the leadership had been through this experience in its own political adolescence and by 1958 had weighed the evidence and chosen a gradualist approach.

The seeds of dissension existed, then, when Acción Democrática reorganized upon returning home in 1958. The first traces of disagreement to reach the public came at the IX National Convention in August of that year. With the veteran leadership sometimes characterized as the Guardia Vieja (GV), the somewhat younger stream within the party—the *arsistas*—followed such men as Ramos Giménez and Paz Galarraga. The fervent young Muchachos were headed by Rangel and Sáez Mérida, among others. The discontented wing at the Convention was the radical group of Muchachos. Having contributed mightily to the struggle against Pérez Jiménez from inside the country, they felt strongly that they should be more fully represented on the reconstituted Comité Ejecutivo Nacional. Although ideological differences existed, the Muchachos were primarily concerned with the winning of greater leverage on the *aparato* through the control of important posts.

The struggle came out in the balloting for party officers after the acclamation of Betancourt as party President. The Muchachos for tactical reasons backed Luis B. Prieto against Raúl Leoni for First Vice-President, but lost. After the selection of Gonzalo Barrios as Second

Vice-President, another contest ensued over the post of Secretary-General. The rivals were Ramos Giménez, Luis Augusto Dubuc, and Rangel. The ARS and GV candidates withdrew in favor of Prieto, who then defeated Rangel by 210-140. Simón Sáez Mérida of the Muchachos was defeated by *arsista* José Manzo González for Secretary of Organization, and when the CEN was completed, not a single member of the revolutionary young group had won a contested race. In every key test the Guardia Vieja and ARS had banded together. Only Rangel as a Political Secretary and Simón Alberto Consalvi as Press Secretary managed to become members of the CEN.[5]

This brush over factionalism was a harbinger of subsequent dissension and rivalry that would rock Acción Democrática to its very foundations. A pair of schisms lay ahead, each of them a major test to the durability and life of the party. The first challenge to the party was largely ideological in nature; the second more a matter of personal ambition. The 1958 Convention had not only made public divisions which had thus far been carefully kept hidden, but it gave the Muchachos in particular their first real taste of intra-party conflict. It was not to be the last.

From the point of view of the Muchachos, Venezuela was suffering from maladies that could and axiomatically should be dealt with immediately. There was no inclination to parry cautiously with the military or to conduct extended fraternal conversations with other political parties. Rather, the Muchachos felt that the task had to be undertaken without delay and, in effect, without consideration of the rest of the political system. The membership of this initially informal group was uniformly young, and but a few had enjoyed more than minimal responsibility in the party before the November 1948 counter-revolution. Many had been educated during the

[5] *Momento*, no. 109, August 15, 1958, pp. 48-49.

dictatorship, and the appeal of marxism and its home-grown variations was strong. Led by such brilliant intellects and leaders as Domingo Alberto Rangel, these young men were radical revolutionaries to the core. Rangel's closest companions were Gumersindo Rodríguez, the ideologue of the group, Américo Martín, and political activist Simón Sáez Mérida.

The prestige of these men was considerable, as a result of their participation in the fight against Pérez Jiménez from inside the country. Their record had been a good one, and they were willing to capitalize upon it to the greatest extent possible. In 1958, although it was later denied, Rangel and his followers had privately encouraged the nomination of a non-partisan presidential candidate representing the entire nation. This, it was hoped, might cut down Betancourt in the process. During the long meetings which discussed the presidential problem, radical *adecos* steadily urged the nomination of an independent. Any such chance was lost with the ballooning of the Larrazábal candidacy, and the party faithful then insisted upon Betancourt.

After elections the radicals continued to maneuver. Rangel himself seemed to be copying Betancourt's original path to success in traveling through the interior regularly, recruiting for the party while arousing support for the new government. His proselytizing stirred particular enthusiasm in Zulia and Lara, two of the major sources of AD strength. Followers also began to step up their activities, and many of the Muchachos were becoming better known to the rank-and-file beyond Caracas.

Support began to collect from the emerging generation of university students. They, like most of their radical leaders, could draw only upon experience under the military dictatorship. There was no practical knowledge of *gomecismo* and after, nor an awareness of the depth and meaning of the long AD struggle. In no position to appreciate the events of the *trienio* and the dangers inherent in attempting to make and institute a revolution overnight, they were vulnerable targets for extremists of the left. Their susceptibility had been underlined by the impact of numerous marxist faculty members whom the dictatorship had permitted to teach throughout the 1950's. Substantial communist literature continued to circulate. Still another factor was the cooperation and collaboration with the communists in late 1957 and 1958 in the fight against the dictatorship.

The moderation and measured pace of the Betancourt coalition administration increasingly seemed to many young people a betrayal of true revolutionary principles. The gradualism of all democratic parties, not just that of Acción Democrática, led the students to a general rejection of the established organizations. With the zeal of flaming idealism untempered by maturity and the lessons of the past, they were ripe for the appeals of skillful leadership, whether opportunistic or genuine.

As early as April 1959 there was evident impatience with the party *aparato*. Unwilling to accept the wishes of the party majority, the students called a meeting of the AD Pleno Juvenil, the youth convention of the organization. Several recommendations were accepted which contradicted existing policy. The Comité Ejecutivo Nacional promptly notified them that such declarations, being contrary to public declarations by the party, would have to be retracted. Furthermore, the AD leadership administered a sharp slap in response to a surprising and ill-reasoned attack on Costa Rica's José Figueres, long a friend of Betancourt and of Acción Democrática. The party youth organization was reminded pointedly: "No wing of the Party, no matter how important, is authorized to declare the lines of national or international policy for Acción Democrática; no wing is ever permitted to discuss the internal organization of the Party or its policy relative to national-revolutionary parties of Latin America. . . . Therefore, . . . the conclusions of the Pleno Juvenil are not and cannot be an expression of the general policy or political orientation of Acción Democrática."[6]

The issue was by no means decided, although the leaders of the Pleno temporarily withdrew. The CEN declaration was followed by a statement from the party's Buró Juvenil Nacional, in effect retracting the attack on Figueres while insisting that there was no intention of deviating from party positions. The conflict subsided briefly as the students bent their efforts toward June elections at the Universidad Central de Venezuela (UCV). Acción Democrática won the university-wide voting by electing 110 delegates as compared with 90 for the communists, COPEI with 45, independents with 20, and the URD with 10.

The next clear confrontation came at the X National Convention in September 1959. Of some 558 delegates in attendance, 401 had been elected through the Sectional Conventions. The remaining 157 came from the national organs: 16 from the CEN, 93 from the CDN, 5 from the TDN, plus 73 regional secretaries.[7] The renewal of party leadership was predictable, First Vice-President Leoni replacing Rómulo Betancourt as party President. Barrios in turn moved up to First Vice-President and Prieto to Second. The vacant Secretary-Generalship was taken by Jesús Angel Paz Galarraga. Asked whether his direction would be centrist or leftist in spirit, he replied that the AD could only move along the road of the national democratic left. As for problems of foreign policy, he reiterated customary party views. ". . . This means the struggle against colonialism, isolation of dictatorships until they are removed ulti-

[6] A.D., no. 48, April 11, 1959, pp. 6-7.
[7] The apparent numerical discrepancy is explained by the fact that a number of delegates were members of more than one organ —as the CEN and CDN, or TDN and CDN.

mately from the Organization of American States, . . .
and establishment of commercial relations with all the
countries of the world. . . ."[8]
The selection of Paz Galarraga, a moderate who was
regarded as a leading *arsista*, was not wholly unacceptable to the young radicals, but they objected to the elevation of Raúl Leoni. More than anyone else from the
Guardia Vieja, Leoni was regarded by the Muchachos
as a plodding party hack whose only virtue was loyalty.
Their feelings were not eased by Leoni's *informe* to the
Convention. Although carefully avoiding names, he
warned that groups within the party and the development of cliques would only lead to multiplicity of purpose and a weakening of the party. A special commission was named to study the problem, and its sixteen
members included such young leaders as Octavio Lepage, Roberto Henríquez Vera, and Carlos Andrés Pérez,
all moderates. The commission delivered a report roundly
condemning existing evidences of factionalism, declaring that the party youth movement in particular needed
to be reminded of the need for submission to party discipline.

The problem was more deep-rooted than that of disciplinary action, however, and by the beginning of 1960
the situation began to head toward a climax. Confident
of support in the universities, Domingo Alberto Rangel
and his followers also believed themselves in control
of a majority of the party in ten to twelve states. He
therefore decided to force the issue; vocally abetted by
Héctor Pérez Marcano and Rafael José Muñoz, he began to differ publicly with both the government and
Acción Democrática.

Two developments in March brought things to a head.
Rangel's colleague Américo Martín wrote a public article
on the Peruvian APRA, with which the AD maintained
cordial relations. Commenting on internal *aprista* dis-

[8] *A.D.*, no. 73, October 3, 1959, pp. 16-17.

order and a rift between the veteran leadership and younger members, Martín drew implicit but obvious parallels between the APRA and Acción Democrática. The Comité Ejecutivo Nacional promptly ordered Martín to cease writing such articles. Five days later, however, he retorted with articles strongly attacking both Figueres of Costa Rica and Puerto Rico's Luis Múñoz Marín, long-time friends of the AD. The resultant furor over this breach of discipline had not yet been resolved when the schism was widened by Rangel himself.

An important contractual renegotiation was taking place at the time between the oil workers' union, FEDEPETROL, and foreign companies. Rangel was assigned by the party to be its representative and *asesor* at the talks. Rangel, who had agreed to the terms of the contract during discussions within the Buró Político of the party, suddenly did an about-face and published a newspaper article differing with the stated position of FEDEPETROL and AD. In a highly partisan polemic he attacked the intentions of the oil interests while questioning the judgment of FEDEPETROL.

The AD labor leaders immediately called a meeting of the party's Buró Sindical Nacional, arguing that the breach of party discipline was irreparable. Such long-time labor leaders as Malavé Villalba, Pérez Salinas, Francisco Olivo, and Salom Mesa angrily determined to carry the issue to the Tribunal Disciplinario. First, however, a full meeting of the Comité Ejecutivo Nacional was held. In a public statement, an overwhelming majority on the CEN expressed through Secretary-General Paz Galarraga the opinion that Rangel and Martín should appear before disciplinary authorities.[9]

The followers of the young radicals mounted their own forces within the Buró Juvenil Nacional, which they effectively controlled. Its relative weakness within the

[9] The text appeared in party journals, as well as *La República* on March 19, 1960.

over-all national leadership, however, made it an inadequate base for support. Although Rangel could have stayed within the party and made a fight, there was little prospect that he could win. Rather than make the effort, he completed the break by refusing to appear before the Tribunal Disciplinario Nacional. He resigned from the party, to be followed immediately by his supporters. They reorganized as a new party, which was first called Acción Democrática Izquierdista—the leftist AD. The first issue of a party journal, *Izquierda*, appeared on May 13, 1960; soon after, the name of the organization was changed to the Movimiento de Izquierda Revolucionaria (MIR).

The separation of these young radicals from Acción Democrática was seemingly inevitable, and the circumstances which led to the break were of secondary importance. As mentioned above, the attitudes and experience of the younger AD leaders, as well as many unaffiliated university students, naturally encouraged impatience with gradualism and a quest for rapid and clear solutions to national problems. There is no apparent way in which the parent organization could have absorbed the energies of the Muchachos and their followers. The generational and age differences were substantial, but the ideological and personal outlook was even more basic. Broad as the AD was, it had little to offer such men as Rangel and others.[10]

The impact of the split on Acción Democrática was potentially grave, for the party's youth movement was shattered. Party leaders have agreed that a good 80 percent of this sector deserted in favor of the MIR.[11] Even more serious was the fact that younger Venezu-

[10] The best single treatment of this conflict is found in R. Arbiza, "Gumersindo Rodríguez, El Ortodoxo," *Momento*, no. 285, December 31, 1961, pp. 10-12, 14, 24.

[11] Interviews with Raúl Leoni, December 6, 1962; Mercedes Fermín, November 19, 1962; and Said Moanack, November 27, 1962.

elans, emerging into the light of political consciousness and participation, would find the MIR an attractive alternative to the AD. Within the next few years, the youth movement within the Unión Republicana Democrática was also devastated, leaving only COPEI of the major parties with a significant following among the Venezuelan students. For the AD, the loss could not be minimized, and the party leaders did not hide their concern. The destruction of all effective organized contact between the party and the young university generation confronted the party with a long-run problem, the implications of which were large.

## Personalistic Factionalism

The wounds left by the *mirista* division were far from healed when a new outbreak of factionalism threatened the immediate survival of the party. The roots of the second division were primarily personalistic rather than ideological, but in a practical sense the episode was more immediately damaging. The existence of the ARS group, which under the leadership of Raúl Ramos Giménez went back to 1947 and 1948, was generally known, yet there was little realization that it constituted a threat to the party. Outward signs of the new struggle manifested themselves in late 1961 when the Comité Directivo Nacional was called to meet on December 27. The message explained that the party had serious problems which demanded swift resolution. The meeting was termed of vital importance, for "the enemies of the Party . . . have been scandalizing the country with repeated charges of an alleged division within our ranks."[12]

The December visit by President John F. Kennedy and his wife turned attention elsewhere, but in early 1962 the nature of the struggle became clearer. What ultimately emerged was a well organized and carefully prepared plan on the part of the *arsistas* to seize control

---

[12] *A.D.*, no. 185, December 23, 1961, p. 1.

of Acción Democrática. ARS had stood firm with the
Guardia Vieja at the 1958 Convention in putting down
the bid of the MIR-to-be, and had also united with the
veteran leadership during the conflict with Rangel and
Martín. In May of 1961, with many *adecos* still reflecting
upon the *mirista* rift, the ARS began to maneuver for
better position.

Although the national leadership had previously decreed that, in the interests of harmony and unity, no
potential presidential candidacies would be discussed,
talk began to be heard about the possibility of *arsista*
leader Ramos Giménez. Several regional organizations
began to mention his availability. Murmurs continued
through the middle of the year; then in October one of
the four Political Secretaries—*arsista* José Manzo González—announced that several AD congressmen were
about to withhold support from the Betancourt coalition
unless administration leaders became more cooperative
and stopped interfering with internal party matters.
Almost simultaneously a series of struggles began to take
place at the round of Sectional Conventions which were
beginning in preparation for the National Convention at
the close of 1961.

The *arsista* drive to seize control of the *aparato* was
far more serious than the earlier threat of the *miristas*.
The XI National Convention in January 1961 had placed
members of the ARS group in 13 of the 22 seats on the
CEN. This preponderance had not been a concern to the
Guardia Vieja at the time, for it took for granted the
loyalty of the *arsistas* and devoted attention instead to
the problem of the young radicals. However, from the
standpoint of the ARS, control of the Comité Ejecutivo
Nacional was a critical accomplishment in the quiet effort
to seize complete control. Recognizing that they still
would be in the minority at a National Convention, the
*arsistas* set about capturing delegates through the Sectional Conventions. Driving for a majority on state delega-

tions, the ARS planned to use the resultant control at the XII National Convention to remove party President Leoni and replace him with Ramos Giménez. Other old-line leaders would also be replaced on the CEN, after which the *aparato* at all levels could be re-formed about *arsistas*.

The Guardia Vieja was late in recognizing the threat, but toward the close of 1961 it began to fight back. As the Convention neared, twenty of the party's twenty-five Sectional Conventions had met. *Arsista* delegates, it was estimated, were in the minority by a margin of 312-209 (see Figure 4).[13] Assuming the figures to be roughly accurate, the ARS was faced with the probability of being outvoted. If that happened, an aroused leadership would clearly purge the *arsistas* from all major posts of leadership. Faced with the apparent reversal of fortune, the ARS proceeded to intervene in the proceedings of the five remaining Sectional Conventions.

The CEN, with its avowedly *arsista* majority, named a set of special commissions to replace Sectional authorities in Anzoátegui, Guárico, and Yaracuy. These commissions were to name the state delegations to the XII National Convention, thereby packing them with *arsista* sympathizers. Delegations were formed in the three states, and similar operations were prepared for the remaining two. The action was not in consonance with party statutes regarding the degree of autonomy in the state organs. It was also an expression of defiance toward Carta Informativa No. 10 of November 5, 1961, in which the Secretary-General had cited party statutes in ex-

---

[13] Allowance must be made for the fact that these figures were never accepted—publicly—by the ARS. However, the state-by-state breakdown is a close approximation of the known centers of *arsista* strength and weakness. Furthermore, newspaper surveys in several states at the time were in agreement with the factional breakdown shown in Fig. 4. Returns in the 1963 national election provide further cause for accepting the figures.

FIGURE 4*

AD CONVENTION DELEGATES—1962

| State[a] | AD-GV | AD-ARS |
|---|---|---|
| Amazonas | 4 | 2 |
| Apure | 2 | 16 |
| Aragua | 7 | 10 |
| Barinas | 1 | 15 |
| Carabobo | 30 | |
| Caracas | 22 | |
| Carúpano | 22 | 4 |
| Cojedes | 2 | 9 |
| Cumaná | 1 | 24 |
| Falcón | 38 | 4 |
| La Guaira | 8 | 1 |
| Lara | 10 | 42 |
| Mérida | 6 | 15 |
| Miranda | | 31 |
| Monagas | 30 | |
| Nueva Esparta | 14 | |
| Portuguesa | 4 | 23 |
| Táchira | 17 | 5 |
| Trujillo | 32 | 1 |
| Zulia | 62 | 7 |
| Totals[b] | 312 | 209 |

[a] AD sectionals diverge from national state boundaries in a few instances. Sucre is divided into Cumaná and Carúpano. The Caracas sectional serves the Federal District, but the La Guaira regional unit is also added.

[b] As indicated in the text, this set of figures preceded the selection of delegates to the national convention by authorities in Anzoátegui, Bolívar, Guárico, Yaracuy, and the territory of Amacuro.

* Figures cited by the convention report of Secretary-General J. A. Paz Galarraga, in A.D., no. 189, January 27, 1962, p. 11. See footnotes for comment on validity of figures.

plaining to state and local authorities the inadmissibility of CEN interference in the holding of conventions.

Although the intentions of the ARS group had become apparent, the aroused Guardia Vieja found itself in a difficult position, for such declarations as that of the Secretary-General could be overriden by the *arsista* majority on the CEN; thus it seemed impossible to block interference in the two remaining Sectional Conventions. In December 1961 the GV therefore adopted the only strategy remaining open to them. Remaining within accepted party channels, the veterans of the party issued a call for the convocation of the Comité Directivo Nacional, which was superior to the CEN in authority. The *arsista* majority on the CEN was unable to prevent the measure, since CDN meetings may be called—as set forth in Article 29 of the party statutes—when requested in writing by fifteen members of the CDN or by three or more sectional organizations.

A formal petition for a CDN meeting was presented on December 8, 1961, bearing the signature of Rómulo Gallegos and twenty-eight other members of the CDN. The ARS group was reluctant to honor the petition, knowing that they would be in a minority on the CDN. Article 30 of the statutes stated that a request for a CDN meeting would be honored within fifteen days at the maximum; it was to be nineteen before the *arsistas* yielded. In the meantime the ARS tried to increase their strength in the states while suspending four non-*arsista* members of the CEN: Paz Galarraga, Lepage, Henríquez Vera, and Salom Mesa. The CDN meeting resulted in the anticipated victory of the Guardia Vieja. Of the 119 who attended on December 27, the party "regulars" held an edge of 63-56. ARS responded that only its fifty-six representatives were legitimate members of the CDN. The following month a pair of "legitimate" AD conventions were held, and Venezuelans saw the once-monolithic AD seemingly represented by two claimants.

The XII National Convention of the party met on January 12, 1962. The regulars headed by Raúl Leoni came together in the Teatro Boyacá, where 567 delegates heard the *arsistas* expelled from the party and saw Rómulo Betancourt give his blessing to the "legitimate" party. On the same day the rival group assembled 373 followers in the Teatro Caracas to hail their own leader, Raúl Ramos Giménez. The non-*arsistas* were declared to be expelled, and the ARS group issued its claim as the true heir of the heritage of Acción Democrática.

The causes of this remarkable chain of events have been variously explained. The first issue revolved about the possible ideological or programmatic nature of the schism. The so-called Guardia Vieja has denied any doctrinal meaning to the dispute. As Gonzalo Barrios said in a radio broadcast at the time, the ARS had tried to impose policies simply as a means of gaining organizational domination; the major concern was that of satisfying personal interests and ambitions. He argued that ideological or doctrinal questions had never been brought up for debate, even after the ARS had won a majority on the CEN.

The *arsistas* consistently maintained, both publicly and privately, that the issue centered about the strengthening and executing of revolutionary party doctrine. The Guardia Vieja were accused of being old, tired, and no longer committed to the revolutionary meaning and spirit of the party. This did not, however, resemble the true revolutionary radicalism of the *miristas*. Rather, the ARS cited three areas of dispute as reflecting the alleged loss of revolutionary doctrine on the part of the veteran leaders: continuation of coalition government, revision of agrarian reform, and restoration of constitutional guarantees.

Each of these issues was tactical in nature rather than a question of basic ideological conviction. As to the first point, *arsista* arguments in favor of ending the coalition government reflected Ramos Giménez' presidential ambitions. There was considerable speculation at the time that Betancourt might agree to a continuation of the AD-COPEI coalition for a second five-year term, headed by COPEI's Rafael Caldera. Although this later failed to materialize, it appeared a definite possibility for some time, and obviously would have blocked the ascension of an *adeco*. ARS therefore demanded the removal of COPEI from the coalition. It is worth noting that several members of the Guardia Vieja shared this view; however, the subject had not been seriously considered by the CEN at the time of the schism. It is not certain that the ARS would not have won the point within the party, whatever the reaction of Betancourt might have been.

The second issue was, again, less than fundamental. Agrarian reform had been enacted in February 1960, and almost immediately was attacked for alleged slowness of implementation. AD peasant leader Ramón Quijada, who joined ARS in the split, strongly opposed the deliberate pace of reform, urging faster action even at the risk of proceeding before necessary court decisions on expropriatory and other legal matters. There was no disagreement over the fundamental tenets of agrarian reform, but only the matter of implementation. Quijada himself was the only *arsista* who expressed public concern over the matter until the party split. The ARS had not loudly championed the revision or alteration of agrarian reform until after the separation.

The third point of disagreement, according to the ARS, was a dispute over the restoration of constitutional guarantees, several of which the government had recently suspended in response to terrorist violence in the capital. To begin with, governmental decisions about the suspension and renewal of such guarantees were made throughout the five-year period without party decisions or declarations one way or the other. And the official statement of the party held merely that it desired the government to restore guarantees at the earliest date consonant with the dictates of internal order and security.

In retrospect, the alleged ideological and doctrinal issues of "fundamental" importance seem to have little validity. *Arsista* claims to the contrary, its interest was simply taking over the control of the party. In the process it expected to remove the prestigious veterans in the party, to purge younger leaders who disagreed with them, and to prepare for 1963 elections through the candidacy of Ramos Giménez. It may well be argued that there was nothing inherently wrong in the effort to seize control of the party machinery. But in politics nothing succeeds like success, and the *arsistas* failed.

It is possible that with a little more patience the *arsistas* might have captured party leadership. With a majority on the CEN, it might have been possible to gain control of most state organs and, through them, to win a popular majority with the party rank-and-file. If anything, the ARS was unduly hasty, and the miscalculation cost them dearly. The effort to win control of the party was a daring one, only narrowly missing. Unlike the *mirista* episode, it was a personal and factional fight for party domination, rather than a basic difference over doctrine or even current policy decisions. When the *arsistas* lost, there was no choice but to break away, re-form a new organization, and try to win public recognition as the "legitimate" Acción Democrática.

On the other side of the dispute, there can be no denial that the Guardia Vieja leadership showed up poorly. The internal problems entailed by the previous division with the younger generation so occupied Leoni and his colleagues that the *arsista* threat was overlooked. The substantial political talent of the *arsistas* themselves further increased GV difficulties once the existence of the challenge became clear. Once the issue was joined, the immense stature of Leoni, Prieto, Barrios, and others in the eyes of the party rank-and-file was a major factor in the triumph of the regular leadership. But had the *arsistas* delayed their drive a few more months, the personal prestige of the veteran leaders would not have been enough. Much speculation—admittedly pointless—has argued that under the direct leadership of Betancourt, the *arsista* factionalism would never have been permitted to reach an advanced stage. This is probable but somewhat irrelevant. The party faithful could only hope that its leadership would be more effective in rebuilding than it had been in dealing with the *arsistas*.

Although the *mirista* schism was dangerous in the long-run implications of the loss of Venezuelan student support, the *arsista* episode held more immediate perils. As shown earlier, the passing of *arsista* congressmen into the opposition cost the AD-COPEI coalition government its majority in the Chamber, and constructive legislation in the lower house was rendered impossible for the duration of the Betancourt administration. On a narrower scale, the loss of the *arsistas* to the AD leadership was a severe blow. Replacements for the CEN were available, but—as further described in the next chapter—much fine talent and ability had been sacrificed.

Some indication of the extent of the loss was given with the formation of a Comité Ejecutivo Nacional by the rival AD-ARS. Among its more prominent leaders, with their previous AD position in parentheses, were the following: President Raúl Ramos Giménez (Political Secretary), Secretary-General José Angel Ciliberto (Sub Secretary-General), Ramón Quijada (Political Secretary), José Manzo González (Political Secretary), Manuel Vicente Ledezma (Secretary of Parliamentary Affairs), César Rondón Lovera (Secretary of International Affairs), Elpidio La Riva Mata (Secretary of Studies), Tomás Alberti (Agrarian Secretary), Héctor Vargas Acosta (Secretary of Organization), Rafael Serfaty (Secretary of Finances), Manuel Alfredo Rodríguez (Propaganda), and Félix Adam (Secretary of Education). Not all of these men were fully recognized as top *adecos* at the time of the split, for a number had been chosen at the most recent convention. However, such men as Ramos Giménez, Ciliberto, Quijada, Manzo González, and Alberti had been very prominent for many years. Furthermore, the defection of three of the party's four Political

Secretaries gave further evidence of the magnitude of the schism.

Throughout 1962 and 1963 the rival organizations waged competition. It was conducted with fierce intensity within the peasant and labor organizations, as related later. It also occurred in a number of states, although *arsista* organizational efforts centered their efforts on metropolitan areas. With the passing of time, two lines of *arsista* tactics emerged: on the one hand, great attention was given to parliamentary affairs, and they used their numbers tellingly in the opposition to harass the government wherever possible. Secondly, they worked toward the establishment of a national opposition candidate about whom the anti-government sectors might coalesce. It was hoped that Ramos Giménez would be the single opposition candidate, but the *arsistas* were willing to cooperate behind a non-partisan or "independent" candidate. The unsuccessful results are related in Chapter XII. In time, it became apparent that the AD-ARS chose not to contest organizationally with the AD in the field. Political activism was conducted within the highly politicized Caracas circles that dominate the headlines but fail to deliver votes at election time. As a consequence, the regular AD leadership had less competition than might have been expected in its drive to rebuild national strength.

Charges and counter-charges about the "legitimacy" of the rival leaders were to continue until December 1963 elections. Only the results could establish beyond any possible doubt the practical legitimacy of Acción Democrática. For the "regular" AD, the forthcoming elections assumed additional importance, for there would be no better way to indicate the extent to which the *aparato* had survived the *arsista* departure. As Leoni and others repeated throughout 1963, the voters would have an opportunity to pass judgment on the true representatives of Acción Democrática.

# CHAPTER VII

# Leadership and Membership

Acción Democrática has from its very inception aimed at the widest possible membership, embracing all levels of society and all geographic regions of the country. The development of party leadership has been an inevitable concomitant. Analyses of both the membership and leadership are less than definitive, for data is not universally available. Some aspects of the party have not proved susceptible to investigation.[1] There are, nonetheless, indications of the basic nature of both the party leadership and membership.

## Biographic Analysis of Leadership

Party leadership has passed through a series of identifiable stages since its first appearance in the protest of 1928. Although delineation between these stages is not always clear, at least six can be noted, each one a reflection of the transitory political situation in which the party leaders found themselves.

The first such stage began in 1936 with the return of young exiles and closed with the *lopecista* expulsion of forty-seven political opponents in 1937. The young members of the Generation of '28 were not politically experienced, nor were they yet thoroughly versed on the nature of Venezuelan problems, although their understanding was rapidly growing. Furthermore, they were political unknowns, and suffered a great handicap due to this lack of public recognition. Those few public figures who had not been closely identified with *gomecismo* were, in most cases, members of the Caracas upper bourgeoisie who were active in the Unión Nacional

---

[1] The author did not have access to AD files, and some of the textual references are therefore imprecise. Relatively few party leaders themselves appear fully informed of and knowledgeable about the nature and background of party membership.

Republicana. Two major efforts were therefore launched in an attempt to minimize these handicaps.

The first aimed at establishing maximum contact with the population, centering the drive on a fight for better living conditions and for the organization of an effective labor force. Thus the young AD leaders-to-be played a major part in the general strike at the close of 1936, as well as trying to win the broadest possible appeal in ORVE and later the PDN. Secondly, the practice was begun of eliciting the cooperation of prominent figures, in many cases intellectuals. This was reflected in the inclusion of the respected Mariano Picón-Salas in ORVE, and was part of the rationale behind the symbolic presidential candidacy of Rómulo Gallego in 1941. The full participation of the poet Andrés Eloy Blanco as an active leader was another illustration.

The clandestine existence of the Partido Democrática Nacional from 1937-1941 not only saw the construction of the foundations of what became Acción Democrática but also included the recruitment into the movement of leaders from various sectors of Venezuelan life. Extensive efforts by Betancourt and his colleagues were directed toward the interior, where party organization had been almost non-existent. The foundation of both the labor and *campesino* movements were laid. The leadership was joined by such figures as Pérez Salinas, González Navarro, and Malavé Villalba from labor, and Quijada and Alberti from the peasantry. By 1941 the organization had progressed substantially beyond its earlier composition of young students and intellectuals.

The 1941 candidacy of Gallegos prepared the party for the official birth of Acción Democrática, and the next four years may be regarded as a third level in the evolution of the leadership. With the emergence from underground activity, propaganda and publicity spread party appeal and created interest. University

students began to flock to the party in droves, and regional organizations became significant in some cases.
Notwithstanding previous attention to the interior, the
over-all movement had been weak outside Caracas,
with the exception of the petroleum workers' region in
Zulia.

Young members of the Generation of 1936-1937 became active in party regional organizations. The development of leadership through participation became increasingly perceptible. The leadership of Betancourt,
Rodríguez, Leoni, Blanco, and others was buttressed
increasingly by such young men as Luis Augusto Dubuc,
Luis Troconis Guerrero, J. M. Siso Martínez, and Raúl
Ramos Giménez. For the first time, legal participation
was providing experience that brought competence to
a new group of young activists.

The October Revolution in 1945 pressed upon the
party requirements far beyond anything that preceded
it. The expansion of the membership taxed party directing organs, and the absence of the most experienced
leaders in the Junta Revolucionaria de Gobierno strained
the capacity of those who remained. The ranks of the
AD labor leadership largely escaped any decline in
ability and competence, but other sectors of the party
were affected. This fourth stage was in some ways a
negative period, for the directors of the party were
forced to fight a set of conditions that made it difficult
to maintain the previous quality of leadership. To some
extent there was a feeling that the leaders were bat-
tling for time, hoping to hold together the party while
additional young activists could be prepared for responsibility.

A characteristic that began to manifest itself during
this period was carried over and magnified during the
fifth stage. The leadership began to include former
youth and student leaders whose total experience was
brief, and for whom the struggles against López Con-

treras and even Medina Angarita were matters essentially of history. These were the members of the young, formative ranks that had barely begun to exert their fullest efforts when the military overthrew the Gallegos government in 1948.

Much of the clandestine struggle during the following decade was conducted by this set of youthful leaders, whose experience in the school of adversity was hardened by the imprisonment and physical torture that many underwent. Prominent in this group were Ciliberto, Manzo González, Octavio Lepage, Rangel, and Sáez Mérida. Most were in their 20's—many were still enrolled in university classes. From their ranks emerged almost the entire leadership of the future MIR as well as some who later joined the *arsistas*. During these years too, the leadership suffered from the attrition of death for the first time. Its veteran ranks were hit by the loss of Blanco, Rodríguez, and Troconis Guerrero. Police repression and assassination inside Venezuela took the lives of such rising young figures as Ruiz Pineda, Carnevali, and Luis Hurtado. The first losses from age and at least partial retirement were Rómulo Gallegos and Cecilia Núñez Sucre.

The most recent stage to be identified has not yet run its course. It began in 1958 when, for the first time, the leadership truly succeeded in permeating all geographic regions with party organs. There were even minor successes within the entrepreneurial ranks which had long resisted the party bitterly. Although soft spots remained—such as the lack of significant youth leadership after the *mirista* defection—the party came closer than ever before to being fully representative of Venezuelan society. The AD claim of being a *policlasista* organization was never more valid. Two further elements, however, darkened the picture.

First of these was the effect of the two internal divisions. The *mirista* affair cut off effective communication with the young students—somewhat ironic in view of the fact that original leadership in 1928 came precisely from this element. Thus the AD now faces the difficulty of recovering its position, and little success has yet been achieved. The effect of the *arsista* schism deprived the party of some of its best political activists. This is a loss that can more readily be handled than that entailed by the *miristas*.

A second current difficulty is one about which much is said but relatively little done—bureaucratization. AD leaders today will almost universally cite the process of bureaucratization as a serious problem to the organization. Yet they speak about the continuing need to improve the quality *and* quantity of administrative secretariats and their staffs. There is an awareness that a qualitative improvement is ever desirable and equally difficult. The tendency of some middle-level party officials to enjoy relative sinecures and to devote themselves to the preservation of their positions, has not yet been attacked.

It may generally be inferred by both public and private statements of many ranking *adecos* that the present challenge to the leadership is only secondarily that of streamlining and improving its organization and personnel. More important is a serious effort to revitalize the entire *aparato*, to infuse it with a renewed spirit that will increase the party appeal to political independents, attract new blood into the directing organs, and rededicate the party toward a set of future goals only dimly perceived at the present time. As is discussed later, the AD leadership recognized after the 1963 elections the importance of widening the party appeal once again. Patronage and political office will always draw additional people, but the problem is to attract the participation of talented young Venezuelans who have in recent years been unwilling to devote themselves to politics.

Party leadership can be traced through evolutionary stages, but this descriptive process tells only a little about the present directors of the party. A compilation of basic biographical data (see Figure 5) provides an outline of twenty-five prominent party leaders. These are believed representative of the contemporary Acción

FIGURE 5*

AD LEADERSHIP—BASIC BIOGRAPHICAL DATA

| Name | Birthplace | A | B | C | D | E | F |
|------|-----------|---|---|---|---|---|---|
| Barrios | Acarigua, Portuguesa | 1904[a] | Dp | Lw | + | + | + |
| Betancourt | Guatire, Miranda | 1908 | Pr | | | + | + |
| Ciliberto | Caripe, Monagas | 1924 | Dp | Lw | + | | |
| D'Ascoli | Caracas, D.F. | 1900 | Sn | Lw | + | + | + |
| Dubuc | Trujillo, Trujillo | 1918 | Dp | | | + | + |
| Fermín | Nueva Esparta | | Dp | Ed | + | + | + |
| González N. | Porlamar, N. Esparta | 1910 | Dp | Lb | | + | + |
| González P. | Valencia, Carabobo | 1920 | Dp | Ps | | | |
| Leidenz | Cumarebo, Falcón | 1916 | Dp | Lw | + | + | |
| Leoni | Upata de Carreros, Bolívar | 1905 | Sn | Lw | + | + | + |
| Lepage | Santa Rosa, Anzoátegui | 1924 | Dp | Lw | + | | |
| Malavé V | Carúpano, Sucre | 1904 | Dp | Lb | | + | + |
| Manzo G. | Caripe, Monagas | 1922 | Dp | Lw | + | | |
| Mesa E. | Guarebe, Miranda | 1919 | Cn | Lb | | | |
| Ordaz | Nueva Esparta | 1918 | Sn | Lb | | | |
| Paz G. | Puertos de Altagracia, Zul. | 1919 | Dp | Md | + | | |
| Peñalver | San Antonio, Monagas | 1918 | Dp | Ed | + | | |
| Pérez S. | Caracas, D.F. | 1906 | Sn | Lb | | + | + |
| Prieto S. | Caracas, D.F. | 1902 | Sn | Ed | + | + | + |
| Quijada | Carúpano, Sucre | 1912 | Dp | Ps | | + | + |
| Ramos G. | San Felipe, Yaracuy | 1917 | Sn | Lw | + | + | |
| Rangel | Tovar, Mérida | 1923 | Dp | Lw | + | | |
| Rondón L. | El Orza, Apure | 1924 | Dp | | | | |
| Siso M. | Upata de Carreros, Bolívar | 1918 | Sn | Ed | + | + | |
| Vargas A. | Valencia, Carabobo | 1922 | Dp | Md | + | | |

Key:   A—Year of birth    F—PDN founder     Lw—Law
       B—Elected post    Dp—Deputy      Ed—Education
       C—Profession     Sn—Senator      Lb—Labor
       D—Univ. degree    Pr—President      Ps—Peasantry
       E—AD founder     Cn—Councilman    Md—Medicine

* Based on data published in party publications.
[a] Barrios' age is not publicized; this is an approximation.

Democrática, although the selection is in some part arbitrary. Of these twenty-five, all but two have been members of at least one of the four Comités Ejecutivos Nacionales between 1958 and 1963.[2] Of these, Pérez Salinas is an AD founder still active in labor affairs, while D'Ascoli, also a charter member of the party, has remained active although outside the formal party hierarchy.[3] Of the remaining twenty-three, fifteen have served on at least two of the four CENs. Put another way, the list includes 14 of the 19 CEN members elected by the IX Convention; 14 of the 20 elected at the Tenth; 11 of the 21 elected at the Eleventh; and 12 of the 21 elected at the Twelfth.[4] Six of the 13 *arsista* rebels are included, plus one of 4 *miristas*.

AD direction is thus studied in terms of its composition since the 1958 return from exile. Chronologically it embraces a period from January 1958 to August 1963. Reliance has been placed upon CEN membership as chosen at the IX Convention in August 1958; the Tenth in September 1959; the Eleventh in January 1961; and the Twelfth, in January 1962. Information has been gleaned primarily from party publications, especially the weekly *A.D.*, although some has come from personal interviews with ranking *adecos*.

The information regarding age is straightforward.[5] The range extends from D'Ascoli and Prieto in their early 60's to Rangel at 40 and Ciliberto, Lepage, and Rondón Lovera at 39. The average age—excluding Mercedes Fermín—comes to 46.4 years. To this data can be added figures on the ages of party founders. As

[2] The composition of the CEN after a revision in late 1963 came too late to be used for the following analysis. The membership of the new CEN is given elsewhere.

[3] Carlos D'Ascoli returned to the CEN in late 1963, assuming the newly created post of Secretary of Economic and Technical Affairs.

[4] Data has been compiled from official lists of the CENs appearing in *A.D.* after each of the four Conventions in question.

[5] Calculations of age are made as of December 1963.

indicated in the accompanying Table, ten of the twenty-five were organizers of the Partido Democrática Nacional, and an additional five are regarded as among the major founders of Acción Democrática. The PDN founders, now the real veterans of the party, average 57.3 years of age. Addition of the five who participated in the 1941 founding of Acción Democrática reduces the average to 53.1 as of the close of 1963.

Geographical data shows little that is startling—in itself perhaps a significant fact. Of the birthplaces listed, 14 of the 20 states plus the Federal District are represented. Nueva Esparta with 4 and Monagas with 3 are the only states with more than a pair. While many of these leaders moved from their birthplaces either because of familial or educational reasons, the distribution is a reminder of the national representation of the leadership. The rural nature of Venezuela—so pronounced early in the century—is underlined by the fact that only 5 men were born in cities which even today have a population of 25,000 or more. Of these, only Caracas and Valencia are to any extent metropolitan cities in the 1960's.

Examination of this material by region rather than by state or city again reflects the national representation of the leadership. Six persons were born along the central coastal region in and around Caracas and the Federal District. Six more came from the eastern coastal state of Sucre and the nearby island of Margarita (Nueva Esparta). Three men came from the deep interior of the country—Apure and Bolívar—while there were also three from the Andes. The latter region can claim Rangel from Mérida and Dubuc from Trujillo, although it is stretching the ordinary connotation of Venezuela's Andean region to include Ramos Giménez from San Felipe, Yaracuy.

Professional backgrounds and education are interesting, for a correlation appears between the two. Sixteen of the 25, or 64 percent, have received degrees, the great majority either a Doctor of Law or Doctor of Political and Social Sciences. Several of these were earned abroad. Carlos D'Ascoli received a degree from the University of Paris in 1932, and Mercedes Fermín at this writing is terminating work for a Ph.D. from Boston University. Raúl Leoni did much of his work during exile in Bogotá, while Gonzalo Barrios studied in Spain during a lengthy stay outside Venezuela. All the others received their degrees from Caracas' Universidad Central de Venezuela, except for Manzo González and Vargas Acosta, who attended the Universidad de los Andes in Mérida.

Of the nine who did not receive degrees, all but two were labor or *campesino* leaders. Detailed biographies disclose a common thread of minimal formal schooling: Pérez Salinas attended school for six years, Ordaz went through primary and secondary school, while Quijada attended for three years. Malavé Villalba and González Navarro were both out of school and beginning working careers as shoemakers while in their early teens. The two non-labor leaders without degrees were Betancourt and Rondón Lovera, both of whom were too involved in political activities to obtain regular degrees. Betancourt never returned to law school following the events of 1928, while Rondón Lovera attended a variety of schools at different times, having received a certificate in humanities at Mexico City in the 1940's.

AD leaders are first and foremost practicing politicians, whatever their special training. Those with law degrees have rarely if ever practiced law as a livelihood. A few of the educators have combined their activities. Thus historian Siso Martínez and geographer Fermín teach at the Universidad Central de Venezuela, and others have devoted occasional periods to university teaching. The two with medical training—pediatrician Paz Galarraga and orthodontist Vargas Acosta—have devoted little time in recent years to their specialized professions.

A footnote might be appropriate regarding women. Acción Democrática was in the forefront of the fight for female suffrage in the early 1940's, and its statutes declare that no separate women's organization should be created within the party, for equality of the sexes means equality of opportunity inside the same machinery. Yet the fact remains that only a few women have been influential as party leaders. A somewhat larger number have been active in the middle ranks of the party; moreover, many were involved during the clandestine activities of 1948-1958. Perhaps only two have consistently been among the formal party hierarchy for an extended period of time, however. Mercedes Fermín remains active in the Chamber of Deputies and has a major voice in high party circles.[6] Furthermore, few men or women have enjoyed a personal friendship or long political intimacy with Rómulo Betancourt.

Cecilia Núñez Sucre has also been prominent for years. Having begun a teaching career in Maturín in 1901, she became well-known even before the death of Gómez. President of the Liga Defensora de Presos Políticos— a civic service group—from 1936-1939, she joined in the early PDN activities and served as finance secretary for one of the first PDN cells, which included both Prieto and the youthful Dubuc. She was a member of the CEN during the first years of Acción Democrática, and at one point filled a vice-presidential post. She still makes occasional appearances at party gatherings, although now in her 80's.

One of the striking characteristics of party leadership that is not revealed by biographical charts is the heavy and constant weight of official duties. The combination of office-holding responsibilities, party duties, and in

[6] In the newest CEN she became responsible for one of the two new posts—the Secretariat of Community Development.

many cases professional or *fracción* obligations, can and often does become an oppressive load. An excellent illustration is José González Navarro. As President of the Confederación de Trabajadores de Venezuela (CTV) he holds one of the most powerful and responsible posts in the country, which he directs from CTV headquarters some two miles from Congress. His political duties are those of a Deputy from the Federal District, and he is also a member of the labor committee. Within the party he is one of the Political Secretaries, which means attendance at regular meetings of the Buró Político as well as the CEN.

During the five months that Congress meets, González Navarro attends sessions of the Chamber Monday through Thursday, generally from 5 p.m. until 10 or 11. Tuesday morning he attends the weekly meeting of the AD congressional wing, and Tuesday afternoon the Political Bureau gathers. If labor matters are important—and usually they are—he is among those who confer with President Betancourt at Miraflores Palace on Wednesday morning. One evening of the week there may be a session of the party CEN, and a congressional committee may hold hearings at 2 or 3 one afternoon. As CTV President he has many further time-consuming chores; besides the requirements of union meetings and routine paperwork, he tries to spend the weekends in the interior whenever possible.

Another major figure in the party is Luis B. Prieto; although without occupational duties such as the labor or *campesino* movement, he is Second Vice-President of the party,[7] therefore attending sessions of the Political Bureau on Tuesday afternoon and often joining the Wednesday morning delegation to Miraflores. He is of

[7] Dr. Prieto moved up to become First Vice-President in August 1963 when Gonzalo Barrios vacated that post to become President in place of Raúl Leoni. When President-elect Leoni appointed Barrios to the cabinet in 1964, Prieto was named Acting President of Acción Democrática.

course a member of the CEN with substantial responsibilities. His role as a Senator demands attendance at the AD parliamentary *fracción* meetings Tuesday morning.

Currently serving as President of the Senate and of the entire National Congress, Prieto is empowered to chair all Senate sessions as well as joint meetings, although often delegating the function to others. As President of the Senate he has a host of official affairs at which attendance is virtually mandatory, and the demands of paperwork in his office are substantial. Tuesday and Thursday mornings he must hold open office hours for the Presidency of the Senate. In the seven months when Congress is not in session, he chairs meetings of the Comisión Delegada, the legislative committee responsible for congressional duties between sessions. As an added filip, he is an editor and occasional contributor to the journal *Política*.

Prieto and González Navarro are by no means extreme examples. Virtually all AD leaders are members of Congress, and while necessary absences are of course excused, the party requires them to attend all sessions as well as gatherings of the parliamentary wing. Those who hold posts in the labor, *campesino*, or teachers' organizations will generally have comparable duties on a congressional committee. Some two dozen are members of the party CEN, and seven are also involved in weekly meetings of the Buró Político. Seemingly futile—and almost always tardy—efforts are made to keep several sets of office hours, including those at Congress, the party headquarters, and a labor or *campesino* building.[8]

Leaders are caught up in a merry-go-round of activities that never stops and rarely slows. Even those who are free of such a wide variety of duties have too little

[8] The author is speaking from personal experience, having spent long hours waiting for tardy interviewees. Delays were rarely due to discourtesy or inefficiency, but from the sheer impossibility of meeting all commitments and appointments promptly.

time. The party itself demands continual visits and trips through the interior, ever testing the grass roots and instilling enthusiasm at organizational rallies. There is little respite, and those who cannot maintain the pace simply slip into the background. One of the results is occasionally slipshod work and overreliance upon office staffs. Here again bureaucratization has been encouraged, for there is a growing necessity for reliance upon technical assistants and administrative advisers for routine tasks. The ease with which this can get out of control is apparent to the leadership, yet little has been done to change the pattern.

To some extent the pressures on the leaders have been ameliorated by the traditional practice of having several expert voices in each major political or economic field. This procedure, encouraged from the early days when knowledgeable leaders were in short supply, has carried down to the present. On labor matters, González Navarro, Malavé Villalba, and Pérez Salinas stand out as recognized figures with high competence and authority. Education has long been a focus of attention for Prieto, Fermín, Núñez Sucre, Leandro Mora, and Siso Martínez. Peasant affairs were handled by Quijada or Alberti, although this has been disrupted by the *arsista* division. Pérez Alfonzo and Betancourt himself have long spoken eloquently on matters of petroleum; in an area of more recent concern such as international affairs, there are voices such as Barrios, Lusinchi, and the independent but pro-AD Marcos Falcón Briceño and Enrique Tejera París. The development of trained staffs of advisers has lessened somewhat the importance of this custom, but it was an important feature of the leadership in years past that remains with Acción Democrática today.

As the AD has reached maturity, the leadership has been faced with various problems. The lack of unity in recent years has been obvious; the *mirista* and *arsista* divisions, along with the so-called "problem of the generations," have combined to form a pattern that is less than monolithic. The question of mobility is a related aspect, to which we now turn.

## Leadership Mobility and Unity

An examination of the composition of the Comité Ejecutivo Nacional over the five years since 1958 is useful in terms of leadership mobility. This 1958-1963 period provides the best criterion to date, for the seven-year period of legal activity in the 1940's was hedged in by too many transitory conditions to be meaningful in terms of analysis relevant to the decade of the '60's. Figure 6 lists the four Comités Ejecutivos Nacionales elected by the most recent National Conventions. Thus all national officers since the return from exile are included, up until the revision of August 1963.[9] The only exception is again the six-month period at the start of 1958 when the restoration of freedom brought continual alteration and re-shifting of party leaders. Returning exiles and emerging underground leaders changed responsibilities frequently, and the formal posts were not in themselves particularly meaningful during this time.

[9] On August 3, 1963, the revised CEN was announced with the following membership: Gonzalo Barrios, President; Luis B. Prieto, First Vice-President; Augusto Malavé Villalba, Second Vice-President; Jesús Angel Paz Galarraga, Secretary General; Ismael Ordaz, Sub Secretary-General; Salom Mesa, Secretary of Organization; Said Moanack, José González Navarro, Armando González, Eligio Anzola Anzola, and Carlos Andrés Pérez, Political Secretaries; Pedro Salazar Aguilera, Secretary of Finance; Francisco Olivo, Secretary of Labor; Pedro Torres, Secretary of Agriculture; Numa Márquez, Youth Secretary; Adelso González, Secretary of Education; Angel Borregales, Secretary of Relations; Héctor Strédel, Secretary of Press; Roberto Heríquez Vera, Secretary of Propaganda; Jaime Lusinchi, Secretary of International Affairs; Antonio Leidenz, Secretary of Studies; Octavio Lepage, Secretary of Parliamentary and Municipal Affairs; Carlos D'Ascoli, Secretary of Economic and Technical Affairs; Mercedes Fermín, Secretary of Community Development.

The last two posts—occupied by D'Ascoli and Fermín—were the newest to be constituted.

Twenty-one national party offices are currently listed. Two additions were made after the IX Convention: a fourth Political Secretary, and the elevation of the post of Sub Secretary-General to full CEN membership.[10] Other offices have remained constant. The four CENs listed in Figure 6 contain from 19 to 21 posts. A total of 46 individuals have held office. Subtracting from this sum the 21 present officers, there are 25 departures from office to be examined and explained.

The prime cause of mobility during this period has been the dissension stemming from the *mirista* and *arsista* schisms. Of the 25 former CEN members who have left that body, 17 joined the rebel groups. The MIR dissidents included Rangel, Sáez Mérida, Gumersindo Rodríguez, and Jorge Dager. Dager later resigned from the MIR to organize his own Frente Democrática Popular (FDP), while the theoretical marxist Rodríguez retired from active politics. Thirteen *arsistas* were elected by the XI National Convention in January 1961. Thus, 68 percent of those who have left the CEN in the past five years have done so as the result of MIR and ARS dissensions.

Of the remaining 8, half took government posts of various sorts, while the others withdrew to pursue essentially private business. Betancourt went to the presidency; Angel Fariñas Salgado was named to a state governorship; Simón Consalvi to a diplomatic post; and Manuel Martínez to the Instituto Agrario Nacional. Those who left the CEN for other causes were Luis Manuel Peñalver, who became director of the Universidad de Oriente in 1961; José María Siso Martínez,

---

[10] The party ordinarily does not list the Secretary-General of the Comité Ejecutivo Seccional for the Federal District and for Libertador, although according to party statutes the post is held by a member of CEN. Therefore, the lists in this text have a maximum of twenty-one rather than twenty-two. And to repeat, the party in late 1963 added the two new CEN posts described previously.

who heads the history department at the Universidad Central de Venezuela; and Mercedes Fermín, who teaches in the geography department at the same institution. Manuel Martínez also became a political commentator on Radio Continente. All eight remain active within Acción Democrática.

A different means of considering mobility is to examine the January 1963 list of CEN members. Of these 21, 11 had belonged to earlier Comités Ejecutivos Nacionales, while 10 were new. Nine of the 10 newcomers assumed posts vacated by the defection of ARS, while the tenth replaced a man who simply switched jobs. With regard to the 11 holdovers, 3 had been members of all 4 CENs—the triumvirate of Leoni, Barrios, and Prieto—while two others were serving on their third Comité since 1958—Paz Galarraga and González Navarro.

In terms of personnel changes, then, the major surge behind leadership mobility has stemmed from the MIR and ARS. Otherwise, revisions have been the result of official governmental duties or of personal preference for private occupations. Furthermore, there have been no effective retirements, for all those who have left the CEN since 1958 have remained interested and active in party matters. In short, the basic changes in personnel over the past five years have been negligible except for the exceptional circumstances of internal feuds.

Now that the question has been viewed in terms of changing personnel, it is also useful to proceed by studying party posts. Political guidance and direction is centered in the eleven-man Buró Político. The leadership in its four top posts has been virtually constant from 1958-1963. At that time, Betancourt was party President, Leoni First Vice-President, Barrios Second Vice-President, and Prieto Secretary-General. With Betancourt's election to the Presidency of the Republic, the other three simply moved up one step. Leoni became AD Pres-

FIGURE 6*

AD LEADERSHIP—MOBILITY

| Post | IX<br>16 Aug. 58 | X<br>27 Sep. 59 | XI<br>15 Jan. 61 | XII<br>20 Jan. 62 |
|---|---|---|---|---|
| Pres | Betancourt | Leoni | Leoni | Leoni |
| 1st VP | Leoni | Barrios | Barrios | Barrios |
| 2nd VP | Barrios | Prieto | Prieto | Prieto |
| Sec-gen | Prieto | Paz G. | Paz G. | Paz G. |
| Pol Secs | Ramos G. (A) | Ramos G. (A) | Ramos G. (A) | Moanack |
|  | Rangel (M) | Rangel (M) | González N. | González N. |
|  | Dubuc | Peñalver | Quijada (A) | Dubuc |
|  |  | Manzo G. (A) | Manzo G. (A) | Malavé V. |
| Org | Manzo G. (A) | Malavé V. | Vargas A. (A) | Mesa E. |
| Press | Consalvi | Henríquez V. | Strédel | Strédel |
| Propag | Dager (M) | Ciliberto (A) | Rodríguez (A) | Henríquez V. |
| Studies | Peñalver | Lariva Mata (A) | Lariva Mata (A) | Leidenz |
| Labor | González N. | Olivo | Olivo | Olivo |
| Agr | Quijada (A) | Quijada (A) | Alberti (A) | González P. |
| Rltns | Ciliberto (A) | Vargas A. (A) | Moanack | Bajares L. |
| Int Rltns | Rondón L. (A) | Rondón L. (A) | Rondón L. (A) | Lusinchi |
| Parl, Munc | López G. | Sáez M. (M) | Ledezma (A) | Lepage |
| Ed, Cultr | Fermín | Siso M. | Adam (A) | A. González |
| Youth | Rodríguez (M) | Martínez | Angarita (A) | Marquez |
| Finance | Fariñas S. | Fariñas S. | Serfaty (A) | Jatar D. |
| Sub Sec-gen |  |  | Ciliberto (A) | Ordaz |

* Based on official lists of party CENs in AD publications.
(A) indicates *arsista* rebels who withdrew at XII Convention.
(M) indicates *mirista* rebels who withdrew between X and XI.

ident, with Barrios and Prieto advancing respectively
to the First and Second Vice-Presidencies. Jesús Angel
Paz Galarraga emerged at the X Convention as new
Secretary-General, and has retained the post since that
time.

There was greater movement among the other posts
on the Political Bureau, with the major factor the same
internal dissension. The three Political Secretaries in
1958 were Ramos Giménez, Rangel, and Dubuc. Rangel
stayed through the X Convention before leaving to
organize the MIR; Ramos Giménez stayed through the

eleventh, then left with other *arsistas*. Dubuc resigned to become Minister of Interior; later he left the Betancourt cabinet and was reincorporated into the CEN. *Arsista* Manzo González served after the X and XI Conventions, while *arsista* Quijada was a Political Secretary on the eleventh CEN before leaving. Labor leader González Navarro, who had been Labor Secretary in 1958, moved up to become a Political Secretary in 1961, and has since retained the post. Finally, attention is directed to the Political Bureau's Secretaries of Organization, Labor, and Agriculture. Labor Secretary González Navarro was succeeded by Francisco Olivo, who remains in the job. Peasant leader Quijada was Agrarian Secretary from 1958 until 1961, then became a Political Secretary while his associate Tomás Alberti took over. When both joined the ARS group, Armando González moved into the position. The Secretary of Organization has changed frequently. In 1958 Manzo González held the job, but his promotion in 1959 opened the job to Malavé Villalba. When the latter became a Political Secretary, he was replaced by *arsista* Vargas Acosta. Following the defection, Salom Mesa assumed the position.

Another standpoint from which to view the leadership is to examine those CEN members in 1963 who were promoted from other duties at the XII Convention. Ten individuals became full-fledged members of the CEN for the first time; it is useful to see where the infusion of new blood originated. The majority rose from the ranks of the party bureaucracy. Both Angel Bajares Lanza and Jaime Lusinchi had been serving as Adjuntos, and simply moved up to the titular position. Antonio Leidenz had been a full member of the CEN some years earlier, and was therefore returning to it. Armando González had become president of the AD-backed peasant confederation after the departure of Quijada and Alberti to ARS, and therefore became Agrarian Secretary almost

automatically. Octavio Lepage had served earlier as an
Adjunto, while Numa Marquez appeared from the depleted ranks of the *adeco* student movement. Jatar Dotti
and Ordaz rose from the *aparato*, although not from
previous positions as Adjuntos.

Aside from questions of mobility, the leadership must
be viewed in terms of unity. This has seemed a mere
chimera in the contemporary era; yet certain features of
the disputes with MIR and ARS stand out in the present
context. One of these is the internal "problem of the generations," which has become a reality to Acción Democrática recently. The emergence of the Muchachos in
1958 and 1959, revealing the presence of young men
holding radical leftist views, was in good part a reflection of peculiar circumstances. The half-hearted persecution of the communists by Pérez Jiménez failed to
root them out of university chairs, and extremists therefore exerted great influence on many students. The
growth of anti-yankee feeling, the appearance of Fidel
Castro as an emotional rallying point, and the return to
Venezuela of political figures who appeared moderate
and even bourgeois in many cases—the confluence of all
these factors led to the loss of the AD university movement under the banner of revolution raised by the
Muchachos. The regular AD leadership had little alternative but to purge this element. In terms of doctrinal
purity, the expulsion was favorable; but the destruction
of the AD's young wing was obviously a bitter blow.

The rise and eventual fragmentation of the ARS group
is less clear in its particulars. As noted before, the *arsistas*
included major figures in the party. Ramos Giménez was
a staunch partisan and one of the outstanding figures
of his generation. Ramón Quijada had been the best-
known political figure among the *campesinos*—barring
Betancourt—for nearly a quarter-century. Rondón Lovera had been a ranking authority on international affairs for some time, while both Ciliberto and Manzo

González were regarded as among the very brightest young politicians to rise from the experience of clandestine opposition to the long dictatorship.

An earlier discussion noted the two divergent arguments: the insistence of the regular AD that the rift was due to the impatience and personal ambition of Ramos Giménez and his close collaborators, that the *arsistas* were traitors to the cause; and the opinion of ARS that the oldtime leadership had lost its vigor, was pursuing ineffectual policies, and had been cut off from the party rank-and-file. Most of all, ARS maintained that the Guardia Vieja was tired and plodding, therefore needed replacement by younger, more vigorous figures.

This derisive term, the Guardia Vieja, proved politically convenient, but in truth it is misleading. The *arsista* faction in 1961-1963 did not include the veteran, founding leadership of Acción Democrática; nevertheless, many regular AD leaders are contemporaries in age and experience of the leading *arsistas*. Secretary-General Paz Galarraga had once been regarded as a member of the ARS group, but he did not join their effort to capture the party machinery. Lepage, Henríquez Vera, Strédel, and many others were of the same age and general background as the *arsista* directors.

Again, one returns to the conclusion that the *arsista* effort was essentially a power drive to seize control of the party, and that its arguments were largely convenient rationalizations without strong meaning. The leaders of the ARS are not to be criticized for such an attempt, but for the miscalculations that led to their failure. This is especially so in view of the narrowness of the margin by which they mistimed their try. Insofar as the present leadership of the AD is concerned, its leaders generally share the view that, to paraphrase one of them, "we are better off without the gangrene that would have spread its poisons; with the *arsistas* gone, we are again whole and healthy."[11] This was possibly true with the *miristas*, whose disagreement was basic and ideological. It was far less certain that the AD could survive the *arsista* splintering without a serious weakening of its position. The 1963 elections later suggested that the regular leadership had survived the defections well; at the same time, the episode strikes an outside observer as an unnecessary and avoidable incident that cost the party first-rate leaders.

A balanced view necessarily casts aspersions on the top leadership of Acción Democrática in 1961 and 1962. Its awareness that the *arsista* peril was real came very late in the day, and the first reaction was sluggish and unconcerned. There were few efforts to strengthen the "regular" leadership when Ramos Giménez' group won a majority on the CEN. The magnitude of the rebellion, which the regular leadership was unable to handle without national publicity, threw into question the quality of the Leoni-Paz Galarraga leadership, which could at best be regarded as uninspired. At the time of the internal struggle, common opinion in Venezuela held that Rómulo Betancourt could have managed the dissension without the eventual scandal of a party airing its disunity in public. This view places understandable but perhaps undue faith in the political wizardry of the President. Certainly his leadership of the party was more astute than that of Leoni, but the *arsista* conflict may have been inevitable. All that could be said without danger of contradiction was that the price of unity within the leadership was high.

The resultant AD determination to run its own presidential candidate in the fall of 1963 was in part a response to the feeling that there was no other way to prove its alleged continuing domination of the Venezuelan populace. Rival claims by the *arsistas* lent added importance to the 1963 elections, at which the struggle

[11] Interview with Mercedes Fermín, November 19, 1962.

for popular support received the national verdict. Only then was the ultimate victory of the regular AD over the competing AD-ARS certain and unquestionable.

## Membership and Discipline

Party directives regarding the recruitment and registration of party members are set forth by the AD in detail. Recruitment is continually exercised on the local level, and general policy encourages the enlistment of members through friends or acquaintances into a *grupo de base*. More carefully organized efforts may be conducted through the labor or peasant movements, which are predominantly AD. Regardless of the method, however, the same basic party directives apply.[12]

Three statutory requirements are set forth. To begin with, the party member must be Venezuelan, politically of age (18), and must "enjoy a good public and private reputation, maintaining wholly proper conduct." Furthermore, he or she may not belong to any other political party. Thirdly, a petition for membership must be made in writing and signed. If unable to read and write, the applicant may use other means of identification. The request for membership must also bear the signature of two members of the party in good standing. They must be prepared to discuss the applicant and to be consulted by the party organ to which the petition has been directed.

Final action on the bid is the statutory responsibility of the relevant Comité Ejecutivo Seccional, although it is permitted to delegate the task to a subordinate party organ—a common practice. Each month the CES will be sent a complete record of all registration by lower party bodies, together with the formal applications and any other relevant papers. The decision on a member-

---

[12] Acción Democrática, *Estatutos* (Caracas: Ediciones de la Secretaría Nacional de Propaganda, 1962), Chapter II, Articles 5-11.

ship petition must be taken and announced within one month of its submission to appropriate authorities. Any rejections of applications—which are unusual—must be explained in writing to the petitioner. Upon acceptance, a new member will be given a temporary document called simply a "Credencial," and within the year this will be exchanged for the party "Carnet" as the form of identification. Carnets are issued from the CEN, distributed through lower organs, and "constitute the only credential to accredit the member."

Once formally accepted as a member, the new *adeco* is expected to fulfill an enumerated set of duties. Many seem politically unsophisticated, but they are believed necessary for the vast majority of members. First is the straightforward admonition "to comply with and defend the Doctrine and Program of the Party and to respect the Statutes of the Organization." Participation is emphasized through the requirement of joining the party *grupos de base* and also any professional or occupational branches or *fracciones* that might be appropriate. Regular attendance is demanded at all such assemblies and meetings. Barring sickness or some other cause for absence accepted by party authorities, the member will be expected to be consistent and reliable in his participation.

Discipline is demanded for all directives and internal resolutions. Should a member disagree with a given party policy, "he has the right to present to the base organ where he belongs, a criticism to that resolution that will be sent to the organs that laid down the policy. . . ." While the matter is pending, however, the member is bound in compliance to the directive. In actual practice this petition of protest is not widely used.

Financial obligations to the party as set forth in AD statutes[13] must be met on a monthly basis. Only the unemployed member is easily excused; otherwise the member who feels unable to pay must present a plea

[13] *Estatutos*, Chapter XII, Articles 123-25.

to party authorities. No set amount is listed in party statutes, although in recent years there have been efforts to encourage the contribution of one *bolívar* monthly. The major purpose of the financial act is less that of collecting funds than of encouraging a feeling of participation by all. The contribution is largely symbolic, and the patent difficulty in collecting a set sum at regular intervals is recognized.[14]

Members are urged to be party propagandists and recruiters at all times, working for the strengthening of Acción Democrática and the addition of new members. Criticisms of party decisions within appropriate organs and meetings are encouraged, but should not be aired outside the party. The strong emphasis upon discussion and debate is underlined with party pride in its "internal democracy." This is reiterated in party rules at different points. The member is reminded with equal force, however, that it is his duty to keep disputes within party circles, however bitter or controversial they may be.

Acción Democrática also recognizes a relationship of a different nature—in addition to the full member (*militante*), there are also *simpatizantes*, or sympathizers. In the words of Article 11, "Acción Democrática will maintain and will widen its influence over persons and sectors unorganized politically through the relationship of *simpatizantes* to the party, systematizing the relations with them through means of information, and orientation . . . in accord with the dispositions of the national leadership."

Members of the party who desire to be politically active are also enjoined by the regulations to follow certain restrictions. The party gives its members the right to campaign and to be elected to any position within the party. The dispositions of Article 133 limit posts to members with specified duration in service,

14 Interviews with Luis B. Prieto, December 11, 1962; and Ismael Ordaz, November 20, 1962.

however. These requirements are placed equally upon those seeking office within the party structure and those who are members of a professional or occupational *fracción* or a peripheral organ.

To be eligible for a national party office, at least six years' membership is required; four years are demanded for those aspiring to sectional posts; district or departmental positions require two years' activity; only one year is necessary for those pursuing jobs at the municipal level or below. The only exception to this schedule of limitations is made for the several levels of the party youth movement, where ordinary restrictions are halved.

A portion of the statutes also deals with party members who seek election to public office or employment in non-elective public jobs.[15] Members ambitious for elective office are subject to expulsion if they offer themselves for election without party authorization. Assuming it is given and the member wins election, he is instructed "always to act in accord with the dispositions of the corresponding *fracción* and of the higher party organ in the locality." He may also be asked by the National or Sectional Conventions at any time to relinquish his post, either temporarily or permanently.

Members desiring a non-elective public post must also obtain express party authorization, and violation of this directive will bring expulsion from the party. Those who hold posts in which public moneys are involved, are required to make a sworn declaration of their wealth and belongings before a judge.[16] A certified copy must be forwarded to the appropriate party organ. Ultimate political authority is also emphasized by directing all members who discharge political, judicial, or adminis-

---

[15] *Estatutos*, Chapters XIV-XV, Articles 126-28.

[16] Betancourt set an example by so doing when he left the Junta Presidency in February 1948. Cf. Betancourt, *Venezuela: Política y Petróleo* (México: Fondo de Cultura Económica, 1956), p. 804 (see note 14).

trative duties for the State to deposit with the leadership a signed letter of resignation with the date left blank. Either Conventions or Executive Committees therefore have the power at any time to remove a party member from office by filling in the date.

Despite the stress placed on discipline by the statutes, one of the fundamental beliefs of the party since its inception has been the importance of full and free debate, of unqualified internal democracy. This has been coupled with strong admonitions to maintain monolithic unity and a solid front outside party circles. A characteristic expression was made, ironically, by Raúl Ramos Giménez after the XI National Convention.

"The election of the CEN and the Political Bureau of the Party has been an electoral product of our internal democracy. We have elected a directorate without impositions of any sort, with every person . . . giving his own opinion. . . .

"The assembly recognized the merits of those it elected as well as those it did not elect, but it considered freely, as happens in our Party, without pressure of any sort. . . ."[17]

The mutually related concepts of internal democracy and party discipline are discussed and reiterated throughout the range of party literature. Excellent excerpts are contained in *La Cartilla del Militante* of 1961, which presented in abridged form the basic outlines of party programs and organization. Widely distributed to the AD rank-and-file, the *Cartilla* admonished members that internal democracy rests upon the perfect exercise of their rights. "The main ones are to discuss *all matters* at meetings; directing organs must always and consistently gather information on the thoughts and views of inferior organs." Furthermore, "messianism, the cult

---

[17] Raúl Ramos Giménez, *La XI Convención Nacional* (Caracas: Ediciones "Leonardo Ruiz Pineda," May 1961), pp. 21-22.

of the personality and the practice of *caudillismo* are ever excluded."[18]

Elsewhere the same document declares that the "counterpart of internal democracy is discipline." Such discipline must be regarded as a member's duty. He is expected to spread and to defend party doctrine, to participate fully at organizational meetings, and to accept the ultimate submission of minority to majority and of lower to higher party bodies. A further declaration underlines the party position on disciplinary matters.

"As a revolutionary party, the internal life of the A.D. is regulated by constant and severe criticism, and of self-criticism in the directing and also the base organizations. . . .

"All members, without exception, must admit to such self-criticism within the open and ample spirit of revolutionary fraternity and companionship. He who does not accept it . . . is incapable of accepting the discipline and collective wish of a democratic organization. To him it becomes necessary to apply sanctions. . . ."

The organs of disciplinary action were outlined in an earlier chapter. The AD's chain of judicial organs parallels the politico-geographical pyramidal arrangement. Decisions are always subject to appeal on a higher level, and may be taken ultimately to the National Convention. The five degrees of severity range from censure and admonition to a definite and irrevocable expulsion from the party. The gravity of the latter leads to the inclusion of a set of conditions under which this ultimate punishment may be applied.

No member of Acción Democrática may be expelled unless he is adjudged guilty of one of five crimes: The misappropriation of party funds; any affiliation with another party, which includes complicity with enemies of the AD; continued and unrepentant violations of dis-

[18] Acción Democrática, *La Cartilla del Militante* (Caracas: Secretaría Nacional de Propaganda, 1961), p. 33.

cipline; deeds committed in basic contradiction to the
party line; or "errors or crimes that compromise the
prestige of the Party . . . incurred in public or private
life."[19]

Procedural protection of rights is given the party member in addition to the ultimate right of appeal. When
a disciplinary body has received a case for judgment, it
must take action within thirty days; this includes the
questioning or appearance of all individuals who may
be involved. The decision itself must follow within a
further period of fifteen days, and this is communicated
to party executive organs during the succeeding five
days. The time limits may be extended if further information seems desirable.[20]

Disciplinary organs are subject to the same regulations, and violation of these statutory requirements may
itself be a cause for reversal of a finding against a party
member. When a final decision is arrived at, it is made
public, with the terms of the sanction set forth in writing. The sole exception comes in the case of the mildest
possible punishment—a declaration of censure or admonition—which will not be widely publicized even within
the party, but will only be sent to the relevant executive
organ, ordinarily the Comité Ejecutivo Seccional. It
should not be assumed that the AD judicial tribunals
are intended merely to enforce discipline on the membership at the lowest level. Their activities have included
the expulsion of the MIR and AD-ARS members, although in these cases the disciplinary power was largely
a formality taken in the wake of those conflicts. A somewhat different example was that of Cirilo J. Brea in the
early 1940's, when that Caracas party official was expelled for financial dealings that were regarded as questionable.

The careful attention given to discipline by Acción

---

[19] *Estatutos*, Article 116.
[20] *Estatutos*, Article 122.

Democrática is illustrated by the practice of the parliamentary *fracción*. The Comité Directivo de la Fracción Parlamentaria, headed by Gonzalo Barrios from 1958-1963, meets once a week when in session. Attendance is mandatory for all party senators and deputies, not excluding even the party President himself. A careful attendance record is kept by one of the parliamentary secretaries. Both absences and tardiness are recorded; unexcused violations can result in a fine of a certain percentage of the legislator's pay for the day. Comparable checks are kept on attendance at congressional sessions themselves. There too the emphasis on regular participation is heavy, and fines are levied against unjustified absenteeism.[21]

An organ that was recently created for disciplinary purposes is little-known and rarely spoken of. The Comisión Nacional de Control y Vigilancia is barely mentioned in a two-line insertion under Article 39, which also draws up the regulations governing it. A newly created organ that has evolved largely as a result of contemporary factionalism, it is empowered to oversee party discipline throughout the organization, from top to bottom. Its existence is not only unpublicized, but it is new enough that the *modus operandi* as well as effectiveness are uncertain. The basic intention is that of strengthening the force of party unity and discipline at all levels.[22]

Unlike the preceding analysis of party leadership, it is not feasible to set forth a detailed breakdown on the nature of the AD rank-and-file. The role of labor and the *campesino* movement in party membership is discussed in Chapter IX.

AD membership figures go no further than the state-by-state listing that results from occasional censuses. The most recent pair were held in August 1959 and May

[21] Interview with Victor Mazzei Gonzalez, November 29, 1962.
[22] Interview with Said Moanack, November 27, 1962.

1962, providing data for the following remarks, as shown in Figure 7. Comparative figures show an increase in membership of nearly 14 percent over the three-year period, as enrollment rose from 795,061 in 1959 to 903,282 in 1962. The state figures show a slight shift in the centers of party strength.

In 1959 the strongest region in terms of membership was Lara with 80,200. Zulia followed with 60,000 and Falcón with 56,000. Sucre was actually second with a total of 78,000 members, but the AD customarily divides it into the regions of Cumaná and Carúpano. By May 1962 the leading state on the basis of membership was Zulia, which had registered a tremendous increase, virtually doubling to a total of 116,561. This was actually a result of renewed and highly vigorous organizing by labor and especially by the petroleum workers' federation. The rapid growth of the working population around Maracaibo gave further impetus to the increase.

Zulia was followed by Lara which, although dropping to second place, registered a slight increase to 81,924. Monagas rose to third position with 56,471, and Falcón fell to fourth with a total of 54,220. The combined sections of Sucre again totaled second highest in the nation—93,797—but were split for party purposes. The most striking increases, other than that of Zulia, took place in Bolívar and Aragua. A population explosion plus an intense campaign of party proselytization more than doubled its membership, from 15,806 to 35,735. In Aragua the swelling of membership went from 11,828 to 24,004. The major reduction came in Yaracuy, which dropped sharply from 43,128 to 21,979. This was a result of the ARS split led by Raúl Ramos Giménez, a native of the state. The most insignificant change was that of the territory of Amazonas, where the alleged reduction was four members.

FIGURE 7*

AD MEMBERSHIP—CENSUS

| State | August 1959 | May 1962 | Change | |
|-------|-------------|----------|--------|--|
| Anzoátegui | 55,802 | 48,600 | − | 7,202 |
| Apure | 19,450 | 12,344 | − | 7,106 |
| Aragua | 11,828 | 24,004 | + | 12,176 |
| Barinas | 18,300 | 10,576 | − | 7,724 |
| Bolívar | 15,806 | 35,735 | + | 19,929 |
| Carabobo | 27,837 | 41,330 | + | 13,493 |
| Cojedes | 15,400 | 14,462 | − | 938 |
| Cumaná | 38,000 | 50,303 | + | 12,303 |
| Carúpano | 40,000 | 43,494 | + | 3,494 |
| Libertador (DF) | 18,500 | 24,999 | + | 6,499 |
| Vargas (DF) | 6,000 | 8,629 | + | 2,629 |
| Falcón | 56,000 | 54,220 | − | 1,780 |
| Guárico | 41,500 | 48,882 | + | 7,382 |
| Lara | 80,200 | 81,924 | + | 1,724 |
| Mérida | 30,000 | 29,320 | − | 680 |
| Miranda | 36,588 | 36,911 | + | 323 |
| Monagas | 55,000 | 56,471 | + | 1,471 |
| Nueva Esparta | 17,472 | 18,473 | + | 1,001 |
| Portuguesa | 31,000 | 35,267 | + | 4,267 |
| Táchira | 32,200 | 33,249 | + | 1,049 |
| Trujillo | 40,000 | 46,328 | + | 6,328 |
| Yaracuy | 43,128 | 21,979 | − | 21,149 |
| Zulia | 60,000 | 116,561 | + | 56,561 |
| Amacuro | 3,650 | 7,825 | + | 4,175 |
| Amazonas | 1,400 | 1,396 | − | 4 |
| Totals | 795,061 | 903,282 | + | 108,221 |

* Figures released by the Comité Ejecutivo Nacional and published in *La República*, July 25, 1962, p. 1. Also *El Nacional*, July 25, 1962, p. 1.

# CHAPTER VIII

# Program and Doctrine

Over the years Acción Democrática has evolved a number of programmatic theses on which to base its pragmatic political decisions. The formative years of the movement saw the beginning of a long evolutionary process, with the gradual refinement of the broad rubrics under which the party formed and grew. The so-called doctrinal thinking of the movement under the semi-organized ARDI tended to lessen the impact of marxism generally, but nothing of a positive nature emerged during the first exile. Under ORVE came the first systematic effort to catalogue the broad areas demanding consideration by the national government.

The *orvista* program made public in July 1936 was broad and general, but the identified areas of emphasis included political democracy, constitutional revision, a reconsideration of social and economic policies, a revision of petroleum policy, and renewed educational efforts. As suggested earlier, the topics were treated in imprecise terms, and the major emphasis was placed on basic constitutional and electoral reforms aimed at the establishment of direct democracy. Non-political aspects of policy were set forth with only a degree of true understanding, and the movement at that time was ill-equipped for detailed, insightful proposals. The identification of problems and of national ills was far easier than the framing of new policies.

With the attempted reorganization into the Partido Democrática Nacional and the expulsion ordered by López Contreras, the PDN found itself occupied primarily in organizational matters. The single important *pedenista* programmatic declaration came as a result of the I National Conference of September 1939. The political thesis adopted at the meeting contained yet another broad analysis of the national transformation believed mandatory for progress. A brief discussion listed the various social factors regarded as basic to a successful balancing of national interests: the *latifundistas* and foreign enterprise, the middle classes, the rural element, and the urban working class.

The official program of the PDN was divided into four sections. The first stated the commitment to a democratic state, resting on a full expression of the national will. Constitutional guarantees were to be made effective and personal liberties extended to all. The municipality was praised as the "true basic cell" for national political life, and a career public administration was cited as necessary to the development of human resources.

The second and most lengthy part of the program was entitled "Economic Reconstruction of Venezuela." Although much was stated in broad terms, there were outlines of future policy for agriculture, banking and finances, and industrial development. The importance of the state was made explicit, marking an important commitment beyond earlier statements. "Analysis leads to the conclusion that the State is, in fact, more capable in Venezuela than in other Latin American countries to exercise . . . a determining influence on the life of the Nation."[1] The PDN document called for the "scientific study of the economic possibilities of the country," and a Council for National Economic Development was also proposed. Equally strong commitments to state action appeared in calls for state assistance in technical and credit programs for agriculture, state corporations for the direct exploitation of subsoil riches, and a controlled parcellation of lands and estates seized from the family of Juan Vicente Gómez.

[1] Major excerpts from the PDN declaration are found in Luis Troconis Guerrero, *La Cuestión Agraria en la Historia Nacional* (Caracas: Editorial Arte, 1962), pp. 203 ff. Less incomplete details also appear in Acción Democrática, *Acción Democrática: Doctrina y Programa* (Caracas, 1962), pp. 42-51.

The same kind of extensive commitment was suggested in the third and fourth sections of the program. The third, dealing with labor legislation, called for an extension of benefits to workers in all sectors and asked for an obligatory social security law. Collective bargaining was advocated, and a statement was included which called for government assistance to labor in the task of constructing a national labor movement. The fourth and final section in somewhat more general language dealt with a reform of education and health. Items to be effected by a PDN government included modernization of secondary education, encouragement of teachers' colleges and vocational schools, and a program to eradicate illiteracy from Venezuela.

The aforementioned official political thesis was brief, but deserves requotation in part: "The Partido Democrática Nacional has a solid doctrinal base, having been organized after extended analyses of Venezuelan reality. Its program and tactics have not been born of capricious will . . . but from a dedicated study of the fundamental problems of the Nation. . . ."

The analysis of national socio-economic problems was summarized in the following words: "Venezuela is a semicolonial, semifeudal country, a country tied to economic, fiscal and political imperialism, with an economy predominantly rural, chained by *latifundismo* and incapable in its present form of assuring for itself economic independence and progress. . . ."

A concluding statement of general concepts reiterated the desire for general democratization of the national economic structure: "We conceive of democracy as nothing less than a government that at the same time permits the free play of social forces and . . . by means of abolishing the *latifundio*, as well as feudal property relations, intervenes in the cities through industrial production and the development of commerce, especially and admittedly protecting . . . in particular the sectors benefitted the least in the present distribution of riches, namely the manual workers and the intellectuals. . . ."[2]

Not until the middle 1940's did the movement—by that time organized as Acción Democrática—begin to present more careful analyses of national problems. Yet once again circumstances made the effort difficult; involvement in the operation of national government during the *trienio* limited the available time. The actual policies of that government give a better idea of the party outlook during those years than can any collection of party statements during the same period.

The decade of clandestinity following the 1948 counter-revolution was a trying experience for the AD in many ways, but one of the positive side effects was the opportunity to engage in extended reconsideration of Venezuelan problems and party doctrine. There was more time for the leaders to discuss and debate such matters. Following the ouster of the dictatorship in January 1958, the AD's massive effort at revitalization included the formation of study groups and commissions charged with the task of revising, expanding, and writing appropriate party "theses," as they are customarily called.

Six such theses were prepared and published separately in booklet form. All but one dealt with programmatic and doctrinal matters, and they have not been superseded as of January 1964. Their organization, logic, and insight are variable; furthermore, they are not as detailed as are many current pronouncements from *adeco* leaders. At the same time, they provide the skeletal structure around which practical political decisions might be formed. Although the documents were somewhat dated by the 1963 presidential campaign, and the original tone had been partially pejorative—in criticizing the Pérez Jiménez

[2] *Acción Democrática: Doctrina y Programa*, pp. 20ff. This 1962 publication brought together all the current party "theses" referred to herein; early pages contain parts of the PDN declarations of 1939.

dictatorship—an examination of them is useful in understanding the broad thrust of AD thinking in policy-making areas.[3]

## Programmatic Bases

All party theses are based to an extent upon the broad programmatic statement adopted in 1958. The latter is divided somewhat unevenly, but eight areas are outlined: political, economic and fiscal, administrative, social, health and general assistance, agricultural, educational, and international. Three identifiable strands run throughout the text of these discussions: political freedom and democratic government, advocacy of state planning in all areas, and state responsibility for the betterment of all segments of Venezuelan society.

General political commitments[4] begin with a statement in support of the principles of authentically democratic government "as the true expression of the will of the national majority." Thus, "sovereignty resides in the people, who exercise it by means of the organs of public power." Attention to elections includes a proclamation of the right of secret and direct suffrage for all Venezuelans of 18 years or more, regardless of sex and literacy. Impartiality by the government in all electoral processes is promised, as well as strong sanctions against any and all forms of fraud or dishonesty.

Freedom and civil liberties are guaranteed in Article 3, and the party further promises "absolute respect for all religious beliefs, reaffirming the principle that religion

[3] The only such party document *not* drawn upon for this chapter was Acción Democrática, *Tesis Organizativa y Estatutos* (Caracas: Editorial "Antonio Pinto Salinas," 1958).

A detailed if highly sympathetic account is contained in Part III of Robert J. Alexander's study of the 1958-63 Betancourt administration and its policies: *The Venezuelan Democratic Revolution* (New Brunswick: Rutgers University Press, 1964).

[4] Acción Democrática, *Bases Programáticas* (Caracas: Editorial "Antonio Pinto Salinas," 1958), Chapter I, Articles 1-7.

is a matter reserved to the individual conscience." The defense of civilian government is stated in a brief treatment of the military that praises its high moral and material state of development. The AD pointedly continues that the armed forces "are conceived as a body that does not deliberate politically, and that submits to the authority of the freely elected organs of the State and to the norms that are determined by the Constitution and the Laws of the Republic."

The same broad principles carry over into the international field.[5] Acción Democrática supports peace and continental friendship. Consequently, it ratifies "conciliation, arbitration, and discussions in the International Organs that must be the means for the resolution of conflicts among States." Sovereign equality for all peoples is defended, and the AD declares its frank solidarity with regions that are struggling to achieve their destinies as independent nations. There is strong support of the principles of international cooperation that constitute fundamental bases for the United Nations and its agencies.

The party makes clear its general position with reference to the Organization of American States and to its hemispheric neighbors. It promises to defend and to work for the OAS, that the latter "may transform its present bureaucratic and inoperative mechanism into that of a living, militant organ, one that represents and reflects the will of the American peoples to live with liberty, eradicating poverty and the lack of culture while advancing their backward economies." There is an additional determination to work for the establishment of an effective, inter-American juridical body, to which private citizens of the Latin American countries can have recourse in seeking to defend themselves against violations of basic rights and freedoms. Then the party shortly but sharply declares its irrevocable opposition to dictatorship

[5] *Ibid.*, Chapter VIII, Articles 1-8.

and to unrepresentative governments, whatever their ideological orientation.[6]

A concomitant paragraph deals with social progress and reform in the hemisphere, and the AD links itself with all efforts to develop the economic resources of Latin America for the welfare of the people. Eventual political and economic integration of the hemisphere is desirable; the party urges "political and cultural understanding with the other nations of Latin America in order to defend democratic institutions and win effective respect for the rights of man and for the flourishing and permanent exaltation of spiritual values."

The AD commitment to state planning continues to be strong and basic. Among the programmatic statements that buttress this position is the set of proposals dealing with economic and fiscal policy. Venezuelan natural resources are to be regulated by the state in order to develop the industries which can contribute to a transformation of the economy. Thus the party insists upon the power of review and, if necessary, revision of existing contractual agreements. This is the philosophy that underlies much of its thinking on petroleum, which is discussed below. The AD favors foreign investment, but asserts that it must be judged wholly in terms of potential or actual contributions to national economic development.

Further economic proposals call for the creation of state enterprises for the greater exploitation of natural resources. Industrialization is to be intensified through

[6] In the early 1960's, the so-called "Betancourt Doctrine" became widely known throughout the hemisphere. As Betancourt himself stated, there was nothing original in this decision not to recognize unconstitutional regimes, for it was basic AD doctrine for years. In essence it parallels the older Tobar Doctrine of inter-American diplomatic practice.

The doctrine was extended and continued when Raúl Leoni succeeded Betancourt in 1964 and soon refused to recognize the military regime which seized power in Brazil early in the year.

the drafting of detailed, expert plans leading to general economic diversification. These measures are to aid in a shift of emphasis away from Venezuela's historic tradition as an importing country. Article 10 calls for the use and management of the national budget in favor of a planned development of the economy, thereby "maintaining the measure of public investment at a high level, orienting public expenses toward a geographic distribution that favors all regions of the country in accord with the needs of progress. The budget will be used to compensate for the variations of the economic cycle, in harmony with the policy that the *Banco Central* applies in the same respect.

Fiscal arrangements also reflect the importance of the role of the state. Article 8 calls for a readjustment of the fiscal system, based on the revision of tax burdens and a redistribution of national income. Later provisions deal with import duties and an official change of commercial policy in order that national industry may thrive and develop, notably in cases where raw materials are being used. The banking system is also to be subject to state intervention, "to the degree necessary for assuring the fulfillment of plans of economic development that will have been elaborated and put in practice." Article 14 continues that the *Banco Central* "will constitute the essential instrument for the direction and selection of credit to benefit in the most rapid fashion the development of the economy."

State planning looms large in party administrative proposals.[7] The party promises governmental participation in the creation of "a national organ within the governmental structure whose task will be the coordination of the planning process on a national, state and municipal scale." An administrative career service is urged, as well as austerity and honesty in the management of public affairs. A judicial career service is endorsed. A passage

[7] *Ibid.*, Chapter III, Articles 1-7.

that cannot be unduly comforting to business interests states that, because private activity is not only useful but necessary for national development, the state will undertake a conciliation with private interests, "reserving to itself the direct control of basic activities and of public utilities."[8]

Chapter IV of the *Bases Programáticas* deals with a series of "social" principles that apply in large part to social security and to labor conditions. They illustrate both the party commitment to a large state role and the lasting concern and responsibility of the government for the improvement of the citizenry. Attention goes directly to the establishment of an effective system of social security as protection against social ills. To make this objective more realizable, Acción Democrática calls for an extension of social security coverage, bringing a larger number of people under its purview. The Instituto de Seguridad Social is to be reorganized as a means of improving services and increasing general efficiency in the application of its loans and indemnities.

The improvement of labor conditions is basic to the series of proposals here advanced. The party urges elevation of the workers' cultural and technical level through technical schools, a workers' university, scholarship programs for advanced training in technical industries, and specialized training programs. The rights of labor are recognized in detail, including equal pay for equal work, the right to strike, a viable minimum wage, a reduction of regular working hours, a gradual increase in the length of annual vacations with pay, special credit facilities, and legislative protection for working women and minors.

Further articles under Chapter IV set forth an additional set of rights applicable to the labor movement. Reform of existing legislation is considered obligatory, while management is required to cooperate with workers

[8] *Ibid.*, Chapter IV, Articles 1-24.

in the negotiation of contracts. Furthermore, the workers are to participate in the over-all benefits of the enterprises in which they are employed; an arrangement in profit-sharing is held appropriate. The right to organize is basic, and Article 24 further declares that parallelism in labor organizations should be eliminated. It concludes that "Acción Democrática supports the right of workers to group in their specific organizations and, as a consequence, considers that the State must guarantee free association and the perfect exercise of labor liberties. Labor freedom must be effective and must be fully guaranteed."

Chapter V extends state responsibility even further, outlining questions of health and social assistance. All Venezuelans have the right to a guarantee of state facilities in the protection of their health, and the state must work out a detailed plan whereby the sectors of the population most vulnerable to social and health infirmities may be provided for. The sanitation program must be intensified to reach all areas of the Republic, and national health services are to be organized through a geographic and functional distribution that contemplates in effective form an equal concern for citizens everywhere.

Acción Democrática reiterates its demand for a raise of living conditions, with particular attention to the peasant population. The latter is to receive greater attention from teachers, social workers, and government employees dedicated to effective collaboration in the rural centers of social assistance. The state is to impose an automatic obligation on all those entering national medical schools, insisting that these young people lend their professional services to rural areas for a specified period, as a part of their over-all training.

The party's programmatic commitment to education is sketchy in outline,[9] but the details are filled in through the proposals of the *Tesis Educativa* traced later in this chapter. Here one should note merely that the party

[9] *Ibid.*, Chapter VII, Articles 1-9.

promises to "make effective the obligation of the state in the creation and support of institutions and services sufficient for the attaining of the country's educational needs." Teachers are to be encouraged in their efforts and are to be made fully cognizant of the true meaning of democracy. There is a pledge to extend and to modernize the newly created pre-school education system, offering greater aid and guidance to mothers during these early years in a child's life. Professional training is reemphasized, new technical and workers' training centers are to be opened, and adult educational programs are also proposed.

An additional section in the *Bases Programáticas* considers briefly the agrarian question, but it is more satisfactorily studied in the specific *Tesis Agraria*. Proposals here[10] urge the transformation of the *latifundista* system of property ownership and the abolition of "the semi-feudal rule of land exploitation." The dispossessed peasants are to be provided with land and with sufficient means of work. A policy of hydraulic development is important, and agricultural credit organs stand in need of expansion. Furthermore, the elevation "of the economic, social and cultural level of the peasant and of the agrarian workers, with an end to increasing the productive capacity of agriculture," will be encouraged by specialized training and extension services under state control.

Such expressions of programmatic principles give but a general picture of the party's over-all commitment, and it becomes fully meaningful only through a reading of the several specific "theses" which were adopted and published at the same time. Although the entire series fits together somewhat awkwardly, its components can generally be grouped under three headings, which will be analyzed in the remainder of the chapter.

[10] *Ibid.*, Chapter VI, Articles 1-6.

## Labor and Agriculture

Students of the Venezuelan labor movement can find a valuable source of information in the first two-thirds of Acción Democrática's seventy-one-page *Tesis Sindical.* Its account of the history of labor is, while anything but unbiased, a highly useful and instructive one. The final third turns to party involvement with and attitudes toward the labor movement, and this is most directly pertinent here. Thus the party declares the labor movement to be its intimate ally.

Labor is not to be considered merely as an offshoot of the AD, for the party insists that the movement must maintain its independence. Labor's own commitments and interests in relation to management and to the representatives of business and commerce must be pursued differently than the party would. At the same time, it is felt that labor "can be an important ally of Acción Democrática in its struggle for a free Venezuela, a Venezuela for Venezuelans, since this is the struggle of the people themselves." Furthermore, ". . . the workers of Acción Democrática will be alert so that the Party does not deviate from its trajectory . . . in the maintenance of internal Party unity, so that no fractionalist bud of any importance can spring forth to weaken the historic role that the Party is called to fulfill."[11]

The AD continues with a frank statement that it conceives of the peaceful Venezuelan revolution as a gradual march toward socialism. "We believe," it explains, "that in the first stages the revolution will be predominantly democratic, but that it may have to travel toward even more distant formulas. . . ." The workers who are party members, then, are committed to the goal of eventual socialism, and to the continuing party effort in this direction that will lead to a system "tinged with purified democratic socialist flavor."

[11] Acción Democrática, *Tesis Sindical* (Caracas: Editorial "Antonio Pinto Salinas," 1958), pp. 70-71.

Acción Democrática discusses the labor movement within the broader context of an alliance of classes fighting for the democratic revolution, and it explains that, for Venezuela, a party is required that blends together the many diverse interests. As the AD declares at one point, it aims to be "a united front of manual and of intellectual workers—nationalistic, revolutionary, antifeudal and anti-imperialistic." This is the basis for its various statements on the revolutionary tasks of the workers, which ultimately take form in a list of concrete proposals.

As the party declares elsewhere, the state must have preeminent control over the national economy. This need not mean the nationalization of industries, but governmental guidance must certainly be great. Control of production and of the level of productive forces will determine the pulse for all society, and therefore the party cannot in good conscience reject its responsibilities. Labor must recognize that its contribution to society can be great.

The full force of Venezuelan labor can only be achieved through a strong, united organization, capable of confronting and defeating the regressive, conservative property holders. In a blunt and uncompromising passage the party states that ". . . workers possess nothing more than their strength and force of labor, and they live by selling it to the capitalists who possess the instruments of production. Between these two classes a continual war is waged, an unceasing war that is . . . ended only when those owners of a progressive mentality agree to make concessions to the workers."

Acción Democrática goes on to cite the individual labor union as the fundamental source of the movement's strength, and the party reiterates the belief that only such an organization can effectively channel the feelings, the needs, and demands of the workers. In a passage that is heavily underscored, the AD states unreservedly that "of all human groupings, the union is the most fundamental and the most permanent. . . ." While the labor movement remains democratic and independent, it can never become an appendage of a political party. For the AD, this is as it should be, for it seeks merely an alliance with the workers' organization.

"A labor organization can be allied to a political party whose parliamentary action guarantees the workers a progressive widening of social legislation, a policy of workers' housing, social security, and legislation on minimum salaries, a strict rule on vacations, etc. For many years, organizations of workers have been oriented toward and guided by the AD political philosophy. . . ."

The *Tesis Sindical* in Chapter XII specifies thirty individual points which are regarded as prerequisites for a minimum program of labor. A brief synthesis indicates at least the highlights. First is a dedication to economic development within an industrial framework. The AD, declaring that the process of industrialization must be founded on essentially new and different bases, continues with the proposition that modern concepts of industrial development include social justice for the worker and responsible cooperation from management. Industrial development means, among other things, an improvement in wages and in the availability of social services. Organized labor can and must fight for the winning and indeed the extension of such measures.

Controls of various types are recommended. One mechanism is a fiscal policy giving preferential treatment from the state to those who are most conscientious in the modernization of equipment and improvement of technical training. A high premium is placed upon the rational organization of production, including series of commissions for import controls, of which the participation of workers is a feature. Labor is to receive further responsibilities through participation in the administration of state-operated enterprises as well as a share in the creation of industrial, commercial, and agricultural co-operatives.

Acción Democrática is convinced that the labor move-ment, through concerted efforts, can itself contribute greatly to the welfare of the working man, and the work-ers themselves are enjoined to struggle relentlessly against all concentration of capital and all monopoly. They are called upon to oppose concessions that may be regarded as onerous. Foreign enterprise is not to be opposed and attacked irrationally, *per se*, but it must not be permitted to exert undue influence. Labor's role should include the tireless struggle for the formation and expansion of state-controlled industries.

In this connection the AD calls upon labor to insist that the export of raw petroleum and raw iron be pro-gressively reduced. Long a champion of refineries on Venezuelan soil, under Venezuelan control, the party stresses the point while repeating its own acceptance of foreign enterprise so long as there is an effective policy of non-intervention in domestic affairs. International ties are to be strengthened through various forms of ex-change and communications, although the Venezuelan labor movement is not encouraged to join a hemispheric or international organization.

Interspersed through the pages of the labor document are occasional references to agriculture and to rural work-ers. At least in theory, Venezuelan agriculturalists are re-garded as but one component of the national labor move-ment; thus the national peasant federation is a member of the massive national labor organization, although in many ways a separate entity. So long as a major portion of the population remains rural, agricultural problems will receive a great deal of interest. Agrarian reform has been a political battlecry and demagogic catch-phrase in Venezuela for years, as indeed in much of Latin America. Yet this is a complex problem, one with which the government is currently wrestling. Official party doctrine is set forth in the *Tesis Agraria*.[12]

The historical evolution of the land problem in Venezuela is the focus for the preliminary discussion in this document, and the over-all tone is more explicative and less provocative than the labor thesis. Yet the underlying sentiment seems identical, namely, that "two great social sectors in Venezuela polarize the struggle between democracy and dictatorship: the people and reaction." The people are understood as those lacking the privileges of power and of riches. Furthermore, three social classes can be distinguished therein: the working class, the peasants, and the middle sectors—the latter including small merchants, artisans, employees, and technicians. The forces of reaction are represented in the city by the commercial, banking, and industrial bourgeoisie, and in the countryside by the tiny *latifundista* minority that has always held something above 80 percent of the tillable land.

The Venezuelan land problem has many facets, of which *latifundismo* is only one. Yet this is undeniably a major obstacle to effective agrarian reform. Acción Democrática observes that it is both a spiritual and material hindrance, and it provides one of the principal points of departure for any comprehensive plan. The party has not wavered from the general tenets of the short-lived Agrarian Reform Law of 1948, three of which were outstanding. First was the belief—still entertained today—that a national consensus has been created in favor of a need for reform, a measured, legislated reform without violence or resort to illegal confiscatory practices. Secondly, reform should not affect large holdings where efficient and modern means of production are employed. Finally, just prices must be paid for all lands expropriated from their owners.

[12] Acción Democrática, *Tesis Agraria* (Caracas: Editorial "Antonio Pinto Salinas," 1958).

The AD's *Tesis Agraria*, having cited its continuing attachment to the general outlines of the 1948 reform legislation, attempts to explain what it calls a rejection of both a capitalist and a socialist approach. The first, it argues, leaves intact the structure of land ownership, merely changing the relations of feudal production to those of capitalist production. This may provide a solution to production problems, but social malaise remains, and the desire for land ownership on the part of the rural masses will not have been fulfilled. "Given the historic obligation of the AD toward the dispossessed peasant masses," says the party, "this solution must be rejected." It would be treason for the AD to adopt an approach whereby a wealthy agrarian bourgeoisie would be encouraged and strengthened.

Having thus disposed of what is allegedly the capitalist approach to land reform, the party turns toward the socialist solution, of which it is equally critical. It believes that the nationalization of land and the socialization of agricultural production would create an economic system in basic contradiction to the juridical structure of a country still founded largely upon private property and free enterprise. The solution, therefore, is in a different direction. "We cannot be collectivists, nor *minifundistas*, nor capitalists in the extreme. We must not be animated by any preconceived prejudice. Each country must realize the agrarian reform that is appropriate to its needs. . . . The political, social, demographic and economic reality of the country . . . is what must stamp its course and the positive forms of change."

Four fundamental objectives are offered as the concluding points of this particular party document. The first deals with the expropriation of lands and their distribution to the landless. According to the AD, an estimated half-million peasants work lands to which they hold no legal claim, or which are no more than three *hectares*. Of these, some 330,000 are heads of family;

neither they nor their offspring are full participants in the nation's economy, although potentially they might contribute substantially. Conditions can be altered so that their lives become essentially rural middle-class. This can be accomplished only through the endowing of the landless with their own property and titles thereof.

The numerous tenant-farmers and share-croppers, sometimes called *conuqueros*, can be converted into valuable contributors to the economy through provisions for credit, for technical aid, for irrigation projects, and modern granaries. These and other such services can be provided through a cooperative service, operated by the state, which "is the ideal system to abolish the disadvantages of small production while retaining the advantages of individualism." The so-called agricultural exploitative services, too expensive or complex for individual use, can be applied on a wide scale. Thus market facilities, credits, machinery, the availability of seeds, and other such aids are possibilities.

A second objective centers on the *tierras baldías*— government-owned lands that are lying unused and undeveloped. On these, the party urges the establishment of special agricultural colonies and communities. Through the formation of such complexes, not only are new fields put into production but the opening of new territory leads to a demographic concentration that facilitates the kind of technical services and health and sanitation improvements that are impossible except on a community basis.

The party's agricultural position includes one seemingly misplaced item, as its third objective refers specifically to the national sugar cane industry. This is on a different level from the other objectives. Finally, the AD insists that agrarian reform should not be applied in such a way as to affect private enterprises that use modern technology in an effort to provide increased production. "Agrarian reform should only affect the unproductive *latifundio* and the feudal system of rental."

## Petroleum

Few aspects of AD doctrine have been expounded at greater length than its petroleum policy. The extraordinary dominance of petroleum in the national economy has made it the keystone of any serious plan for diversification. The earnings of the industry must provide in large part for the financing of educational and welfare programs. AD attention to the subject has been long-standing. The very complexity of the subject and its wide range of economic implications render impossible a detailed presentation within the scope of this work. The historical evolution of AD petroleum policy, as well as detailed legislative efforts from 1945-1948, are set forth at length in various portions of Betancourt's *Venezuela: Política y Petróleo*. More recent analysis has come from Betancourt's Minister of Mines Juan Pablo Pérez Alfonzo, in a study which examines the *perezjimenista* policies at length, as well as offering comparisons between Venezuela and other major oil-producers.[13]

In its *Tesis Petrolera*, Acción Democrática provides a basic outline of the principles from which detailed policy has sprung forth. Its central thesis holds that petroleum can, through proper planning, be used to encourage and hasten a more balanced economic development. Until the late 1950's, in the party view, the rapid growth of the petroleum industry was so oriented that there was no substantial variation to the national economic structure. A large part of the income derived from concessions and sales was used merely to pay for the enormous volume of imports that had built up during the ten-year dictatorship.

[13] Juan Pablo Pérez Alfonzo, *Petróleo: Jugo de la Tierra* (Caracas: Editorial Arte, 1961).

The AD strongly argues that increased petroleum exports failed to provide a true index of national prosperity. As evidence it notes that oil has represented up to 98 percent of the total value of exports, yet occupies less than 3 percent of the economically active Venezuelan population. Foreign investment has traditionally benefited itself more than it has contributed to the progress of Venezuela. It is this which leads the party to regard as mandatory the intervention or participation of the state in the continuing development and expansion of the industry. "Investments effected by foreign capital in our country . . . have converted it into a specialized producer of primary exports, to the detriment of the remainder of the national economy. These investments . . . basically benefit the industrial importers first and then, to a lesser extent, the country where the investment is realized."[14]

Referring back to the policies of the *trienio*, the *Tesis Petrolera* recalls the creation of the famous "50-50" policy, whereby Venezuela shared the profits evenly with foreign enterprise. In 1945 the party set an international precedent that was soon followed in the petroleum centers of the Middle East. On June 26 of the following year the AD government adopted the policy of receiving royalty payments in kind and not in money, in this fashion avoiding possible losses that might accrue through the devaluation of crude oil. Despite serious concern on the part of the petroleum interests, no precipitous action was taken. Fears of massive expropriation or of nationalization were never realized.

Indeed, the AD has always been forthright in its denial of intentions to nationalize the oil industry. In March 1948 the Gallegos administration designated a special commission to study the fundamental bases for the establishment of a state-owned refinery, with over-

[14] Acción Democrática, *Tesis Petrolera* (Caracas: Editorial "Antonio Pinto Salinas," 1958), pp. 24-25.

all diversification one of the anticipated results. Implementation of all proposed revisions was pending when the counter-revolution smashed hopes for reform at that time.

The concluding statements enunciated in the *Tesis Petrolera* are indicative of the AD position in recent years. "To construct a new Venezuela it is necessary to develop national industry. But the industry cannot prosper if a free, democratic, independent atmosphere does not exist. . . . We must gradually develop heavy industry as much as light." The AD therefore aspires to develop its over-all economic policy along the general lines set forth by Betancourt in *Política y Petróleo* when he insisted that a people who failed to manipulate and to develop its own natural resources would axiomatically find these riches exploited by foreign capital, with the danger being that of a deformed colonial mentality.

A ten-point set of "general propositions" attempts to outline positions that are consistent with preceding declarations. A national petroleum company was to be established that would deal in production, refining, sales, and transportation. This might be enforced and supported by the creation of a national petroleum fleet. The increased role of the state in the over-all direction and formulation of petroleum policy, would be buttressed by the denial of further concessions to private enterprise. State involvement, in short, becomes increased in the belief that "the participation of the Venezuelan state in all conversations of Governments and Enterprises on the sharing of markets . . . is irrenounceable. . . ."[15]

These proposals were to some extent intended for the transitional period following the return from exile and the recovery from the final years of Pérez Jiménez. The policies enacted by the Betancourt administration under the direction of Pérez Alfonzo were far more advanced. This is not a discussion of official policies dur-

[15] *Ibid.*, p. 39.

ing a given administration, but several features were outstanding. The government set up its own state agency for the development of petroleum, and by the end of the Betancourt term of office it was beginning to expand its activities. Pérez Alfonzo was personally prominent in the creation and strengthening of the Organization of Petroleum Exporting Countries (OPEC) to which Venezuela and several producers of the Middle East were charter members. Efforts to bring rationality to the setting and maintenance of prices on the international market led to collaboration among member states. The new administration inaugurated in March 1964 pursued similar goals.

An excellent summary of the importance of petroleum policy in the future of the nation was penned by Pérez Alfonzo while writing from Washington exile in June 1954.

"Venezuela has a great resource in its petroleum, but it is also faced with great responsibility. It must not impede a use of this resource to satisfy the needs of other peoples, but in protecting its own national interest, it must never let the industry become dilapidated.

"Petroleum is the principal of all indispensable fuels in modern life. . . . The future of the product is absolutely certain; its prices will continue to rise. Venezuela needs to maintain and even to increase the income it receives from petroleum. With a policy of just participation, the exploitation of present concessions is enough for the country."[16]

## Education

Educational policy has also been important in the framework of party doctrine, and the party leadership has included several of those prominent in the teachers' movement, such as Prieto, Núñez Sucre, Fermín, and Mora. The party "considers the educational process as

[16] Pérez Alfonzo, op.cit., pp. 83-84.

an important part of national reality. . . ." The resolution of educational problems implies the effort in turn to resolve all problems that confront the nation in political, cultural, and economic terms. Acción Democrática therefore argues that education requires a clear and definite orientation; this it attempts to set forth in its educational declaration.[17]

The party specifies three major goals for national education. First is the promotion and defense of the democratic way of life. Next is the interpretation and transmission of the benefits of Venezuela's historical and social patrimony, with a view to the enrichment of national culture. Third is the effort "to form the personality of the Venezuelan within a concept of human solidarity, making him able to understand and to exercise the principles of democracy, . . . [helping him] to acquire an economic conscience as a good producer and good consumer; [and] to create and to enjoy the blessings of culture. . . ."

National education is intended to permit a solidification of the feeling for peace and coexistence among all nations—notably those of the Latin American community—while it also aims at helping the citizenry to become truly aware of Venezuela's geographic, socioeconomic and cultural reality, increasing the concern over and attention toward the great and pressing national problems that the masses are generally unequipped to confront. Fundamental to all proposals and goals is that public education will be free at all levels. Moreover, "the state should also lend social assistance to persons who for economic reasons cannot take advantage of educational services. Primary education will be obligatory for all inhabitants of the country and when the present levels of educational maladjustment have been

[17] Acción Democrática, *Tesis Educativa* (Caracas: Editorial "Antonio Pinto Salinas," 1958).

overcome, this obligation will be extended to middle-level education as well."

The party's broad educational policy rests in large measure on its belief that the entire educational system must be controlled as a coordinated, systematic entity. The existing gaps at various levels of learning are such, in the AD view, that unified control is necessary to tie together effectively the individual efforts being advanced at different planes of learning. The details need not be repeated here, but six areas are cited: pre-school education, primary, middle or secondary, normal training for non-university teachers, special or technical programs, and finally, university studies.

Considerable attention is given to the administration of education. The party believes that the inefficiency and incompetence of educational administration in the past has been seriously prejudicial to the nation's best interests. Only through careful organization and the integration of functions into a general, logically consistent framework, can such administrative obstacles be minimized and eventually eliminated. As the party puts it, "the direction, orientation, administration and supervision of the educational system, at all levels, will be exercised in the Ministry of Education, in which will be centralized and unified all activities, services, and educational establishments of the Republic." Only the military schools are excluded.

Educational supervision is felt to be an appropriate function of the state, a responsibility that cannot be delegated, even though intermediaries can serve in the implementation of policy. Supervision must be thorough and effective, and a gradual elevation in the quality of teaching is mandatory. An extensive program of recruiting and training of new school teachers is intended to provide for the necessary personnel. Above all else, perhaps, the *Tesis Educativa* stresses in this context that education must be carefully *planned*. The role of the state is once more a significant one, and it is upon the wisdom and intelligence of the Ministry of Education that the AD rests its hopes for the vitality of educational reforms.

Private education in Venezuela is predominantly Catholic, and this fact has given the party no end of difficulty. Its disputes with the clergy over the years have been aired previously, especially the divergence of views experienced during the *trienio*. The problem of government control over church-operated schools may always be ticklish. It seems pertinent to pursue a briefly tangential examination of the broad *adeco* attitude toward the Church. There has been uneasiness on the part of the clergy in the past—a distrust that has only recently been dissipated to a degree. The party views on religion have been consistent ever since the years of the PDN.

Carlos D'Ascoli in November 1936 expressed the general opposition of the movement to the introduction of the clergy into politics, at the same time insisting that there was no basic concern with dogma. "In confessional matters the PDN permits the amplest freedom of conscience; its members will be able to profess religious ideas of any creed. At no time and in no way and under no circumstances will the Party intervene in questions that it considers the internal matters of its associates. Never will it adopt positions that might wound the religious sentiments of the Venezuelan citizenry."[18]

Controversy over its position vis-à-vis the Church first plagued the party seriously during the debates of the Constituent Assembly early in the *trienio*. A major point of disagreement revolved about religion and private education. The AD insisted that, while it was fully respectful of the Catholic Church, it was determined in its advocacy of religious freedom. Disagreement at the time over a Junta decree favoring state support for pri-

[18] *Ahora*, November 4, 1936, pp. 1, 6.

vate schools fed the flames of dissension. A later proposal to change the constitutional reference to church-state relations as regulated by the 1824 Law of Ecclesiastical Patronage brought further debate over the true intentions of the AD concerning the Church in the field of religion.

The party's doctrinal position has been made quite clear; the declarations in the *Tesis Educativa* are scarcely equivocal.[19] The party "respects the freedom of teaching, interpreting it as a right that any person with accredited abilities may possess and enjoy. . . . Freedom of education . . . has the support of Acción Democrática, so long as its exercise is realized within the limitations demanded by the proper formation of a democratic conscience." Operating on this basis, the AD believes that the state should be privileged to authorize the creation of private institutions insofar as is deemed preferable. Furthermore—a point of much sensitivity—it believes that all private education falls under the purview and vigilance of the state. Thus, all private schools that desire official recognition, must receive certification from the Ministry of Education.

Private institutions, in the opinion of the AD, must not practice any form of discrimination. In the words of Chapter IV, Article 4, equal access should be available to all students under the same standards, "without limitations of race, religion, nationality, social position, condition of birth or philosophical creed." The state will have the power to cancel or withdraw any and all forms of authorization previously conceded to an institution of private education, if in its judgment the conditions of learning are not conducive to proper educational

---

[19] This is not to imply that there is no anti-clerical sentiment in the AD. Especially among the older leaders of the party—whose experience included antagonism from the Church in years past—there is still a heritage that is highly suspicious of the least hint of clerical intervention in politics.

methods, or when the learning is administered in a fashion "not in accord with the democratic principles [of] the Constitution."

The party stand on education has been fairly consistent through the years. Perhaps the best brief statement of fundamental principles came from the opening articles of the 1948 Organic Law of National Education.

"Education is an essential function of the State and all the inhabitants of the Republic have the right to receive it freely in official facilities. . . .

"Education has as its object the achieving of the harmonious development of the personality, forming citizens preparing for life and for the exercise of democracy, fortifying the sentiments of nationality, nourishing the spirit of human solidarity and promoting national culture. In its content . . . it is oriented preferentially toward the value of work as a fundamental civic duty . . . and the development of the productive capacity of the Nation."[20]

## International Affairs

Although no single party thesis in recent years has been focused specifically on international affairs, there have been frequent references to related questions. As suggested in the brief mention of the AD programmatic bases, the party has established two broad objectives. The first advocates political democracy and independence universally, while the second centers on the importance of Latin American solidarity. Each of these goals has been encouraged or supported in various ways during recent years; on at least one occasion, interestingly, there has been a divergence between the official party position and the policy adopted by the government.

One major element of the first objective is the insist-

[20] Chapter I, Articles I and 2 of the 1948 Organic Law of National Education, passed shortly before the overthrow of the Gallegos government.

ent withholding of diplomatic recognition from non-constitutional governments of the hemisphere. This policy was pursued during the *trienio* and resumed under Betancourt in 1959. Thus Venezuela withheld recognition of the regimes which seized power by unconstitutional means in Peru in 1962, Honduras, the Dominican Republic, and Guatemala in 1963, and Brazil (by the Leoni administration) in 1964. This so-called Betancourt Doctrine, simply a modern version of the Tobar Doctrine, was adopted even on occasions when the immediate practical repercussions—as with Brazil in 1964—appeared unfavorable.

Within hemispheric circles the AD-dominated government followed a policy demanding multilateral action against dictatorships both of right and left. Thus the Betancourt administration at the Sixth Consultative Meeting of Foreign Ministers at San José in August 1960 voted for sanctions against the Trujillo dictatorship, which had launched an assassination attempt against Betancourt from the Dominican Republic. Equally stern positions were taken against the Castro regime in Cuba, culminating in the discovery of clandestine, Cuban-supplied arms in November 1963, the subsequent investigation, and the July 1964 foreign ministers' gathering which called for the breaking of all ties with the island nation.

Recognition policy has also provided a source of dispute with regard to the position of the Soviet Union. During the *trienio* there had been no relations with the USSR. Betancourt also withheld recognition after 1959 although the party itself officially backed a reestablishment of relations. Another such disagreement—again concerning a temporary rather than fundamental issue—came with the party reception given Dominican presidential candidate Viriato Fiallo shortly before 1963 elections in that country. Betancourt himself preferred Fiallo's opponent Juan Bosch, and was reportedly highly displeased when Fiallo was as cordially received as Bosch.

Two additional occurrences reflect the broad AD approach to international affairs, although not specified in basic party doctrine. First was the founding in 1950 of the Inter-American Association for Democracy and Freedom. Meeting in Habana with the participation of Betancourt and other *adecos*, it was succeeded a full decade later by a second gathering, held in Maracay. National revolutionary and Christian democratic parties from throughout the hemisphere attended to discuss matters of common interest. One further example of party dealings with the hemisphere followed the creation of the Latin American Free Trade Area (LAFTA). Despite statements in praise of this regional development, the Betancourt administration delayed a final commitment to it; Raúl Leoni came to office in 1964 before the creation of conditions in Venezuela which the AD felt should precede its membership in the organization.

The general direction of the AD's international policy through the years, in short, has sought an independent position which demands full support of political democracy in the hemisphere, collaboration with the United States on a basis of mutual respect and equality, opposition to totalitarianism of either right or left, and an effort to give meaning to hemispheric multilateral action intended to strengthen and unify democratic sentiment throughout the region.

# PART THREE

The Party and Venezuelan Society

CHAPTER IX

# The Party and Organized Labor

In addition to its continuing contact with the people through a heavy and unremitting schedule of rallies, meetings, or educational and social events, Acción Democrática has established and maintained ties with most of the nation's major interest groups.[1] Indeed, much of its electoral strength is so founded. Although precise figures are lacking, party leaders estimate that at least 50 percent of the total AD vote in 1958 came from the labor movement. The two major organizations, the Confederación de Trabajadores de Venezuela (CTV) and the Federación Campesina de Venezuela (FCV), currently comprise some 1,300,000 members.[2] The electoral importance is seen when this figure is compared with the 1963 electorate of slightly over three million.

The dominance of the AD in these organizations underlines the degree to which the party relies on labor support.[3] While efforts to be in the fullest sense a *policlasista* party have been reflected in various segments of national life, the preponderance of the party's labor activities makes feasible a separate treatment. The next chapter will then devote itself to certain of the organized elements of society that do not fall effectively within the purview of the national labor organization and the peasant federation.

[1] In the present context a broad definition of interest groups is used. The relative lack of functional specificity in some areas of Venezuelan society and politics makes a narrow definition of limited value.

[2] Confederación de Trabajadores de Venezuela, *Federaciones Nacionales* (Caracas: Imprenta de la CTV, 1962), p. 3.

[3] *Adeco* leadership does not deny the importance of labor to the party, although there is a universal denial that the party resembled in any real way a "labor party."

### Relations with the Labor Movement

The origins of organized labor in Venezuela can be traced back at least as far as 1919, when workers in the graphic arts founded the Gremio de Profesionales de Artes Gráficas. They even had the temerity to organize a strike of a day-and-a-half in January 1920, and won their demands for a salary increase. They were soon followed by the shoemakers with the Gremio de Zapateros in Caracas, under the leadership of a Spanish socialist, José Tostón. A variety of small societies were also born, and helped provide a minor escape valve for tensions during the Gómez era. The dictator himself founded a Federación de Trabajadores, and Venezuela became a member of the Organización Internacional del Trabajo.[4]

A democratic labor movement under Gómez was wholly impossible, but some small beginnings were made, and they swiftly took root following his death. The real impetus to organized labor came in 1936 and 1937. The pioneering union of the modern labor movement was founded in 1936, the Asociación de Linotipistas under the leadership of Pedro Bernardo Pérez Salinas. Valmore Rodríguez also founded the first union of petroleum workers in Cabimas on February 27, 1936.[5] The subsequent spread of locals through the oil regions was rapid, culminating in the historic if mismanaged strike at the close of 1936. Although López Contreras ended the work stoppage by decree on January 22, 1937, it is regarded as a milestone in the evolution of Venezuelan labor.

The gathering of the first national congress of workers in December 1936 also provided encouragement. Over 200 delegates, claiming to represent 150,000 workers,

[4] The reminiscence of a pioneering figure is P. B. Pérez Salinas' "El Momento Obrero en Acción Democrática," *A.D.*, no. 170, September 13, 1961, p. 15.

[5] For a detailed account, see Jesús Prieto Soto, *El Chorro: Gracia o Maldición* (Madrid: Industrias Gráficas España, 1960).

met in Caracas shortly before the official crackdown. It gave impetus to the subsequent clandestine campaign for improved workers' rights, and the founders of the illegal Partido Democrática Nacional included a substantial number of young labor leaders, most of whom are prominent in the AD. Their numbers embraced Pérez Salinas, Malavé Villalba, the late Valmore Rodríguez, González Navarro, Luis Tovar, and Juan Herrera.

During the following years under López Contreras, the quiet struggle between the democratic leadership of the PDN and the communists was paralleled by competition inside the nascent labor movement. With the former led by Betancourt and the latter by the Machados and Juan Bautista Fuenmayor, the fight was an extended one; until the coming of the Medina administration in 1941, it was generally believed that the communists held the upper hand, especially among the petroleum workers. The early months of the Medina government saw, if anything, further progress in the communist effort.

After initial uncertainty, the communists under Fuenmayor became allied with Medina, giving extensive support to the regime. In return, paragraph six of the existing constitution, which prohibited the communists to organize, was removed. And as the commitment of the government to the Allied cause in World War II became unqualified, the communists became even more loyal to the President. As late as a 1943 congress of petroleum workers in Caracas, the communist position was strong. The combination of gradual concessions from the regime and superior financing of communist-controlled labor unions prevented Acción Democrática from winning the upper hand. The situation was startlingly reversed in March 1944, however, at the second Convención Nacional de Trabajadores in Caracas.[6] The

[6] The first such congress had been that of late 1936.

presumed purpose was the founding of an official national labor organization, and among the foreign visitors was the Mexican Vicente Lombardo Toledano of the Confederación de Trabajadores de América Latina (CTAL), who provided unofficial advice to the communists.

Some ninety-three unions were represented, including twelve of fourteen petroleum locals. At a meeting to choose members of an executive committee, an AD participant proposed a fifty-fifty split in representation. The communist refusal, based on their alleged control of a majority of the delegates, caused a crisis that concluded with the withdrawal of AD members. Shortly thereafter the Medina government decided to withhold legal recognition from all unions whose delegates had not withdrawn with the AD forces. This perplexing move has never been adequately explained. In any event, its upshot was that the AD labor organizers were able to revise a number of the unions whose legal recognition had been withdrawn.

The curious nature of the affair was further underlined by the immediate reaction of the AD, which was to lash out at the government action as sharply as at the communists. On April 1, 1944, Raúl Leoni called the dissolution a throwback to the days of Gómez. "This stroke of the executive pen," he charged, "destroyed in seconds the work of several years, while the liquidation of loyalty on the part of many unions threatens to be followed by still further arbitrary moves on the part of the President."[7] The end result, nevertheless, was a great boost to Acción Democrática in a critical time.

Toward the close of the Medina period, then, the labor movement was progressing, and the position of the AD had picked up perceptibly. The October Revolution, as Pérez Salinas has written, "opened a new era

---

[7] A.D., no. 109, April 1, 1944, p. 1.

for our labor movement, because it permitted the application of true freedom of association, the right of contracts and of collective bargaining, and the success of important labor matters. . . ." For political as well as ideological and historical reasons, the AD turned to the workers as a major source of support, and labor was given sympathetic encouragement in the series of disputes that dotted the next three years. Creation of a separate Ministry of Labor under Raúl Leoni permitted a fuller degree of collaboration.

During the *trienio* Acción Democrática proclaimed a lengthy set of principles that went far in the establishment of modern trade unionism in Venezuela. A partial list includes a maximum eight-hour day, equal pay for equal work, annual paid vacations, indemnification in case of a breach of contract, the right to strike except in public services, and shared benefits for all. The AD also provided for the special protection of women and minors, official government mediation or conciliation in the resolution of labor-management conflicts, and collective bargaining in the negotiation of labor contracts.[8]

Minister of Labor Leoni was active in official encouragement of the organization of both industrial and agricultural unions. Fully half were *campesino* groups, which was something of an innovation. Including unions of both types, in 1946 alone some 500 new unions were organized, more than doubling the number that existed when the AD took power. The most powerful single organization was the petroleum workers' federation (FEDEPETROL), formed in March 1946 at Caracas. A national labor organization was created for the first time; in November 1947 the Confederación de Trabajadores de Venezuela (CTV) was founded, with *adeco* Pérez Salinas serving as Secretary-General.

Organizational skills within the CTV were evident,

---

[8] Luis Lander, "La Doctrina Venezolana de Acción Democrática," *Cuadernos Americanos*, IX, julio-agosto 1950, pp. 29-30.

and the support of a virtually unchallenged government was of inordinate assistance. By the time of the fall of Gallegos there were an estimated 300,000 members. Three years earlier there had been no more than 50,000.[9] It was a palmy time for labor, given the abrupt and extraordinary change in official attitudes. Government mediation resulted in a series of pro-labor decisions as consistent and unbroken as the anti-labor policies of earlier regimes. It was small wonder that remaining communist elements were shunted aside. And the AD electoral victories in the three contests from 1945-1948 were so great that the divided communists were out-polled 21-1. As Luis Lander later remarked, such a margin of triumph fortified the thesis that the major barrier to communism was simply "giving satisfaction to the just desires of the masses."

While the labor movement abetted the aggressiveness of the AD during the *trienio*, it was not an adequate counterweight to the armed forces when the military stages its counter-revolution. This is not to minimize labor's influence in supporting the regime through moments of unrest and violence that did not include organized military opposition. During an attempted right-ist revolution in April 1947, for example, FEDEPETROL publicly declared that the oil workers backed the National Constituent Assembly and the government against any and all attempted insurrections. It promised "to respond with all means at our disposal . . . [to combat] the enemies of democracy and the working class."[10]

The rise of dictatorship brought a revival of unhappy times for Venezuelan labor. With AD leaders hounded into exile, remaining communist labor leaders tempo-

[9] Interview given by P. B. Pérez Salinas to Robert J. Alexander, cited in Alexander, *Communism in Latin America* (New Brunswick: Rutgers University Press, 1957), p. 263.

[10] Edwin Lieuwen, *Petroleum in Venezuela; A History* (Berkeley: University of California, 1954), p. 105.

rarily stepped into the vacuum. Their ascendency proved transitory, for the regime began extending its repression to all workers' organizations. Soon one wing of the communist party was urging a unity pact with the AD, although the appeal was denied. Only a single union—the Federación de Trabajadores del Distrito Federal—was permitted to enjoy some degree of freedom, and it maintained ties with the communist World Federation of Trade Unions. In due course its operations were restricted, and early in 1952 the military regime created its own trade union federation, the Movimiento Obrero Sindical Independiente de Trabajadores (MOSIT). A few leaders were ex-communists, but the federation was carefully watched by the authorities. By the end of 1954 communist labor leader Rodolfo Quintero had been forced to leave the country, and communist influence lessened slightly with the passing of time.

The eventual establishment by the regime of its Confederación Nacional de Trabajadores (CNT) aided in Pérez Jiménez' control of labor. Despite the construction of a characteristically luxurious and inappropriate labor center in Caracas, the size of the labor force was cut back some 25 percent. Collective bargaining and meaningful strikes were prohibited. During the dictatorship, AD labor leaders set up a CTV-in-exile as a propaganda organ. Clandestine pamphleteering within Venezuela included messages aimed at the workers; the first of these appeared less than a month after the counter-revolution. Yet little could be done inside the country until January 23, 1958, and the ouster of the regime.

The year 1958 was one of turmoil and activity for labor. The formation of an informal coordinating committee soon took the form of the Comité Sindical Unificado Nacional, which set about the lengthy reconstitution of the democratic labor movement. In August 1958 the acting head of this body, José González Navarro, reported that seventeen state and four industrial federations had been constituted, with a national Congreso de Trabajadores de Venezuela meeting in November to rebuild the CTV. Designated the third such congress—succeeding those of 1936 and 1947—it met on November 14, 1959, and ran through the next eight days.

At the first meeting the delegates came together in the Nuevo Circo to hear collective greetings from their leaders. González Navarro declared that a total of 685 industrial and commercial unions and 1,250 peasant leagues had been organized, grouped into 22 regional or state federations and 9 industrial federations. An estimated 1.1 million workers were affiliated and represented at the congress.[11] Of 1,065 delegates, the AD represented the greatest number. The party claimed the membership of 561 delegates, followed by 210 communists, 152 *copeyanos*, and 142 *urredistas*.

Supporters of other parties, however, placed representatives on the CTV board of officers for the first time. There were three communists on the Comité Ejecutivo, two each from COPEI and URD, and one unaffiliated. The six *adecos* included President González Navarro, Secretary-General Malavé Villalba, Secretary of International Relations Pérez Salinas, Secretary of Agriculture Quijada, Secretary of Press and Propaganda Andrés Hernández Vásquez, and Secretary of Statistics and Employment José Marcano.[12]

The labor movement continued to widen its membership and to extend the organization. By mid-1961 it claimed 1,935 unions, 23 state federations, and 12 indus-

[11] Basic information about the conference, the composition of delegates, and the texts of speeches is found in José González Navarro, *Discursos de la C.T.V.* (Caracas: Litografía Barcelona, 1960).

[12] Confederación de Trabajadores de Venezuela, *Recopilación de Informes, Acuerdos, Resoluciones y Recomendaciones; III Congreso de Trabajadores de Venezuela* (Caracas: Imprenta Nacional, 1960).

trial federations, with a total membership of some 1,300,000. Of the industrial federations—omitting for the present all discussion of the peasant federation—the largest membership was that of the Federación de Trabajadores de Construcción, which claimed 125,000 construction workers in 33 affiliated unions. Next came 44,000 members of 23 affiliates of the sugar cane workers, the Federación de Trabajadores de la Caña de Azúcar, and fourth was the politically powerful Federación de Trabajadores Petroleros de Venezuela (FEDEPETROL), with 40,000 members belonging to 43 unions.

Only a few labor organizations have not affiliated with the CTV, of which the most prominent politically is the Comité de Sindicatos Autónomos (CODESA), founded a few months after the fall of Pérez Jiménez and based on some 20,000 workers whose leaders saw a need for a Catholic labor movement.[13] Other non-CTV organizations of some prominence can be mentioned. One is the teachers' Federación Venezolana de Maestros (FVM), while another is the powerful journalists' Asociación Venezolana de Periodistas (AVP).

The industrial federations of the CTV are normally national in scope, and they negotiate contracts on an industry-wide basis. The regional or state federations, on the other hand, include all kinds of workers. Unions may often embrace all workers in a given enterprise or establishment, and individual variations are substantial. Financial bases are laid by member dues, which are collected only in certain industries through checkoff arrangements, while in others the problem of dues-collection is difficult. Outside financial help from the government is relied upon, and under present circumstances this understandably strengthens labor's ties with Acción Democrática.

[13] The christian democratic COPEI, however, has continued to work within the CTV itself; several *copeyanos* have been officers of the CTV Comité Ejecutivo.

The political affiliation of the CTV with the government and with the AD sometimes follows curious lines. The national labor law prohibits the trade unions from having political affiliations; AD party doctrine is also firm on this point.[14] Nearly all major labor leaders are national figures in their political parties, however, and the clear majority of these are members of Acción Democrática. While other parties have been represented, the majority of AD labor leaders has permitted the party to maintain close ties with the national confederation.

Labor leaders of the three major parties have emphasized since 1958 that the CTV does not participate in partisan politics; they claim that those who run for political office on a party ticket do so as individuals rather than as CTV leaders. There are no "official" labor slates of candidates or even lists of preferences. Although perhaps theoretically accurate, however, this is drawing an exceedingly fine line. President González Navarro in his New Year's address on December 31, 1960—his last such message before the division of the labor movement—reiterated this view while strongly endorsing the major aspects of the governmental economic program, including details regarding employment and related labor problems.[15] The government coalition of AD and COPEI was paralleled within the CTV, where *adecos* and *copeyanos* easily combined to form an effective majority on all major issues.

The Venezuelan labor movement entered a new phase in mid-1961, the termination of which was uncertain as late as 1963. A series of events led to the virtual creation of two labor movements, the dominant one re-

[14] Acción Democrática, *Tesis Sindical* (Caracas: Editorial "Antonio Pinto Salinas," 1958), p. 42.

[15] José González Navarro, *Discursos del Presidente de la Confederación de Trabajadores de Venezuela* (Caracas: Publicaciones de la C.T.V., 1961), pp. 6-8.

maining the official CTV, democratic in outlook, favorable to the Betancourt government, and controlled by AD and COPEI leaders; the so-called "non-official CTV" was formed by extremists and communists following their expulsion from the CTV. The division developed into an additional split when the *arsista* faction broke away. Eventually the rival organization became known as the Central Unica de Trabajadores de Venezuela (CUTV), which itself splintered at the end of 1963. The prospects for the complete reassertion of supremacy by the regular CTV were strong at that point.

These virtual defections from the CTV were tied up with political party disunity, and the division became perceptible when the revolutionary marxist faction of the AD separated in early 1960 to form the Movimiento de Izquierda Revolucionaria. By the close of 1960 the *miristas* had aligned themselves closely with the communists, and a continuing squabble among the leaders of the CTV found the pro-government AD-COPEI majority warring with the extreme leftist, anti-government PCV-MIR coalition, to which a few URD labor leaders joined for purposes of political gain. The constant haggling back and forth on the Comité Ejecutivo proved increasingly detrimental to the advancement of labor.

As the rift within the leadership widened, González Navarro called an extraordinary meeting of CTV leaders in Caracas on June 16, 1961. It was decided that action was mandatory, thus the next national convention was called into session. The fourth labor congress was held from December 8-11, 1961.

Long preparation in both industrial and regional federations had preceded the gathering, and a number of locals had held new elections. Extremist hopes of broadening their strength within organized labor were dashed by the overwhelming triumph of the pro-government forces. Although votes in some instances were close, the

AD won in 32 of the 36 member federations.[16] In local elections the AD won 188 of 243 times without any alliance. In conjunction with COPEI it won 12 more, while COPEI took 7 on its own. Thus 207 of 243 contests went to supporters of the government coalition. The PCV-MIR alliance won but 16 elections, adding 9 more when joined by the URD. The URD won 9 times by itself, and there were 2 cases in which unusual non-AD alliances won.

With its control thereby assured, the regular leadership pushed at the meeting for the expulsion from the CTV of ideological elements which were unwilling to coexist with the majority. "We are . . . going to eradicate . . . the illegal strikes planned in certain areas behind the backs of the workers' majority. . . . We are going to fight to the very last the present policy of violence against public services and utilities, a policy exemplified by the burning of public vehicles and the assault of local stores."[17]

The majority on the Comité Ejecutivo found its task lightened due to the collaboration and—in a sense—intervention of Rómulo Betancourt. The President of the Republic at the opening session extolled the freedom of the labor movement, pledging continued cooperation from his administration. While giving tacit support to the purging of extremist labor leaders, he sought increased sympathy and support for his government by condemning roundly the recent metropolitan violence, bus-burning, and rioting that had caused a suspension of several constitutional guarantees. "I want to ask you," he called out, "if in any form the suspension of guarantees has affected you?" The delegates cried their denial, and Betancourt went on to add, "I was about to reestablish

[16] *Hispanic American Report*, XIV, no. 12, February 1962, p. 1106.

[17] José González Navarro, *Ante el IV Congreso de Trabajadores de Venezuela* (Caracas: Imprenta Nacional, 1962), p. 11.

them, but then came the recent events, including an act of piracy through the hijacking of an Avensa plane, thereby endangering over forty persons, as well as violent street demonstrations when we broke relations with the totalitarian and despotic Cuban regime."

Delegates subsequently heard a report calling for a new executive committee. One was duly elected, while communist, *mirista*, and *urredista* labor leaders were expelled. Thus the division with the extremists was completed, but the unity of the movement was also shattered. Those who were ousted then called their own convention, organizing the so-called "non-official CTV" and undertaking a set of policies in opposition to those of the original confederation and of the government. Later the ranks of the new organization were swollen by *arsista* rebels, although with a very few exceptions the AD labor leaders were the staunchest allies of the veteran party leadership. The ARS dispute actually had relatively little effect on the labor movement; its impact was far greater on the peasant organization. The conflict within the Federación Campesina de Venezuela over the *arsista* challenge was also discussed, as will be seen in the next section.

Expulsion of the extremists and creation of a rival confederation had little immediate effect on the regular CTV. The most recent compilation of national figures—dated September 1962—listed a total of 331 locals, while the 21 regional or state federations embraced 431 affiliates. Thus a total of 762 held some 600,000 Venezuelan workers, while an additional 700,000 came from the 2,249 peasant leagues and unions.

Labor ties with Acción Democrática continued strong, and the AD has strengthened further its dominant position. With communist rivals outside the regular CTV and with COPEI labor strength still developing, the AD easily held a majority in virtually all unions. In January

1963, 7 of the 11-member CTV Comité Ejecutivo were *adecos*. All state directories or committees were controlled by the AD, with the sole exception of Táchira, where the *copeyanos* held a 4-3 margin. The majority of the committees of the industrial federations were also controlled by the AD, including 5 of 7 directors of FEDEPETROL, all 9 of the construction workers, 8 of 9 from the transport workers, and so forth (see Figure 8).

The history of the rival group has been a checkered one. In April 1963 the official name of Central Unica de

FIGURE 8*

CONFEDERACIÓN DE TRABAJADORES DE VENEZUELA

| I. *Industrial Federations* | *Affiliates* | *Directory*a |
|---|---|---|
| Federación de Trabajadores Petroleros de Venezuela (petroleum workers) | 40 | 7-5 |
| Federación de Trabajadores de la Industria Gráfica (graphic arts) | 9 | 7-6 |
| Federación de Trabajadores Portuario de Venezuela (port workers) | 11 | 9-9 |
| Federación Nacional de Trabajadores de la Industria de la Construcción (construction workers) | 34 | 9-9 |
| Federación de Trabajadores de la Caña de Azúcar y sus Derivados de Venezuela (sugar cane workers) | 28 | 7-7 |
| Federación de Trabajadores de Transporte de Venezuela (transport workers) | 34 | 9-8 |
| Federación de Trabajadores de la Industria de Bebida (food and liquor workers) | 15 | 9-9 |
| Federación Unificada de Trabajadores del Distrito Federal y Estado Mirando (DF, Miranda workers) | 68 | |
| Federación Nacional de Trabajadores de la Salud (health workers) | 46 | 9-7 |
| Federación Sindical de Obreros de Comunicaciones de Venezuela (communications workers) | 14 | 7-4 |
| Federación de Trabajadores Cigarrilleros y sus Similares (tobacco workers) | 3 | 9-7 |
| Federación de Trabajadores de la Industria Eléctrica de Venezuela (electricity workers) | 21 | 10-7 |
| Federación Nacional de Empleados (employee-types) | 8 | 7-6 |
| | 331 | 99-84 |

FIGURE 8 (Continued)

II. *State Federations*

| | Affiliates | Directory | | Affiliates | Directory |
|---|---|---|---|---|---|
| Aragua | 45 | 9-8 | N. Esparta | 15 | |
| Anzoátegui | 24 | 10-8 | Portuguesa | 11 | 9-8 |
| Apure | 8 | 9-8 | Sucre (Cumaná) | 25 | 7-7 |
| Bolívar | 21 | 9-5 | Sucre | | |
| Barinas | 9 | 7-4 | (Bermúdez) | 12 | 7-7 |
| Carabobo | 46 | 13-9 | Táchira | 19 | 7-3 |
| Cojedes | 9 | 7-6 | Trujillo | 31 | 9-7 |
| Falcón | 21 | 9-5 | Zulia | 60 | 7-6 |
| Guárico | 13 | 8-6 | Terr. Amazonas | 1 | |
| Lara | 26 | 9-8 | Terr. Delta | | |
| Mérida | 15 | 8-5 | Amacuro | 3 | 9-3 |
| Monagas | 17 | 7-5 | | | |
| | | | | 431 | 160-118 |

| | | |
|---|---|---|
| Industrial Federations | 331 | |
| State Federations | 431 | |
| | 762 | |

NOTES TO FIGURE 8

* Federations and affiliates taken from mimeographed material issued by the Confederación de Trabajadores de Venezuela on September 5, 1962. Figures regarding *adeco* leaders were cited by Raúl Leoni in a speech reported in *A.D.*, no. 238, January 19, 1963, p. 4. There were no rival denials of the figures, although it must be remembered that URD, AD-ARS, and extremist elements had been removed from the CTV.

a First column indicates total number of members for the federation's directory or board of officers; the second indicates those who are members of Acción Democrática.

Trabajadores de Venezuela was adopted and the pretense of being the "legitimate" CTV was dropped. The CUTV, including communists, *miristas, urredistas,* and *arsistas,* proclaimed a set of proposals which in many particulars resembled those of the CTV itself. Several wholly political declarations were issued, however, most notably a demand that the government release alleged "political prisoners" whose anonymity was never endangered. Perhaps its major criticism of the CTV was that it was essentially a partisan political organ of the government party rather than a representative of national labor interests.

The CUTV leaders in the rivalry with the CTV were President Horacio Scott Power of the URD, longtime communist Rodolfo Quintero as Secretary, and *mirista* José Marcano as Secretary of Labor. By the spring of 1963 the CUTV was claiming the control of 21 national and state federations, this in contrast to nearly 40 for the CTV. With the approach of 1963 elections the CUTV became increasingly strife-ridden. While the running battle with the CTV was increasingly articulated in terms of pro- or anti-government political declarations, the leadership of the CUTV began to crumble. What might have presented a substantial challenge to the CTV virtually collapsed as a result of inter-party rivalry within the CUTV leadership.

The dissension first arose from disunity within the URD itself. The party's labor experts divided down the middle; the moderates were unwilling to cooperate effectively with the communists and *miristas*, hoping that a non-revolutionary position might help them to strengthen their labor base after the December national elections. Such men as Scott Power were from the left wing of the Unión Republicana Democrática, however, and were not disposed to abandon a fairly radical and intransigent position. The continual disagreement rendered the CUTV almost totally ineffectual. By the end of 1963 Scott Power had fallen into serious disfavor with Jóvito Villalba and others within the URD, and the significance of the CUTV seemed past. In early 1964 individual CUTV unions began to move over to the CTV, drawn by continual appeals for unity from González Navarro. By May Day of 1964 the CTV's position was unchallengeable.

Even at that date a major disagreement centered about the question of affiliation with an international labor group. From 1948-1958 the exiled *adeco* labor leaders

had worked closely with the Organización Regional Interamericana de Trabajadores (ORIT), in some cases serving as active ORIT officials. It had been assumed that
the reconstituted CTV would join both ORIT and its
parent International Confederation of Free Trade Unions
(ICFTU). Communist influence in the immediate post-
1958 period opted in favor of their own Confederación
de Trabajadores de América Latina (CTAL) and the
communist World Federation of Trade Unions (WFTU).
Further disagreement stemmed from the preference of
some Catholic trade unionists for the International Federation of Christian Trade Unions (IFCTU). The issue
remained unresolved through several CTV gatherings,
until in 1962 the decision was finally made to join
ORIT and the ICFTU.

The development of the Venezuelan labor movement,
to sum up, has clearly been beneficial to the average
worker, and much of the credit must go to Acción Democrática. Always highly sympathetic to labor and convinced of its importance both to the nation and to the
party itself, AD contributed virtually all the non-communist labor leaders of importance. One of the major
factors in the continuing primacy of the CTV is the
presence of González Navarro, Malavé Villalba, Pérez
Salinas, Herrera, and others—all of them among the
founders of the modern labor movement, all of them
loyal *adecos.*

The AD when in power has been generous with labor,
beginning with the labor ministry of Leoni during the
*trienio* and continuing with the same man's presidency
twenty years later. Until 1958 the major competition had
come from the communists, who had been defeated during the *trienio.* The increasing vitality and strength of
the other democratic parties after 1958, however, was
reflected in the reduced unity within the CTV. Had it
not been for the continuing AD-COPEI coalition in

national government, the schisms within the CTV might have been more serious than they were.

One must note that the AD labor leaders are staunch and sometimes unyielding partisans. The party's labor wing was the first to denounce the disloyalty of Rangel and the Muchachos; it was also the labor wing that worked for the nomination of Leoni in 1963, a time when many others regarded him as the most partisan candidate the AD might put forward. And it has been the AD labor leaders who have been consistently the most stubborn in opposing extremist terrorism, urging when necessary the partial suspension of constitutional guarantees.

The record of the party in the history of the Venezuelan labor movement must be regarded as outstanding, but in the past few years it is somewhat mixed. The CTV has been a major bulwark of the government in opposing the lawlessness and terror of the far left, while it has been improving relations with the Venezuelan military to remove all suspicion of ambitions to arm the workers, as was the case in 1948. Yet the CTV leadership has also been exceedingly firm in maintaining its control over all labor, and has been aided mightily by governmental paternalism. The subsidy decided upon in 1958 by all the democratic parties has grown substantially, and CTV ties with the AD government have augmented the *adeco* position immeasurably.

With the change in government coalition in 1964, COPEI was no longer a partner in the administration. Given this fact, growing *copeyano* inroads into the AD's labor position may bring about a substantial revision in the makeup of national labor leadership. At the present writing, however, the ties of the party and the CTV remain close, and the AD is unlikely to yield its present position willingly. Although the CTV did not deliver the AD vote as anticipated in 1963 elections, most Venezuelan workers still favor the party. Nothing less than a collapse of the party or a major eruption within the labor movement seems likely to topple the AD. While the party remains in office, significant levers of power continue to be theirs.

## Relations with the Peasant Movement

The Venezuelan peasantry has always been a potential source of political power. Its sheer numbers are impressive, yet the backwardness of agricultural methods, the regional and local isolation undisturbed by an adequate communications and transportation system, and calculated avoidance of the land problem by many governments, have combined to relegate the *campesino* to a politically negligible position. Only within the past generation has this begun to change, until today the support of the peasantry has become an important pillar on which the constitutional government rests.

From early times the structure of territorial ownership in Venezuela has followed the familiar pattern of *latifundismo*, and this was, if anything, strengthened and consolidated during the Gómez era. The extreme centralization of land ownership led to continued decadence in the nation's agriculture, and the sudden rise of petroleum as the overwhelming economic determinant led to even greater neglect of agriculture. As in other areas of Venezuelan life, the death of Gómez marked a turning point; indeed, it made feasible the organizing of the peasantry into a group politically capable of making its demands heard.

Among the early leaders who appeared in 1936 was Ramón Quijada, who had briefly belonged to the Partido Republicano Progresista before joining the PDN. Perhaps the only *campesino* leader of significance to emerge at such an early date, he served on the executive committee of the 1936 labor congress, and was among the opposition figures expelled by López Contreras in 1937.

Formal organizational efforts among the peasants in the late 1930's were slight, but Quijada and a small band of colleagues began to make themselves known in the interior, as did Rómulo Betancourt.

Later *medinista* liberalization included the drafting of an agrarian law in 1945 at the instigation of the President. Yet the officially heralded incorporation of the peasant into national life was carefully designed to avoid any disturbance to the *latifundia*. Only *tierras baldías* could be used and, according to critics of government policy, the entire piece of legislation was but a facile maneuver intended to lull the awakening Venezuelan *campesinado* back to sleep. Thus the organization of the peasantry had been minimal until the October Revolution.

With Acción Democrática in power, however, party leaders began to work actively with the farmers and peasants. Quijada, Carlos Behrens, Tomas Alberti, and Daniel Carías began to organize peasant leagues. All members of the AD, they worked for the structuring of an effective organization to work in harness with sympathetic government officials. The original leagues were set up by Quijada in Aragua and Carabobo, and others soon formed in Sucre. Encouragement by the Labor Ministry was helpful, and two years after the overthrow of Medina it was feasible to organize a national peasant congress.

On November 15, 1947, the first Convención Nacional de Campesinos was held in Caracas' Teatro Coliseo. Assembled delegates formed the Federación Campesina de Venezuela (FCV) and elected Ramón Quijada President. Behrens, Carías, Alberti, and Luis Moreno filled out the five-man Comité Ejecutivo Nacional. Representation was by no means national, and the organization was rather fragmentary, yet it was a beginning that hinted at the potential importance of an organized peasant movement. A political thesis and program was adopted that set down for the first time in some systematic fashion an outline of necessary or desirable measures.[18]

The FCV report on land ownership—based at the time on 1937 data, the most recent then available—pointed out that the population included 59 percent who lived in groups of less than 1,000, while 75 percent of the population derived its sustenance directly from agricultural activities. Some 4.4 percent of the owners held 78.7 percent of the land, an estimated 2,705,888 *hectares*. The remaining 95.6 percent of land owners held only 21.3 percent of the land. Additional *informes* filled in the bleak picture, including an account of the social as well as agricultural problems resulting from the system of landholding, the prevalence of *conuqueros*, and the unproductive results of existing conditions generally.

The FCV arrived at the conclusion "that only resolute and energetic intervention by the Venezuelan State can prevent the bankruptcy of the national economy, achieving the material and spiritual emancipation of the *campesinado*. Only the Nation is able . . . to create a truly national agriculture . . . and to incorporate the peasantry into large-scale production. . . . Only the Nation can mobilize the peasantry to create an agriculture without *latifundistas*." A strong and united peasant movement was called an indispensable means of working with government authorities in the realization of necessary programs.

The over-all orientation suggested a sense of urgency on the part of agrarian leaders, and there were ideological touches of socialism. The FCV in this spirit proclaimed as a fundamental political principle "the democratization of territorial ownership . . . democracy under which the Federación Campesina de Venezuela will exercise its doctrinal and organizational action on the rural masses,

[18] Federación Campesina de Venezuela, *La Cuestión Agraria Venezolana; Tesis Política y Programática de la Federación Campesina de Venezuela* (Caracas: Tipografía Americana, 1948).

to the end of preparing them for socialism." Yet there were none of the proposals so common to revolutionary programs of land reform, and only scattered references to possible collectivism. FCV leaders were not ideologically sophisticated, but they knew from personal experience the woes of the peasantry, and they devoted themselves to organizing their followers while turning to the government for aid.

Agrarian reform and a basic restructuring of Venezuelan agriculture had been among the earliest programmatic goals of the men who in 1945 entered the revolutionary Junta, and the provisional government swiftly passed a decree dealing with the seizure of certain unoccupied private holdings, while the creation of the Corporación Venezolana de Fomento (CVF) in May 1946 was dedicated to the increase of agricultural production through central guidance. The program included improvement of livestock, financial credits for peasants, rapid mechanization, the improvement of feeder roads, and irrigation projects.

The land problem was fundamental; the Junta soon realized that basic reform was necessary rather than gradual or partial alterations. The result was the drafting of an agrarian reform project. Distribution of *tierras baldías* was stepped up, while plans were laid for the expropriation of further unoccupied lands, although only after judicial hearings setting a just indemnification for the owners. The commitment to an over-all program was formalized in Article 69 of the 1947 Constitution, and in 1948 the congress passed a reform law signed by Rómulo Gallegos on the third anniversary of the October Revolution. An Agrarian Reform Institute was established with statutory backing set at 3 percent of the national budget. This was in its formative stages when the military staged the November *golpe de estado*.

The peasant movement was frozen into inactivity by the dictatorship, and occasional outbursts were met with stern measures. Several hundred *campesino* organizers were jailed, the majority from Oriente and Zulia, where the movement had made early inroads.[19] Yet the initial efforts were not forgotten, and the return of democracy in 1958 brought a renewed cry for aid. It increased with the presidential campaign of Rómulo Betancourt, and peasant leaders from Acción Democrática campaigned tirelessly in their cause.

The return from exile freed Quijada and others for renewed organizational efforts, and in June 1959 the first Congreso Campesino de Venezuela was convened in Caracas.[20] Some 4,000 delegates came together in a massive meeting, elected a Comité Ejecutivo presided over by Quijada, and heard a lengthy speech by Betancourt setting forth his plans for agrarian reform. The reorganized Federación Campesina de Venezuela became an integral part of the national CTV, and several peasant leaders joined the CTV directorate. While organizational plans were laid, publicity centered on the eventual form of agrarian legislation. Quijada had already stated his conviction that "only with its perfect realization can be laid the bases to sustain the democratic regimes during the transformation from a backward and deformed national economy." The establishment of a democratic regime, based on true social justice, could only be achieved through the rapid implementation of agrarian reform, in Quijada's view.

"Agrarian Reform . . . must incorporate the great rural sector of Venezuelan society into the ownership of land, of financial and technical means of making the lands productive. . . . Agrarian Reform, I repeat, is the *desideratum* of those who struggle not for a democratic liberal bourgeoisie, but for a democracy that by adequate and just distribution of riches, becomes a model of

[19] Interview with Armando González, November 23, 1962.

[20] This was titled the "first" peasant congress despite the 1947 meetings.

democracy that serves as an example . . . to all the Latin American peoples."[21]

The government proceeded to enact agrarian reform, and on February 22, 1960, it was promulgated and signed into law by Betancourt on the famous battlefield of Carabobo, site of the final decisive battle in Venezuela's struggle for independence. The President declared that the nation, while enjoying the greatest per capita income in Latin America, had some 350,000 families—roughly one-third of the population—living on a bare subsistence level without owning property. He promised the investment of 2.5 billion *bolívares*—then some $550,000,000— in the next four years, devoted not only to the distribution of land but to such items as rural schools and sanitation, electrification of the countryside, and the construction of additional feeder roads. At the same time he warned against violent or illegal occupation of lands, "because in a rule of law such as we now have in Venezuela, nobody is authorized to take justice into his own hands."[22]

FCV President Quijada also spoke, expressing general satisfaction but including certain reservations. Referring to the older policy of simple colonization of new lands, he praised it as useful while adding that alone it was inadequate. He indirectly suggested that the new law might be placing undue reliance on colonization, and asked for further consideration of the size of lands being distributed to the peasants. He called on large landowners to reduce their traditional reliance on salaried agricultural workers.

Thus Venezuela began once more a serious effort to cope with its land problem. The present program is a

[21] *A.D.*, no. 40, February 7, 1959, p. 15.

[22] Rómulo Betancourt, *Reforma Agraria; Liberación Económica de Venezuela* (Caracas: Imprenta Nacional, 1960), p. 13. The text of speeches by Betancourt, Quijada, and lesser officials is included.

long-range project. While an interim assessment cannot yet be made, implementation of the program led to a schism in the peasant movement. The main factor was human—the sincerely dedicated but unyielding and intractable Ramón Quijada. The culmination of controversy over reform came in 1961, less than two years after initiation of the program. Even earlier, Quijada was at odds with directors of the Instituto Agrario Nacional (IAN) and the Banco Agrario y Pecuario (BAP), as well as *copeyano* Minister of Agriculture Víctor Giménez Landínez.

Impartial estimates of the dispute generally concur that the crux of the matter centered about two questions: the speed of implementation, and the personal ambition of Quijada. Quijada seemed unwilling to wait for gradual means to take effect; even at the cost of other government programs, he wanted rapid action on the agrarian front. His public statements increasingly reflected the thought that government measures were centered almost totally on the distribution of *tierras baldías*. He became disenchanted with what government spokesmen believed to be a mixed system including colonization, expropriation of lands through legal means, and related measures such as electrification and sanitation. Quijada set forth his concern at the AD Pleno Agro in the spring of 1961, where he found himself in a minority that opposed the views of IAN director Pérez Segnini, also an *adeco*.

The summer of 1961 was the lull before the storm; Quijada reopened the issue in September, voicing three major criticisms of the program. He forthrightly insisted that recent claims by the IAN that 35,000 families had been settled on one million *hectares* were outright lies. He stated that only 10,000 families had been placed, while the other 25,000 had been promised parcels of land that were not delivered. A sharp attack was also launched on the policy of colonization, which Quijada maintained was a deliberate deviation from the intended land re-

form in order to avoid a revision of *latifundista* structure
to that of democratic ownership. He also added gratuitous
attacks on Pérez Segnini, whose position he was widely
believed to covet. He hinted that occasional outbursts
of rural violence would increase substantially unless the
whole orientation and pace of the program were drastically revised.[23]

A joint press conference by Giménez Landínez and directors of both the IAN and BAP repeated previous
figures, pledging that the figure of 35,000 families was
correct. The following day Quijada reappeared to concede the distribution of lands for 35,000 families, but
he still claimed that many had not actually been settled.
At this point of uncertainty Quijada's increasing flirtation with the *arsista* wing of the AD complicated things,
for the peasant leader began to hint at his own possible
defection from the party.

Ramón Quijada, concerned with the fate of the peasantry, clearly was genuinely interested in promoting the
well-being of the *campesinado*. Unlike many AD leaders, his own views had been closely circumscribed by
his narrow interests, to the exclusion of other considerations. As the *arsista* schism began to develop, Quijada
rarely spoke in criticism or derision of veteran party
leaders. Certainly he did not share the deep mistrust of
Betancourt that motivated certain of the *arsistas*. Yet
such was his determination to recast the mold of the
agrarian program that he tenaciously refused to retreat
or even to entertain suggestions for compromise. The
other *arsistas* cultivated him assiduously, desirous of
obtaining his power and influence with the peasantry.

At the outset, perhaps, Quijada's personal ambitions
were relatively modest; it is not believed that his eyes
were on the presidency when the dispute began. How-

[23] An excellent if journalistic treatment is that of Enrique Rodríguez, "El 'affaire' Quijada," *Momento*, XXIII, no. 273, October
8, 1961, pp. 26-28.

ever, he was convinced that the estimated half-million rural votes for Betancourt in 1958 were actually his. Quijada then sought a greater share of autonomous power, and felt that Acción Democrática would be crippled without the support that he alone could deliver at the polls. Quijada was fully convinced that half of Betancourt's electoral support lay in his own hands, and that his personal position was undeniably ascendent within the AD.[24]

Increasingly embroiled in controversy within the Political Bureau of the AD as well as the Comité Ejecutivo of the CTV, Quijada announced that the Federación Campesina de Venezuela would boycott the fourth CTV congress in December 1961. When the labor leadership threatened to replace Quijada and the entire FCV directorate, he declared himself in favor of the ARS, and complications were multiplied yet again. December 1961 and January 1962 were in many ways the most turbulent and chaotic months in the history of Acción Democrática. While the party struggle raged within the CEN and the CDN, the labor movement expelled the extremists and saw them form a splinter group; the *campesino* leadership divided almost exactly in half. The future of the party was hanging in the balance, and the AD survival may well have been due to the decisive action by party leaders. Certainly they were instrumental in the eventual resolution of the series of disputes, as well as working to reorganize and rebuild following the expulsions.

Fighting Quijada after his declaration in favor of ARS, the CTV promptly intervened throughout the country in an effort to gain control of the state-level peasant organizations. The division was sharp, and ultimately 11 of the 23 FCV sectionals sent delegates to the CTV meeting, while the remaining 12 stood by Quijada and absented themselves. With virtually half the FCV rep-

[24] Interview with Carlos Behrens, November 23, 1962.

resented, therefore, the CTV proceeded to reshape *campesino* leadership, placing it under the presidency of Armando González, who had refused to follow Quijada out of Acción Democrática. The equal division of the FCV was further illustrated by the fact that, of its 13-man directorate, 7 broke away to form the Quijada nucleus, while 6 remained loyal to the AD and to the labor confederation.[25]

At the beginning of 1962 the issue was very much in doubt. With 11 sectional organizations and 6 peasant leaders supporting the "official" FCV, while 12 sectionals and 7 leaders followed Quijada and AD-ARS, the struggle was bitter. Agents for both groups fought for support in the interior, and the conflict was by no means bloodless. By February all but 4 state peasant organizations were controlled by the González leadership, and of those, the Lara *campesinos* ambiguously declared themselves in favor of Quijada but simultaneously in support of constitutional government and the official agrarian reform law.

Quijada insisted that the peasant masses were loyal to him and not to local leaders, but his own organization soon found itself defeated by a combination of persuasion and muscle. The peasant movement had still been in some ways poorly organized; Quijada had through the years become well-known with the country people, and his supporters had staffed various local or regional organs. At the same time, however, the amorphous quality of the *campesinado* made effective organization almost impossible. Confronted by the superior finances and manpower of the government-supported and CTV-backed peasant organization, Quijada had little real chance. The intervention of the government and of Betancourt himself further contributed to the final outcome.

Betancourt had spoken in favor of CTV-controlled forces publicly, and he spent hours welcoming delega-

25 Interview with Armando González, November 23, 1962.

tions of "loyalist" peasants in Caracas. Then in February he took an eleven-day tour of the interior, during which time he spoke at rallies in seven states, delivering titles of land each time. He announced that of 54,759 requests to the Instituto Agrario Nacional, 42,119 had been delivered. A total of 1,377,386 *hectares* valued at 325 million *bolívares* were involved.[26] Betancourt's trip—only one of many such jaunts during his presidency—was attacked by opponents as opportunistic campaigning. Supporters pointed out the value of Betancourt's appearing whenever possible as a way of personifying the government to uneducated and unsophisticated peasants whose support was important to the survival of the regime. There was some truth in both positions. For the present context, the value of Betancourt's popularity in the *campesino* fight was substantial.

The future of the González-directed FCV gradually improved throughout 1962. As late as June the challenge of the Quijada group was still substantial, and that month his supporters met in Caracas to proclaim his leadership. The official FCV also held a convention, with 3,825 delegates representing 3,124 organizations with a total of 743,725 members. González' presidency was reiterated and a new FCV symbol was adopted—that of an ear of corn, machete, and hoe. From June forward the weight of the CTV and of government support became tremendous. The administration aided through the use of the agricultural subsidy, as González himself admitted. All the parties in 1958 had agreed upon the need for a subsidy to the peasantry; in 1962 and after, such financial assistance went to followers and supporters of González' organization rather than that of Quijada. Additionally, peasant representatives to the Instituto Agrario Nacional and the BAP were named from the official FCV. It was also the official group that

[26] *Hispanic American Report*, XV, no. 2, April 1962, p. 146.

worked with the government in the implementation of agrarian reform.

Because of the subsidy, official recognition of *campesino* unions has to come from the government; the Minister of Labor sends a letter of certification to newly formed organizations.[27] Added to such official assistance was the continual awarding through the months of titles of land by the President. His popularity with the peasants little diminished after some four years in power, Betancourt lent all his prestige to the cause of the official FCV under González' direction. Quijada was powerless to prevent the loss of his remaining followers.

As has been seen, virtually half of the CTV members are actually peasants of the FCV. While the votes of petroleum workers and others can to some extent be delivered at election time, the same is not true of the scattered, often isolated *campesinos*. Under Quijada there was serious question about the unity of the peasants, and there was little to suggest that the situation would be basically different under González. The almost universal support for Betancourt in 1958 was less a sign of a monolithic peasantry than an overwhelming faith in one man, buttressed by a major organizational effort that involved many party leaders as well as avowed *campesino* directors. This became even more apparent when Raúl Leoni in 1963 was far less successful in the interior.

If the effective political control of *campesino* votes by FCV leaders is in question, the fact of a growing organization is not. Today's FCV includes both *sindicatos* and *ligas campesinas*, which are slightly different although the terms are commonly used interchangeably.

[27] González took pride in showing the author a large stack of documentary accreditations from the government to local unions and leagues. He also pointed to a permanent gold plaque on which the official FCV and his slate of officers was recognized as representative of the peasant movement.

The distinction is not an important one, however; the original peasant locals were formed as leagues, and even today tend to be smaller and more informal. The *sindicatos* are more fully organized, and invariably have a complete slate of officers and regularly scheduled meetings and elections. *Sindicatos* ordinarily will have no fewer than forty or forty-five members, while the leagues may in isolated areas be considerably smaller.[28]

The last set of public figures was released by Armando González at the time of the June 1962 "official" convention. At the time there was a membership of an alleged 460,425 peasants, formed into 2,249 organizations. To these were added 875 *fraternales* with a representation of 283,300. *Fraternales* were neophyte groups in the process of formation, applying for FCV membership and asking the government for recognition. Thus a total of 3,124 organizations with a combined membership of 743,725 attended the conference. In the next five months, according to a subsequent interview, an additional 122 organizations came into the FCV, adding yet another 50,000 members.

As President of the FCV, Armando González sees a dual role for the peasant movement at present: first is service to its membership, and second is cooperation with the government. In the case of the former, the FCV must serve its members in relation to land owners and employers, dealing in problems of wages, hours, and living conditions. The second function is that of operating through the Instituto Agrario Nacional to aid in the implementation of the agrarian reform program. Both are believed to contribute to the encouragement of democracy and the support of constitutional government. Although recognizing many weaknesses in the present agrarian legislation, González and his supporters have argued that implementation of its better features will more swiftly alleviate rural miseries than scrapping the

[28] Interview with Carlos Behrens, November 23, 1962.

entire project and beginning once again to map out a new piece of law-making.

A final effort by the leadership is the counseling of moderation to the frequently impatient *campesinos*. Whether progress is rapid enough to forestall peasant restlessness is uncertain, although there had been no serious violence as of early 1964, and the peasants were still supporting the constitutional government. As to the concerns of the AD itself, efforts to harness the peasantry for political purposes have met with only partial success. It is true that no other party has been able to win the sympathies of the peasantry, but the AD strength has been largely that of party organization and mostly of its candidates' popularity. The FCV can be controlled and its leadership maintained through intervention from the CTV and from the government itself, but this is far different from saying that the FCV leadership has organized the peasants into an effective political group.

Any political party that succeeds in politicizing the peasantry and wielding it for partisan purposes will have taken a long stride toward replacing the AD as Venezuela's major party. Thus far, however, such a result has proven impossible, given the political experience and educational aspects of the principles and doctrine of the AD.

CHAPTER X

# The Party and Non-Partisan Groups

The relations of Acción Democrática with the various sectors of Venezuelan society are nowhere more extensive than with organized labor, the latter construed as including the peasantry. Although the laborers and peasants are not organized as mere adjuncts of the party, there is undeniable evidence that both groups are largely controlled and directed by the party. In recent years, the paternalism of the government has prevented the development of fully independent labor organizations. The situation in other areas of Venezuelan life is somewhat different, however.

A number of important sectors, although involved in politics occasionally, are non-partisan in a different sense. Several civilian sectors will be considered briefly; a more detailed examination is necessary for the role of the military as it affects and interacts with Acción Democrática. Only after these groups are understood can one turn to AD relations with rival political parties.

## Relations with Civilian Sectors

Among the more important non-partisan civilian groups, three in particular stand out: the teachers' movement, the university students, and the feminine movement. The AD has been proud of its contributions in education especially, doctrinal aspects of which were noted earlier. So far as teachers are concerned, the earliest glimmerings of organization came with the founding of the Sociedad Venezolana de Maestros de Instrucción Primaria (SVMIP) on January 15, 1932,[1] under the shadow of dictatorial persecution. A group of young educators and primary school teachers, convinced of the

[1] This is now celebrated as the anniversary of the Día de los Maestros—Teachers' Day.

need for an enlightened national movement, devoted themselves to pedagogical efforts aimed at awakening both the public and fellow teachers from the educational lethargy. Prieto, Núñez Sucre, Miguel Suniaga, and Alirio Arreaza were among the founders.

With the death of Juan Vicente Gómez the educators came into the open for the first time, calling into session the first Convención Nacional del Magisterio Venezolano in August 1936. Assembled delegates expanded the original SVMIP to include pre-university educators of all levels, not merely primary school instructors. According to Article 1 of the organizational statutes, the new federation would include teachers from all branches of public and private education, as well as students in their final course prior to beginning their own teaching careers. The new organization, called the Federación Venezolana de Maestros (FVM), vowed to work in the most intense and effective fashion for the education of the populace, operating as an organization outside political parties and religious institutions.[2]

In its Declaration of Principles the FVM pledged its dedication to the permanent values of culture and to the interests of children, school, and teaching. It also set forth a series of goals that has been carried down to the present. These embraced commitments to work "for the improvement of conditions in school"; to increase the spirit of international solidarity while "strengthening the ideals of peace and co-fraternity among peoples"; to unify the Venezuelan teachers' movement to the maximum; to improve living conditions for all teachers, including better remuneration along with social and cultural assistance; and to work for the assigning of administrative educational posts and the operation of school directorates without political influence.

[2] Venezuela, Presidencia de la República, *Documentos Que Hicieron Historia; Siglo y Medio de Vida Republicana, 1810-1961* (Caracas: Ediciones Conmemorativas del Sesquicentenario de la Independencia, 1962, Vol. II), pp. 219-20.

Organizational provisions of the FVM statutes called for the election of a Consejo Directivo Central (CDC), and delegates chose as their first president Luis B. Prieto. Soon to assume prominence in politics, Prieto told interviewers of his interest in both the FVM and the newly formed ORVE. Explaining his recent affiliation with the political movement, Prieto also spoke of his faith that it could achieve necessary reforms, notably in the educational field.

Prieto's position was interesting as the first close tie between the teachers' movement and the political organization that became the AD. The passage of years was marked by increasingly active efforts to further the cause of education. Such young educators as Reinaldo Leandro Mora and Mercedes Fermín joined the movement, and the legalization of the AD in 1941 made the party the first major political voice crying out in the interests of non-university educational reforms. At the founding meeting of Acción Democrática in September, Luis B. Prieto proclaimed the party's educational position in an address entitled "'Acción Democrática' y los Problemas de la Educación Nacional."

Declaring that the party believed education to be the only adequate way of incorporating the masses into a life of justice and law, Prieto assured his audience that the AD gave its educational proposals a preferential position. While university reforms were included, priority would be given to lower-level education.

"Our central preoccupation will be the primary school, especially the rural school. Let each population nucleus have its school. We will fight poor attendance by attacking the source of its causes. . . .

"If the primary school is the central preoccupation, that does not mean abandonment of other branches of education in the system that Acción Democrática proposes, but on the contrary it will be our goal that secondary education . . . be put within the reach of all apt and capable persons."[3]

The AD continued to voice its educational commitment during the next four years and, once in power, its encouragement was unremitting. With Prieto and Fermín most active in calling for and helping to lay down reforms, the *trienio* gave a major impetus to education. First in Junta decrees and later in the October 1948 education legislation, the party gave substance to its statements. Faced with a situation in which nearly two-thirds of school-age children were not in class, while illiteracy was well over 50 percent, the party set about an aggressive policy. By the 1948 counter-revolution, the AD had tripled the budget as well as primary school enrollment. The program of adult literacy featured the creation of special schools in which some 25,000 were taught to read.

Reforms came to a grinding halt after the change of regime, and the FVM itself was subject to obstruction and the congenital antagonism of the dictatorship. Hamstrung throughout the next ten years, the FVM struggled to maintain a degree of autonomy, surviving to return in 1958 and grow more vigorous than ever before. The reconstituted Federación Venezolana de Maestros continued to operate strictly in terms of its own professional interests. Holding itself aloof from the service of political parties, the FVM underwent no pressure to become an active partisan. The AD made no effort to incorporate the teachers within its organization, and the FVM was among the few groups which deliberately held itself apart from the Confederación de Trabajadores de Venezuela, preferring to remain aloof while formulating and advancing policies at the service of teachers and students alike.

By 1962 the FVM claimed over 26,000 members in 25 state and regional federations, while its international affiliations included association with the Conference of

[3] *Ahora*, September 16, 1941, pp. 2-3.

American Educators in the United States. The strong position of the AD and its sympathizers is not to be denied, despite the effective separation of strictly partisan matters from FVM educational concerns. Seven of the 13 national leaders are AD members, and by 1963 the party held a majority on state directorates throughout Venezuela, with but three exceptions: Táchira, Yaracuy, and Miranda (Petare). Leandro Mora had become Minister of Education, and the continued concern of the AD-COPEI coalition government with educational problems at all levels assured a lasting influence within the movement.

The FVM continues to pursue a strongly independent position, and even its *adeco* leaders join with independents and members of the other parties to maintain the integrity and autonomy of the organization. Today the general educational goals of the several parties are essentially alike; there is little real point in injecting party politics into the FVM and its operations. The same is generally true of the various state and regional teachers' organizations of various sorts. With all Venezuela largely committed to major strides in the educational field, the non-partisan flavor of this sector can be expected to continue indefinitely.

Quite another situation prevails, however, with the university students of the nation. At first glance the change of attitudes and orientation seems little short of extraordinary, and the student movement of the 1960's impresses one as wholly unrecognizable from that of a generation earlier. The position of the AD with the students has also gone from one extreme to another. However, on closer examination there are at least a few similarities between the present university students and their predecessors.

The Generation of '28 was initially active on the student level, and in the brief period of political freedom in 1936, the student orientation toward the democratic left was essentially the same. A new group of politicized students emerged as the Generation of 1936-1937, sharing the same basic outlook and later joining Acción Democrática. Only a small number of students became active in the communist movement; youthful protests and the struggle for a better Venezuela could better find an outlet through the AD, and most students recognized the fact. While it is true that the Catholic-oriented UNE and its successors held the loyalties of a few students, the majority certainly affiliated themselves with the AD. During the *trienio* this was especially true. *Copeyano* strength was revealed only in Mérida's University of the Andes. Communist strength was relatively unimportant.

The dictatorial decade brought together a set of forces that encouraged an extreme leftist outlook in Venezuelan students. At several institutions—most notably the Universidad Central de Venezuela in Caracas—the influence of the communists increased substantially. Venezuelan communists continued to direct their efforts toward intellectuals rather than workers and laborers. When the dictatorship fell, the students found themselves possessed of a drive and zest that was impatient over the restoration of freedom, eager to implement needed socioeconomic reforms. Speed was believed to be of the essence. As already noted, the decade-long absence of AD had erased practical knowledge of the party for many. Students often regarded the AD as but one more group of office-seekers, more proficient electorally than its competitors, but a patronage-minded group that was massively organized and militantly partisan, with relatively little genuine concern for the plight of the masses.

The rising generation in Venezuela, as in much of Latin America, saw the tide of international communism on the march, and believed that it rather than the United States was the bearer of the true message for the future. The continued cooperative cordiality between the Betancourt administration and the United

States seemed to emphasize the alleged subordination of the former to whims of the State Department in Washington. North American policies in the hemisphere contributed to a common belief that economic interests were dominant, while such ill-conceived measures as the decoration of Marcos Pérez Jiménez with the Legion of Merit seemed to provide adequate proof. The rise of Castro in Cuba's Oriente added another factor—the appearance of a great charismatic leader about whom great emotional attachment could be centered.

With the moving of Fidel Castro toward the Soviet Union and international communism, interference in Venezuelan affairs by *fidelista* agents heightened in intensity. Sabotage, robbery, and lawless violence in Caracas and elsewhere forced several suspensions of constitutional guarantees by the Betancourt government. Students seized upon this as a further spur to explosive irresponsibility and ignored the occasional loss of innocent lives and accompanying property damage that government measures were designed to offset.

By 1963 student disorders began to decrease slightly, although on at least one occasion a small group of students stopped and burned a set of buses and swiftly fled to the sanctuary of university grounds in order to avoid apprehension. Nonetheless, the UCV was in class more than in 1961-1962, when the academic year was repeatedly interrupted by strikes, protests, and demonstrations of various sorts. Furthermore, the psychological blow incurred by the disclosure of Soviet missile bases in Cuba—while not shaking the faith of the most ardent students—clearly disillusioned a substantial number who had been unwilling to concede the existence of Soviet dominion over major Cuban policy decisions.

The parallels between the students' attitudes today and a generation ago are in some particulars more superficial than real. The visitor to Caracas' UCV will see the walls adorned with placards and the halls decorated with overarching signs attacking the government in particular and all non-extremist parties in general. There and elsewhere are encountered suggestions that the present student effort is as concerned with the Venezuelan masses as were the demonstrators of '28. There are also references to the AD-supported seizure of power by non-constitutional means in 1945, suggesting that a change of government in 1962 or 1963 would be morally acceptable.

The student revolutionaries of 1928 and 1936-1937 saw themselves as fighting for political democracy and the representative forms through which effective reforms might take place; the contemporary students attempt to place their emphasis also on political matters. While claiming to desire the socio-economic changes that national problems demand, the university students today face a frustration that their predecessors did not have. The wide unpopularity of the Gómez regime in 1928, and the popular revulsion against officialism in 1936-1937, permitted substantial public opinion to coalesce behind the revolutionary students of those days. Thus in 1928 and a decade later there was some valid reason for the students to regard themselves as the intellectual guardians of the nation, fighting in the vanguard of the peoples' cause for political and social justice.

This cannot be said for today's students. Finding themselves without significant support from the Venezuelan public, the students in despair and frustration permit themselves to be driven into a lawlessness and terrorism that is new to Venezuela. Seeing the major parties—the AD, COPEI, and the URD—as well as moderate splinter groups winning the backing of the populace with a set of essentially moderate goals, the anxious students angrily drift further to the left, seeking political ideas and forms whereby they may help the people of the nation in spite of themselves. The innate conceit and gross unreality of such a view are but two of the temperamental weaknesses of the contemporary student leaders. A characteristic statement was delivered by a leading student revolutionary after the national elections of December 1963 when, conceding the failure to prevent the people from voting, he vowed that the people would be "liberated" from the yoke of existing parties and policies and educated until they understood their true interests.

Cut off from the masses and unsuccessful in winning broad support, today's students turn to extremism, lawlessness, and acts of physical daring and bravery that provide psychological solace to replace the desire for public acclaim. Generational irresponsibility has become a national illness that fits the entire student fabric to a degree, although it is far more serious in Caracas than in the interior. Mariano Picón Salas observed in 1963 after his return from a diplomatic mission to UNESCO that the years of Pérez Jiménez had cut off the nation's youth from all authority, either parental or academic. The restoration of normal liberty and freedom in 1958 found the young people in many cases psychologically unable to cope with their duties and responsibilities either individually or collectively, and and the result was seen in the continued outbursts of lawlessness.[4]

Another of the inherent emotional elements at the present time is the lack of drama and sensation in the gradual, planned, ordered effort to construct a new economic reality. In 1928 and after, the effort to oppose Gómez was a dangerous one, and those engaged in the quest felt themselves caught up in a great service to their people while justifying it with some risk to life and limb. The same situation does not pertain today, and the appeal of defiance and the bravado of attacking at night, robbing or looting, and then fleeing be-

[4] *El Nacional*, January 24, 1963, p. 10.

fore the arrival of the authorities—this is the kind of thrill that the student today cannot get by working within a democratic framework and regular, routine, daily activities.

The Acción Democrática in 1958 made the explicit decision to urge upon its student followers an emphasis on studies and work rather than continual politicking. This judgment, approved enthusiastically and forthrightly by Rómulo Betancourt, has since been called into some question as the result of student extremism. Nevertheless, the AD has directed its students to refrain from undue political participation. University walls are covered with extremist banners, interspersed only infrequently with emblems of *copeyano* or *urredista* students; AD mottoes are very rarely seen.

The decision to restrict undue student participation was a rational one, but it also made easier the extremist path to university domination. The AD's movement was devastated by the MIR separation in 1960, and the later strengthening of moderate student forces came essentially through the gradual rise of COPEI's strength with the students. For by 1963, the URD's own youth movement—the Vanguardia Juvenil Urredista (VJU)— had also been virtually decimated. Aside from *copeyano* sympathizers, virtually all the politicized students were committed to extremism of the left.

The Betancourt government exerted its efforts in the strengthening and diversification of university training. For the first time a major policy was adopted to give substantial support to universities outside the city, and it was significant that, by 1961 and 1962, many of the strike calls issued by student officials at the UCV were ignored by institutions outside the capital. Increasingly the extremist sentiments centered in Caracas, while students elsewhere became more engrossed in finishing their educations and pursuing careers. The growing realization that careers for university graduates are remunerative in today's Venezuela has also led to a slight weakening of political activism on the part of students outside Caracas. The government has been active in the founding and expansion of the Universidad de Oriente, which has branches in several eastern towns. It bears mentioning that the first President of the Organizing Commission was former AD Political Secretary Luis Manuel Peñalver, while his assistant was José Lorenzo Pérez, son-in-law of President Betancourt.

Student domination by extremists of the left has had unfortunate results for Venezuela, entirely aside from the AD's loss of appeal with this element. The apparent weakening of communist influence is hopefully the beginning of a trend toward moderation and constructive studies. Yet this cannot be assumed, and both the AD and URD face a long period of rebuilding. In the meantime, the present generation of university students is sadly failing to produce leaders with promise of future national leadership. Intellectual young men are inclined to be active in student harangues and in small bands of terrorists; the circumstances that permitted the emergence of Villalba, Betancourt, Leoni, Caldera, and many others do not seem to exist in Venezuela today. The loss is far more than that to any single party, but to the Republic itself.

A few words will suffice concerning the feminine movement, for it is necessary merely to note the role of the party in the advance of women in recent years. The great and historic accomplishment was that of winning suffrage in 1945. Outstanding participants in the struggle were *adecas* Cecilia Núñez Sucre and Mercedes Fermín, although several among the early band of young feminists later joined other parties. Fermín was writing in the student journal *FEV* as early as 1936, examining the position of women in Venezuelan history. The formation of political organizations for the first time gave a small group of women real hope for political emancipation, and they were incorporated into political factions and parties of the time. Nearly all politically conscious women had been anti-Gómez, and had followed the symbolic trail-blazing of Núñez Sucre. With the outlawing of the PDN in 1937, its ranks soon came to include Ana Luisa Llovera, Lola Morales Lara, and Ana Esther Gouverneur. Many other women began to join the PDN, most notably women students—the future professional women. A "pro-women's vote" movement developed and was advanced with the cooperation of a pioneering group known as the Cultura Femenina, and the first Congress of Women was called in Caracas, signaling a renewed demand for the vote.

When suffrage was subsequently delivered during the rule of the AD Junta, women streamed to the polls in 1946 to cast more than 50 percent of the total vote. By this time the restructuring of the PDN as the AD had carried with it the majority of those women politically active at the time. In the feminine movement as in a number of sectors of national life, the AD's early success was in part a function of the lack of competition from other truly democratic parties. In the early 1940's the logical place for politically interested women was Acción Democrática. After 1945 a few drifted to COPEI and the URD, a number which increased after 1958. However, the AD had already established itself.

During the *perezjimenista* era, women of all political persuasions joined the struggle; for the first time Venezuelan women saw the inside of prison walls, while countless others suffered through depredations to families and loved ones. The eventual return of democratic life in 1958 released a new surge of feminine adherents into the stream of partisan politics, although a hesitancy bred of social tradition constrained many from public activity. Only a few women were actively prominent in national politics: besides Deputies Fermín of the AD and Vidalina de Bártoli of the URD, others included AD activists Evelyn Trujillo and Ana Luisa Llovera.

For Acción Democrática, its Comité Ejecutivo Nacional had in the 1940's included a separate Secretaría Femenina, but this was eliminated at the 1948 convention on the grounds that such a separation was false. Since that time the party has encouraged women to be active within the regular membership alongside their male counterparts. The AD has also organized and supported the annual convocations of its feminine members in Plenos Femeninos, where the effort is that of political education and of arousing interest and renewed participation.

## Relations with the Military

At the time of Venezuelan independence, Simón Bolívar, a native son of Caracas, described his homeland as a barracks. Through much of its history, Venezuela has indeed been ruled by force of arms. Throughout the nineteenth century and well into the twentieth, Venezuelan "general-presidents" have exercised political dominion through military power. Even today the role of the military in the nation's political affairs is substantial, and less than a decade ago a military dictator sat in Miraflores Palace.

The heritage of military involvement in politics should not be construed as presenting a simple picture of brute force run amuck. For in point of fact, the Venezuelan military has been evolving and has not yet reached its final and fully matured state. The relationship of civilian elements with the military in recent times—and most specifically the dealings of the AD with the armed forces—has been uneven and irregular. The erratic course of these relations says something about the evolution of the party as well as the changing attitudes and experience of the military.

The founders of AD were adolescents and grew up under the rule of the Gómez dictatorship. That regime was in several ways the last militarily based government that resembled the classic tradition of the nineteenth century. The armed forces were anything but modern or professional; rather, they were formed in large part by regional and sectional bands of armed men whose loyalties were to individual *caudillos*. One of the several keys to Gómez' success was his ability to win the lasting support of individual leaders whose armed supporters could maintain peace and order in their given geographic areas.

The military force of the country early in the twentieth century, then, was little more than a group of sectional bands tied together by allegiance to one man. Those few dissident figures unwilling to accept Gómez' rule were defeated and driven into exile. Only toward the later years of the dictator's long rule did the armed forces begin to show signs of modernization. Gradually the cadets produced by the military schools began to develop a concern for status, for adequate weapons and more advanced training. An indication of this nascent interest came at the time of the uprising on April 7, 1928.

With junior- and middle-rank officers irked by frequent assignments as overseers of cane-cutting laborers on *gomecista* holdings and comparable non-military, caretaker kinds of jobs, dissatisfaction was ignited during the February student demonstrations. By April a series of somewhat disorganized discussions between students and young officers led to a military uprising that was put down only through the astute leadership of loyalist forces under General Eleazar López Contreras at Caracas' San Carlos barracks. The rebellious officers were imprisoned indefinitely, their treatment harsher than that meted out to the students.

The years to follow almost imperceptibly saw a gradual trend toward a more professional attitude on the part of young graduates of the military schools. Under both López Contreras and Medina Angarita, new blood began to enter the armed forces. Internal unity and singleness of purpose lessened as the younger, professionally oriented officers found themselves unable to advance in rank because of the presence of old *gomecista* veterans whose retirements had been delayed. Many of the latter were semi-literates whose experience was scarcely military by modern standards. Friction and resentment between the two groups increased, and the general situation by 1944 and 1945 became more inflammatory as the senior officers began to divide behind the rival aspirations of López Contreras and of outgoing President Medina.

Among the junior officers in the mid-1940's were a number who had received advanced training abroad. Several had been students in Lima at the Peruvian military school, and their increased awareness of the modern potentialities of militarism left them fully convinced that drastic action was needed. From such circumstances came the will to revolt in 1945; and from the political crisis of that summer came the first dealings between Acción Democrática and the Venezuelan military. As recounted earlier, the initial contact was made by the military through the intermediary of Edmundo Fernández, a personal friend of Rómulo Betancourt. The latter, at first skeptical, eventually agreed to a meeting, and on the night of July 6, 1945, the AD and young military rebels conferred for the first time.[5]

Betancourt and Raúl Leoni met with five officers at Fernández' home, learning to their surprise of the existence of the secret Unión Patriótica Militar (UPM). The officers, whose spokesmen on this occasion included

[5] An interesting version of this relationship and its background is included in Ana Mercedes Pérez, *La Verdad Inédita* (Caracas: Editorial Artes Gráficas, 1947).

Major Carlos Delgado Chalbaud and Captain Mario Vargas, explained in detail the growing dissatisfaction shared by other junior officers. *Gomecista* holdovers refused to retire; promotions were slow or non-existent; technical improvements were blocked by superior officers; a wide variety of military reforms were rejected by the leadership. Salaries for middle- and junior-level officers were low, and prospects of raises were slight. Comparable military men elsewhere in Latin America were proceeding with alterations and a general modernization that seemed possible in Venezuela. In short, a stagnation existed which these officers were determined to dispel. To do so, collaboration with a civilian political organization was deemed necessary, and the obvious choice seemed to be Acción Democrática.

The justification for intended rebellion on the part of the military rebels-to-be, then, was a mixture of professional concern, patriotic dedication, and a desire for material improvements and personal advancement. And from 1944 until the revelations to AD leaders in July 1945, they had slowly laid their plans. Political reforms to which the UPM was at least nominally committed included universal suffrage, constitutional reform, administrative competence, and most especially, professional military service. These goals, as the AD was told, were to be upheld by the armed forces following the revolutionary uprising; the uprising, the AD learned, was to be carried out within a few months, whether or not civilian or *adeco* support was given.

The leadership of Acción Democrática quietly discussed the situation within the top hierarchy of the party. More than mildly astonished by the revelations of the UPM, they were confronted with an issue of no little complexity. In the past they had attacked military involvement in politics. Vocal in their defense of the Venezuelan military as a wholly apolitical force, Acción Democrática had also been a consistent champion of purely civilian government, decrying unconstitutional interference in the nation's political evolution.

Balanced against this was the tempting prospect of gaining power, of reaching a position from which the several and deeply desired reforms could be implemented. In the face of existing political conditions, there was little practical prospect that the AD would soon reach national office through the decision of an indirect electoral system. Given the rising tide of *medinista-lopecista* rivalry, the offer could scarcely have been more intriguing. As a series of meetings were held with military leaders following the first contact on July 6, detailed possibilities for joint action became the subject of talks between *adeco* Gonzalo Barrios and the military's Mario Vargas. As Betancourt later wrote—and party leaders recently have reiterated in interviews—Vargas made a highly favorable impression. More than any other single person he helped nourish the growing belief of the AD in the sincerity of democratic convictions which the UPM repeated.

The eventual decision of the AD to join with the military rebels has been criticized by many rivals on the Venezuelan political scene. There is no disputing the cooperation of Acción Democrática in the eventual *golpe de estado*; it is also clear that this action ran contrary to frequent expositions of party doctrine which criticized any intrusion whatever by the military into the sphere of national politics. At the least, however, it is equally certain that the party did not leap at the offer immediately. Rather, it delayed for some time while the possibility of a single unity candidate was explored with General Medina and his advisers.

The tentative candidacy of Diógenes Escalante drew the support of the AD; all existing evidence suggests that the party was sincere in proffering its support to an Escalante presidency, from which it believed itself to have assurances of greater political freedoms. With the collapse of the Ambassador's health, however, the issue was reopened. As discussions continued, UPM representatives insisted upon their determination to carry through the revolution even without any civilian assistance whatever, if necessary. With the eventual selection of Biaggini by Medina as his successor—a man totally unacceptable to Acción Democrática—the party's decision to cooperate in the military uprising became firm.

Once the agonizing choice was made, the top leadership joined wholeheartedly with the UPM, although necessarily continuing to conduct daily party affairs as if a constitutional solution to the political crisis was still both possible and desirable. At first December was set as the date, but news leaked out to the government earlier, and so, unexpectedly on October 17, the AD and military rebels made their move. A few hours after a mass meeting of the AD in Nuevo Circo, military insurgents captured the Escuela Militar and continued to Miraflores and its barracks. AD members on the 18th also moved into the streets, engaging in sporadic battle throughout the afternoon with police and soldiers loyal to the regime. By day's end the revolutionaries had won control in Caracas, and it was easily extended to the rest of the nation. The victory belonged to the UPM and the AD.

For Acción Democrática, the decision to participate in the uprising was one of the more momentous in its history. In view of countless public denunciations of military interference in political matters, it was embarrassing in the extreme to be so involved. Furthermore, revolution against Medina was less easily justified than an uprising against Gómez or someone of his ilk. Even today this AD action is occasionally flung back at the party by political opponents. All things considered, however, there is little regret over the choice; placed in the same set of circumstances, today's party leadership agrees that the same path would be followed. Rightly or wrongly, it is felt that normal approaches to power had been effectively blocked, and there were no constitutional means of reaching a position from which political and economic reforms might have been introduced.

AD leaders in justifying their involvement have also cited the fact that military rebels were determined in any event to proceed with their plans. Perhaps the final word, so far as Acción Democrática is concerned, can be taken from Betancourt's message to the National Constituent Assembly as Junta President. Although one can argue with his position, he did at least set it forth on January 20, 1947. "Like all politically organized collectivities with a vocation for power, Acción Democrática wanted to govern. Its men and women were not iconoclasts with anarchic inclinations. . . . They wanted to contribute, with hands and hearts, to the building of a new order, based on effective democracy, with economic nationalism and social justice. In such circumstances, the proposition of the Unión Patriótica Militar was particularly tempting. . . ."[6] When the possibility of an evolutionary solution to the situation vanished through the disability of Escalante, Betancourt added, the AD's decision was clear. He might have added that the immediate future of AD-military relations was also to be colored by the experience they shared during the brief conspiratorial period and then the subsequent provisional government.

Initially the relations between the party and young officers were excellent. The two military members of the Junta, Vargas and Carlos Delgado Chalbaud, appeared sympathetic to AD aspirations for the nation; moreover, their own actions were circumscribed so that matters of security and internal order were their primary functions. The implementation of the intended national socio-economic revolution was left in the hands of the AD leaders.

[6] Rómulo Betancourt, *Trayectoria Democrática de una Revolución* (Caracas: Imprenta Nacional, 1948), p. 324.

Ranking *adecos* continually articulated their belief in civilian politics, urging upon the military a fully non-partisan, professional role. References to the subordination of military leaders to civilian authority were usually tactfully avoided, but there were occasions on which the position was stated bluntly.

While emphasizing the nature of non-political military responsibility, the AD attempted to appear responsive to the needs of the military. The old-guard officers were removed from active service following the October Revolution, while the lower-ranking officers received 30-percent pay hikes. A variety of fringe benefits was also provided, including commissary and related services that exceeded those of the past. Less than a year after the revolution, leading officers of the Unión Patriótica Militar declared in a public letter to Eleazar López Contreras that "in only eight months, the Revolution has done more for the army than your government, in which we of the Armed Forces had so many hopes, hopes that were ultimately disappointed."[7] Further reference was made to the lack of modern equipment and absence of professional training that were characteristic of earlier days.

On the surface, relations between the party in power and the military were unruffled almost throughout the *trienio*. The sincerity of the most prominent *adecos* in supporting and encouraging apolitical armed forces was genuine and initially unquestioned; at the same time, the party was aware that a military *golpe* was not beyond the range of possibility. And while the armed forces in many cases were willing to accept civilian control, there were exceptions. A small but influential group of military men—most notably Delgado Chalbaud and Pérez Jiménez—nursed doubts as to the continuation of non-political duties. Moreover, the armed forces

[7] *El Nacional*, July 4, 1946, p. 1.

gradually began to suspect that the AD was determined to destroy its status and reduce it to little more than a small internal security force. As this sentiment began to surge, officers who felt little affinity for the AD and its program began to spread rumors that nourished military disaffection. In 1948 there were widely circulating tales that Acción Democrática was accumulating a cache of arms with which the workers might in an emergency be supplied. The militancy of AD-dominated labor did little to calm the doubts of many military men.

The flavor of anti-military views inside the AD began to increase, particularly among the party rank-and-file. The leadership itself, which had been plagued with a series of attempted coups almost from the outset, grew increasingly concerned, and public statements occasionally reflected this critical inclination. The party began to consider not arming the workers, but winning military officers into the party itself. Rising opposition by the small but noisy URD and COPEI further dramatized the gravity of the situation, and private businessmen and landholders, demoralized before the onslaught of the AD's zealous reformism, encouraged the military to move against the government.

By the early fall of 1948 the situation was increasingly shaky, and nearly three weeks of semi-crisis preceded the November counter-revolution. Public attention was diverted, however, by the cacophony of political turmoil and the rush of new governmental programs. Not until November 20 were there public hints of difficulty, when newspaper stories reported that ranking officers had conferred with Gallegos the previous day. That the situation was perilous became clearer November 21 with the suspension of constitutional guarantees. The President decreed the measure "inasmuch as circumstances have developed which create a state of alarm affecting the nation's economic and social life." Press and radio were censored, outgoing cables were checked, and party assemblies were abolished temporarily.[8]

The military demands upon the President followed almost at once. He was informed that additional cabinet posts were demanded, as well as the expulsion of Betancourt and the participation of COPEI in government. The President, whatever the possible lack of political insight that had contributed to the situation, forthrightly rejected the demands, thus making the seizure of power inevitable. The ultimatum—delivered by Delgado Chalbaud, Pérez Jiménez, and Luis Felipe Llovera—brought Mario Vargas hastily back to Venezuela. A leader of the UPM since 1944 and perhaps the best friend of the AD in the higher military echelons, he had been recuperating from treatment at Saranac Lake, New York. His desperate flight back to Caracas and subsequent pleas with his colleagues went unheeded, however, and on November 24 the counter-revolution was carried out. Acción Democrática was driven from office and into the lengthy decade of exile that lay ahead. The experience of its relationship with the military was not to be forgotten.

Justification of the coup by the new provisional government attempted to lay the blame entirely on elements of the party. The official version declared that "an extremist faction of the AD party" began maneuvers designed to dominate the military. Allegedly, a general strike was in the works, which contributed to the necessity of forcible intervention by the military. Furthermore, the AD was dissolved because of the effort "to incite the people . . . because it tried to destroy the institutional integrity of the armed forces . . . and because an extremist faction of the party was attempting to maintain itself in power by diverse means of social disruption."[9]

[8] *El País*, November 20, 1948, p. 1.
[9] Venezuela, Oficina Nacional de Información, *Documentos*

The natural denial of the AD was expounded most fully by Rómulo Betancourt in later years. He argued that the party accepted the importance of a regular army and attempted to encourage and support it. Thus the AD had contributed to technological improvement and to necessary betterment of living conditions generally. This, he felt, was consistent with the military function of providing professional service subordinate to civilian control. However, "military conspiracies continued. . . . Acción Democrática lacked the elements to arm the people in confronting subversion. . . . When the revolution came there were popular strikes and protests, but the war material of the army, used with Prussian brutality, ended the resistance. . . ."[10]

Granting the grievances and suspicions on both sides, the deterioration of party-military relations was most strongly influenced by the broad ambitions of a few leaders who were reluctant to concede the abrogation of the tradition of military involvement in politics. The social revolution being planned and implemented by the AD had little appeal to several of the key military leaders, and thus the reluctance to overthrow the constituted government was less than substantial. The initial hesitation of Delgado Chalbaud in uniting with anti-AD officers was also overcome in time, and indications in 1949 suggested that, but for his assassination, he would have stood for president in 1950, thus assuming the leadership which instead devolved upon Marcos Pérez Jiménez.

Acción Democrática had ample time to reflect upon the cause of its fall during the years ahead; the exercise in self-criticism tended to be sharper in areas other than that of relations with the military. Yet it was recognized

Relativos al Movimiento Militar de 24 de Noviembre de 1948 (Caracas: Imprenta Nacional, 1949), pp. 20, 29.

[10] Rómulo Betancourt, Venezuela: Política y Petróleo (México: Fondo de Cultura Económica, 1956), pp. 469-70.

that the complete neutralization of the military as a political force would be impossible for an indefinite period. Since the armed forces would remain a crucial factor in the stability and survival of any government, it behooved the party to reestablish and maintain the best possible ties and closest understanding. It was to this effort that the AD in general and Betancourt in particular was dedicated in the post-1958 years.

The military in Venezuela had undergone certain changes during the decade in absolute power. At least superficially, Pérez Jiménez had ruled in a fashion reminiscent of another *tachirense*, Juan Vicente Gómez. A pallid public speaker and ineffective popular figure, Pérez Jiménez relied upon armed might as directed by the advice of some half-dozen fellow colonels from Táchira. Policy was decided by a small number of men, and with the passing of time the gulf between the dictator and the military widened. Such measures as the strengthening of the security police as a counterweight to the regular military were harmful to the *rapport* the dictator desired. Moreover, the experience of the younger officers was injurious to the regime.

Whereas Pérez Jiménez and those of his generation had learned of modern military techniques in academies elsewhere in Latin America, the next group of young officers experienced much of this foreign training in Europe and the United States. There was a regular stream of trainees to such U.S. bases as Fort Leavenworth and Fort Bragg, to mention but two. Part of the result was contact with and some understanding of political democracy and the tradition of an apolitical military institution. A large number of officers regarded by Pérez Jiménez as untrustworthy was sent abroad as military attachés and advisers during this period, and reflected the broadening influence of contact with non-Latin American military men as well as doubts over Pérez Jiménez' entire approach. Long before the events

of January 1958, the hold of the President on the loyalties of the military had weakened.

Popular revulsion against the ousted regime was
strong in early 1958, and many officers were impressed
with the unfortunate nature of the intervention during the preceding decade. There were concerted efforts
to rid the armed forces of unrepentant *perezjimenistas*,
and the sense of responsibility to the public was heightened. Circumstances made the military leadership sensi-
tive to overtures from civilian political groups, and the
AD was not long in making its peace with the armed
forces. Betancourt and other AD leaders had conferred
frequently with military officers well before the inauguration of the new government in 1959. The following
years showed a continual courtship of the military by
the new President, one which proved of critical importance.

At this writing, true civilian government has survived
in Venezuela longer than ever before. The armed forces
have been loyal to existing civilian leaders, although by
no means subordinate. Betancourt spoke out countless
times during his five-year administration in exaggerated
praise of the innate importance of the military as defenders of Venezuelan soil. The total establishment,
numbering between 25,000 and 30,000, was praised both
for its non-involvement in partisan politics and its fundamental contribution to national sovereignty. Both the
government and the regular AD leadership imposed
upon its subordinates and supporters the most stringent
commands not to give the military cause for mistrust.
Strongly anti-military labor leaders of the *trienio* spoke
frequently of the importance of the armed forces, and
useful personal friendships were for the first time ce-
mented between CTV officials and high-ranking officers.

A noted student of the Latin American military, Edwin
Lieuwen, has described the relationship as a kind of

gentleman's agreement.[11] The armed forces operate and administer their affairs with a free hand, while receiving a minimum of 10 percent of the annual budget—a figure below that of several Latin American countries. Jet aircraft and comparable modern "hardware" has been purchased for the armed forces; promotions have been awarded in most cases on the basis of merit; benefits include credit for off-post housing. Officers whose motives were questionable found themselves pensioned off handsomely, and the measure was generally accepted.

As President, Rómulo Betancourt carefully paid attention to various aspects of living conditions for the military. Thus the Ministry of Defense revised drastically its policy of individual loans to officers for the purchase of personal homes. As Betancourt noted in a speech to Congress on March 11, 1961, the program was a dynamic but inexpensive one in that it was "in no sense a donation, since amortization and interest are taken out monthly from the pay of the officers and non-commissioned officers who benefit."[12] Comparable policies led to generally better treatment in the social sphere than had been the case under Pérez Jiménez.

Accorded such treatment, the military have remained loyal throughout the Betancourt years and into the administration of Leoni. Betancourt's personal role was also substantial. Ever a peripatetic president, his many trips into the interior usually included courtesy calls at barracks and training camps; he was known to visit during the Christmas holidays, sharing in the camaraderie of the occasion. The personal touch was also employed in bringing military leaders into policy-making circles. While advice was rarely sought from officers on non-military questions, they were kept informed of all

[11] Edwin Lieuwen, *Venezuela* (New York: Oxford University Press, 1961), p. 161.

[12] Rómulo Betancourt, *Mensaje del Presidente ante el Congreso Nacional, 11 marzo 1961* (Caracas: Imprenta Nacional, 1961).

major developments, and many of them came to develop a genuine personal attachment to the President. Especially with regard to policy toward Cuba and the long struggle against internal subversion. Betancourt leaned upon his ranking officers.

There could be little faulting of the military in its determined opposition to armed mutiny. A rightist effort launched in April 1960 at San Cristóbal with support from the Dominican regime was swiftly squelched. A pair of uprisings in 1962 were also suppressed; marines at the Carúpano base were overcome by regular army troops in May, and a more serious outburst of fighting the following month at the naval base of Puerto Cabello was put down by civilian elements fighting alongside army units. The latter two efforts were leftist in coloration, encouraged and supported by the MIR in particular, one of whose leaders was seen on the scene of the fighting. In none of these cases was there support or sympathy from ranking officers nor from the two major garrisons, those of Caracas and Maracay. Later, the armed forces were steadfast in their support of the administration during the months of subversion in 1962 and 1963. General Antonio Briceño Linares, the Defense Minister, shrewdly handled military operations throughout the period.

Much of the success during this phase of military-AD relations was the reflection of Betancourt's personal genius rather than that of party accomplishment. At the same time, other party members became more appreciative of the function played by the military. With the inauguration of Raúl Leoni, the possibility of greater party activity became a possibility. While Betancourt's successor was also scrupulous in beginning a personal courtship of the military, his temperament and personality increased the likelihood of greater ties between officers and the party itself. Few expected his personal esteem to rival that of Betancourt among ranking officers; thus more reliance was necessarily placed upon the party. At the same time, Leoni appointed to his cabinet a general known for his pro-AD proclivities. Whether or not this move was wise cannot be stated yet, but it represented something of a shift from Betancourt's practice.

A notable development on the military side of the relationship was the establishment of the so-called Fuerzas Armadas de Cooperación, dedicated to assisting the campaign against adult illiteracy. Detachments of the military spent their duty hours in organizing and directing literacy classes. To this was added a set of schools designed to teach improved agricultural techniques to *campesinos*, and there was also military participation in the administration's program of economic development. A new engineering battalion was organized for highway construction, and there were further indications of support from the military leaders for various projects generally falling within the scope of community development and nation-building.

After saying the preceding, it must be added that the armed forces in Venezuela today remain—potentially— the major single arbiter of national politics. Thus today's relationship of Leoni and the AD with the military bears great importance. The course of future dealings must await the coming of events presently unforeseen. Time can help to create a permanent civilian tradition in government that will bring necessary realignments within the military itself. In all this, the tact, intelligence, and insight of the AD will be a determinant at least as influential as the temperamental and pragmatic proclivities of the officers themselves.

# CHAPTER XI

# The Party and Inter-Party Relations

The Venezuelan political universe was simplistic and tightly circumscribed when the founders of Acción Democrática first became politically active. However, among the recent developments has been the evolution of a party system that in both 1958 and 1963 showed great vitality. The vigor of campaigning and the nature of competing claims are examined in Chapter XII. Before a consideration of national elections in the democratic era following 1958, preliminary attention must be given the party system itself. Crucial to an understanding of the present status of Acción Democrática is a prior knowledge of its relations with rival parties over the years.

For the AD, three periods are perceptible. The first was one of stubborn and unyielding opposition to rival political organizations. Covering the hectic *trienio* and the early part of the decade in exile, this time was marked by a partisanship that adamantly refused to cooperate with other parties or to recognize the value of effective competition. The second, beginning with the events of the 1952 elections, reflected a change in which the party found it necessary for the first time to enter into at least informal exchanges with its competitors. Finally, coming down to the present is a period in which the bitterness of past experience has taught the AD the limitations of power. The necessary element of toleration in a mature and relatively stable polity has been recognized, with collaboration understood in the tri-party coalition created in 1959 and subsequent events which carried through into 1964 and beyond.

## Organized Opposition and Intransigence

The establishment of the forms of political democracy, of civil liberties, and of universal suffrage led during the *trienio* to the creation of parties which later became principal contestants in national politics. Although the opposition to Acción Democrática at the outset was more noisy than effective, it included the creation of two organized rivals—COPEI and the Unión Republicana Democrática. Of these, the former was more outspoken in its criticism of the AD. Christened the Comité de Organización Política Electoral Independiente, COPEI represented a political element which had first emerged in student politics in 1936-1937.

The earliest glimmerings of what became COPEI were recorded in 1934 at the Congreso Internacional de la Juventud Católica in Rome. This youth meeting helped to provide the initial impetus for what later developed into the Christian democratic movement in Latin America. Those in attendance included a number of later Catholic leaders: Eduardo Frei of Chile, Mario Polar of Peru, Venancio Flores of Uruguay, and Venezuela's Rafael Caldera. The Venezuelan movement began to evolve at home following the death of Gómez, first taking form in the anti-FEV Unión Nacional Estudiantil (UNE). Rejecting the demand of FEV president Jóvito Villalba in that year for a public declaration demanding the expulsion of the Jesuits from Venezuela, these Catholic students under the leadership of Caldera withdrew from the FEV to form their own organization.

Created on May 8, 1936, the UNE included among its charter members Caldera, Lorenzo Fernández, Miguel Angel Landáez, and Víctor Giménez Landínez. Upon graduation they organized the Acción Electoral, which was briefly active politically in the Federal District. Later it became known as Acción Nacional, electing Caldera and Pedro José Lara Peña as national deputies, while three members served as Caracas councilmen. The group generally supported López Contreras during his presidency; conservative thought was dominant, and most members held a conviction that *lopecismo* offered the best practical hope for national progress. Years later, in 1954, Rafael Caldera wrote a letter to the then-exiled former president; reflecting upon the disillusionment of the experience, he observed that "we had the expectation of seeing in your Government the beginning of a rectification of our history, [but now] we lament that, although you were undoubtedly a skillful politician, you never became a genuine statesman, capable of giving future solidity to the collective dreams of that era."[1]

Throughout the final *lopecista* period and the administration of Medina, the group was fairly inactive. Caldera himself left Congress and turned to the teaching of sociology in the Universidad Central. After the October Revolution he served briefly as Solicitor-General, but soon resigned and went into political opposition. The organization known as COPEI was, as its name suggests, initially intended as an electoral committee. Its official installation took place on Sunday, January 13, 1946, before a gathering of 500 persons opposite the Plaza Candelaria in Caracas. The first Directorio Nacional included such now-familiar names as Pedro del Corral, Caldera, Fernández, Landáez, and Edecio La Riva Araujo. Del Corral was named party president, work was begun to form units in the interior, and on April 13 Caldera announced his formal separation from the government.

During its formative period COPEI was fairly imprecise in ideology. A general declaration favoring democracy and a dedication to "social Christian" thought was issued, but little was spelled out. As the campaign for the Constituent Assembly progressed in 1946, COPEI underlined its democratic convictions in the face of AD criticism by attacking the majority party as desirous of establishing an official party of the state. "The position of COPEI toward the October Revolution is clear and distinct. We are with the Revolution, with its ideals and

[1] *La Esfera*, May 14, 1954, p. 7.

promises. . . . But we are . . . against the tendency that may make of the Revolution a sewer of hates. . . . We fight against ambition and indifference."[2]

In September 1946 a party manifesto set forth the *copeyano* commitment to progress and reform. "COPEI fights for social justice with the same tenacity with which it fights for democracy." Furthermore, continued the statement, the party was firmly devoted to improvement of conditions for the worker, although not to the exclusion of other social sectors. Thus, "COPEI proclaims that social justice demands, on the one hand, the recognition of the rights of the workers and, on the other, the respect of rights of the other classes. . . ."[3] The Church-state relationship was an obvious question, and COPEI stated its position in vaguely imprecise terms. There was also a statement recognizing the fundamental importance of the family as the basis of national life. Caldera indicated publicly his intention of establishing for the party a broad popular base through the advocacy of social welfare measures, but he was hard-put to paint such policies as more than a pale reflection of long-established AD doctrine.

In 1946, as in the next few years, the influence of unreconstructed *lopecistas* continued strong, while less enlightened clerical circles also made themselves felt within COPEI. Caldera's public statements in this period frequently were expressed in language incomprehensible to many citizens, as, for example, a claim that "like the European movements inspired by the christian democratic current . . . [COPEI] has in its political essence and being the defense of the democratic ideal, a defense

[2] Venezuela, Presidencia de la República, *Documentos que Hicieron Historia; Siglo y Medio de Vida Republicana, 1810-1961* (Caracas: Ediciones Conmemorativas del Sesquicentenario de la Independencia, Vol. II, 1962), p. 388.

[3] Manuel Vicente Magallanes, *Partidos Políticos Venezolanos* (Caracas: Tip. Vargas, 1960), p. 153.

based on the dignity of the person and the realization of liberty. . . ."[4]

*Copeyano* conservatism in its early years was further underlined by the regional nature of the party. The heart of its strength lay in the conservative and highly Catholic states of the Andes, the same geographic section from which previous military dictators had emerged, and the historic isolation of this area from Venezuelan affairs cast a shadow on COPEI. The future of the party was to be dotted with efforts to extend its appeal beyond the Andes, a goal which neared fruition only in December 1963 elections.

Unlike COPEI, confronted in its adolescence with problems of regionalism, the second opposition party during the *trienio* was nationally based but even weaker in over-all appeal. The Unión Republicana Democrática was another offshoot of the October Revolution, and had no prior ancestry. Organized in December 1945 by the so-called "Grupo del Rosal," the URD leadership was initially composed of Isaac Pardo, Elías Toro, Rafael Vegas, and former *adeco* Inocente Palacios. The original manifesto declared the party to be the creation of men "concerned over the future of democracy and of republican institutions."[5] They promised to help achieve the program formulated by the Junta Revolucionaria de Gobierno, to fight for a direct presidential vote, and to aid and abet full public debate on the contents of the coming constitutional reform. None of this offered the voter anything different from the AD, but it marked the modest beginning of what later became a major political party with national appeal.

Where COPEI was influenced during the *trienio* by former *lopecistas*, the URD found itself infiltrated by *medinista* forces, including many former members of the PDV. Humberto Bartoli and Alfredo Tarre Murzi had

[4] *Ibid.*
[5] Venezuela, Presidencia de la República, *op.cit.*, p. 353.

been prominent in the *medinista* party; others who joined the URD in this formative period included Ignacio Luis Arcaya, Luis Hernández Solís, and J. M. Domínguez Chacín, all of them associates of Jóvito Villalba in forthcoming years.[6] Villalba himself, isolated from political power following the Revolution, employed his personal prestige to assert himself in the party, and he sought control of the URD as a personal vehicle for advancement. The original founders of the party were soon shunted into the background, and before the close of 1946 Villalba was paramount; *urredista* founders formally resigned in late 1947.

Known almost from the outset as a party of oratory, the URD gave but occasional doctrinal statements, all of them fairly nebulous. On no clear issue could the URD be differentiated from the AD, favoring as it did the implementation of similar policies. Villalba demanded the inclusion of his party in the government, a suggestion that had little electoral value during the *trienio*. With Villalba himself having been earlier an outstanding figure in the same movement from which Acción Democrática had come, there was in truth no programmatic or ideological reason for the party's existence. At the URD's first national meeting in the fall of 1946, Villalba presented a rhetorical set of proposals that included agrarian reform, anti-imperialism, and a reaffirmation of the commitment to the Revolution in its broad outlines. The party's general declaration of intent was less than concrete. "In social matters we are revolutionaries. . . . Our pronouncements against imperialism are categoric. In politics we are liberals, because we conceive that the transformation of the country will have to rely upon the effort of all Venezuelans. Since our founding we have predicated our existence as a party on the struggle for a

[6] A publication necessary to the study of the URD today is J. M. Domínguez Chacín, *El Partido Político; Estructura y Organización de Unión Republicana Democrática*, 2d ed. (Caracas: n.p., 1961).

unity of all political forces in a government of National Integration."[7]

Relations between the parties during the *trienio* were virtually non-existent. Acción Democrática, having stood alone while leading the fight for reforms since 1941, declared forthrightly that the tasks of carrying out the social revolution were its exclusive property. The URD was scornfully dismissed as an instrument of Villalba's *caudillismo* and of personal ambition; there was almost a disdain for such a small group, and recollections of Villalba's national prominence during student days were far from complimentary. For the AD, the URD was simply attempting to share in the rewards of office and to interfere for personal purposes in an historic undertaking to which Acción Democrática had exclusive rights.

Hostility between COPEI and the AD also ran high, and the immoderation of partisanship left precious little room for maneuver or accommodation on either side. The AD was unwilling to grant the credentials of COPEI as a genuine reformist organization. Rather, the party was viewed as a contemporary manifestation of strongly clerical elements with intellectual ties to the more extreme elements of *lopecismo*. The experience of the AD founders under the López Contreras government in the late 1930's was not to be wiped out so swiftly. The memory of harassment by the *lopecista* security forces was embittered, and feeling was generally far stronger against the government of López Contreras than that of Medina. The somewhat disunited *copeyano* group responded to AD attacks by charging that the latter was attempting to build a monolithic government party, one which could be expected to follow extreme lines where the religious issue might be involved. AD educational policies were especially suspect to COPEI.

During the period of the *trienio*, then, the relations of

[7] "La Convención de U. R. D. Marcará el Fin de la Jefatura Unica," *Momento*, no. 111, August 29, 1958, pp. 33-34.

the AD with both the URD and COPEI were charged with animosity, and the thought of even minimal accommodation was alien to the *adeco* mentality. It was true that the rank-and-file felt angrier toward its opponents than did the leadership. Even so, the most to be said for AD directors in this period is to note that they regarded COPEI and the URD as minor but bothersome annoyances which merely made more difficult the construction of a new, "modern" Venezuela. Nowhere within Acción Democrática was there awareness or recognition of possible benefits which might accrue from party cooperation. To the AD, the opposition parties were totally negative in approach and utterly devoid of the slightest likelihood of constructive contributions.

The November 1948 overthrow of Acción Democrática was carried out by the armed forces themselves, but the response of COPEI and URD hardened the AD's attitude toward them. The continued participation of COPEI and the URD in political affairs for a brief period after the military counter-revolution tarred them—in the AD view—with at least intellectual participation in the movement. Antagonism toward its two rivals continued in the AD through the early years of the military regime. The first encouragement of the later collaboration of the parties, however, came with the events surrounding the 1952 elections. The vote itself and the subsequent experience of all the parties in exile gradually led to the fuller collaboration which became possible after 1958.

### 1952 Elections and Exile Understanding

The military junta which seized power from the AD had organized a commission to draft an electoral statute, and its proposals were in government hands by 1950, shortly before the assassination of Carlos Delgado Chalbaud. On April 19, 1951, its provisions went into effect through the issuance of Decrees 118 and 119.[8] The

[8] For a detailed account of these events, see Leo B. Lott, "The

former raised the minimum voting age from eighteen to twenty-one, and denied parties the right to dispatch observers to voting sites. Suffrage became mandatory, with fines and sanctions applied against those who abstained. Decree 119 set forth additional details, and Acción Democrática was forbidden from participation. Thus, "those who have formed national or local directing organs of dissolved parties cannot be registered, nor can they take part in the functioning of parties or political organs."

The AD denounced the decrees as a vehicle for fraud and the perpetuation of the regime, but COPEI and the URD were both uncertain. COPEI, although guardedly optimistic, in October 1951 issued a statement attacking a possible postponement of elections, declaring that more than two years of *de facto* government was quite sufficient. The URD also regarded the government action with mixed feelings. Although Jóvito Villalba was openly optimistic, his friend and 1952 electoral colleague Mario Briceño-Iragorri was far from sanguine. He was to observe that he had little confidence in the course of events. "I shared at the outset the abstentionist thesis of Acción Democrática that . . . the presence of the opposition at the polls would give improper moral support to the farce that the military Government was preparing. . . ."[9]

The question of abstention or participation was critical to COPEI and the URD. Not until April 1952 did the regime even slightly relax the restrictions on public assembly; at the same time, party gatherings were "subject to future restrictions and prohibitions which the government might from time to time decree." Only on

1952 Venezuelan Elections: A Lesson for 1957," *The Western Political Quarterly*, X, no. 3, September 1957.

[9] His account was later published in Mario Briceño-Iragorri, *Ideario Político* (Caracas: Editorial "Las Novedades," 1958). He had generally been opposed to Acción Democrática.

May 4, 1952, was the URD permitted to stage a major rally in Nuevo Circo, the first such gathering since the overthrow of Rómulo Gallegos. Official restrictions continued, however, and included such matters as a complicated set of documents and programmatic statements which were required before a party could register and participate.

Perhaps inevitably, an official party gradually took shape. The pro-government organization began as an allegedly spontaneous movement that produced 1,600,-000 "adhesions" to the cause of Pérez Jiménez in the Federal District alone. This evolved into a Movimiento Pro-Adhesión, and three other "independent" organizations[10] soon banded together in forming the Frente Electoral Independiente (FEI). The Frente called for a series of mild reforms that were pale reflections of the planks proposed by the other parties.

The combination of restrictions on campaigning, creation of a pro-government party, and the general temperament of the regime fed doubts about the possibility of a free and meaningful vote. Acción Democrática could not accept the nature of elections, and indicated its abstentionist policy on the party's eleventh anniversary. Betancourt and clandestine leader Leonardo Ruiz Pineda issued the declaration "Ante la Farsa Electoral," in which party members were urged not to vote.[11] They reiterated the growing complaints of official intervention by COPEI and the URD in underscoring *adeco* objections.

COPEI, which had preceded the URD in calling for free elections in the preceding year,[12] also was first in proclaiming its decision to take part. On September 14, 1952, the party issued a strongly worded critique of existing internal conditions, further charging that the likeli-

[10] The Frente Electoral, the Unión Nacional, and the Organización Independiente.

[11] Acción Democrática, *Ante la Farsa Electoral* (Caracas, 1952).

[12] COPEI, *Copei Frente al Estatuto Electoral y la Actual Situación Política* (Caracas: Avila Gráfica, s. a., 1951).

hood of free elections was dubious. At the same time, however, the party declared itself morally compelled to seek at least a handful of delegates to the proposed 1953 Constituent Assembly, in order to fight against and to condemn anticipated abuses of democracy by government forces.

Thirteen days later the Unión Republicana Democrática released a statement which was similar in tenor. It rejected abstention as not in keeping with "democratic revolutionary movements." The URD manifesto denounced electoral conditions in more outspoken terms than had COPEI. The illegalization of Acción Democrática was criticized as closing political activity to large sectors of the population. Furthermore, "those of us who enjoy the relative possibility of acting legally, are nonetheless persecuted at each step—are menaced, are spied upon." The URD concluded that, if the seemingly inevitable fraud did take place on election day, the entire nation would turn against the government.

Toward the close of the campaign in late 1952, official harassment grew by leaps and bounds. The *urredista* and *copeyano* campaigns differed both in tone and program. The URD pursued an ultra-nationalistic line— far more so than in previous elections. Denouncing the imperialism of foreign capital and attacking COPEI as reactionary and clerical, the URD advocated the refinement of Venezuelan oil inside the country and under Venezuelan controls. The party platform called merely for the nationalization of gasoline sales in the country, but at least one *urredista* leader called for total nationalization of the petroleum industry. Public works were promised in terms of irrigation and electrification projects in the interior. The regime's public works program in Caracas was attacked as grandiose, extravagant, and unnecessary.

COPEI followed a more moderate course. While still including representatives of more conservative thought in Venezuela, the party could not fairly be charged—as it was by the communists—of representing the same interests as did the government.[13] Moderate reforms were proposed, and particular attention was given to honest administration, government aid to private industry, and the complete protection of human rights and the dignity of the individual. Rafael Caldera toured the interior to whip up support for the anti-government cause, as did Villalba and URD leaders.

The climax of the campaign came on November 26, 1952, with the closing rally of the URD. Major addresses were delivered by Villalba and Briceño-Iragorri, while the anti-government flavor was indicated by a moment of silence in observation of the recent death of AD underground leader Ruiz Pineda. The fluttering of white handkerchiefs in the crowd suggested the AD sympathies of many who attended.[14] The regime attempted to minimize the gathering by calling fifteen FEI meetings in Caracas the same night, providing free transportation by government vehicle. The device was unsuccessful, however, for most of the FEI meetings were sparsely attended while more than 50,000 went to Nuevo Circo to cheer Jóvito Villalba at his oratorical best.

A major element in the inter-party relations of the period was the decision of Acción Democrática to reverse its abstentionist policy. Although prohibited from open participation and highly dubious about the chances of a free vote, the party was mildly surprised by the continued activity of COPEI and the URD. Grasping at the slim chance of a change in regime, the party chose to instruct its followers. Fearing that a public declaration might provide the regime with an excuse to postpone elections or annul the results, the party did not announce

---

[13] Partido Comunista Venezolano, *La Actuación de los Partidos; la Farsa Electoral* (Caracas, 1952).

[14] White was the traditional color of Acción Democrática, and the waving of handkerchiefs at political meetings was a common occurrence.

its change in plans. However, clandestine leaders spread the word as widely as possible, and supporters were urged to vote for Jóvito Villalba's party.[15]

The choice of the URD rather than COPEI was less than a major dilemma. Opposition from the latter party during the *trienio* had been more fundamental and in large part doctrinal; the same could not be said of the URD. On the personal level, ties of friendship with Villalba existed, and his personal beliefs were considered more attuned to those of the AD than were Caldera's. As a final practical point, there was the fact that Villalba was the best-known politician at liberty in the country. The AD therefore reasoned that its interests in opposing the government would best be served by supporting the Unión Republicana Democrática.[16]

Generally orderly voting was held on November 30, 1952, and early returns that evening suggested an overwhelming victory for the URD. The Consejo Supremo Electoral first announced that the URD had 147,065 votes, while the FEI was barely over 50,000 and COPEI was a distant third. Over 30 percent of the votes had been counted, when a bulletin from the International News Service in Caracas told the world that the URD had won all but two states—the Andean strongholds of COPEI. Shortly after, the stream of official returns was cut off, and Venezuelans crowding about their radios heard nothing but music and commercials until the night of December 2, when Marcos Pérez Jiménez unexpectedly broadcast from Miraflores Palace.

A stunned nation was informed that the junta had resigned, giving full power to the military, who in turn had designated Pérez Jiménez as Provisional President. The junta resignation was taken, he announced, "with the purpose of giving the representations of the national armed forces the freedom to constitute a government that

[15] Interview with Octavio Lepage, January 10, 1963.
[16] Interview with Gonzalo Barrios, November 27, 1962.

is best in accord with the national interest. . . ." It was later added that the military had conferred on Pérez Jiménez all powers it had possessed "in the Constitutive Act of Provisional Government dated 24 November 1948, as modified 27 November 1950."[17] The proclamation was signed by Pérez Jiménez, Llovera Páez, and commanders of the several military branches.

This blatant maneuver was climaxed by a new set of election returns announced by the Consejo Electoral Supremo. The official final returns gave the government forces 788,086 votes to 638,336 for the URD, while COPEI was credited with but 300,309. International opinion swiftly mobilized in condemning the virtual *golpe de estado* on December 1, but had no effect on the outcome. In a telegram to URD leaders Villalba and Arcaya, Pérez Jiménez charged that much of the URD vote had come from communists and, more importantly, from Acción Democrática. The armed forces, he stated, would not accept results in which, allegedly, "the prestige of the nation will be damaged, seriously compromised by the electoral victory of Acción Democrática and of the Communist Party that the URD has taken advantage of."[18]

The government then called Villalba and others for a private interview with the Minister of Interior Relations. When they refused to accept the official verdict, they were taken into custody and exiled. Remaining steps to "legalize" the dictatorship were crisp and effective. The Constituent Assembly met on January 9, 1953, with COPEI and the URD members not in attendance. In ten days' time a draft constitution was ready, and it was soon promulgated. Included was a passage naming Pérez Jiménez as constitutional president for a five-year term.

The entire course of events affected AD relations with

---

[17] The text of the announcement is found in Venezuela, Presidencia de la República, *op.cit.*, pp. 416-18.

[18] The text is available in Briceño-Iragorri, *op.cit.*, pp. 229-30.

rival democratic parties in two ways. On one hand, a controversy with the URD was created which has never been resolved to the satisfaction of partisans. The obvious victory of the URD before the annulment of elections has been hailed by that party as a great triumph. As late as 1963 the *urredistas* recalled their opposition to dictatorship in 1952 and the smashing verdict which had been achieved. The quiet decision of the AD to join behind the URD is regarded as entirely unimportant. *Urredistas* argue that, since the AD's earlier public declaration had called for abstention, the votes amassed by the URD were positive indications of genuine URD strength.

Acción Democrática has naturally insisted on its own interpretation, remarking that the results of elections both during the *trienio* and after 1958 suggest the continued domination of pro-AD sentiment in the country. While conceding that the URD was more popular in 1952 than either COPEI or the military regime, the AD views the massive vote for the URD as the result of its own support of the Villalba forces.

Circumstances make an evaluation of rival claims less than precise, although AD arguments are more persuasive. Less than five years earlier it showed a consistent record of 70 percent or better, while the URD in three attempts had failed to win 5 percent of the vote. Further support for this contention came in a letter by Rutgers professor Robert J. Alexander to *The New York Times* shortly after the election. He reported that URD leaders had told him the previous June that they expected a large portion of AD votes.[19] Others to share this view included the London *Economist*, the Paris *Monde*, and Washington *Post*.

Beyond this particular controversy, however, the expulsion of *urredista* leaders and the subsequent creation of complete authoritarianism under Pérez Jiménez placed the URD and COPEI in much the same position as the

[19] *The New York Times*, December 9, 1952, p. 10.

AD. Although the persecution began somewhat later, by the end of 1957 these two parties had themselves suffered greatly at the hands of official repression. The sharing of this common experience with Acción Democrática tended to soften the past bitterness of partisan exchange, and all three parties eventually came to the realization that their interests would best be served by mutual action in opposing the dictatorship. The adoption of the "Nueva Táctica" by Acción Democrática at the 1956 conference of exiles was an expression of this attitude, one which was at great variance with that of the *trienio* period.

The adoption by the AD of a policy of full and active cooperation with COPEI and the URD was intended to be implemented through consultation and discussion. Gradual cooperation inside Venezuela among underground groups was followed by talks among exile leaders. Preliminary plans were made to establish effective interparty cooperation through a single exile directorate located in Bogotá, Colombia. The unexpectedly rapid rush of events at the end of 1957 led to the overthrow of the regime before the center could be opened. However, interparty cooperation led to a formal AD proposal in January 1958—before Pérez Jiménez' flight—that all three parties unite for the reestablishment of representative democracy in Venezuela. Included was a call for the selection of a single, unopposed presidential candidate in the next free elections.

Jóvito Villalba was contacted in the United States, while a personal letter was sent from Betancourt to *copeyano* leader Caldera in Venezuela. Traveling from Costa Rica with the message sewn into the sole of his shoe, Enrique Tejera París narrowly eluded authorities while seeking out Caldera, himself at this time a hunted man.[20] The message could not be delivered, and Caldera himself was arrested and exiled. Yet the attempted formalization of party cooperation along these lines

[20] Interview with Enrique Tejera París, November 2, 1962.

indicated the distance away from unbridled partisanship which all three parties had traveled. From this point it was a relatively short step to the kind of collaborative understanding which was undertaken following the return to Venezuela.

## Collaboration and Coexistence

The tri-party effort to collaborate during the recuperative period following the restoration of constitutional government in Venezuela proved unable to select a single candidate, but the spirit of conciliation nonetheless prevailed. It was formalized by the public signature of the Pact of Punto Fijo on October 31, 1958. In addition to the cooperative commitment to representative democracy, a common minimum program was accepted. Future exchanges of views and a continuation of cordiality behind the elected president were promised. National enthusiasm was reflected in the commentary of the popular weekly *Momento*. "Failure of a single candidacy under a triparty pact has now led to creation of a possibility no less fertile or promising for the maintenance of unity: the constitution of a legal government of coalition."[21]

The immediate result was the formation by Rómulo Betancourt of a cabinet that included representatives of COPEI and the URD in addition to his own party. The inevitable rise of partisanship developed, however, soon after the 1959 inauguration of the government. Almost from the outset there were strains between the AD and the Unión Republicana Democrática. Temperamental differences developed which proved difficult to smooth over. For the URD, a vivid memory of what was believed a great victory in 1952 enforced a feeling that the party needed to go its own way. Although differences of policy were largely ones of degree, the area of foreign policy proved a source of constant friction. The ultimate withdrawal of the URD from the government coalition in

[21] *Momento*, no. 121, November 7, 1958, p. 53.

1960 was a direct result of clashing views over such policy.

The rise of Fidel Castro in Cuba captured a great deal of sympathy in Venezuela in 1959 and 1960. The URD, influenced by its younger membership, felt itself strongly attuned to the Cuban Revolution at the outset. Whereas AD and *copeyano* leaders were suspicious from the beginning, the URD committed itself firmly to the Cuban Revolution, which it was later to negate only with difficulty. In the meantime, however, the divergent AD-URD views toward Castro came to a head in 1960. At San José, Costa Rica, in August and September 1960, a pair of Foreign Ministers' Conferences were held, one of them considering the matter of possible sanctions against Trujillo's Dominican Republic, the other against revolutionary Cuba. Heading the Venezuelan delegation was the *urredista* Foreign Minister, Ignacio Luis Arcaya.

In the course of conference discussions concerning possible action against Cuba, Arcaya pursued a less than unsympathetic course—one which was advocated by the URD but was contrary to the governmental decisions taken in cabinet meetings before his departure from Caracas. As reports filtered back to Venezuela, consternation in the government was noticeable. In the confusion that ensued, Arcaya for a time withdrew from the delegation as its official head, considered his resignation, then withdrew it just as most observers expected Betancourt to accept it. Back in Caracas Jóvito Villalba had just returned from an extensive tour, found the situation tense, and at once tried to patch up differences. Betancourt and Arcaya were personally inclined to continue their official relationship, but the task was rendered more difficult by recriminations between rank-and-file members of both parties.

*Urredistas* attacked the developing anti-Castro sentiment of official policy, hailed Arcaya as a hero, and demanded that the party withdraw from the coalition.

Many *adecos*, on the other hand, stated that Arcaya had put party before nation by ignoring policy directives laid down at cabinet meetings, and therefore he should be ousted from the coalition along with the party. Somewhat abrasive personal encounters at the cabinet level also heightened ill will, and Villalba was more confusing than effective in trying to make political capital from the episode without leaving the government. Two months after the San José episode, the URD finally took the inevitable step and withdrew from the coalition. There were few recriminations on either side at the time, and Rómulo Betancourt's lack of concern over the *urredista* decision was paralleled by URD satisfaction at being free of the constricting ties of governmental participation.

From late 1960 on, the URD adopted a position of increasing criticism toward the government, and the AD in particular retorted in kind. With the accession of *mirista* and *arsista* rebels in Congress, the URD found itself the most numerous member of the anti-government majority in the Chamber of Deputies from 1962 to 1964. Criticism of government policy and also of official intentions regarding national elections became extreme, and no one was more vocal than Jóvito Villalba. Yet the response from *adecos* was less outspoken, due at least partially to great concern over healing two internal wounds while supporting the government against extremist terrorism.

The relations between the AD and URD grew rather acrimonious, then, and remained so until after 1963 elections. In contrast, COPEI and the AD maintained close ties throughout. *Copeyanos* headed several important ministries, including that of agriculture, from which policy emanated for the execution of the agrarian reform program. Legislative relations between the *fracciones* or parliamentary wings of the two parties were good; especially after the loss of a government majority in the lower house, *copeyano* Herrera Campins and *adeco*

Barrios worked closely and effectively in combatting the opposition on behalf of government policy. *Rapport* between the two parties' legislators was frequently close and almost always effective.

In the sweep of political events in contemporary Venezuela, among the more important developments has been the growing maturity and experienced efficacy of COPEI. In large measure this can be credited to the five years of cooperation with the AD, fighting to resist the various pressures that threatened the government on numerous occasions. The opportunity to share in the making of policy and the administering of existing programs was important to the party, and by the conclusion of the Betancourt government there could be little question about the maturity and general responsibility which characterized AD-COPEI relations.

Little certainty is possible in speaking of AD dealings with the other groups which grew up after 1958. The existence of MIR and ARS, both of them composed of former *adecos,* provided a special case. In the first instance, the eventual participation of the MIR in actions of violence and non-constitutional opposition led to unyielding opposition from the AD. The *arsista* case varied slightly, conditioned by rival claims about the legitimacy of twin AD parties. The virtual annihilation of the *arsistas* in the 1963 elections made the relationship of negligible future importance.

Only the relations with communists and *miristas* were marked by an attitude of intransigence; leftist extremism brought violence and destruction to which the government, AD, and COPEI responded with stern opposition. The first major outburst came in November 1960 with an attempted leftist insurrection sparked by a strike of telephone workers. Students staged demonstrations, burned automobiles in Caracas, and followed communist and *mirista* directives to attempt full-scale revolt. Nearly four days of rioting and violence ensued until Betancourt reluctantly ordered army troops into the streets, at the same time declaring a state of emergency and suspending several constitutional guarantees.

This first such suspension under the Betancourt government was to continue nearly eighteen months. An investigation led to the lodging of charges against *mirista* Domingo Alberto Rangel and communist Teodoro Petkoff. The former was exonerated, but Petkoff was finally brought to trial. The *comisión permanente* of Congress concluded its own investigation with the decision to lift Deputy Petkoff's immunity, and he was subsequently tried, found guilty of attempted subversion, and jailed. The restoration of full guarantees in December 1961 was interrupted several times in the months ahead, and constituted a major source of partisan criticism by the opposition.

On these occasions the constitutional suspensions were only partial. As Alexander has recently observed, four limitations on democratic rights were noticeable: press freedom was limited, outdoor political meetings were forbidden, the government was permitted to raid homes without warrant and could also arrest citizens without an obligation to bring them before the courts in a given period of time.[22] Press restrictions were applied primarily to the communist daily *Tribuna Popular* and the *mirista* weekly *Izquierda*, although the URD's daily *Clarín*, which came to provide an outlet for extremist editorial polemics, was also censored and frequently shut down temporarily. The restrictions on outdoor political meetings—applied against the AD and COPEI as well as extremist organizations—was but a minor hardship. In contrast, the two suspensions regarding the raiding of homes without warrant and unlimited detention of suspected lawbreakers were more serious in their impact.

Supporters of the government argued that the limita-

[22] Robert J. Alexander, *The Venezuelan Democratic Revolution* (New Brunswick: Rutgers University Press, 1964), p. 127.

tions on liberties were necessitated by the insistence of the non-democratic opposition to act outside the bounds of political legitimacy. Furthermore, it was argued that average citizens were not affected by the restrictions. Opponents seized upon the actions as arbitrary, repressive, and designed to spare the government serious criticism and open attacks. It should be noted that Congress remained in session throughout the five-year term. Perhaps more significantly, the election year 1963 was totally without constitutional restrictions until the brutal murders of several National Guardsmen on an excursion train toward the end of the campaign. The public outrage at the opposition—as noted elsewhere—permitted official action intended to outlaw both the PCV and MIR. The action was still before the courts at election time; leading congressmen from the two parties had in several cases been apprehended and taken into custody. It is significant that even the URD and AD-ARS recognized public acceptance of official actions and muted their criticism of the action.

In the aftermath of 1963 elections, there were early indications of growing responsibility within the democratic party system. Acción Democrática became far more moderate in its partisanship. COPEI eventually refused to join the government of Leoni after extended conversations in early 1964, but while there was sentiment in both COPEI and the AD against continued cooperation, there was little acrimony in the negotiations. *Copeyano* demands in terms of cabinet positions and state governorships were higher than the new President was willing to pay, but COPEI's return to its self-proclaimed "independent judgment" gave no sign of returning to the kind of exaggerated partisanship that had existed during *trienio* days.

There were also indications that URD relations with the AD were heading for smoother waters. With the URD's expulsion of its extremist wing early in 1964, the party established better relations with the AD. Jóvito Villalba, long a friend of many prominent *adecos*, led his party in a moderation of attitudes toward the AD. By the summer of 1964 the URD enjoyed better relations with Acción Democrática than ever before. A final indication of general improvement was the moderation of forces grouped about a former "independent" senator and 1963 presidential candidate, Arturo Uslar Pietri. Following elections Uslar organized his congressional supporters into the Frente Nacional Democrático (FND). Although his intellectual and programmatic position was more at variance with that of the AD than were other parties', Uslar gave early signs of adopting a moderate opposition which would further contribute to political responsibility.[23]

The evolutionary stage reached by the national party system by 1964, buttressed by the successful completion of elections and the formation of a new government, was distinguished by a spirit of conciliation and of coexistence that was new to Venezuela. Acción Democrática was no longer arrogant in insisting that all policy responsibility should be a party monopoly; it conceded that the cooperation of its competitors was both desirable and necessary. In turn, the democratic opposition accepted the *adeco* attitude in viewing national affairs as the domain of all loyal Venezuelans. No longer convinced that the AD was plotting their eradication by means either electoral or illegal, the opposition parties were inclined to operate within the bounds of a competitive system. Although future events might well change conditions drastically, there were clear indications as of late 1964 that inter-party relations were both more responsible and less destructive than ever before.

[23] By fall of 1964, President Leoni organized a three-party coalition in which the URD and Uslar Pietri's FND joined Acción Democrática in the cabinet.

# CHAPTER XII

# The Party and Elections

The overwhelming proportion of AD electoral victories during the *trienio* held steady at some 70 percent of the vote. Given the relative insignificance of the opposition and the AD domination of government, results could scarcely have been otherwise. With the return of contested elections in 1958, the party found itself pressed as never before to prove again its position as leading vote-getter in Venezuela. The triumph of Rómulo Betancourt with a shade less than 50 percent of the 1958 vote returned the party to office, but its position—shaky from the outset—was further weakened by first the *mirista* and later the *arsista* defectors. By 1963 the party had little choice but to stand for election alone; only through such a contested battle could the relative strength or weakness of Acción Democrática be proved.

The 1963 elections were of historic importance not only for Venezuela but, on a different level, for the hemispheric struggle against communism. For the AD itself, the returns charted the course of government for future years while indicating the party's popular strength in comparison with that of its opponents. Analysis of the returns also promised to reveal party soft spots. No evaluation of Acción Democrática in the decade of the sixties is possible without a detailed study of the 1963 elections and a comparison with the returns of 1958.

## The 1963 Campaign[1]

In late 1962 and early 1963 the major parties were occupied with the search for possible coalitions. Given

---

[1] Portions of this chapter are taken from a more detailed account by the author. For the fuller analysis, see Martz, *The Venezuelan Elections of 1963* (Washington: Institute for the Comparative Study of Political Systems, 1964).

the general pro- and anti-government groupings at the time, a variety of possibilities existed. Both Acción Democrática and COPEI indicated genuine interest in a continuation of their collaboration. A uniting of forces seemed to make victory certain in December, and the general thrust of national policy would at the same time have been preserved. The possibility of a single opposition candidate made more attractive the possibility of an accord between the AD and COPEI.

Party loyalties proved too strong, however. AD Party President Raúl Leoni and other leaders had stated that the party had to run its own flag-bearer, and much the same situation existed for COPEI. Chafing in its position as junior partner in government, confident of its growth, and assured of a brightening future under the popular Rafael Caldera, COPEI was not prepared to accept an *adeco* as its candidate. The quiet suggestion that Caldera run as a unity candidate was rejected by the AD, and eventually the chances of agreement dimmed. By midsummer the prospects for a single candidate were virtually nil.

Acción Democrática met first, holding its XIII National Convention in Caracas' Teatro Boyacá on July 2. There were 671 delegates, and for the first time in party history the choice of a candidate was not fully obvious. Leading contenders were two of Betancourt's early colleagues in building the party: President Leoni and First Vice-President Gonzalo Barrios. Dark horses included a rising Betancourt protégé, ex-Minister of Interior Relations Carlos Andrés Pérez, and Eligio Anzola Anzola, another former cabinet minister and a staunch partisan with regional support from his home state of Lara.[2]

While the choice seemed to be Leoni or Barrios, a complicating factor was Rómulo Betancourt's own preference

[2] For a useful journalistic account, see "La Convención de AD," *Momento*, no. 36, July 7, 1963, pp. 26-29.

for a five- or six-man slate of candidates. To leave open the door for joint action with COPEI, the President advised such a list, from which the Comité Ejecutivo Nacional might choose a candidate in conference with leading *copeyanos*. The proposal was received with considerable coolness, and Betancourt eventually withdrew in the face of obvious preference for a single candidate. The balloting for a nominee gave Leoni 474 votes, Barrios 117, Anzola Anzola 43, and Luis Augusto Dubuc, 27. The defeated candidates called for unanimity, which was immediately granted.

Raúl Leoni had begun nearly a year earlier to project himself toward a possible nomination, and frequent trips to the interior as Party President had bettered his chances. Strong and effective support came from the party's Labor Bureau, whose leaders were personally close to Leoni while indebted to him for assistance as Minister of Labor from 1945-1948. The presence of 180 labor delegates and 140 from the AD's agricultural sector gave Leoni a substantial bloc of support from the outset, and his first-ballot victory followed with ease. Only Gonzalo Barrios had credentials as a party founder which rivaled those of Leoni himself, but most of his backing came from the Youth Bureau of the party, which was not strong. A few others preferred him to Leoni because of their belief that the Party President was at best an uninspired if conscientious party worker lacking in the vision necessary to forge a coalition government while dealing with both terroristic and military pressures.

The nomination of Leoni was significant in several respects. In the first place, it was perhaps the first basic decision the party had taken in contradiction of Betancourt's wishes. While the latter was not opposed *per se* to his old collaborator, he strongly desired an agreement with COPEI and rightly acknowledged the unacceptability of a Leoni candidacy to the *copeyanos*. Beyond this, the party for the first time was presented with a definite choice, and serious internal fighting was avoided. Thirdly, the possibility of a joint campaign with COPEI disappeared, and COPEI's nominee at its own convention in August became a foregone conclusion.

On August 23 the IX National Convention of COPEI opened before 450 delegates; on the 25th the party platform was adopted, and the following night Rafael Caldera was nominated by acclamation. *Copeyano* support for the AD candidate had become academic once Leoni was chosen, and the party had no alternative to Caldera. There had been some concern that a fourth defeat might close the door to any chance of Caldera's ever obtaining the presidency. But the absence of other party leaders with the proven stature or national appeal of Rafael Caldera forced his nomination upon COPEI.

With the government forces each going separate ways, the opposition attempted to arrive at a single candidate, but without success. Among the earlier possibilities mentioned in the press were the URD's Villalba, ex-junta president Larrazábal, lawyer-writer Arturo Uslar Pietri, philanthropist Eugenio Mendoza, and *arsista* President Raúl Ramos Giménez. In the end, all but Mendoza became active candidates. In the URD, Jóvito Villalba had been engaged since the fall of 1962 in a struggle to retain control of the party; in addition to left-wingers who opposed him, others believed that a repeat of the 1958 support for Larrazábal would be advantageous.

Villalba's months-long effort finally won the necessary grass-roots support, assuring his candidacy before the URD convention met. This left before him the task of gathering other anti-government forces behind his candidacy, but the URD "maestro" was unsuccessful. The first who rejected his overture was the AD-ARS, by this time referred to as AD-Op, or Acción Democrática en Oposición. Increasingly rent with internal difficulties of its own, the *arsista* group regarded Villalba as but another party nominee, and at its convention Raúl Ramos Giménez was selected. One of the results was the withdrawal from the party of its *campesino* leader Ramón Quijada, who had bitterly argued in favor of independent Senator Arturo Uslar Pietri.

The latter become the third announced opposition candidate when, on July 13, he declared himself at a celebration in San Cristóbal, an Andean town near the Colombian border. In the absence of an established organization or formal convention, he was chosen by a so-called Independent Electoral Committee composed of the minuscule Movimiento Republicano Popular (MRP) and the peasant groups of Quijada recently rechristened the Comité Electoral Campesino. A prime mover in the administration of Medina Angarita, Uslar had long been engaged in both a personal and programmatic fight with Acción Democrática.[3] He immediately introduced a basic anti-party approach that was to continue throughout the campaign.

One further candidacy was that of retired Admiral Larrazábal, who on July 31 appeared in Caracas' Plaza Urdaneta to speak of the tragedy of hungry Venezuelans and to reiterate past statements calling for a broad change in the entire socio-economic structure of Venezuela. His speech was preceded by a message from Jorge Dager— an ex-*adeco* and later ex-*mirista*—who announced the organized backing of his own one-man Frente Democrático Popular (FDP). The August selection of Caldera, then, put six major candidates in the field: Leoni, Caldera, Villalba, Larrazábal, Uslar Pietri, and Ramos Giménez.

Party activities during the summer months also included participation in the national electoral census, and

---

[3] One of the more striking evidences was his sharply critical review of Professor Lieuwen's *Venezuela*, in which the AD is treated sympathetically and much of the interpretation of the *trienio* relies upon the writing of Rómulo Betancourt.

those groups with significant organizations worked strenuously to register all eligible voters. Interest lagged at first, and by mid-July the parties began to share general concern. Gonzalo Barrios, acting AD President in lieu of Leoni, announced the dispatching of directives to the AD membership; disciplinary sanctions were threatened for any who failed to register. The party concentrated on Caracas during the week of July 21-28, and later turned to other regions. COPEI conducted an extensive telephone campaign in urban areas, and the URD was notably active in the interior. By the end of the official sixty-day registration period, the Consejo Supremo Electoral announced that over two million had been recorded. Two further fifteen-day extensions carried on until the close of August. Final figures—not released until late October—listed 3,369,986 registered voters; this was out of an estimated 3,586,000 eligible voters, or 93.97 percent.

In a very real sense the campaign had been going on informally for many months, but not until August did all the candidates begin the semi-official phase of the contest. For Acción Democrática, the exposition of its platform was, as always, of great campaign importance. Raúl Leoni had first stated the broad goals of the party during his acceptance speech, and these were developed more fully in his subsequent Program of Government.[4] The AD divided its platform into four major spheres: the political, social, economic, and institutional. As the principal representative of the government, the party placed strong emphasis in its political proposals on the maintenance and consolidation of the democratic system. There were echoes of the past in statements favoring direct and secret universal suffrage. Extremist parties might be rehabilitated into the body politic, but only upon their own initiative. In the international field the

[4] Acción Democrática, *Programa de Gobierno* (Caracas: Italográfica, 1963).

AD urged a strengthening of international cooperation and continuing opposition of the strongest sort toward the "totalitarianism imposed upon the Cuban people."

Turning to social matters, there was a continuing commitment to state capitalism, with the party "sustaining the obligation of the state to promote opportunities of all sorts; to broaden the rule of Social Security and to create the opportunities for employment; and to guarantee workers' rights to organize. . . ." With the population expected to rise by 2.7 million in the next five years, it was held necessary to create at least 400,000 jobs. Economic matters also stood out; among these was a promise to continue and to expand the existing program of agrarian reform. Leoni promised to extend land ownership by 200,000, relying substantially upon large unproductive areas to be supported by technical assistance and an improved extension service.

Industrialization was to reach the point at which dependence on foreign producers would effectively be reduced, and public credit was to become a more influential tool in the stimulation of economic development. The gravity of the housing shortage demanded the construction of 75,000 homes annually, or a total of 375,-000. Finally, institutional reforms were to include an administrative strengthening of the provinces, as Leoni often reiterated during his tours through the interior.

With few exceptions, the platforms of opposing candidates differed only in degree. The *copeyano* Program of Government covered virtually the same points, except that the party criticized certain areas of governmental policy which the AD necessarily had to defend. Social security projects were termed inadequate, with COPEI promising a "unification and simplification of administrative structures and a progressive extension of . . . services." An innovation was suggested through a Law of Family Loans, based on the spirit of social-minded papal encyclicals, under which a family subsidy would be available. Most dramatic of specific socio-economic proposals was a flat promise to build 500,000 homes in the next five years. Basing its argument on the existing housing deficit of some 700,000 and the predicted five-year increase of 300,000, COPEI criticized government policy as inadequate.[5]

Differences between the AD and COPEI centered largely over plans for 75,000 or for 100,000 new homes annually, as well as the family subsidy called for by COPEI. However, a perceptible consensus on most important issues existed when the several party platforms were compared. For the URD, a basic five-point statement set forth sharp criticism of government policy. Proposals for change were essentially imitative in content, however. Villalba campaigned with a set of socio-economic policies similar to those of Leoni and Caldera. Social security was to be expanded, educational opportunities improved, and broader health and medical services were promised. Employment was to be encouraged by a variety of measures that were in large part tied to the concomitant goal of increased industrialization. The latter point was a major *urredista* economic objective, as was a program of improved agrarian reform so designed as to avoid alleged shortcomings of official policy that merely led to a multiplication of ownership on unproductive lands.

URD criticism in the political sphere centered on charges of official AD *continuismo* and the possibility of electoral fraud to perpetuate the AD in office. The URD promised "a national democratic government to bring peace and understanding to all Venezuelans and to guarantee work for all as well as the full national development of the country." Government inflexibility in dealing with leftist extremists was attacked, and the URD called for the

[5] According to the 1963-1966 Plan de la Nación, 260,000 would be built; 193,500 to be partially or wholly financed by the public sector, and 66,500 exclusively by the private sector.

incorporation of the MIR and PCV into the circle of legitimacy once again. Extremists were promised an amnesty, and Villalba called for a "restoration" of the constitutional system, which he charged the Betancourt government with having shattered.

The opposition of Arturo Uslar Pietri, while perhaps in more basic disagreement with AD policy than that of the other candidates, was spelled out in broad terms that gave little indication of the areas of conflict. Uslar joined in criticism of government policy toward the MIR and PCV, arguing that the AD had failed to lead the nation within legal boundaries. He promised a climate of peace and order within which socio-economic adjustments might be made. As the most conservative of major candidates, Uslar muted to a degree the specifics of his program which might have indicated a brake on the pace of reforms.

The official platforms of the two remaining opposition candidates were characteristic of their personal inclinations. Wolfgang Larrazábal appealed to the electorate for a "revolution of coexistence and eradication of misery." Urging cordial relations with the Church (where no serious dispute existed), he pledged the continued merger of the armed forces into the mainstream of democratic attitudes and procedures. *Arsista* Raúl Ramos Giménez apparently felt no compunction about promising the sky, and his five-point program included "Venezuelan food for all," free books for students at all levels, and a minimum of 750,000 new jobs for workers.[6]

As active campaigning picked up in intensity, each of the contestants threw all available resources into the contest. Seeking maximum exposure, they emphasized personal contact, and the nation was subjected to a more active campaign than ever before. The two

[6] For an analysis of *arsista* difficulties in 1963, see Gonzalo Alvarez, "La Ultima Crisis del ARS," *Momento*, no. 368, August 4, 1963, pp. 56-59.

most effective over-all campaigns were those of COPEI
and of Uslar Pietri's "non-party" group, while Acción
Democrática revived the same electoral mechanism utilized five years earlier.[7] A Comisión Electoral was established under the direction of 1958's winning electoral
manager, Luis Lander. With sub-commissions headed
respectively by the party's national Secretaries of Press,
Propaganda, and Organization, Lander exercised over-
all supervision from Caracas.

The Comisión tried to channel the efforts of Leoni
himself, constantly setting up and clearing his itinerary
with the candidate's personal staff. Regional electoral
commissions also functioned under the rule of the national group; requests for party leaders or for the candidate, renewed efforts in critical areas, and reports on
existing currents of sentiment were funneled back to
headquarters. As the campaign proceeded, it became apparent that its organization was superior to that of 1958.
Unlike his predecessor, Leoni had a full three months
to campaign, and the Comisión Electoral was in operation even before that.

Lander remarked that the Comisión had a dual educational function which preceded the more usual campaign role. In one aspect this related to the shift of
party colors on the voters' tarjeta[8] as a result of the decision by the Consejo Supremo Electoral regarding the
claims of the AD and of AD-ARS.[9] The AD choice of

[7] Detailed factual information on the mechanics of the AD
campaign was provided by Luis Lander, interviewed on February
4, 1964. Interpretations here rely upon the views of rival cam-
paigners as well as independent observers.

[8] With the granting of the vote to illiterates by the AD government in the 1940's, the use of colored ballots or tarjetas and
party symbols was adopted as an effective means of identification.

[9] The AD and ARS had entered claims to the traditional white
tarjeta and party symbol before the Consejo Supremo Electoral.
The former had registered the symbol and names under terms
of the national Industrial Property law, while arsistas had done

black, despite negative connotations which made some *adecos* initially dubious, demanded extensive publicizing. After twenty years' identification with white, this mattered greatly to the party.[10] Viewing the choice of black as the simplest change, the AD then began the task of propagandizing it; this was to prove the most successful facet of the entire AD campaign, for Venezuelan voters virtually without exception learned of the change.

A second educational task was the preparation of rank-and-file members to act as observers at the thousands of individual voting tables. Training classes were held throughout the country to explain the duties and responsibilities, the kinds of situations that might arise, and the various responses which were possible. Much of this effort actually preceded the national convention in July, and Luis Lander had set up his office well before the party nominee was decided. Both before and after the convention, however, the broad educational function of the campaign was emphasized. Especially in view of leftist attempts to block elections, the party regarded them as an educational function in which civic participation and democratic forms were of vital importance.

AD leaders were aware of their position as the dominant government party and the connotations that much of their campaigning therefore bore. Demonstration

---

the same thing under a separate section of the copyright and patents law. The CSE was forced to eliminate the white *tarjeta* and symbol for 1963, promising to validate its use for the party which ran strongest in the elections. Relevant data and documents in photostated form are found in Acción Democrática, *La Batalla por el Nombre y Símbolos de Acción Democrática* (Caracas: Publicaciones de la Secretaría Nacional de Propaganda, 1963).

[10] The *arsista* determination to win the use of traditional AD symbols underlined concern about electoral prospects. The opportunity of capitalizing on old party loyalties seemed promising as a way of increasing its vote in December.

that a party in power could hold honest, contested elections received great emphasis. There was some expectation that party strength would decline from 1958 as a result of inevitable erosion of popularity after five years in office. Nonetheless a firm decision was made that the first priority was the holding of elections and the defense of the constitutional system. Although the AD campaign was clearly a partisan one, the leadership placed its own victory second to the overriding goal of a free vote and selection of a new government.[11] Thus there was no hesitation in retorting to opponents' charges, but in most cases this meant an enunciation of the existing government record.

The tone of moderation was echoed by Raúl Leoni. Aware of his image as an unyielding and inflexible partisan, and also recognizing the eventual necessity of forming another coalition government should he win, Leoni bore down heavily on the responsibilities of constitutional government. A shrewd but quiet politician whose forte lay outside the delivery of campaign speeches, Leoni repeatedly called for national conciliation. If his personality was not likely to capture many undecided voters, it at least was presented in such a way as to make him acceptable in the event of victory.

Some of the sharpest electoral attacks came from AD's junior partner in government, COPEI. At the outset COPEI faced the apparent difficulty of being associated in the popular mind with the government. There was the danger that unpopular measures largely the work of the AD would be tied to COPEI as well. The appeal to the electorate therefore demanded some differenti-

[11] This statement, while accurate, should not be regarded as a partisan claim of a selfless and disinterested attitude on the part of AD leaders. There was no serious question in their minds about ultimate victory, and campaign managers never felt that the moderation in campaigning would mean a difference between victory and defeat. The only question was that of the winning margin.

ation from the AD. In time, the party succeeded with remarkable skill in having the best of two worlds—of taking credit for government achievements while disassociating itself from less popular matters. The response on election day testified to the *copeyano* success in this delicate juggling act.

Specifics of the COPEI program were spelled out repeatedly, and the single item which caught fire was the promise of 100,000 new houses annually. The party at the same time was vocal in taking credit for the favorable aspects of agrarian reform—reminding voters that it had held the Ministry of Agriculture—while tarring the AD with the brush of ineffective implementation through the AD-directed Instituto Nacional de Reforma Agraria. The AD was also criticized for continuing national terrorism and governmental handling of extremism. COPEI represented itself as strongly anticommunist while insisting that all official measures be strictly legal and constitutional. There were broad hints that police inefficiency and AD inflexibility contributed to the continuing rancor and violence of extremist activities.

Rafael Caldera also helped the cause through an effective personal campaign. By 1963 he seemed, both nationally and internationally, second only to Rómulo Betancourt in political stature. Earlier campaigns had helped to make his face a familiar one, and at 46 he radiated a youthful spirit that appealed to the growing number of young Venezuelan voters. His winning television personality was an additional asset, and at one point he even debated with Arturo Uslar Pietri,[12] something that Leoni prudently avoided. If the *copeyano* organization lacked the smoothness of the well-oiled AD apparatus, it was adequate to mount an effort throughout the entire Republic.

---

[12] *El Debate Caldera-Uslar Pietri; Texto Completo del Debate por Televisión el 22/10/63* (Caracas, 1963).

The unqualifiedly anti-government campaigns were more diverse in organization and tactics. Only the Unión Republicana Democrática enjoyed anything approaching a national organization, and it was rent by a continuing internal struggle. National supervision of the campaign was weak, and Villalba ran it in large part from his traveling party. The URD's historic organizational weakness was a drawback, for the candidate's intense personal campaign failed to capitalize on the popular *rapport* he did indeed establish on many occasions. Jóvito reached many remote parts of Venezuela and ordinarily drew an enthusiastic response, but the day after his visit to a town or hamlet there would be little effective organizational follow-up.

The URD in large part called for the same broad policies as did the two government parties, but with the customary promise of accomplishing them better. Villalba attacked the government as being politically bankrupt, and not until late summer did he grow confident that elections would actually be held. Representing himself as the only truly national figure who might "reunite" all Venezuelans, he was often inspired by the plaudits of his audiences, and in oratorical terms was probably the most effective campaigner.

Arturo Uslar Pietri's bid for office was striking at the lack of organizational strength. The anticipated influence of Ramón Quijada's *campesino* leagues failed to materialize. At the same time, Uslar ran a campaign that was without monetary limitations, and his use of radio, television, and newspaper advertisements outstripped that of his competitors. If anything, overreliance was placed on such media, and his major appeal focused on the urban centers.

The urbane and sophisticated Uslar Pietri was often ill-at-ease in dealing with ordinary peasants, proving more effective with city dwellers. Notable in his campaign was the single most effective symbol of the entire race—adoption of a bell as his label. Radio and television ran innumerable spot announcements with the ringing of a bell and a few brief words about "Arturo el Hombre"—Arturo the Man. The slogan was effective, and bell-ringing at political rallies was a useful attention-getter. Throughout his campaign Uslar reiterated the evils of party government, the inevitable growth of nepotism, of spoils and official corruption. Insisting that Venezuela could never achieve true reforms under party rule, he asked for a vote of confidence in his independent role.

The efforts of Wolfgang Larrazábal and Raúl Ramos Giménez were somewhat lackluster. The former, lacking adequate financial support, was thereby restricted in his efforts. Travels to the interior were less extensive than those of his opponents, and even in urban areas he had to rely primarily on his own broad popularity. This had receded in the five years since 1958, and efforts to revive it met with mixed results. As for Ramos Giménez, campaigning was half-hearted. The defection of Quijada after the convention had reduced public support even below its previous level. In retrospect it seems that the *arsistas* recognized their weakness and campaigned largely in hopes of retaining their congressional seats in metropolitan Caracas. Although Ramos Giménez and his colleagues had fully demonstrated their political talents while members of the AD, their 1963 performance was inferior. Early in the campaign a major rally in Ramos Giménez' home town—San Felipe, Yaracuy—drew a modest crowd of a few hundred, and from that time forward knowledgeable observers discounted the magnitude of *arsista* strength.

## Electoral Results

The battle between government and extremists continued down to election day on December 1,[13] with the

[13] A detailed discussion of the running struggle is found in

leftists trying desperately to force a military *golpe*. During the pre-election week alone there was an abortive general strike, gunfire in the workers' districts of Caracas that led to the death of 21 and injury of at least 100, the kidnapping of a North American officer assigned to the military mission, an attempted mass assassination of presidential candidates through the mailing of bombs, and the highjacking of a two-engined Avensa airliner during a flight from Ciudad Bolívar to Caracas. A cache of arms and ammunition from Cuba was also uncovered, later leading to the July 1964 action of the hemispheric foreign ministers in branding the Cuban regime as an aggressor. Elections were nonetheless held in the face of all threats, and 91.33 percent of registered voters went to the polls.

In examining the returns, a brief digression is necessary to describe the environmental setting, for the usual fourfold geographical classification is not particularly useful in this context. Five "political" regions can be identified for the purposes of electoral analysis: the Metropolitan Center, the Coastal Range, the Llanos-Guayana interior, the Maracaibo Basin, and the Andean region. Although not uniformly consistent in geographic terms, they recommend themselves for electoral analysis.

The Metropolitan Center, largest with 28.22 percent of the population (2,329,828), includes the Federal District and the neighboring states of Miranda and Aragua. Caracas itself spills over the district line into Miranda. Although certain areas of Miranda and Aragua are rural, both are influenced by the nearby capital, heart of Venezuelan political and economic life. The next largest urban center is Maracay, with nearly 150,000. In an electoral sense the influence of Caracas voters is overwhelming.

Next comes the Coastal Range, in which six states (Falcón, Lara, Yaracuy, Carabobo, Nueva Esparta, and Sucre) contain 24.02 percent of the population (1,982,-713). This categorization omits at least two states that also appear relatively "coastal" in nature. These, however—Anzoátegui and Monagas—are low-lying rather than elevated and, for political reasons as well, more appropriately fit the Llanos-Guayana interior. The Coastal Range includes important manufacturing and industrial areas as well as rural sectors. Major cities are Barquisimeto and Valencia, each in the vicinity of 200,000. Politically the Coastal Range is somewhat more heterogeneous than the others; in both 1958 and 1963 the electoral pattern was mixed.

Third is the Llanos-Guayana interior, numbering eight states (Barinas, Apure, Portuguesa, Cojedes, Guárico, Anzoátegui, Monagas, and Bolívar) and two federal territories (Delta Amacuro and Amazonas). While geographic distinctions between the Llanos and the Guayana region are significant, in the politico-electoral sense the region is fairly homogeneous. Essentially rural, still provincial and isolated in many parts, it has the lowest population density of all the regions. Although the territorial expanse is nearly 80 percent of the Republic, the population of 1,838,258 is but 22.27 percent of the national total. The most populous city, Ciudad Bolívar, is still under 100,000. Party domination by the AD has been traditional.

The Maracaibo Basin is composed of the single state of Zulia. Containing the center of Venezuela's major petroleum deposits, Zulia's population of 1,044,047 represents 12.65 percent of the population. As a center for organized labor its political sympathies have long run toward Acción Democrática.

The same cannot be said for the distinctive Andean mountainous section to the southwest. Composed of three states (Táchira, Mérida, and Trujillo), 12.84 percent (1,060,610) of the population lives in this remote section. The area from which a half-century or more of military dictators has emerged, the most conservative and most Catholic portion of Venezuela, the Andes have consistently produced strong political support for COPEI.

Analysis of the returns the week after elections suggested a number of things about the strength of Acción Democrática and of its party rivals. The still-undefeated AD won, but by a drastically reduced margin. Although Leoni was an easy winner, his 32.8 percent of the vote was far from Betancourt's 1958 figure of 49.2. This general drop was matched by congressional returns, with the party falling from 49.5 in 1963 to 33.2. Both times the presidential candidate received a slightly smaller percentage of the vote than did the congressional slate. Once the mathematics of proportional representation and the electoral quotient were worked out, the AD held 21 of 45 Senate seats and 65 of 177 in the lower house (see Appendix, p. 394). This was a drop from 1958's 32 of 51 in the Senate and 73 of 133 in the Chamber, although the *mirista* and *arsista* divisions had reduced the number of AD "loyalists."

Second place was won by Rafael Caldera and COPEI. Climbing from a third-place position in 1958, Caldera's total of 396,293 rose in 1963 to 588,372 votes; this was a full 5 percent increase, from 15.2 to 20.2. (Appendix, p. 398). *Copeyano* congressional slates followed with a 6 percent rise from 15.2 to 21.2 (Appendix, p. 399). The congressional delegation added 3 senators to the 1958 total of 6; in the Chamber it more than doubled its number, from 19 to 40 (Appendix, p. 401).[14]

[14] To illustrate the use of proportional representation in Venezuela we can use 1958 elections in Miranda, which was allotted six seats in the Chamber on the basis of population. In the con-

The multi-candidate nature of the 1963 race added further dimensions to what had been relatively simple in 1958. Jóvito Villalba ran third with 18.9 percent of the vote, a drop of 12 percent from the 1958 record of the URD's candidate. Likewise, the *urredista* congressional vote fell from 26.8 to 17.6 percent, reflecting in part the value of the Larrazábal coattails to *urredista* congressional candidates in 1958. The independent Uslar Pietri was meanwhile sweeping Caracas while polling 469,240 votes, just above 16 percent. His followers, organized as the *ad hoc* Independientes Pro-Frente Nacional (IPFN), trailed with 381,507 votes for congress. Among the 45 Senators, three were from the IPFN, including Uslar himself; 20 *uslaristas* won entry into the Chamber of Deputies (Appendix, pp. 395 and 401).

Remaining candidates and organizations trailed far behind. Larrazábal polled 275,304 votes with the minor aid of the FDP, some one-third of which came from the Federal District (Appendix, p. 395). Larrazábal himself was one of four Senators, while 16 deputies were chosen. Raúl Ramos Giménez and AD-Op did more poorly than most had expected; the former polled but 2.29 percent of the total, while the party's congressional representa-

---

gressional vote, the URD led with 60,740 votes, followed by the AD with 50,583, COPEI with 27,016, and the PCV with 9,853. Seats were then allocated through the division and recalculation of such totals.

The URD, having led the vote, received the first seat. Its total was then divided in half, or 30,371. Since this figure was less than the AD total, the latter was awarded the second seat. Then its total was halved, dropping to 25,291. The URD again headed the list, receiving the third Miranda deputy, after which its total was reduced to 15,185. The fourth seat then went to COPEI, whose 27,016 became the greatest. After dividing it in two, or 13,508, the next highest figure was that of the AD, which received the fifth seat. With the AD total then reduced to 12,645, the highest remaining figure was the URD's 15,185; therefore the *urredistas* were awarded the final seat. Miranda's delegation to the Chamber was thus composed of three *urredistas*, two *adecos*, and one *copeyano*.

tives ran somewhat stronger (Appendix, p. 397). Ramos Giménez won a chamber seat from the Federal District— the only member of the party to win a national seat by means other than the electoral quotient.[15] The *arsista* senator and 4 additional members of the lower house were later seated through the quotient. A seventh presidential candidate, Germán Borregales,[16] received 0.32 percent of the vote. The operation of the quotient awarded one deputy apiece to a pair of minor factions, the Partido Socialista Venezolana (PSV) and the Movimiento Electoral Nacional Independiente (MENI).

Further analysis included a comparison of collective government and opposition totals (B-17).[17] The combined AD-COPEI presidential vote of 1,546,071 represented 53.0 percent of the vote. Using congressional rather than presidential totals, the same pair received 54.5 percent of the vote—1,532,307. The AD-COPEI margin in the Senate became 30-15, and 105-72 in the Chamber. A different dichotomy was that of party and

[15] Beyond the application of PR is the electoral quotient. First the vote total for Congress is calculated—in 1958 it was 2,580,217. In the Chamber's application of population figures, the number of deputies was set at 127. The division of 127 seats into 2,580,217 votes came to 20,001; in 1958 this became the electoral quotient for the Chamber. A parallel arithmetical process produced a Senate quotient. In the Chamber, then, the COPEI total of 392,305, when divided by the quotient of 20,001, came to 19. Since the party had elected only 15 deputies through PR, it received 4 more. In the Senate, the quotient entitled the party to 6 seats; having won but 3, the party received an additional 3 senators. All such additional deputies and senators are customarily allotted to states where a party has no representatives or, at the least, is underrepresented. This judgment is made by the Consejo Supremo Electoral.

[16] Borregales was a journalist of the far right who campaigned sporadically.

[17] The probability of a continuing AD-COPEI alliance under Leoni made such figures initially important, although the eventual failure of negotiations between Leoni and Caldera over a new coalition led to the naming of an essentially non-partisan cabinet in March 1964 by the new president. A coalition embracing the AD, URD, and FND was formed late in the year.

"non-party" forces. The distinction was important, for the AD, COPEI, and URD had enjoyed years of experience, formal national structure, and customary organizational trappings. Their rivals were basically "non-party" and Uslar Pietri was explicitly anti-party.

Described in these terms, the 1963 election contrasted sharply with that of 1958. Previously only some 5 percent of the electorate voted for a candidate or list other than that of AD, COPEI, or URD. The 1963 participation of Uslar Pietri and Larrazábal changed this. Using presidential totals, the three parties polled 2,097,191 votes, or 71.9 percent of the total; opposing "non-party" forces received a substantial 820,705 votes, or 28.1 percent (B-17). The congressional pattern was similar, with the former grouping receiving 72 percent with its 2,029,732 votes, while the non-party won the remaining 28 percent, or 787,136 votes. Translated into congressional seats, this gave the "party" group a lead in the Senate of 37-8, and in the Chamber of Deputies 134-43.

Regional analysis of the figures relies upon the division discussed above. The relative weakness of the formally organized parties in the Metropolitan Center was striking. In 1958 the poor showing of Acción Democrática and COPEI had been overshadowed by the smashing 57.8 percent of *urredista* candidate Larrazábal, but this was a function of the "Larrazábal phenomenon" rather than URD strength. This was borne out in 1963 when the AD led the three parties although *dropping* to 16.3 percent, while the URD with Villalba received only 13.5 percent. A full 57 percent of the vote in the Metropolitan Center went to non-party candidates.

The organized parties showed strongly in the next most populous area, the Coastal region. Acción Democrática, the URD, and COPEI led in that order, polling some 82 percent of the vote. The AD ran first in five of these six states, while the URD captured the native state of its presidential candidate, Nueva Esparta. In the more sparsely populated Llanos-Guayana section this configuration was repeated. The order was again AD, URD, and COPEI, with the three winning 86.4 percent. Of the eight states and two federal territories, Acción Democrática won all but Amazonas, where the URD led in a total vote of less than 5,000. COPEI ran second in three of these, the URD in the remaining six.

Toward western Venezuela the Maracaibo and Andean regions proved more diverse. In the state of Zulia, given the strength of labor and the domination of generally leftist sympathies, the AD's leading total of 37.6 was nevertheless a major drop from 1958. The URD narrowly squeezed into second place ahead of COPEI, but both Larrazábal and Uslar Pietri drew significant support, and the non-party total was 29 percent, its largest figure outside the Metropolitan Center. Finally, the three-state Andean southwest continued to be a *copeyano* stronghold. Indeed, its percentage rose in five years from 45.5 to 50.2, and the party for the first time led in all three states. An arduous effort by the AD did not prevent its own sharp decline; the three parties together received 86.7 percent. The AD reduction was taken up partially by COPEI but primarily by Uslar Pietri, who offered a fairly conservative appeal for votes in the region.

The politico-regional cleavage of the 1963 elections between the Metropolitan Center and the rest of the country was striking. The so-called "Caracas Question" had plagued Acción Democrática since 1958,[18] and the existence of the "Larrazábal phenomenon" was but a partial explanation. In 1963 the political and electoral division between Caracas and surroundings and the rest of the country was extreme. The over-all electoral outcome was obviously dependent upon the results in the national population center. Yet for the second consecu-

[18] An analysis of AD difficulties in Caracas which preceded the 1963 vote appeared in Gabriel Moro, "Por Qué Perdió AD en Caracas," *Momento*, no. 355, May 5, 1963, pp. 28-34.

tive presidential race the winner ran no better than third in the political heart of the nation.

Given these circumstances, it is instructive to view the national returns *excluding* the Metropolitan Center (B-16). The distortion of Raúl Leoni's victory is negligible; excluding the Metropolitan Center, he would have received 38.9 percent rather than 32.8. The narrow gap between Caldera and Villalba would not have changed substantially, but the vote for Uslar Pietri would have been nearly halved—from 16.08 to 8.9—while that of Larrazábal would have fallen from 9.43 to 5.8 percent. Proportions of the Metropolitan Center vote are magnified when first government-opposition, then party-"non-party" dichotomies are recorded. In the former instance, the AD-COPEI forces would have increased their lead from 54.4-45.6 percent to a more substantial 61.7-38.3; the margin would have been 23 percent instead of 9. As for the party-"non-party" distinction, the first grouping would have swept 82.6 percent of the total instead of 71.88. The "non-party" element assumes far greater political significance when its electoral appeal goes from 17.4 percent to 28.12.

Several interpretations can be drawn from these figures and percentages. An obvious fact of much importance was the weakening of Acción Democrática. Although the party had long since conceded that the 1945-1948 days of 70-80 percent support were gone forever, not even the virtual 50 percent of 1958 had been achieved. Most party leaders had anticipated some 40 percent, and the decline to one-third was unexpected. The drop was founded on several factors: the lesser stature and electoral magnetism of Leoni relative to Betancourt; internal schisms that had cost the party capable leaders and the entire youth movement; the weakness of its appeal to essentially non-partisan urban middle sectors; the weight of unpopular or unsuccessful government policies; and, perhaps most importantly, the five-year accumulation of anti-government sentiment so characteristic of Venezuelan politics.

In the light of the returns, party leaders began concerned post-mortems for Acción Democrática. The party was still endowed with the best organizational machinery in the country. On the other hand, its appeal to political independents—at least through the determined but plodding Leoni campaign—was almost nil. The 1962 party census had claimed 926,663 full members, only 30,000 less than the vote Leoni received. Party domination over the labor sector was less effective than usual. The Confederación de Trabajadores de Venezuela claimed at the time a membership of some 1.3 million. Largely the creation of AD leaders, the group had been counted on to provide more votes than leaders believed it had delivered.[19] In many workers' sectors—most notably those of Caracas—either Larrazábal or Uslar Pietri ran strongest. In Zulia the party lead was far less than it had been in 1958. Although city totals were imprecise, AD leaders themselves agreed that they also did less well than anticipated in Maracaibo, Valencia, Maracay, and Barquisimeto.

The lack of appeal to non-committed voters was observable at different levels. Although Leoni was less than spell-binding, the answer was not this simple. The campaign had placed great reliance on the party machinery. Furthermore, there were references to dated issues over political rights and universal suffrage, former AD-inspired achievements that by 1963 had lost all vitality as issues. Detailed expositions of the party program were above all else dull, and there was a failure to capitalize upon the genuine popularity of agrarian reform. The entire campaign lacked much of the verve

[19] Although labor leaders disagreed, several party leaders indicated in private discussions that the CTV may well have emphasized the defense of constitutionality in the preceding five years to such an extent that much of its partisan influence over CTV membership was lost.

that had been characteristic of the party in the past. More than a little complacency had been involved, notwithstanding the recent splits with MIR and the ARS.[20] Perhaps the one factor for which the party was not responsible in electoral terms was the erosion of public support over such a turbulent five-year period. For this was an inevitable fact of political life that no party could have been expected to nullify completely. At least a few votes were alienated in some of the urban areas from the increasingly firm anti-terrorist measures adopted in the fall of 1963. Such events as the forced evacuation of a city block to flush out a sniper, the occasional arrest and overnight jailing of an innocent bystander, were among the kinds of occurrences that weakened still further the AD position. Both in the urban centers and in the interior the party slumped from its 1958 totals, with no single region standing out. The party vote declined in each of the five geographic regions, and in three of these it was a drop of more than 20 percent.

If the over-all picture was disappointing for Acción Democrática, there were some bright spots. The aberration of AD-Op had been dissipated, and *arsistas* no longer had grounds for disputing the legitimacy of the regular AD. Furthermore, the admittedly hollow achievement of leading the URD and COPEI in the Federal District was at least an improvement over the situation in 1958. And the sheer fact that an AD-dominated government had completed its constitutional period, had conducted and won honest elections, and was to effect the change of administration, was an achievement of great magnitude. The overriding goal of the party throughout the campaign had been the holding of elections and defense of the constitutional system; party

[20] Rómulo Betancourt himself reportedly commented that perhaps the results for the AD would be propitious, for the need of invigorization and rethinking of appeals to the citizenry were evident.

moderation and responsibility were evident. Future tasks both in government and within the party were challenging. Yet the leadership recognized their magnitude, and in 1964 set out to solidify and to rebuild, instilling the vigor and zest that had recently been lacking. With more than half the population in its twenties or less, the importance of appealing to Venezuelan youth had clearly become almost impossible to exaggerate.

Of AD's rivals, COPEI appeared in a sense the electoral victor. In climbing past the URD into second position, it had also increased its national distribution of strength. Strong races were run in Lara, Portuguesa, Yaracuy, and Barinas, where COPEI won Senate seats by direct vote for the first time. *Copeyanos* also won Chamber seats for the first time in Anzoátegui and Bolívar. Representation on municipal councils increased across the nation. The party campaign had been hard-hitting, and went far in overcoming the handicap of running as junior coalition member. By the time results were known, the entire party shared a genuine belief that it was riding the wave of the future. Recent successes of a relative kind by christian democratic parties elsewhere in Latin America made this faith more persuasive.

COPEI clearly exaggerated the proportions of its victory. Still substantially weaker than Acción Democrática, with regional soft spots in the Llanos-Guayanas and in the Metropolitan Center, and enjoying only a small margin over the URD and the supporters of Uslar, it further shared in the AD and URD problem of urban areas, especially Caracas. At the same time, there could be no denying that only COPEI had increased its position in the 1963 elections; the surge was definitely an upward one.

Of the three permanent, organized parties, the Unión Republicana Democrática came out of elections with the most serious wounds. The influence of the URD left—the *ala negra*—was a detrimental one which in early 1964 was purged from the party. Yet the Villalba campaign appeared as an unsuccessful crusade that might not be repeated. The URD still had little in the way of an identifiable programmatic message; its call for a change in government had been essentially negative, and the organizational structure was not developed to the point of taking up the slack left by the absence of a special niche in the Venezuelan party spectrum. The strength suggested by the 1958 election had clearly been that of Wolfgang Larrazábal's transitory popularity, rather than a broad basis of popular support for the URD.

The "non-party" candidacies of AD-Op and the *larrazabalista* FDP showed that both groups had little claim to popular support. The dissident *arsistas* proved themselves to have been a transitory faction without permanence on the political scene. Even in Ramos Giménez' own Yaracuy the group won but 12.7 percent of the vote. The removal of the *arsista* group was paralleled by the conclusion of Larrazábal's brief but once meteoric political career. Although he continued to be regarded sympathetically in the capital, his over-all national standing was slight.

Arturo Uslar Pietri waged an effective campaign, despite doubts as to his commitment to regular political action. A four-month campaign moved at a rapid pace and was well-conceived but for its urban bias. Had Ramón Quijada been able to deliver rural votes, Uslar's general position would have been far higher than it was. Instead, most of his support was urban, including new members of the growing middle class, often non-religious and hostile to COPEI, who were strongly protective toward their *status quo*. Uslar's votes were clearly the result of his own campaigning, reflecting in part the emphasis upon partisan independence and criticism of the shortcomings of party politics. He was also something of a "new" name to most of the electorate, although well-known in intellectual and higher political circles for a generation. The formation of his congressional followers into a formal party in 1964 suggested his intention of remaining politically active, but this robbed him of his non-partisan appeal, and many of his opponents regarded his aversion to the tasks of political life as an indication that his major electoral successes were already past.

Beyond the many assorted details already itemized, several broad conclusions can be drawn from the elections. These include a popular commitment to democratic process in repudiation of communist appeals and terrorism, a broad programmatic consensus reflected in the similarity of party proposals, a continuation of the multi-party system;[21] an urban-rural socio-economic cleavage that translated in political terms to an anti-party bias in the Metropolitan Center; and an increasingly youthful electorate that presented a challenge to all political organizations.

For Acción Democrática, the greatest challenge of all lay in the last fact; yet it was the same problem that confronted COPEI and the URD. What had until recently been regarded as purely AD problems with the nation's youth came into focus as something plaguing all organized parties. With the electorate assuming an extraordinarily youthful caste, every political organization found itself faced with the necessity of making inroads on new voters. Indeed, so long as democratic processes and electoral choices marked the road of national progress in Venezuela, the single most critical political area was that of the youth. For the political direction these Venezuelans may follow and the choices to be made will in large part decide not only the coming pattern of the party system, but the very future of the Republic itself.

[21] This contradicted several pre-election predictions that the eclipse of the URD would result in a two-party system revolving about COPEI and the AD.

# CHAPTER XIII

# Epilogue: The Party in Perspective

At mid-day on March 11, 1964, the Venezuelan presidential sash was lowered upon the shoulders of Raúl Leoni. In a brief but impressive ceremony Rómulo Betancourt concluded his five-year constitutional term and passed on the authority of office to his duly elected successor. In that act, one of the major events in contemporary Latin American politics became reality. For this, the first transfer of power in Venezuelan history from one democratically elected chief executive to his legitimate successor, represented simultaneously a victory for the forces of representative government, a defeat of international communism and the influence of Castro Cuba, and a remarkable reaffirmation of the civic virtue and patriotism of the Venezuelan people. Neither the party system in general nor Acción Democrática in particular could claim more than a part of the credit. Amid the relative euphoria of the event, however, it provided a significant historic point from which an assessment of the AD might be made.

## Acción Democrática: A "Modern" Political Party

Three major areas were set forth in the introduction as necessary for a Latin American party to qualify as "modern." These were, in order, ideology, permanent organization, and the multi-faceted aspect of party rather awkwardly termed popular acceptance. A survey of the AD experience over the years shows it to qualify in each of these areas. As for the first, the party's ideology is applied in terms of program and platform; it is programmatic, rather than ideological in a narrowly doctrinal sense. The highly detailed set of proposals and statements, of policy declarations and statements of principle by Acción Democrática can be regarded as programmatic. With the AD proposals establishing certain guide lines within which daily pragmatic decisions must be made, it is difficult to deny the programmatic base of the party.

A closer examination of ideology and program is necessary in order to arrive at a satisfactory means of characterizing the party. The AD is often referred to as one of the *aprista* parties, but it should be noted that *adeco* leaders themselves reject the descriptive term *aprista*. This rejection is in part a function of emotion and of pride. Regarding itself as uniquely Venezuelan, the AD understandably has little taste for being tagged by a name created by another party in a different country. To the AD, the APRA is distinctly Peruvian in outlook, program, and composition; to regard it as a prototype is simply unacceptable to the AD leaders. There is the additional factor of the Peruvian *aprista* difficulty in achieving national power through some 40 years' existence, a clear contrast to the record of the AD. And finally, AD leaders maintain that the Peruvian *aprista* movement in their minds is a rather vivid reflection of marxist thought. Rightly or wrongly, the AD will add that the *aprista* organization is scarcely viable; certainly it is not the effective national apparatus that the AD has constructed.[1]

There are also semantic difficulties over a wide use of *aprismo* as a popular classification in recent years. Loose usage has thrown together as *aprista* such diverse parties as the AD, Costa Rica's Partido Liberación Nacional (PLN), the Liberal Party of Colombia, the Dominican Revolutionary Party, the Liberal Party of Honduras, and the Movimiento Nacionalista Revolucionaria of Bolivia. Although certain similarities exist,

[1] Interview with Raúl Leoni, October 29, 1962; with Mercedes Fermín, November 19, 1962; with Gonzalo Barrios, November 27, 1962.

there is serious question as to whether or not these and additional parties can validly be described by the same term. In short, there are several reasons for discarding *aprista* as descriptive of the AD.

One alternate possibility would be to label the AD either marxist or socialist. These very terms, of course, can involve a sticky exercise in interpretation. Aside from the partially irrelevant fact that Venezuelan communists and marxists today regard the AD as petit-bourgeois, the latter shows little remaining impact from the brush with marxism experienced by many of its leaders in their youth. The party pays great attention to the working class, to be sure, and there are scattered references in party literature suggesting historic hostility between management and labor. This is the closest approach to marxism in contemporary AD writings. The term "socialist" was not uncommon for a time in the past. In the 1940's, Rómulo Betancourt himself often used the term. Yet there is little in today's Acción Democrática which resembles pure socialism. Massive nationalization, thorough and total economic controls, rigid limits upon foreign investment and private enterprise, and full direction of the distribution of the national product are not and have never been significant. While the role of the state in the economy has been and will continue substantial, this is a far cry from effective nationalization. Even the taking of lands for redistribution through agrarian reform has been undertaken by a moderate rather than radical program.

A more recent tendency has been to refer to the AD as a labor party. In Venezuela itself this is occasionally seen in print or heard in private conversation. Political rivals argue that organized labor is the real source of strength for the party and there is no disputing the long AD domination of organized labor, although today it is less monolithic than it once was. The applicability of the term may be questioned, however, in view of the uncertain hold of the party on the *campesino* movement, which comprises roughly half the CTV membership. This cataloguing of Acción Democrática not only implies a hold over organized labor that seems less solid than it once was, but is also suggestive of a one-class party, which the AD definitely is not. As far back as 1936 the old ORVE aimed at being the spokesman and representative of the whole spectrum of Venezuelan social life, and the PDN and then the AD continued with reiterations that the party was *policlasista*. Observation of the party does nothing to dispel this contention.

In some of its more pugnacious declarations, the party has seemingly restricted somewhat its appeal. In a 1961 document it informed party faithful that "Acción Democrática . . . represents several social classes, but not all, only the three exploited popular classes, those affected by identical problems and tied together by a common purpose. The three most energetic and conscious classes thus join together in an historic task: the workers, the peasants, and the middle class."[2] Even in such a statement, however, the party is far from a single-class organization. Its external relations as described in earlier chapters give further testimony to its multi-class composition and interest.

Doubtless there are inherent dangers in any given label. There may well be something to recommend Silvert's phrase "social democratic," although the European connotations of the phrase are misleading. The preference here is a term which, although less common than *aprista*, is by no means rare. Suggested by Raúl Leoni in an interview while he was Party President, "national revolutionary" will henceforth be relied upon. It is possible to protest that the more apt phrase would be national *evolutionary*. In the Latin American *milieu*, however, the use of "revolutionary" as implying a commitment to

---

[2] Acción Democrática, *La Cartilla del Militante* (Caracas: Secretaría Nacional de Propaganda, 1961), p. 14.

non-violent political and economic transformation is customary.

Second of the criteria for classification as a modern party is that of permanent party organization; relevant aspects of organization are leadership, membership, the operating structure, and articulation as political education. For Acción Democrática, the leadership has gradually been shaped and formed by the experience of well over a quarter-century. As outlined in Chapter VII, six evolutionary stages can be delineated, beginning with the legal opposition to López Contreras in 1936. From the days of 1936 when the leadership was politically inexperienced and publicly unknown, the climb gradually gained altitude. Even the decade of exile and illegal resistance did not prevent a renewed strengthening of the leadership in the post-1958 period. The pair of rifts in 1960 and after seriously shattered the degree of complacency with which the leadership had previously regarded itself, but the eventual result was a reinforcing of the party hierarchy in preparation for the 1963 elections and the subsequent personnel shifts following the inauguration of Raúl Leoni in March 1964.

The public disillusionment toward the *miristas* by 1963 and the rejection of the *arsista* appeal by the electorate in December of the year not only eliminated these groups as forces representing popular opinion but in turn strengthened the position of the reorganized AD leadership. The 1963 presidential campaign, although lacking at times in zest and in wide popular appeal, was a smoothly coordinated effort in which a large number of regional and local party members were directed and supervised by national headquarters, while the Comando Electoral worked effectively with candidate Leoni's own staff. There seems little question as to the essential cohesion, collaboration, and over-all supervision as carried out by the leadership.

The party membership is not subject to as direct and

simple analysis as that of the leadership, and certain facts are blurred. At the same time, this is no reason to deny the existence of an effective, working, and durable national party organization. The membership can at least be cited as evidence of the national base of Acción Democrática, since its 900,000-plus card-carrying supporters are found throughout the Republic and even the two federal territories. In the recent three-year period between the party censuses of 1959 and 1962, there was an increase of nearly 14 percent, this in the face of *arsista* and *mirista* defections. The fundamental accuracy of the figures was reflected in the 1963 elections, with AD vote strength by state closely paralleling the party membership in the same place.

The geographic distribution of the party, then, is nothing if not national. Class and group interests of the membership are broadly representative. The national labor movement today is less AD-dominated than ever before, but most CTV members still cast votes for Acción Democrática. The *campesino* vote cannot be taken for granted, but it is agreed that the Betancourt electoral victory in 1958 relied in large part upon peasant backing in the interior, and the same element was significantly present for the election of Raúl Leoni. Like the other organized democratic parties, the AD clearly slipped in the loyalties of many urban dwellers, but there continued to be important support from many professional people and at times from independents who do not enter actively into politics. The representation of classes and interests, in short, is varied and changing within Acción Democrática; the appeal is far more than that of one class, and the various groups ebb and flow in terms of impact upon the party.

The structural framework of the party need not be described again in detail; in the present discussion of party modernity, only a few organizational points need to be stressed. To begin with, the organization is national while reaching down to small villages and towns. This is not an organization with a head and no body, with a brilliant group of national legislators and parliamentarians who enjoy little if any significant support and backing at the regional and local level. The activities of the *grupos de base* in Acción Democrática are perhaps the most important in terms of the internal health of the party. When these are not functioning actively and imaginatively, the party organization stagnates. The converse is also true.

The emphasis at all levels throughout the party is officially on the ultimate authority of the convention, whether local, regional, or national. In actual practice the major policy decisions are made by the executive or administrative organs and officials. The organizational configuration is pyramidal, and the flow of messages, directives, and information is rapid, whether going to or from the top hierarchy. The party in ordinary times—that is, in the absence of national crisis or of elections—encourages the decision-making activities at the lower levels. While this by no means is intended to indicate a lack of authority on the highest hierarchical level, it is worth noting that, when feasible, local officials are permitted to make local decisions in accord with the particular issues and problems at hand.

Tied in with the kind of participation carried out by local members of the party is the problem of articulation and, broadly speaking, of political education. At the present time any hope of providing incontrovertible data that can support contentions about party activity or lack of it in terms of political education is unrealistic. Direct observation can provide a general impression of the matter that is more than intuitive, but it is simply not possible to base statements in this area on empirical evidence. Most observers would agree that the educational activities of both the AD and of COPEI—the URD to a much lesser extent—are dedicated to the participation of the individual. There is in each of the first two parties an awareness of the importance of broad participation, and thus efforts are strong and determined in seeking to broaden the party base and to increase the political knowledgeability of the rank-and-file member and supporter.

What has rather unsatisfactorily been termed "popular acceptance" embraces the other norms which must be met if a party is deservedly called modern. These are essentially direct and uncomplicated. First is the matter of truly broad and national appeal as reflected in elections. For Acción Democrática there can be no doubt on this count. The three *trienio* elections were conducted virtually without effective organized opposition, and the regularity with which the AD received at least 70 percent of the vote was to be expected. In the post-Pérez Jiménez era, however, the party has continued as the nation's leading vote-getter. While its national percentage in 1963 was only one-third, this still outstripped the competition. More importantly, the distribution continued to be national. States which the party did not win usually saw the AD coming in second; only the *copeyano* stronghold in the Andes seemed out of reach, and the AD was consistently second there. The problem of the Metropolitan Center has come to afflict each of the organized parties, a kind of aberration that is reviewed in the final section of the chapter.

Probably the simplest of all criteria is that of at least a decade's duration. For Acción Democrática, even if one chooses not to include the pre-1941 years of preliminary action or, for that matter, the ten years in exile, its active and legal life is easily more than a decade. With the exception of the Venezuelan communist, the AD is the oldest and longest-established party in Venezuela. The concluding aspect of party modernity as reflected in terms of popular acceptance is that of the inner justification felt through governmental authority or the probability of sharing in it. Here too the AD experience is incontrovertible; except for its first four years of existence, the party has had at least a portion of national power throughout the periods of democratic government and honest elections. Only once has there been a shadow of possible doubt—following the defection of AD-ARS from the party. The outcome of 1963 elections laid all such doubt to rest.

Acción Democrática, then, meets each of the norms necessary for a party to qualify as modern. In the terms set forth, Venezuela's first modern party has been the AD. It is no longer alone as a modern party, for COPEI has recently succeeded in achieving the same goals and qualities. For both, the evolutionary process has been an arduous and a lengthy one, but its completion has meant and will continue to represent yet one additional sign of the progress which has characterized Venezuela in nearly all sectors of its life and society.

## National Revolutionary Party in an Emergent Polity

At least a few of the methodological difficulties in the comparative analysis of Latin American political parties have been set forth in the introduction; a more extended consideration of the matter has appeared elsewhere.[3] The present study is essentially that of a single party, rather than being explicitly comparative in treatment and arrangement. However, there are potential benefits in examining Acción Democrática in terms of its experience as a national revolutionary party in such a polity as that of Venezuela. The set of conditions found in Venezuela as the AD gradually grew to maturity have been paralleled in a number of other Latin American countries. It therefore behooves us to set down in general outline the nature of these conditions. Then it will be possible to ex-

[3] John D. Martz, "Dilemmas in the Study of Latin American Parties," *Journal of Politics,* XXVI, no. 3, August 1964.

amine the patterns of action adopted and pursued by the AD, analyzing these through revolutionary strategy and tactics, attitudes, forms of leadership, and the evolving organized opposition within the polity.

Venezuela in the late 1930's and early 1940's was a country in need of reform in all areas of national life. The political heritage of Bolívar's "barracks" was institutionally and non-constitutionally primitive. Indirect elections were employed for the selection of all national officials, and the representative nature of such authorities was usually questionable. The ruling military leaders at a given time either held national power or exercised it indirectly from behind the scenes. Political participation for the masses was ordinarily non-existent, and the kind of activism associated with political parties was negligible. Constitutional rights for the protection of the individual were violated by successive governments with impunity; only with a successful *golpe de estado* could redress be taken against a government.

Socio-economic conditions in general were also primitive. Like many of its Latin American neighbors, Venezuela was essentially agrarian; an estimated two-thirds of the population was engaged in agricultural pursuits. And at the same time the country was dependent upon the income of a single product as the base of the economy. By the end of the 1930's, the discovery of vast petroleum deposits had brought a surface prosperity that was grossly maldistributed. Profits were ploughed into government activities, both legitimate and otherwise; projects were usually aimed at the construction of bridges, office-buildings, roads, and comparable items.

Little was done to improve the lot of *campesinos* living as *conuqueros* on land owned by absentee members of the socio-economic elite. Conditions of bare subsistence were common, while illiteracy and poverty ran unchecked. The expanding population—not as dramatic in the early 1940's as it is today—nonetheless contributed to a gradual worsening of already appalling conditions. In the cities, what was at first only a slow trickle from the countryside nonetheless worsened the standard of living for the average Venezuelan. The middle class was yet minuscule, and those who emerged from the universities to enter the professional world found their opportunities limited and advancement slow. The over-all low level of education in the country proved a major hindrance to urban as well as rural sectors, while shortages and inadequacies continued in the fields of health, housing, public welfare, and social security.

Given the confluence of these political and socioeconomic grievances, the emergence of a reformist-minded, nationalistic group was inevitable; the natural protest was mounted by a younger generation in Venezuela, and those with direct political concern in most cases joined the movement which in 1941 was christened as Acción Democrática. From its inception the party advocated a set of basic reforms that might well be characterized as revolutionary. Yet they were intended as duly approved measures to be adopted by a government truly representative of the Venezuelan people. Notwithstanding the revolutionary cast of its long and detailed set of proposals and projects, Acción Democrática first sought the reins of power through legal means, thus attention was particularly devoted to political reforms.

The pattern followed by the AD as a national revolutionary party can first be traced in terms of over-all strategy; it called for the achievement of political reforms which would bring the entire populace into the electoral process. Outspoken in its criticism of military intervention in political affairs as well as non-constitutional changes of government, the AD sought national power in order to implement its demands for structural change in Venezuela's society and economy. It was the apparent impossibility of winning power under a system of limited suffrage and indirect elections that eventually contributed to the controversial AD participation in the October Revolution of 1945. Convinced that the winning of power by legal means was simply impossible, the party joined with military rebels in mounting the successful attack against the constitutional Medina government.

Interpretations of this AD decision have been summarized earlier; in the broader pattern of national revolutionary movements, the act permitted the capture of power which had been regarded as a prerequisite to subsequent socio-economic reforms. Although political reforms had not been employed in its rise to power, the party nonetheless set about the adoption of political and electoral reforms. While the provisional regime was issuing decrees necessary to the continued operation of national affairs, attention was directed toward political reforms. Universal suffrage and direct voting were adopted in the selection of a Constituent Assembly, and that body in due course sanctioned the electoral changes as a method of broadening the electorate and bringing to each citizen the responsibilities of the vote.

Only by early 1948 did this political process bring to office the elected government of Rómulo Gallegos, and at least a start had already been evident in the area of non-political reforms. Many of the striking efforts of the *trienio*—anti-illiteracy campaign, the eradication of malaria, revision of petroleum contracts, a commitment to housing and to hospitals, the establishment of a national economic body, and the promise of basic agrarian reform—were undertaken by the provisional government. The Gallegos government was in the process of extending and honoring these commitments when the counterrevolution came. The adoption of a national agrarian reform law, for one example, came scant weeks before the military seized power, hence the bill was never implemented.

Even during the *trienio*, all organized political groups tended to accept the general outlines of *adeco*-inspired reforms. The URD subscribed to similar revolutionary

ideals while promising to carry them out more effectively. COPEI, even with the influence of *lopecista* elements
in 1945-1948, also advocated significant reforms in health,
housing, agriculture, education, and the like. The basis
of a more extensive consensus between the political
parties was therefore laid by 1948, and the decade of
repressive military rule did little to change the thinking
of the parties or the sentiments of the populace. The return of party government after 1958 demonstrated an
even more complete commitment by democratic organizations to similar socio-economic reforms. The pre-election statement of principles to which the three parties
willingly subscribed suggested the breadth of agreement.

For the national revolutionary AD, the very winning
of a consensus which revolved about its original goals
created both programmatic and practical difficulties. It
was not accidental that the party's 1963 campaign relied
unduly on references to the political reforms and broad
economic policies first advocated nearly a generation
earlier. It was difficult to make political capital with
proposals to which the major opposition fully agreed.
And for a party in power, there were problems in combatting the innate anti-government bias which rival
parties utilized in promising to carry out similar policies
more effectively and efficiently. The adoption of policies
and reforms earlier proposed and initiated by the AD
was a testimony to its credentials as the party which
brought to the country the entire panoply of important
changes. Yet the problem of adopting new and appealing
policies and electoral promises was difficult, and by 1964
the *adeco* leadership was still grappling with the question.

In addition to the pattern of programmatic strategy is
the matter of revolutionary attitudes. This meant for
Acción Democrática an early intransigence toward opposition that was not fully modified until the post-1958

era. Rarely abashed over the responsibilities and potentialities of national power, *adecos* were enthused with
their sudden accession to power. There was little reluctance in beginning the programs and policies which
had been expounded in theoretical terms for several
years. The attitude was not only one of zestful ardor at
the accomplishment of basic reforms but also a perceptible narrow-mindedness toward the opposition. The
"johnny-come-lately" stance of the URD in particular,
as well as its apparent *medinista* influences and the
*lopecista* ones in COPEI, led many *adecos* to disdain the
opposition. There was little willingness to accept the
possibility that non-*adecos* could themselves contribute
significantly to the restructuring and modernizing of
Venezuela.

In a sense, the revolutionary phase of the party—at
least, the first years of political power and of inexperienced immoderation—was past when Pérez Jiménez fled
the country in 1958. Certainly the attitudes had changed
fundamentally. Although both the party leadership and
rank-and-file tended to retain a certain feeling of supe-
riority, they recognized that the party was neither monolithic or all-knowing. The participation of non-*adecos*
and of partisans of other parties was seen as a further
means of winning wide acceptance of policies. The
spirit of conciliation was more than a temporary ex-
pedient. With the realization that its days of almost unlimited domination were forever gone, the AD made
the kind of adjustments which, one might submit, are
necessary from every national revolutionary party when
it encounters significant activity on the part of an organized democratic opposition.

Party leadership of the citizenry can be viewed as
having evolved through a pattern in which first ideological, then personal, and finally organizational considerations were paramount. With the AD relying upon
popular support as its fundamental source of strength,

its leadership has been required to shift emphases over the years. As a new organization the movement was virtually without a reputation; its leaders were young and unknown, hence charismatic leadership was out of the question. In order to become known to the public, the leadership chose a pair of specific policies. The first called for the exposition of policies and proposals, while the second brought into the movement figures who already enjoyed national repute.

The programmatic appeal was therefore the first effort by the leadership to stir the popular imagination. There were attacks on first the Gómez, then the López Contreras governments, hitting at corruption, nepotism, the violation of human rights, and the intrusion of the military into politics. Economic measures were criticized, while the movement adopted a set of positive policies which included political and electoral reforms on one hand and economic and social revisions on the other. The prominence of the movement in the public eye, as noted earlier, was enhanced during the early years by the occasional or regular participation of Picón Salas, Gallegos, and Blanco, whose reputations had already been made.

Revolutionary leadership changed in the mid-1940's with the increased national prominence of not merely Rómulo Gallegos but also such men as Betancourt, Rodríguez, Barrios, Prieto, and Leoni. Programmatic appeals were by no means shelved, but it was no longer necessary to arouse public support through attacks on military dictatorship and promises of direct democracy, representative government, and fundamental socio-economic reform. Top AD figures were true popular leaders, and their strength with the citizenry was only secondarily a function of their policies and promises.

The period of institutionalization and of the party's reliance on its organization came in the years after 1958. It became current within the party to regard the *aparato* as the single most important factor in its continuing primacy. Reliance upon the machinery rather than the leadership or program was a hallmark of Acción Democrática in the early 1960's. The 1963 campaign was illustrative of the fact, for Leoni's personality was not attractive to political independents, while the party platform and 1963's "Programa" leaned heavily upon a listing of past reforms which the party had achieved years earlier. The inability of the party to draw non-party and unaligned votes testified to the overweening faith in the machinery as a means of retaining national popularity.

A final element in the AD experience as a national revolutionary party is that of its relationship with party rivals in the Venezuelan polity. During most of the 1940's, Venezuela had what might be called a "dominant one-party" system. First Medina's PDV, then Acción Democrática itself assumed the leadership of such a party arrangement. The former could loosely be regarded as a party, at least in terms of the definition introduced previously. Under the Medina administration the AD was relatively unencumbered in strengthening its organization and building for future responsibility. During the *trienio,* both the URD and COPEI found themselves often harassed by the AD, and there was no serious possibility for either of them to win national power.

After the long years in exile, however, the return of political parties saw a multi-party system unlike that of earlier years. Both COPEI and the URD had gradually evolved until they were on the verge of achieving status themselves as modern parties. With the 1963 elections, there was little serious question about the modernity of COPEI. With a program identified as christian democratic, the party leadership gave every appearance of being able to survive the disappearance even of Rafael Caldera, and the organization seemed as important as personal leadership. The party, although still stronger in the Andes than elsewhere, had established itself as an important electoral force throughout Venezuela, and old charges of regionalism were unconvincing. The durability of the party seemed unquestioned, while the possibility of winning power in the future was bright. The share in government under Rómulo Betancourt had already given COPEI a taste of what it might later achieve on its own.

The position of the URD following the 1963 elections was still somewhat uncertain. If the Venezuelan system was definitely multi-party, the modernity of the URD was somewhat debatable. Its program remained similar to that of the AD; if not original, it was at the same time essentially that of a national revolutionary party. With an existence stretching back to 1946, the URD could not be regarded as a temporary splinter group. Yet the judgment as to party organization was difficult, for in many areas the party's strength was that of Villalba's personal leadership, and local *urredistas* were either disorganized or totally unorganized. With serious question about the URD organization, about its possible collapse if Villaba disappeared from the political scene, its classification as a modern party under the present definition was uncertain.

Effective competition within the party system has been healthy for Venezuela as well as for the parties. The withdrawal of the right to participate from the communists and also *miristas* is not construed as a denial of party competition; the basis for their exclusion has been the explicit unwillingness to operate within the restraints of constitutional democracy. With Venezuela now enjoying a competitive party system, the national revolutionary Acción Democrática has seen its position challenged more basically than ever before. An assumption that is entertained here—not presented as a formal hypothesis for the lack of adequate comparability in this Venezuelan study—suggests that in a competitive party system, the modern party will always win in direct

competition with traditional parties. The AD is no longer
Venezuela's only modern party, however, and the battle
to remain the country's leading party is therefore more
difficult than before.

Only comparable studies of national revolutionary
parties in Latin America would make possible a set of
hypotheses concerning the evolution of such parties, including their role in the emergence of the particular country toward full-fledged nationhood. It may well be that
the experience of Acción Democrática is characteristic
of other national revolutionary parties in similar circumstances. One cannot posit these as hypotheses, however,
in the absence of parallel studies. A final contention regarding today's AD may well have validity elsewhere,
however. This revolves about the multiplication of modern parties within the given polity.

So long as the national revolutionary party is opposed
by traditional parties, its domination is relatively secure.
Only anomic disturbances or nonconstitutional intervention is likely to remove the party from primacy. The
winning of modern status by other parties, however,
creates a situation in which the national revolutionary
movement finds itself seriously challenged. So it is today
that Acción Democrática, while still Venezuela's leading
party in electoral and organizational terms, must prepare for the most serious challenge of its history. The
problem of reorienting programmatic appeals to meet
the changing needs of the nation is a difficult one. Yet
it is the kind of problem the party must solve, if it is to
accommodate itself to the competition and the political
setting of Venezuela in the mid-1960's. Having won the
political changes it advocated, the party now sees its
socio-economic positions adopted by its competitors.
With consensus achieved on the issues which contributed
to the AD's national revolutionary programmatic appeal,
it must identify issues and proposals so that it may carve
out a position for the future. This search is a test which

many national revolutionary parties may ultimately face, and the future of Acción Democrática in substantial part will be determined by the degree of success it encounters.

## Acción Democrática: Problems for the Future

The challenge of the future toward the AD takes many different forms, at least a few of which have been presented earlier. In a final consideration of the party's present position, two distinct yet closely related areas stand out. The first applies to the electoral problems confronted within various sectors of the Venezuelan electorate. The other is the matter of organizational appeal and internal strength that can encourage and give impetus to a renewed drive for support from these sectors.

Electoral problems can be identified in terms of party appeal to such elements as the urban middle sectors, the youth, labor, and the peasant movement. Before even these, perhaps, comes the "Caracas problem" earlier alluded to. The weakness of the AD in the Metropolitan Center and in Caracas itself in 1958 was understandable. The weaknesses had been created in part by the AD's absence of a full decade and in part by the natural appeal of Wolfgang Larrazábal. Furthermore, the participation and direction of the AD campaign in the Federal District by such figures as *mirista* Simón Sáez Mérida meant a less than enthusiastic effort in planning the party campaign there.[4] The party's internal dissension, although not public at the time, was a debilitating factor in the process.

Fully conscious of its miserable showing in Caracas and environs, the AD determined to change the situation

[4] An examination of the AD's "Caracas Problem" which was optimistic for the party's future was Gabriel Moro's "Por Qué Perdió AD en Caracas," *Momento*, no. 355, May 5, 1963, pp. 28-34.

by 1963. Concerted planning and dedicated organizational groundwork preceded the election by years. A
pair of winning and experienced leaders, Octavio Lepage
and Guillermo Salazar Meneses, began to rebuild the
party in the Federal Districts. It was divided into 28
party zones, which in turn were subdivided into 145
Comités de Barrios, 10 of them in the workers' section, 23
de Enero. The 28 zonal leaders met regularly each fifteen
days, and plans were carefully laid in anticipation of the
election. Despite occasional interference from national
headquarters—too close to district offices—there were
expectations that the AD would recover its position in
1963.

The anticipated recuperation of Acción Democrática
in the Federal District was not realized in the elections.
At the same time, the support for both the URD and
COPEI dropped measurably, leaving the AD in third
place in presidential and congressional contests, yet
somewhat ahead of its regular party rivals. Thus the
three major organized democratic parties found themselves in the post-election period facing a comparative
absence of popular support in the nation's capital. For
Acción Democrática, its success in defeating the URD
and COPEI was more than canceled out by the overwhelming preference of *caraqueños* for either Uslar
Pietri or Larrazábal.

The nature of the party's Caracas problem relates in
part to the contemporary aversion of the growing urban
middle sectors to align themselves with the organized
parties. The anti-government bias that has been nationally characteristic has now been broadened in the
capital region into an anti-party bias. Caracas voters in
1963 clearly preferred the explicitly non-party, *anti-*
party Uslar Pietri; those who did not flocked to the banner of the still-popular and basically unaffiliated Wolfgang Larrazábal. The regular parties were left to fight
over the electoral crumbs. Thus the latter were faced

with the need to reestablish popular appeal in the eyes of the urban middle sectors.

The evolution of the urban middle sectors in Venezuela is very recent, and little scholarly examination has yet been given to the subject in this particular country. Nonetheless, none would deny the rapid enlargement of this group, first during the relative economic prosperity of the early Pérez Jiménez days, then under the Betancourt administration with its efforts at broadening the effective, productive segment of the population. With the growth of professional men, the increase in both small and middle-size businessmen and entrepreneurs, the rise in basic standards of living and income contributed to the accentuation of bourgeois middle-class attitudes.

The inclination of these Venezuelans has been increasingly toward maintenance of the status quo. For those who desire genuine socio-economic reforms on a national basis, the regular parties are seen as less than ideal instruments for such changes. The electoral appeal of an Uslar Pietri, sound and sane in his statements while implicitly determined to slow down economic change during the process of removing inequities, was naturally strong. Uslar, more than any of his rivals, suggested a sedate approach to many problems, leading to a very gradual treatment that was guaranteed not to disturb the newly developing interests of the middle sectors.

For the AD itself, this situation meant a continuing obstacle through the difficulties related to city-rural rivalries. Under Raúl Leoni in 1964 the residents of Caracas continued to complain that the AD government gave major assistance to the interior while effectively ignoring Caracas. There was an inverted kind of urban provincialism which was little concerned with the rest of the country if its own primacy was to be slighted or reduced. And beyond this, the AD was confronted with a number of metropolitan voters who simply regarded it as old, tired, and lacking the drive that might totally restore public order while vigorously protecting urban business interests. The image of a patronage-minded party which the AD has been projecting in Caracas is not designed to attract unaffiliated or independent voters.

In labor and the peasantry the position of Acción Democrática is strong, although it is by no means secure. The moderate drop in AD support from labor has been viewed as partially a result of the commitment of CTV leaders to protect and defend the constitutional system above all else. Additionally, the growing strength of COPEI within the labor movement is not to be discounted. Today, although most national labor figures continue to be ranking *adecos,* there is no eschewing the fact that the automatic delivery of more than a half-million labor votes can no longer be taken for granted. As for the *campesinos, adecos* themselves recognize that neither they nor any other group has yet effectively organized the peasants and molded them into a significant and controllable voting bloc. Certainly the AD is far more likely to achieve this goal than any of its rivals; at the same time, the construction and strengthening of the FCV is far short of being able to reach, let alone to control the vote of every Venezuelan peasant.

The party's situation with regard to the nation's youth is especially serious. With over half of the electorate in 1969 expected to be voting in national elections for the first time, the sheer political importance of this group is overwhelming. Here as with the problem of the urban middle sector, the AD is far from alone in its problems. The URD is no better off; only COPEI has enjoyed noticeable support from the students in recent years, and this may be somewhat transitory in nature. Certainly there are many new voters emerging into the electorate, searching for allegiances and for leadership. The challenge for the AD is once again great. Given the strong anti-AD bias of revolutionary student leaders, the AD will be contested bitterly in the struggle.

Apart from the question of the sectors of the voting population to which Acción Democrática must direct its campaigns, the party faces organizational issues which center in large part on personality and personnel. One can point out, thus, that the party does not have great appeal to the urban middle sector or the emerging young student; but this begs the question of why.

The over-all image which the party has come to project before the uncommitted, reasonably educated Venezuelan is far from favorable. The strong feeling of personal *rapport* and of common goals and ideals that characterizes the party—and contributes to its organizational strength in the interior—seems to more sophisticated urbanites like a selfish, closed group which operates primarily for the purpose of its own support and self-preservation. Many have a feeling that the AD is most concerned in perpetuating its position of dominance for individual rather than for national purposes. For at least a few, there is the thought that the AD has retained its strength through a hoodwinking of sincere but uneducated *campesinos*. While there are certain injustices in this, the fact remains that such an impression *does* exist within important electoral sectors of Venezuela. Although the AD still has an organizational apparatus and party membership that is jealously admired by its opponents, this same apparatus and membership signifies to some the self-seeking nature of the party today.

Problems of bureaucratization within the party apparatus do exist, although in many cases there is still a shortage of competent office-workers and dedicated full-time organizational aides and assistants. Over and above this is the basic need of the party to remove the picture of a patronage-oriented fraternal organization composed of politically adept but nationally unconcerned men. The pre-1964 popular impression of Raúl Leoni as something of a political hack has been breaking down since he assumed office, but it typifies the attitudes of various sectors toward the party generally. Whether justified or not, it represents a public feeling that the party cannot afford to ignore.

Insofar as the internal workings of the machinery are concerned, the generational problem seems to have been accommodated. The AD can function effectively when its direction comes in large part from such men as Paz Galarraga, Moanack, Carlos Andrés Pérez, Lepage, and Dubuc. With Leoni and Barrios occupied by problems of national administration, nearly the only remaining veterans with major national popularity are Prieto and, to a lesser extent, D'Ascoli and labor leaders such as Pérez Salinas and González Navarro. To the public, however, there is some degree of sameness, and this can only be overcome by growing emphasis on lesser figures within the party. Since COPEI and the URD are also handicapped by the overwhelming public domination respectively of Caldera and Villalba, the time is ripe for a new set of fresh political figures. Acción Democrática would be well rewarded by meeting such a need.

And if the fairly common popular view of the party demands a renovation of its public leaders, much the same reinvigoration is needed for the party's programmatic proposals. While the adoption of an entire new program would be inconsistent with the party's past, there is nothing to prevent a readaptation of the same basic principles to the needs of the mid-1960's. The 1963 AD campaign has already been described as one in which there was a rather tired and familiar ring to old declarations that had lost the immediacy of earlier years. Notwithstanding the existence of a relative consensus on the part of most Venezuelans, there is no reason for the party to ignore or neglect the framing and presentation of new programs, at least insofar as implementation is concerned.

The confrontation of Acción Democrática with such matters lies ahead. It is not impossible that the next few years will see the rise of a new party which will capture support in the Metropolitan Center, spread its organization nationally and become a significant modern party. The permanence of Acción Democrática and COPEI is more certain than that of the URD; yet the continuation of any or all of the three does not assure that national leadership will not pass into different hands. The successful survival of the AD in the face of recent factionalism and inner disunity suggests a lengthy future for a party that has established itself as one of the most prominent in the hemisphere. At the same time, past and recent victories cannot guarantee continuing primacy within the Venezuelan party system. Acción Democrática has risen to meet major challenges before; if it is to maintain its position, the party must rise again to confront and overcome the conditions and circumstances which threaten its power and influence.

# National Electoral Data

## 1. CIVIC PARTICIPATION—1963

| | Estimated Population[a] | Registered Voters[b] | Sen. | Dip. | Presidential Vote Totals |
|---|---|---|---|---|---|
| Distrito Federal | 1,440,450 | 557,239 | 2 | 29 | 478,466 |
| Anzoátegui | 410,117 | 165,091 | 2 | 8 | 149,479 |
| Apure | 132,233 | 49,108 | 2 | 3 | 38,220 |
| Aragua | 343,520 | 145,811 | 2 | 7 | 128,264 |
| Barinas | 159,155 | 62,381 | 2 | 3 | 54,202 |
| Bolívar | 246,598 | 106,811 | 2 | 5 | 93,322 |
| Carabobo | 412,630 | 178,591 | 2 | 8 | 156,211 |
| Cojedes | 79,693 | 32,763 | 2 | 2 | 29,916 |
| Falcón | 351,830 | 150,164 | 2 | 7 | 134,974 |
| Guárico | 270,670 | 107,859 | 2 | 5 | 94,839 |
| Lara | 514,255 | 226,771 | 2 | 10 | 185,625 |
| Mérida | 287,447 | 126,258 | 2 | 6 | 110,572 |
| Miranda | 545,858 | 223,564 | 2 | 11 | 197,970 |
| Monagas | 265,217 | 110,472 | 2 | 5 | 96,211 |
| Nueva Esparta | 91,933 | 45,808 | 2 | 2 | 43,935 |
| Portuguesa | 228,436 | 92,635 | 2 | 5 | 77,852 |
| Sucre | 427,295 | 177,113 | 2 | 9 | 157,464 |
| Táchira | 431,626 | 152,798 | 2 | 9 | 131,947 |
| Trujillo | 341,537 | 150,169 | 2 | 7 | 127,776 |
| Yaracuy | 184,770 | 81,872 | 2 | 4 | 71,047 |
| Zulia | 1,044,047 | 406,356 | 2 | 21 | 339,595 |
| T. Amazonas | 12,072 | 4,356 | – | 1 | 4,080 |
| T. Delta Amacuro | 34,067 | 15,959 | – | 1 | 13,929 |
| | 8,255,456 | 3,369,986 | 42 | 168 | 2,917,896 |

| | | | | |
|---|---|---|---|---|
| Estimated population | 8,255,456 | Registered voters | | 3,369,986 |
| Estimated voters | 3,586,000 | Total valid | | 2,917,896 |
| Registered voters | 3,369,986 | Invalid | | 161,014 |
| Difference | 216,014 | Total votes cast | | 3,078,910 |
| % Registered | 93.97 | % Voting | | 91.33 |

[a] Official census figures for December 1, 1963.
[b] Official registration figures as announced October 30, 1963.

2. PRESIDENTIAL VOTE, CONGRESSIONAL REPRESENTATION BY STATE—1963

| | Leoni | *Sen.* | *Dip.* | Caldera | *Sen.* | *Dip.* | Villalba | *Sen.* | *Dip.* |
|---|---|---|---|---|---|---|---|---|---|
| DF | 65,333 | | 4 | 50,665 | | 3 | 62,669 | | 4 |
| Anzoátegui | 62,822 | 1 | 4 | 13,640 | | 1 | 53,051 | 1 | 3 |
| Apure | 19,304 | 2 | 2 | 7,762 | | 1 | 5,102 | | |
| Aragua | 24,923 | | 1 | 16,875 | | 1 | 22,909 | | 1 |
| Barinas | 21,495 | 1 | 2 | 17,524 | 1 | 1 | 8,904 | | |
| Bolívar | 40,963 | 1 | 3 | 10,853 | | 1 | 22,232 | 1 | 1 |
| Carabobo | 39,746 | 1 | 2 | 26,226 | | 2 | 30,799 | | 1 |
| Cojedes | 12,311 | 1 | 1 | 5,839 | | | 8,881 | 1 | 1 |
| Falcón | 52,811 | 1 | 3 | 33,005 | | 2 | 39,211 | 1 | 2 |
| Guárico | 39,230 | 1 | 3 | 16,124 | | 1 | 25,043 | 1 | 1 |
| Lara | 70,004 | 1 | 4 | 47,586 | 1 | 3 | 29,691 | | 2 |
| Mérida | 27,297 | | 2 | 63,699 | 2 | 4 | 7,648 | | |
| Miranda | 43,576 | 1 | 3 | 39,184 | | 3 | 23,153 | | 1 |
| Monagas | 57,791 | 2 | 4 | 7,469 | | | 25,260 | | 1 |
| N. Esparta | 19,339 | 1 | 1 | 1,092 | | | 22,821 | 1 | 1 |
| Portuguesa | 33,332 | 1 | 3 | 18,691 | 1 | 1 | 16,391 | | 1 |
| Sucre | 93,894 | 2 | 6 | 10,654 | | | 46,112 | | 3 |
| Táchira | 33,398 | | 2 | 66,555 | 2 | 6 | 7,508 | | |
| Trujillo | 41,510 | 1 | 2 | 55,733 | 1 | 4 | 17,928 | | 1 |
| Yaracuy | 21,689 | 1 | 2 | 20,878 | 1 | 2 | 11,333 | | |
| Zulia | 127,955 | 2 | 9 | 56,315 | | 4 | 58,034 | | 3 |
| Amazonas | 1,415 | | 1 | 994 | | | 1,540 | | |
| D. Amacuro | 7,561 | | 1 | 1,009 | | | 4,900 | | |
| Totals | 957,699 | 21 | 65 | 588,372 | 9 | 40 | 551,120 | 6 | 27 |
| Elec. quotient | | | | | | | | 1 | 2 |
| Percentages | 32.81 | | | 20.19 | | | 18.88 | | |

2. CONTINUED

| | Uslar | Sen. | Dip. | Larrazá-bal | Sen. | Dip. | Ramos Giménez | Sen. | Dip. | Borre-gales | Sen. | Dip. |
|---|---|---|---|---|---|---|---|---|---|---|---|---|
| DF | 191,028 | 1 | 10 | 98,129 | 1 | 7 | 8,357 | 1 | | 2,285 | | |
| Anzoátegui | 6,356 | | | 7,820 | | | 5,523 | | | 267 | | |
| Apure | 4,099 | | | 833 | | | 1,032 | | | 88 | | |
| Aragua | 33,575 | 1 | 2 | 27,143 | 1 | 2 | 2,224 | | | 615 | | |
| Barinas | 4,091 | | | 415 | | | 1,594 | | | 179 | | |
| Bolívar | 9,825 | | | 6,943 | | | 2,294 | | | 212 | | |
| Carabobo | 25,826 | | 1 | 30,589 | 1 | 2 | 2,420 | | | 605 | | |
| Cojedes | 924 | | | 340 | | | 1,569 | | | 52 | | |
| Falcón | 4,945 | | | 2,173 | | | 2,465 | | | 364 | | |
| Guárico | 9,144 | | | 2,408 | | | 2,643 | | | 247 | | |
| Lara | 24,698 | | 1 | 9,246 | | | 3,720 | | | 680 | | |
| Mérida | 9,153 | | | 702 | | | 1,849 | | | 224 | | |
| Miranda | 55,170 | 1 | 3 | 27,261 | | 1 | 8,819 | | | 807 | | |
| Monagas | 2,222 | | | 1,940 | | | 3,402 | | | 127 | | |
| N. Esparta | 344 | | | 158 | | | 167 | | | 14 | | |
| Portuguesa | 5,537 | | | 1,416 | | | 2,204 | | | 281 | | |
| Sucre | 2,251 | | | 3,243 | | | 1,124 | | | 186 | | |
| Táchira | 21,520 | | 1 | 1,111 | | | 1,575 | | | 280 | | |
| Trujillo | 9,041 | | | 1,689 | | | 1,592 | | | 283 | | |
| Yaracuy | 3,317 | | | 4,409 | | | 9,068 | | | 353 | | |
| Zulia | 45,983 | | 2 | 47,169 | | 3 | 2,981 | | | 1,158 | | |
| Amazonas | 68 | | | 30 | | | 30 | | | 3 | | |
| D. Amacuro | 123 | | | 137 | | | 185 | | | 14 | | |
| Totals | 469,240 | 3 | 20 | 275,304 | 3 | 15 | 66,837 | 1 | | 9,324 | | |
| Elec. quotient | | | | | 1 | 1 | | 1 | 4 | | | 2[a] |
| Percentages | 16.08 | | | 9.43 | | | 2.29 | | | 0.32 | | |

[a] One deputy apiece for Partido Socialista Venezolana (PSV) and Movimiento Electoral Nacional Independiente (MENI).

3. Presidential Vote, Congressional Representation by State—1958

| | Betancourt | Sen. | Dip. | Caldera | Sen. | Dip. | Larrazábal (URD) | Sen. | Dip. | Larrazábal (PCV) | Sen. | Dip. |
|---|---|---|---|---|---|---|---|---|---|---|---|---|
| DF | 59,832 | | 3 | 64,734 | | 4 | 252,750 | 2 | 12 | 29,997 | | 4 |
| Anzoátegui | 92,472 | 2 | 5 | 6,334 | | | 36,139 | | 1 | 4,730 | | |
| Apure | 28,832 | 2 | 2 | 3,580 | | | 4,263 | | | 385 | | |
| Aragua | 26,280 | | 1 | 11,738 | | | 61,660 | 2 | 4 | 4,616 | | |
| Barinas | 28,078 | 2 | 2 | 9,845 | | | 5,301 | | | 569 | | |
| Bolívar | 43,938 | 2 | 2 | 4,504 | | | 23,500 | | 1 | 1,584 | | |
| Carabobo | 53,039 | 1 | 3 | 13,167 | | | 60,275 | 1 | 3 | 3,261 | | |
| Cojedes | 14,996 | 2 | 2 | 3,427 | | | 6,660 | | | 223 | | |
| Falcón | 71,489 | 2 | 4 | 16,858 | | | 30,011 | | 1 | 3,400 | | |
| Guárico | 55,482 | 2 | 3 | 7,287 | | | 17,338 | | 1 | 1,350 | | |
| Lara | 117,463 | 2 | 6 | 18,606 | | 1 | 34,189 | | 1 | 6,244 | | |
| Mérida | 39,388 | 1 | 2 | 51,827 | 1 | 2 | 5,037 | | | 525 | | |
| Miranda | 50,569 | 1 | 2 | 28,158 | | 1 | 70,606 | 1 | 3 | 4,936 | | |
| Monagas | 66,821 | 2 | 4 | 3,699 | | | 14,808 | | 1 | 2,248 | | |
| N. Esparta | 19,796 | 1 | 1 | 748 | | | 15,926 | 1 | 1 | 412 | | |
| Portuguesa | 49,823 | 2 | 3 | 5,945 | | | 8,979 | | | 2,077 | | |
| Sucre | 109,597 | 2 | 6 | 5,468 | | | 28,854 | | 1 | 2,828 | | |
| Táchira | 46,446 | 1 | 3 | 61,717 | 1 | 4 | 8,238 | | | 665 | | |
| Trujillo | 68,583 | 1 | 4 | 38,397 | 1 | 2 | 11,878 | | | 1,214 | | |
| Yaracuy | 45,387 | 2 | 3 | 8,229 | | | 10,171 | | | 1,857 | | |
| Zulia | 186,346 | 2 | 10 | 30,376 | | 1 | 89,697 | | 4 | 11,102 | | 1 |
| Amazonas | 1,237 | | 1 | 724 | | | 1,255 | | | 55 | | |
| D. Amacuro | 8,198 | | 1 | 925 | | | 3,181 | | | 173 | | |
| Totals | 1,284,092 | 32 | 73 | 396,293 | 3 | 15 | 800,716 | 7 | 34 | 84,451 | | 5 |
| Elec. quotient | | | | | 3 | 4 | | 4 | | | 2 | 2 |
| Percentages | 49.24 | | | 15.2 | | | 30.71 | | | 3.2 | | |

4. COMPARISON OF NATIONAL VOTE BY PARTY—1958 AND 1963

| Party | 1958 | |
| | President | Congress |
|---|---|---|
| AD | 1,284,092 | 1,275,973 |
| COPEI | 396,293 | 392,305 |
| URD | 800,716 | 690,357 |
| PCV | 84,451 | 160,791 |
| IR | 15,564 | 19,424 |
| PST | 11,405 | 15,476 |
| MENI | 18,312 | 14,908 |
| PSV | | 10,983 |
| Totals | 2,610,833 | 2,580,217 |

| Party | 1963 | |
| | President | Congress |
|---|---|---|
| AD | 957,699 | 936,052 |
| COPEI | 588,372 | 596,255 |
| URD | 551,120 | 497,425 |
| IPFN | 469,240 | 381,507 |
| FDP | 275,304 | 274,100 |
| AD-OP | 66,837 | 94,211 |
| PAN | 9,324 | |
| PSV | | 37,318 |
| | 2,917,896 | 2,816,868 |

5. Comparison of Presidential Vote by Party—1958 and 1963
(percentage)

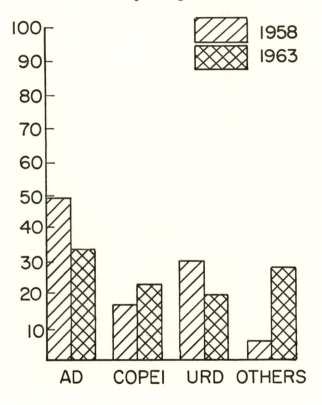

6. Comparison of Congressional Vote by Party—1958 and 1963
(percentage)

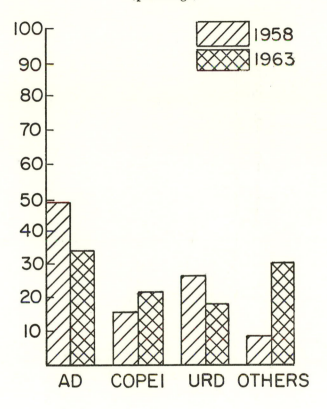

7. Presidential Vote by Candidate—1963
(percentage)

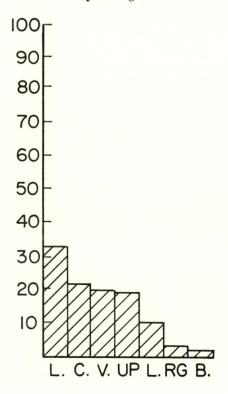

8. COMPARISON OF CONGRESSIONAL REPRESENTATION BY PARTY—1958 AND 1963

SENATE

| Total | AD | COP | URD | PCV | AD-OP | MRP | FDP | IPFN | Year |
|---|---|---|---|---|---|---|---|---|---|
| 51 | 32 | 6 | 11 | 2 | | | | | 1958 |
| 51 | 26 | 6 | 11 | 2 | 4 | 1 | 1 | | 1963[a] |
| 45 | 21 | 9 | 7 | | 1 | | 4 | 3 | 1964 |

[a] Composition of 1958-elected Congress following party realignment but before installation of new Congress in 1964.

CHAMBER OF DEPUTIES

| Total | AD | COP | URD | PCV | AD-OP | FDP | MIR | IPFN | Year |
|---|---|---|---|---|---|---|---|---|---|
| 133 | 73 | 19 | 34 | 7 | | | | | 1958 |
| 133 | 36 | 19 | 34 | 5 | 22 | 2 | 15 | | 1963[a] |
| 177[b] | 65 | 40 | 29 | | 5 | 16 | | 20 | 1964 |

[a] Composition of 1958-elected Congress following party realignment but before installation of new Congress in 1964.
[b] Total includes single deputies from the MENI and PSV.

# APPENDIX B

# Regional Electoral Data

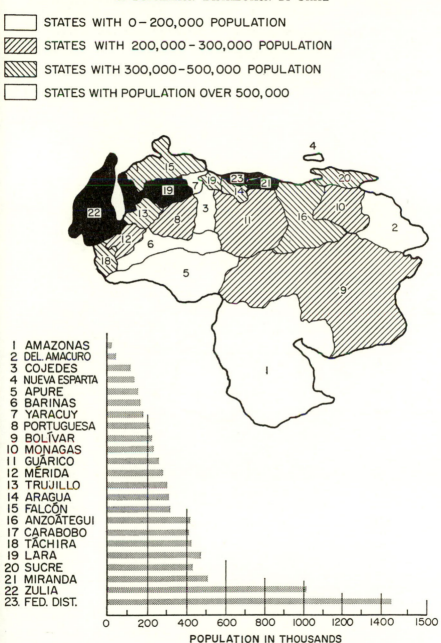

STATES WITH 0 – 200,000 POPULATION

STATES WITH 200,000 – 300,000 POPULATION

STATES WITH 300,000 – 500,000 POPULATION

STATES WITH POPULATION OVER 500,000

1 AMAZONAS
2 DEL. AMACURO
3 COJEDES
4 NUEVA ESPARTA
5 APURE
6 BARINAS
7 YARACUY
8 PORTUGUESA
9 BOLÍVAR
10 MONAGAS
11 GUÁRICO
12 MÉRIDA
13 TRUJILLO
14 ARAGUA
15 FALCÓN
16 ANZOÁTEGUI
17 CARABOBO
18 TÁCHIRA
19 LARA
20 SUCRE
21 MIRANDA
22 ZULIA
23. FED. DIST.

POPULATION IN THOUSANDS

10. Population Distribution by Politico-Electoral Region

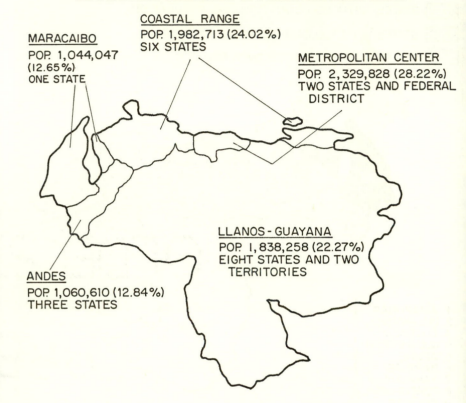

COASTAL RANGE
POP. 1,982,713 (24.02%)
SIX STATES

MARACAIBO
POP. 1,044,047
(12.65%)
ONE STATE

METROPOLITAN CENTER
POP. 2,329,828 (28.22%)
TWO STATES AND FEDERAL
DISTRICT

LLANOS-GUAYANA
POP. 1,838,258 (22.27%)
EIGHT STATES AND TWO
TERRITORIES

ANDES
POP. 1,060,610 (12.84%)
THREE STATES

## 11. DISTRIBUTION OF VOTERS BY STATE—1963 PRESIDENTIAL ELECTION

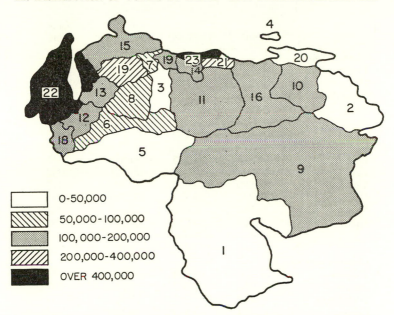

0-50,000
50,000-100,000
100,000-200,000
200,000-400,000
OVER 400,000

## 12. REPRESENTATION IN CHAMBER OF DEPUTIES, BY STATE—1964

13. Presidential Vote by Region—1963

|  | Leoni | Caldera | Villalba | Uslar Pietri |
|---|---|---|---|---|
| **Metropolitan Center** | | | | |
| DF | 65,333 | 50,665 | 62,669 | 191,028 |
| Miranda | 43,576 | 39,184 | 23,153 | 55,170 |
| Aragua | 24,923 | 16,875 | 22,909 | 33,575 |
|  | 133,832 | 106,724 | 108,731 | 279,773 |
| **Coastal** | | | | |
| Falcón | 52,811 | 33,005 | 39,211 | 4,945 |
| Lara | 70,004 | 47,586 | 29,691 | 24,698 |
| Yaracuy | 21,689 | 20,878 | 11,333 | 3,317 |
| Carabobo | 39,746 | 26,226 | 30,799 | 25,826 |
| Nueva Esparta | 19,339 | 1,092 | 22,821 | 344 |
| Sucre | 93,894 | 10,654 | 46,112 | 2,251 |
|  | 297,483 | 139,441 | 179,967 | 61,381 |
| **Llanos-Guayana** | | | | |
| Barinas | 21,495 | 17,524 | 8,904 | 4,091 |
| Apure | 19,304 | 7,762 | 5,102 | 4,099 |
| Portuguesa | 33,332 | 18,691 | 16,391 | 5,537 |
| Cojedes | 12,311 | 5,839 | 8,881 | 924 |
| Guárico | 39,230 | 16,124 | 25,043 | 9,144 |
| Anzoátegui | 62,822 | 13,640 | 53,051 | 6,356 |
| Monagas | 57,791 | 7,469 | 25,260 | 2,222 |
| Bolívar | 40,963 | 10,853 | 22,232 | 9,825 |
| D. Amacuro | 7,561 | 1,009 | 4,900 | 123 |
| Amazonas | 1,415 | 994 | 1,540 | 68 |
|  | 296,224 | 99,905 | 171,304 | 42,389 |
| **Maracaibo** | | | | |
| Zulia | 127,955 | 56,315 | 58,034 | 45,983 |
| **Andes** | | | | |
| Táchira | 33,398 | 66,555 | 7,508 | 21,520 |
| Mérida | 27,297 | 63,699 | 7,648 | 9,153 |
| Trujillo | 41,510 | 55,733 | 17,928 | 9,041 |
|  | 102,205 | 185,987 | 33,084 | 39,714 |
| Totals | 957,699 | 588,372 | 551,120 | 469,240 |

13. CONTINUED

| | Larra-zábal | Ramos Giménez | Borre-gales | Total |
|---|---|---|---|---|
| Metropolitan Center | | | | |
| DF | 98,129 | 8,357 | 2,285 | 478,466 |
| Miranda | 27,261 | 8,819 | 807 | 197,970 |
| Aragua | 27,143 | 2,224 | 615 | 128,264 |
| | 152,533 | 19,400 | 3,707 | 804,700 |
| Coastal | | | | |
| Falcón | 2,173 | 2,465 | 364 | 134,974 |
| Lara | 9,246 | 3,720 | 680 | 185,625 |
| Yaracuy | 4,409 | 9,068 | 353 | 71,047 |
| Carabobo | 30,589 | 2,420 | 605 | 156,211 |
| Nueva Esparta | 158 | 167 | 14 | 43,935 |
| Sucre | 3,243 | 1,124 | 186 | 157,464 |
| | 49,818 | 18,964 | 2,202 | 749,256 |
| Llanos-Guayana | | | | |
| Barinas | 415 | 1,594 | 179 | 54,202 |
| Apure | 833 | 1,032 | 88 | 38,220 |
| Portuguesa | 1,416 | 2,204 | 281 | 77,852 |
| Cojedes | 340 | 1,569 | 52 | 29,916 |
| Guárico | 2,408 | 2,643 | 247 | 94,839 |
| Anzoátegui | 7,820 | 5,523 | 267 | 149,479 |
| Monagas | 1,940 | 3,402 | 127 | 96,211 |
| Bolívar | 6,943 | 2,294 | 212 | 93,322 |
| D. Amacuro | 137 | 185 | 14 | 13,929 |
| Amazonas | 30 | 30 | 3 | 4,080 |
| | 22,282 | 20,476 | 1,470 | 654,050 |
| Maracaibo | | | | |
| Zulia | 47,169 | 2,981 | 1,158 | 339,595 |
| Andes | | | | |
| Táchira | 1,111 | 1,575 | 280 | 131,947 |
| Mérida | 702 | 1,849 | 224 | 110,572 |
| Trujillo | 1,689 | 1,592 | 283 | 127,776 |
| Totals | 3,502 | 5,016 | 787 | 370,295 |
| | 275,304 | 66,837 | 9,324 | 2,917,896 |

14. PRESIDENTIAL VOTE BY REGION—1958

|  | Betancourt | Caldera | (URD) Larrazábal | (PCV) Larrazábal | Total |
|---|---|---|---|---|---|
| *Metropolitan Center* |  |  |  |  |  |
| DF | 59,832 | 64,734 | 252,750 | 29,997 | 407,313 |
| Miranda | 50,569 | 28,158 | 70,606 | 4,936 | 154,269 |
| Aragua | 26,280 | 11,738 | 61,660 | 4,616 | 104,294 |
|  | 136,681 | 104,630 | 385,016 | 39,549 | 665,876 |
| *Coastal* |  |  |  |  |  |
| Falcón | 71,489 | 16,858 | 30,011 | 3,400 | 121,758 |
| Lara | 117,463 | 18,606 | 34,189 | 6,244 | 176,502 |
| Yaracuy | 45,387 | 8,229 | 10,171 | 1,857 | 65,644 |
| Carabobo | 53,039 | 13,167 | 60,275 | 3,261 | 129,742 |
| Nueva Esparta | 19,796 | 748 | 15,926 | 412 | 36,882 |
| Sucre | 109,597 | 5,468 | 28,854 | 2,828 | 146,747 |
|  | 416,771 | 63,076 | 179,426 | 18,002 | 677,275 |
| *Llanos-Guayana* |  |  |  |  |  |
| Barinas | 28,078 | 9,845 | 5,301 | 569 | 43,793 |
| Apure | 28,832 | 3,580 | 4,263 | 385 | 37,060 |
| Portuguesa | 49,823 | 5,945 | 8,979 | 2,077 | 66,824 |
| Cojedes | 14,996 | 3,427 | 6,660 | 223 | 25,306 |
| Guárico | 55,482 | 7,287 | 17,338 | 1,350 | 81,457 |
| Anzoátegui | 92,472 | 6,334 | 36,139 | 4,730 | 139,675 |
| Monagas | 66,821 | 3,699 | 14,808 | 2,248 | 87,576 |
| Bolívar | 43,938 | 4,504 | 23,500 | 1,584 | 73,526 |
| D. Amacuro | 8,198 | 925 | 3,181 | 173 | 12,477 |
| Amazonas | 1,237 | 724 | 1,255 | 55 | 3,271 |
|  | 389,877 | 46,270 | 121,424 | 13,394 | 570,965 |
| *Maracaibo* |  |  |  |  |  |
| Zulia | 186,346 | 30,376 | 89,697 | 11,102 | 317,521 |
| *Andes* |  |  |  |  |  |
| Táchira | 46,446 | 61,717 | 8,238 | 665 | 117,066 |
| Mérida | 39,388 | 51,827 | 5,037 | 525 | 96,777 |
| Trujillo | 68,583 | 38,397 | 11,878 | 1,214 | 120,072 |
|  | 154,417 | 151,941 | 25,153 | 2,404 | 333,915 |
| Totals | 1,284,092 | 396,293 | 800,716 | 84,451 | 2,565,552 |

15. Regional Comparison of Presidential Vote by Major Party—1958 and 1963

| Regions | AD | | COPEI | | URD | |
|---|---|---|---|---|---|---|
| | 1958 | 1963 | 1958 | 1963 | 1958 | 1963 |
| Metropolitan Center | 20.5% | 16.3% | 15.7% | 13.2% | 57.8% | 13.5% |
| Coastal | 61.5 | 39.7 | 9.3 | 18.6 | 26.6 | 24.0 |
| Llanos-Guayana | 68.2 | 45.0 | 8.1 | 15.3 | 21.2 | 26.1 |
| Maracaibo | 58.7 | 37.6 | 9.5 | 16.5 | 28.3 | 17.0 |
| Andes | 46.4 | 27.6 | 45.5 | 50.2 | 7.5 | 8.9 |

16. National Vote Excluding Metropolitan Center—1963
A. PRESIDENTIAL CANDIDATES

| | Leoni | Caldera | Villalba | Uslar Pietri | Larra-zábal | Ramos Giménez | Borre-gales |
|---|---|---|---|---|---|---|---|
| Natl. | 957,699 | 588,372 | 551,120 | 469,240 | 275,304 | 66,837 | 9,324 |
| M.C. | 133,832 | 106,724 | 108,731 | 279,773 | 152,533 | 19,400 | 3,707 |
| | 823,867 | 481,648 | 442,389 | 189,467 | 122,771 | 47,437 | 5,617 |
| | 38.9% | 22.8% | 20.9% | 8.9% | 5.8% | 2.4% | 0.3% |

B. COMPARISON OF GOVERNMENT AND OPPOSITION

| Government | | | Opposition | | |
|---|---|---|---|---|---|
| AD | 823,867 | 38.9% | URD | 442,389 | 20.9% |
| COPEI | 481,648 | 22.8% | IPFN | 189,467 | 8.9% |
| | | | FDP | 122,771 | 5.8% |
| | | | AD-OP | 47,437 | 2.4% |
| | | | MAN | 5,617 | 0.3% |
| Totals | 1,305,515 | 61.7% | | 807,681 | 38.3% |

C. COMPARISON OF PARTY AND "NON-PARTY"

| Party | | | "Non-Party" | | |
|---|---|---|---|---|---|
| AD | 823,867 | 38.9% | IPFN | 189,467 | 8.9% |
| COPEI | 481,648 | 22.8% | FDP | 122,771 | 5.8% |
| URD | 442,389 | 20.9% | AD-OP | 47,437 | 2.4% |
| | | | MAN | 5,617 | 0.3% |
| Totals | 1,747,904 | 82.6% | | 365,292 | 17.4% |

17. Miscellaneous Data on Presidential Returns—1963

### A. comparison of government and opposition

| Government | | | Opposition | | |
|---|---|---|---|---|---|
| AD | 957,699 | 32.81% | URD | 551,120 | 18.88% |
| COPEI | 588,372 | 20.19% | IPFN | 469,240 | 16.08% |
| | | | FDP | 275,304 | 9.43% |
| | | | AD-OP | 66,837 | 2.29% |
| | | | MAN | 9,324 | 0.32% |
| Totals | 1,546,071 | 53.00% | | 1,371,825 | 47.00% |

### B. comparison of party and "non-party"

| Party | | | "Non-Party" | | |
|---|---|---|---|---|---|
| AD | 957,699 | 32.81% | IPFN | 469,240 | 16.08% |
| COPEI | 588,372 | 20.19% | FDP | 275,304 | 9.43% |
| URD | 551,120 | 18.88% | AD-OP | 66,837 | 2.29% |
| | | | MAN | 9,324 | 0.32% |
| Totals | 2,097,191 | 71.88% | | 820,705 | 28.12% |

Bibliography

Index

# Bibliography

## I. BOOKS

### A. Writings of Acción Democrática

Barrios, Gonzalo. *Los Días y la Política.* Caracas: Editorial "El Nacional," 1963.

————. *Por Qué Han Sido Suspendidas las Garantías Constitucionales.* Caracas: Colección "Pueblo y Parlamento," 1963.

Betancourt, Rómulo. *Con Quién Estamos y Contra Quién Estamos.* San José: n.p., 1932.

————. *Dos Años de Gobierno Democrático, 1959-61.* Caracas: Imprenta Nacional, 1961.

————. *Dos Meses en las Cárceles de Gómez.* Barranquilla: n.p., 1928.

————. *En las Huellas de la Pezuña.* Santo Domingo: n.p., 1929.

————. *Interpretación de su Doctrina Popular y Democrática.* Caracas: Editorial Suma, 1958.

————. *Posición y Doctrina.* Caracas: Editorial Cordillera, 1958.

————. *Problemas Venezolanos.* Santiago: Imprenta y Editorial Futuro, 1940.

————. *Rómulo Betancourt: Pensamiento y Acción.* México: n.p., 1951.

————. *Rómulo Betancourt: Semblanza de un Político Popular, 1928-1948.* Caracas: Ediciones Caribe, 1948.

————. *Trayectoria Democrática de una Revolución.* Caracas: Imprenta Nacional, 1948.

————. *Tres Años de Gobierno Democrática, 1959-1962.* 3 vols. Caracas: Imprenta Nacional, 1962.

————. *Una República en Venta.* Caracas: n.p., 1937.

————. *Venezuela; Política y Petróleo.* México: Fondo de Cultura Económica, 1956.

Gallegos, Rómulo. *Una Posición en la Vida.* México: Ediciones Humanismo, 1954.

Jatar Dotti, Braulio. *Inhabilitación de la Extrema Izquierda y Guerrillas Corianas.* Caracas: Colección "Pueblo y Parlamento," 1963.

Machín, José María. *Caudillismo y Democracia en América Latina*. México: Ediciones Humanismo, 1955.

Paz Galarraga, Jesús Angel. *Violencia y Suspensión de Garantías*. Caracas: Colección "Pueblo y Parlamento," 1963.

Pérez Alfonzo, Juan Pablo. *Petróleo; Jugo de la Tierra*. Caracas: Editorial Arte, 1961.

————. *Venezuela y su Petróleo; Lineamientos de una Política*. Caracas: Imprenta Nacional, 1960.

Prieto Figueroa, Luis Beltrán. *De una Educación de Castas o una Educación de Masas*. La Habana: Editorial Lex, 1951.

————. *El Concepto del Líder; El Maestro como Líder*. Caracas: Editorial Arte, 1960.

————. *El Humanismo Democrático y la Educación*. Caracas: Editorial Novedades, 1959.

Rangel, Domingo Alberto. *Una Teoría para la Revolución Democrática*. Caracas: Editorial Arte, 1958.

————. *Venezuela: País Ocupado*. Caracas: Pensamiento Vivo, 1960.

Rodríguez, Valmore. *Bayonetas sobre Venezuela*. México: Editores Beatriz de Silva, 1950.

————. *Los Caminos Inefables*. Maracaibo: Editorial Excelsior, 1925.

Ruiz Pineda, Leonardo. *Ventanas al Mundo*. Caracas: Editorial Arte, 1961.

Tejera París, Enrique. *Dos Elementos de Gobierno*. Caracas: Editora Grafos, 1960.

Troconis Guerrero, Luis. *La Cuestión Agraria en la Historia Nacional*. Caracas: Editorial Arte, 1962.

B. VENEZUELAN POLITICS AND HISTORY

Acevedo, Javier Pérez de. *Dos Años en Venezuela Bajo la Dictadura de Gómez; Impresiones y Recuerdos*. La Habana: Molina y Compañía, 1940.

Alexander, Robert J. *The Venezuelan Democratic Revolution*. New Brunswick: Rutgers, 1964.

Allen, Henry Justin. *Venezuela: A Democracy*. New York: Doubleday, Doran & Co., Inc., 1941.

Arcaya, Pedro Manuel. *Venezuela y su Actual Régimen*. Baltimore: The Dial Press, 1935.

Arellano Moreno, Antonio. *Guía de Historia de Venezuela, 1492-1945.* Caracas: Ediciones EDIME, 1955.

Baptista, Octavio. *Venezuela; Su Historia y sus Métodos de Gobierno.* Guadalajara: Talleres Linotipográfico "Grafica," 1942.

Baralt, Rafael María. *Resumen de la Historia de Venezuela.* Paris: Desclée de Brouwer, 1939.

Blanco Peñalver, Pedro Luis. *López Contreras ante la Historia.* Caracas: Tipografía Garrido, 1957.

Briceño-Iragorri, Mario. *Ideario Político.* Caracas: Editorial "Las Novedades," 1958.

————. *Mensaje sin Destino; Ensayo sobre Nuestra Crisis de Pueblo.* Caracas: Tipografía Americana, 1951.

————. *Sentido y Vigencia del 30 de Noviembre (Exámen Esquemático del Drama Electoral Venezolano).* Madrid: Ediciones Bitacora, 1953.

Caldera Rodríguez, Rafael. *Moldes para la Fragua.* Buenos Aires: Editorial Ateneo, 1962.

Christ, Raymond E. *Venezuela.* Garden City: Doubleday & Company, 1959.

Colmenares Díaz, Luis. *La Espada y el Incensario: la Iglesia bajo Pérez Jiménez.* Caracas: n.p., 1961.

Cova, Jesús Antonio. *Quinta y Sexta Columnas.* Caracas: Impresores Unidos, 1945.

Dávila, Antonio. *La Dictadura Venezolana.* Maracaibo: Tip. Criollo, 1954.

De Leeuw, Hendrik. *Crossroads of the Caribbean Sea.* New York: J. Messner, 1935.

Diez, Julio. *Historia y Política.* Caracas: Tipografía Vargas, 1963.

Domínguez Chacín, J. M. *El Partido Político; Estructura y Organización de Unión Republicana Democrática.* 2 vols. Caracas: n.p., 1961.

Feo Calcaño, Guillermo. *Democracia vs. Dictadura.* Caracas: n.p., 1963.

Fergusson, Erna. *Venezuela.* New York: Alfred A. Knopf, 1939.

Forero Manzano, Eloisa y Federico Alamo Fuentes. *Pérez Jiménez Explica su Caída.* Caracas: Editora Grafos, 1962.

Gabaldón Márquez, Joaquín. *Archivos de una Inquietud Venezolana.* Caracas: Ediciones EDIME, 1955.

Gallegos Ortiz, Rafael. *La Historia Política de Venezuela; de Cipriano Castro a Pérez Jiménez.* Caracas: Imprenta Universitaria, 1960.

Gil Fortoul, José. *Historia Constitucional de Venezuela.* Caracas: n.p., 1955.

Gilmore, Robert L. *Caudillism and Militarism in Venezuela.* Athens: Ohio University Press, 1964.

Iduarte, Andrés. *Veinte Años con Rómulo Gallegos.* México: Ediciones Humanismo, 1954.

Irazábal, Carlos. *Hacia la Democracia; Contribución al Estudio de la Historia Económico-Político-Social de Venezuela.* Caracas: Pensamiento Vivo, 1961.

Jankus, Alfred P., and Neil M. Malloy. *Venezuela; Land of Opportunity.* New York: Pageant Press, Inc., 1956.

Jones Parra, Juan. *Pocket Atlas of Venezuela.* Caracas: Miangolarra Hermanos, 1957.

León, Ramón David. *Hombres y Sucesos de Venezuela: La República desde José Antonio Páez hasta Rómulo Gallegos.* Caracas: Tipografía Americana, 1952.

Lavin, John. *A Halo for Gómez.* New York: Pageant Press, Inc., 1954.

Lieuwen, Edwin. *Venezuela.* London: Oxford University Press, 1961.

Liscano, Juan. *Rómulo Gallegos y su Tiempo.* Caracas: Biblioteca de Cultura Universitaria, 1961.

Lizardo, Cesar. *Espacio y Voz del Paisaje.* Caracas: Tipografía Garrido, 1954.

López Contreras, Eleazar. *El Triunfo de la Verdad; Documentos para la Historia Venezolana.* México: Edición Genio Latino, 1949.

————. *Páginas para la Historia Militar de Venezuela.* Caracas: n.p., 1945.

Lott, Leo B. "Venezuelan Federalism: A Case Study in Frustration." Madison: University of Wisconsin, unpublished Ph.D. dissertation, 1954.

Lugo, Francisco Aniceto. *Pérez Jiménez; Fuerza Creadora.* Caracas: Imprenta Nacional, 1954.

Luzardo, Rodolfo. *Notas Económico-Históricas*. Caracas: n.p., 1962.

Magallanes, Manuel Vicente. *Partidos Políticos Venezolanos*. Caracas: Tip. Vargas, 1960.

Márquez, Pompeyo. *Hacia Dónde Va el 23 de Enero?* Caracas: Pensamiento Vivo, 1959.

Marsland, William D., and Amy Marsland. *Venezuela Through its History*. New York: Thomas Y. Crowell Co., 1954.

Medina Angarita, Isaías. *Cuatro Años de Democracia*. Caracas: Pensamiento Vivo, 1963.

————. *La Nueva Lucha y la Acción Nueva; el Ideario Político del señor general Isaías Medina Angarita*. Caracas: Oficina Nacional de Prensa, 1943.

Oropesa, Juan. *4 Siglos de Historia Venezolana*. Caracas: Librería y Editorial del Maestro, 1947.

Osorio, Luis Enrique. *Democracia en Venezuela*. Bogotá: Editorial Litografía Colombia, 1943.

Parra, Francisco J. *Analectas: Compilación de Artículos y Documentos Políticos, Administrativos, Económicos y Financieros*. New York: Las Américas Publishing Company, 1958.

Peñalver, Juan Blanco. *Historia de un Naufragio*. Maracay: Editorial Nuestra América, 1962.

Pepper, José Vicente. *Fichas de Romulato*. Ciudad Trujillo: Editorial Montalvo, 1949.

————. *Reconstrucción Integral de Venezuela*. Valencia: Editorial "Aborigin," 1953.

Pérez, Ana Mercedes. *La Verdad Inédita*. Caracas: Editorial Artes Gráficas, 1947.

Pérez Jiménez, Marcos. *Pensamiento Político del Presidente de Venezuela*. Caracas: Imprenta Nacional, 1954.

Picón Lares, Eduardo. *Ideología Bolivariana*. Caracas: Editorial Crisol, c.a., 1944.

Picón Salas, Mariano. *1941; Cinco Discursos sobre Pasado y Presente de la Nación Venezolana*. Caracas: Editorial La Torre, 1941.

————. *Hora y Deshora*. Caracas: Editorial Vivo, 1963.

Planas Suárez, Simón. *Venezuela Soberana; Panamericanista no Regionalista*. Caracas: Tipografía Americana, 1954.

Plaza, Salvador de la. *Desarrollo Económico e Industrias Básicas.* Caracas: Universidad Central de Venezuela, 1963.

Pocaterra, José Rafael. *Gómez; Shame of America.* Paris: A. Delpeuch, 1929.

Quevedo, Numa. *El Gobierno Provisorio 1958.* Caracas: Ediciones Conjuntas Pensamiento Vivo, 1963.

————. *Política y Parlamento.* Caracas: Editorial "Las Novedades," 1951.

Quijada, Ramón. *Reforma Agraria en Venezuela.* Caracas: Editorial Arte, 1963.

Quintero, Rodolfo. *Elementos para la Sociología del Trabajo.* Caracas: Universidad Central de Venezuela, 1963.

————. *La Universidad y la Política.* Caracas: Universidad Central de Venezuela, 1961.

Rivas Rivas, José (ed.). *Compilación y Fotógrafos de la Vida Venezolana; de Gómez a Betancourt.* 4 vols. Caracas: Historia Gráfica de Venezuela, 1962-63.

Rodríguez, José (ed.). *Quién Derrocó a Gallegos?* Caracas: Tip. Garrido, 2d ed., 1961.

Rondón Lovera, César. *Problemas Políticos de Venezuela.* Caracas: n.p., 1963.

Rourke, Thomas. *Gómez; Tyrant of the Andes.* Garden City: Halcyon House, 1936.

Russell, William Richard. *The Bolivar Countries: Colombia, Ecuador, Venezuela.* New York: Coward-McCann, 1949.

Serxner, Stanley J. *Acción Democrática of Venezuela; Its Origins and Development.* Gainesville: University of Florida Press, 1959.

Siso Martínez, J. M. *Historia de Venezuela.* México: Servicio Impreso, 1954.

Tarnói, Ladislao. *El Nuevo Ideal Nacional de Venezuela; Vida y Obra de Marcos Pérez Jiménez.* Madrid: Ediciones Verdad, 1954.

Umaña Bernal, José. *Testimonios de la Revolución en Venezuela.* Caracas: Tip. Vargas, 1958.

Uslar Pietri, Arturo. *La Universidad y el País.* Caracas: Universidad Central de Venezuela, 1962.

————. *Venezuela; Un País en Transformación.* Caracas: Tip. Italiana, 195?.

Vallenilla Lanz, Laureano. *Cesarismo Democrático.* Caracas: Imprenta Garrido, 3d ed., 1952.

Ward, Edward. *The New El Dorado: Venezuela*. London: Robert Hale, Ltd., 1957.

Watters, Mary. *A History of the Church in Venezuela*. Chapel Hill: The University of North Carolina Press, 1933.

Wohlrabe, Raymond A. *The Land and People of Venezuela*. Philadelphia: Lippincott, 1959.

C. VENEZUELAN ECONOMY AND SOCIETY

Arcaya, Pedro Manuel. *Estudios de Sociología Venezolana*. Madrid: Editorial América, n.d.

Arraíz, Antonio. *Geografía Económica de Venezuela*. Caracas: Cultural Venezolana, 1956.

Bolívar Coronado, Rafael. *El Llanero; Ensayo de Sociología Venezolana, con un Estudio sobre el Gaucho y el Llanero*. Buenos Aires: Editorial Venezuela, 1947.

Caldera Rodríguez, Rafael. *Idea de una Sociología Venezolana*. Caracas: Alma Mater, Librería y Editorial, 1954.

Carrillo Batalla, Tomás Enrique. *La Economía del Comercio Internacional de Venezuela*. Caracas: Editorial Mundo Económico, 1963.

Dil Espejo, Pedro José. *Ideas Sociales; Esquema sobre el Origen, Desarrollo y Soluciones de la Cuestión Social*. Caracas: Universidad de Caracas, 1958.

Falcón Urbano, Miguel A. *Nuestro Petróleo; Riqueza Instrumental del Desarrollo Venezolano*. Caracas: Editora Didascalia, S. A., 1962.

Fernández y Fernández, Ramón. *Reforma Agraria en Venezuela*. Caracas: n.p., 1948.

González C., Ricardo. *La C. V. F. y su Doctrina Económica*. Caracas: Imprenta Nacional, 1956.

Hill, George William, and Ruth Oliver Hill. *Some Social and Economic Bases for Immigration and Land Settlement in Venezuela*. Caracas: n.p., 1945.

Inter-American Regional Organization of Workers of the ICFTU. *El Movimiento Democrático Internacional contra la Dictadura Venezolana*. México: n.p., 1955.

International Labour Office. *Freedom of Association and Conditions of Work in Venezuela*. Geneva: International Labour Office, 1950.

León, Ramón David. *De Agro-pecuario a Petróleo*. Caracas: Tipografía Garrido, 1944.

Lieuwen, Edwin. *Petroleum in Venezuela; A History*. Berkeley: University of California Press, 1954.

Maza Zavala, Domingo Felipe. *Paradojas Venezolanas: Crónicas de Economía y Angustia Social*. Caracas: n.p., 1959.

Plaza, Salvador. *Estructuras de Integración Nacional*. Caracas: Pensamiento Vivo, 1959.

Prieto Soto, Jesús. *El Chorro: Gracia o Maldición*. Madrid. Industrias Gráficas España, 1960.

Siso, Carlos. *La Formación del Pueblo Venezolano; Estudios Sociológicos*. Madrid: García Enciso, 1955.

Uslar Pietri, Arturo. *Sumario de Economía Venezolana*. Caracas: Academía de Ciencias Políticas y Sociales, 2d ed., 1958.

D. LATIN AMERICAN POLITICS

Alexander, Robert J. *Communism in Latin America*. New Brunswick: Rutgers University Press, 1957.

————. *Labor Movements of Latin America*. New York: League for Industrial Democracy, 1947.

Gomez, Rosendo A. *Government and Politics in Latin America*. New York: Random House, 2d ed., 1963.

Hanson, Simon G. *Economic Development in Latin America*. Washington: Inter-American Press, 1951.

Herring, Hubert. *A History of Latin America*. New York: Alfred A. Knopf, Inc., 2d ed., 1961.

James, Preston E. *Latin America*. New York: Odyssey Press, 2d ed., 1959.

Jorrin, Miguel. *Governments of Latin America*. New York: D. Van Nostrand Co., Inc., 1953.

Lieuwen, Edwin. *Arms and Politics in Latin America*. New York: Frederick A. Praeger, Inc., 2d ed., 1962.

Pierson, William Whatley, and Federico Guillermo Gil. *Governments of Latin America*. New York: McGraw-Hill Book Company, Inc., 1957.

Poblete Troncoso, Moisés, and Ben G. Burnett. *The Rise of the Latin American Labor Movement*. New York: Bookman Associates, 1960.

Silvert, Kalman H. *The Conflict Society: Reaction and Revolution in Latin America.* New Orleans: The Hauser Press, 1961.

Szulc, Tad. *Twilight of the Tyrants.* New York: Henry Holt and Company, 1959.

Whitaker, Arthur Preston. *The United States and South America; The Northern Republics.* Cambridge: Harvard University Press, 1948.

## II. DOCUMENTS AND PAMPHLETS

### A. WRITINGS OF ACCIÓN DEMOCRÁTICA

Acción Democrática. *A. D. y la Lucha por Libertad.* One-page leaflet signed by Comité Ejecutivo Nacional, 1951.

————. *Acción Democrática ante la Ley de Hidrocárburos.* Caracas: Editora Futuro, 1943.

————. *Acción Democrática contra Maniobra Anti-Nacional Monstrua.* One-page leaflet signed by Comité Ejecutivo Nacional, 1951.

————. *Acción Democrática en el Debate Económico.* Caracas: Secretaría Nacional de Propaganda, September 1961.

————. *A La Rebelión Civil Llama Acción Democrática.* Six-page leaflet signed by Alberto Carnevali, 1952.

————. *Ante la Farsa Electoral.* Mimeographed sheet signed by Comité Ejecutivo Nacional, 1952.

————. *Bases Programáticas.* Caracas: Editorial "Antonio Pinto Salinas," 1958.

————. *Batalla por el Nombre y Símbolos de Acción Democrática.* Caracas: Secretaría Nacional de Propaganda, 1963.

————. *Cartas de los Presos Políticos y otros Documentos.* Caracas: n.p., 1951.

————. *Declaración del Comité Ejecutivo Nacional.* Three-page leaflet signed by Leonardo Ruiz Pineda, 1952.

————. *Discurso Programa de Gobierno de Raúl Leoni.* Caracas: Secretaría Nacional de Propaganda, 1963.

————. *Disección del Presupuesto de la Dictadura Militar.* Caracas: n.p., 1950.

——. *Informe sobre Actividades de la "Quinta Columna"
en Venezuela.* Caracas: Lit. y Tip. Vargas, 1942.

——. *La Caída de la Dictadura.* One-page leaflet signed
by Eligio Anzola Anzola, 1953.

——. *La Cartilla del Militante.* Caracas: Secretaría
Nacional de Propaganda, 1961.

——. *La Juventud de Acción Democrática y las Pasadas
Elecciones Universitaria.* Puerto La Cruz: Tipografía
Peñalver, 1961.

——. *La Voz de la Resistencia.* Four-page leaflet signed
by Leonardo Ruiz Pineda, 1951.

——. *Pacto Suscrito el 31 de Octubre de 1958 y Declaración de Princípios y Programa Mínimo de Gobierno de
los Candidatos a la Presidencia de la República en la
Elección del Día 7 de Diciembre de 1958.* La Nación,
1958.

——. *Ratificación de Principios Teóricos y de Orientación Programática Normativos de Acción Democrática.*
Caracas: Secretaría Nacional de Prensa y Propaganda,
1958.

——. *Tesis Agraria.* Caracas: Editorial "Antonio Pinto
Salinas," 1958.

——. *Tesis Educativa.* Caracas: Editorial "Antonio Pinto
Salinas," 1958.

——. *Tesis Organizativa y Estatutos.* Caracas: Editorial
"Antonio Pinto Salinas," 1958.

——. *Tesis Petrolera.* Caracas: Editorial "Antonio Pinto
Salinas," 1958.

——. *Tesis Política.* Caracas: n.p., 1962.

——. *Tesis Sindical.* Caracas: Editorial "Antonio Pinto
Salinas," 1958.

——. *Venezuela Bajo el Signo del Terror; Libro Negro
de la Dictadura.* México: Editorial Centauro, 1953.

Barrios, Gonzalo. *AD, el Partido Comunista y el Banco In-
teramericano.* Caracas: Secretaría Nacional de Propaganda,
March 1960.

——. *Bloque de Abril.* Caracas: Lit. y Tip. Vargas, 1936.

Gallegos, Rómulo. *La Libertad y la Cultura.* Caracas: Secretaría Juvenil de Acción Democrática, 1958.

——. *Yo Invito a Serenidad y a Reflexión.* Caracas: Secretaría Nacional de Propaganda, April 1960.

Leoni, Raúl. *Mensaje de Fé y Disciplina.* Caracas: Secretaría Nacional de Propaganda, May 1960.

Muñoz, Guillermo. *El Presente Malestar de Venezuela; Un Fenómeno Estructural.* Secretaría Nacional de Propaganda, October 1960.

————. *La Economía Nacional y el Mensaje del Presidente Betancourt.* Caracas: Secretaría Nacional de Propaganda, May 1961.

————. *La Economía Nacional y Las Medidas de Urgencia.* Caracas: Secretaría Nacional de Propaganda, June 1961.

Paz Galarraga, Jesús. *Doctrina de Acción Democrática y su Estrategia en la Transición.* Caracas: Ediciones "Leonardo Ruiz Pineda," March 1961.

————. *Hay Dos Conspiraciones en Venezuela?* Caracas: Secretaría Nacional de Propaganda, August 1960.

————. *Un Reto a la Dictadura.* Maracaibo: n.p., 195?.

Prieto Figueroa, Luis Beltrán. *Antonio Pinto Salinas; Militante y Poeta.* Caracas: Editorial Arte, 1962.

————. *Tareas para la Juventud.* Caracas: Secretaría Nacional de Propaganda, 1962.

Ramos Giménez, Raúl. *La XI Convención Nacional.* Caracas: Ediciones "Leonardo Ruiz Pineda," May 1960.

Rodríguez, Manuel Alfredo. *La Universidad y el Régimen Democrático.* Caracas: Secretaría Nacional de Propaganda, December 1960.

————. *Política y Universidad.* Caracas: Ediciones "La Estrella en la Mira," 1960.

Venezuela, Junta Revolucionaria de Gobierno. *El Gobierno Revolucionario de Venezuela ante su Pueblo.* Caracas: Imprenta Nacional, 1946.

————. *La Revolución Venezolana ante la Opinión de América.* Caracas: Imprenta Nacional, 1946.

————. *Leyes y Estatutos. Decretos y Resoluciones de la Junta Revolucionaria de Gobierno.* Caracas: Imprenta Nacional, 1945-46.

## B. Venezuelan Politics

Calcaño, Antonio Simón. *Recuerdos del Sufragio (Crónica Electoral).* Caracas: Cooperativa de Artes Gráficas, 1937.

426 BIBLIOGRAPHY

Caldera Rodríguez, Rafael. *Libertad y Democracia; Su Vigencia y Proyección Social.* Caracas: Imprenta Nacional, 1960.

Confederación de Trabajadores de Venezuela. *Estatutos.* Caracas: Publicaciones de la C. T. V., 1962.

———. *Federaciones Nacionales.* Caracas: Imprenta de la C. T. V., 1962.

———. *Recopilación de Informes, Acuerdos, Resoluciones y Recomendaciones; III Congreso de Trabajadores de Venezuela.* Caracas: Imprenta Nacional, 1960.

Copei. *Copei Frente al Estatuto Electoral y la Actual Situación Política.* Caracas: Avila Gráfica, s.a., 1951.

Corporación Venezolana de Fomento. *Obras de la Corporación Venezolana de Fomento, 24 de Noviembre de 1948 a 2 de Diciembre de 1953.* Caracas: Editorial Bellas Artes, 1953.

*Debate Caldera-Uslar Pietri; Texto Completo del Debate por Television el 22/10/63.* Caracas: 1963.

Dominican Republic, Secretaría de Relaciones Exteriores. *Libro Blanco (Contiene una Declaración de la Cancillería Dominicana Provocada por los Recientes Ataques del sr. Rómulo Betancourt contra el Gobierno y el Pueblo Dominicanos.* Ciudad Trujillo: Prensa Nacional, 1946.

Federación Campesina de Venezuela. *La Cuestión Agraria Venezolana; Tesis Política y Programática de la Federación Campesina de Venezuela.* Caracas: Tipografía Americana, 1948.

Ferrer, Diego Bautista. *Con Jóvito Villalba, por Edmundo Chispa* (pseud.) Caracas: Editorial Atlantida, 1940.

González Navarro, José. *Discursos del Presidente de la C. T. V.* Caracas: Litografía Barcelona, 1960.

———. *Discursos del Presidente de la Confederación de Trabajadores de Venezuela.* Caracas: Publicaciones de la C. T. V., 1961.

Movimiento Electoral Nacional Independiente. *Normas para la Orientación Organizativa del Comité "Catuche" pro candidatura del Contralmirante Wolfgang Larrazábal, a la Presidencia Constitucional de la República.* Caracas: n.p., 1958.

Movimiento Republicano Progresista. *Manifiesto Constitutivo del Movimiento Republicano Progresista (MRP)*. Caracas: Secretaría Nacional de Prensa y Propaganda, 1961.

Partido Comunista Venezolano. *II Congreso del Partido Comunista, 1948*. Caracas: n.p., 1948.

————. *Construyendo Partido*. Caracas: n.p., 1949.

————. *Homenaje Revolucionario a los Fundadores de la Primera Célula Comunista en el Estado Lara (1934-1948)*. Caracas: n.p., 1948.

————. *La Actuación de los Partidos; la Farsa Electoral*. Caracas: n.p., 1952.

————. *La Crisis que nos Amenaza; Un Programa de Cuadernos de Capacitación Política Salvación Nacional*. Caracas: n.p., 1958.

————. *La Vida Revolucionaria de Gustavo Machado*. Caracas: E.T.C.A., 1946.

Partido Demócrata Venezolano. *El "Partido Demócrata Venezolano" y su Proceso (Documentos)*. Caracas: Editorial Elite, 1938.

Partido Democrático Venezolano. *La Libertad Económica y la Intervención del Estado*. Caracas: Tip. La Nación, 1945.

————. *Proyecto de Bases y Estatutos del Partido Democrático Venezolano*. Trujillo: n.p., 1943.

Silva Tellería, Ernesto. *Venezuela; República Democrática?; Proyecciones sobre la Constitucionalidad Venezolana*. Caracas: Editorial Bolívar, 1936.

Unión Republicana Democrática. *La Dirección Nacional Estudiantil de Juventud Urredista al Estudiantado Universitario*. Mérida: n.p., 1962.

————. *URD y la Revolución Cubana*. Caracas: Editorial Doctrina, 1961.

United States, Bureau of Foreign and Domestic Commerce. *Investment in Venezuela; Conditions in Venezuela*. Washington: U.S. Department of Commerce, 1953.

————, Department of Labor. *Labor Law and Practice in Venezuela*. Washington: U.S. Government Printing Office, 1961.

————, Department of State. *Venezuela; Oil Transforms a Nation*. Washington: U.S. Government Printing Office, 1949.

Venezuela, Asamblea Nacional Constituyente, 1946-48, Comisión Permanente. *Diario de Debates*, 24 nov. 1947–3 feb. 1948. Caracas: Imprenta Nacional, 1947-48.

———. Congreso Nacional, Cámara del Senado y Cámara de Diputados, *Diario de Debates; Recopilación*. Caracas: Imprenta Nacional, 1952 and after.

———. Consejo Supremo Electoral. *Procedimiento para Efectuar la Votación el 15 de Diciembre de 1957*. Caracas: Imprenta Nacional, 1957.

———. *Resultado de la Votaciones Efectuadas el 7 de Diciembre de 1958*. Caracas: Estadística del C. S. E., 1959.

———. *Síntesis de las Labores Realizadas por el Consejo Supremo Electoral desde el 7 de Noviembre de 1936 hasta el 28 de Febrero de 1937, o sea, durante la Formación del Censo Electoral en la República*. Caracas: Imprenta Nacional, 1937.

———. Constitution. *Constitución de 5 julio de 1947*. Caracas: Imprenta Nacional, 1947.

———. *Constitución de 23 enero de 1961*. Caracas: Imprenta Nacional, 1961.

———. Dirección Nacional de Información. *Venezuela; Expresiones del Nuevo Ideal Nacional*. Caracas: Imprenta Nacional, 1953.

———. Leyes y Estatutos. *Compilación Legislativa de Venezuela, 1946*. Caracas: Imprenta Nacional, 1947.

———. *Decretos de Garantías y Estatuto Electoral. Conforme a Publicación Hecha en la Gaceta Oficial de Los Estados Unidos de Venezuela no. 169 Extraordinario, del 15 de marzo de 1946*. Caracas: Editorial Tamanaco, c.a., 1946.

———. *Estatuto Electoral, 1947 (Copia Fotostática de la Gaceta Oficial Número 199 Extraordinario, Fecha 19 de septiembre de 1947)*. Caracas: Editorial "Almeda Cedillo," 1947.

———. *Estatuto para la Elección de Representantes a la Asamblea Nacional Constituyente y Garantías ciudadanas, Acordadas por el Gobierno Revolucionario*. Caracas: Imprenta Nacional, 1946.

———. *Gobierno y Nacion Defienden en Venezuela el Régimen Democrático; Actos contra el Terrorismo Comu-*

*nista.* Caracas: Publicaciones de la Secretaría de la Presidencia de la República, 1964.

————. *Ley de Censo Electoral y de Elecciones.* Caracas: Edición Oficial, Imprenta Nacional, 1936.

————. *Ley de Censo Electoral y de Elecciones.* Caracas: Edición Oficial, Imprenta Nacional, 1941.

————. Ministerio de la Defensa. *La Agresión a Mansalva.* Caracas: n.p., 1963.

————. *Nuevo Estatuto Electoral de Venezuela.* Bogotá: Publicaciones de la Embajada de los Estados Unidos de Venezuela en Colombia, 1950.

————. Oficina Nacional de Información y Publicaciones. *Documentos Oficiales Relativos al Movimiento Militar de 24 de noviembre de 1948.* Caracas: Imprenta Nacional, 1949.

————. Presidencia de la República. *Documentos que Hicieron Historia; Siglo y Medio de Vida Republicana, 1810-1961.* 2 vols. Caracas: Ediciones Conmemorativas del Sesquicentenario de la Independencia, 1962.

————. Servicio Informativo. *Venezuela Bajo el Nuevo Ideal Nacional: Realizaciones durante el Año de Gobierno del General Marcos Pérez Jiménez.* Caracas: Imprenta Nacional, 1954.

————. *Victoria Democrática en Venezuela.* Caracas: Publicaciones de la Secretaría de la Presidencia de la República, 1964.

Villalba, Jóvito. *Continuismo? Autocracia? No! Democracia (Prólogo Andrés Eloy Blanco).* Caracas: n.p., 1941.

Wolf, Ernesto. *Tratado de Derecho Constitucional Venezolano.* 2 vols. Caracas: Imprenta Garrido, 1945.

## III. SIGNED ARTICLES

### A. WRITINGS OF ACCIÓN DEMOCRÁTICA

Betancourt, Rómulo. "A Dónde Va Venezuela?" *Cuadernos Americanos*, XV, noviembre-diciembre 1956, 7-37.

————. "América no Puede Vivir sin Justicia y sin Libertad," *Repertorio Americano*, XXIX, noviembre 1948, 209-15.

————. "Comunidad Interamericana sin Dictaduras," *Combate*, II, no. 11, julio-agosto 1960, 7-9.

Betancourt, Rómulo. "Evolución Histórica de Venezuela," *Boletín de la Unión Panamericana*, LXXX, julio 1946, 376-82.

———. "La Opinión Continental Frente a la X Conferencia Interamericana," *Cuadernos Americanos*, XII, septiembre-octubre 1953, 7-36.

———. "Panorama in Somber Colors," *The Nation*, CLXIX, July 30, 1949, 101-04.

———. "The Venezuelan Miracle," *The Reporter*, August 13, 1964, 37-41.

Blanco, Andrés Eloy. "Denuncia ante los Soldados de América," *Bohemia*, 15 agosto 1949, 17-22.

Lander, Luis. "La Doctrina Venezolana de Acción Democrática," *Cuadernos Americanos*, IX, julio-agosto 1950, 20-39.

Leoni, Raúl. "View from Caracas," *Foreign Affairs*, XLIII, no. 3, July 1965, 639-47.

Prieto Figueroa, Luis Beltrán. "Inmunidades Parlamentarias," *Política*, no. 16, enero 1961.

———. "Juicio y Prejuicios sobre la Política y los Políticos," *Política*, I, septiembre 1959, 48-66.

Rangel, Domingo Alberto. "Explicación Histórica de la Revolución Venezolana," *Cuadernos Americanos*, VI, mayo-junio 1947, 7-20.


B. VENEZUELAN POLITICS

Alexander, Robert J. "Betancourt on Venezuela," *American Economic Review*, XLVII, no. 6, December 1957, 1024-26.

———. "Democracy Dawns in Venezuela," *Canadian Forum*, XXVIII, no. 331, August 1948, 103-04.

Alvarez, Gonzalo. "487 Delegados en una Maratón de Elogios," *Momento*, no. 117, 10 de octubre 1958, 26-33.

Arbiza, R. "Gumersindo Rodríguez, El Ortodoxo," *Momento*, no. 285, 31 de diciembre 1961, 10-12, 14, 24.

Beatty, W. Donald. "Venezuela: A New Era," *Current History*. XXXVIII, no. 223, March 1960, 144-49.

———. "Venezuela: Rich Abroad—Poor at Home," *Current History*, XXIV, no. 139, March 1953, 149-55.

Caldera, Rafael. "The Christian Democratic Idea," *America*, CVII, no. 1, April 7, 1962, 12-16.

———. "Venezuela on Election Eve," *Commonwealth*, XLIV, October 4, 1946, 590-92.

————. "Una Nueva Constitución para Venezuela," *Política*, no. 2, octubre 1959, 38-50.

Cusack, Thomasine. "A Reappraisal of the Record of Venezuela, 1939-1959," *Journal of Inter-American Studies*, III, no. 4, October 1961, 477-96.

Espina, Alberto. "Los Cinco Hombres Claves de Acción Democrática," *Momento*, no. 105, 18 de julio, 1958, 48-53.

Griffin, Charles C. "Regionalism's Role in Venezuelan Politics," *The Inter-American Quarterly*, III, no. 4, October 1941, 21-35.

Haubert, C. A. "Venezuela under Betancourt," *Current History*, XL, no. 236, April 1961, 232-40.

Holmes, Olive. "Army Challenge in Latin America," *Foreign Policy Reports*, XXV, December 1949, 166-75.

Kantor, Harry. "The Development of Acción Democrática de Venezuela," *Journal of Inter-American Affairs*, I, no. 2, April 1959, 237-55.

————. "The Development of a Democratic Venezuela," *Vital Speeches of the Day*, XXVI, no. 4, December 1, 1959, 102-05.

Lear, John. "The Surprised Democracy," *Saturday Evening Post*, CCXVII, March 31, 1945, 14-15, 74, 76.

Lott, Leo B. "Executive Power in Venezuela," *American Political Science Review*, L, no. 2, June 1956, 422-41.

————. "The Nationalization of Justice in Venezuela," *Inter-American Economic Affairs*, XIII, no. 1, Summer 1959, 3-19.

————. "The 1952 Venezuelan Elections: A Lesson for 1957," *Western Political Quarterly*, X, no. 3, September 1957, 541-58.

Martz, John D. "The Growth and Democratization of the Venezuelan Labor Movement," *Inter-American Economic Affairs*, XVII, no. 2, Autumn 1963, 3-18.

————. "Dilemmas in the Study of Latin American Political Parties," *Journal of Politics*, XXVI, no. 3, August 1964.

————. *The Venezuelan Elections of 1963*. Washington: 1964.

————. "Venezuela's 'Generation of '28': The Genesis of Political Democracy," *Journal of Inter-American Studies*, VI, no. 1, January 1964, 17-33.

Matthews, Herbert L. "New Era in Venezuela," *Foreign Policy Bulletin*, XXXVII, no. 12, March 1, 1958, 89-90, 96.

Pedrozo, Ciro. "El Proceso Electoral de 1963," *La Esfera*, 21-23 de octubre 1962.

Rangel, Carlos. "Las Elecciones 1963," *Momento*, no. 324, 30 de septiembre 1962, 36-39.

Rivas, Lolita. "U.R.D.: Un Partido en Crisis," *Elite*, no. 1934, 20 de octubre 1962, 32-33.

Rodríguez, Enrique. "El 'affaire' Quijada," *Momento*, no. 273, 8 de octubre 1961, 26-29.

Romualdi, Serafino. "Venezuela Crushes Labor," *American Federationist*, LIX, no. 2, February 1952, 23-24, 30.

Shapiro, Samuel. "Betancourt's Venezuela: Alternative to Castroism?" *Commentary*, XXXI, no. 6, June 1961, 479-85.

Stucki, Lorenzo. "Venezuela's Alternative to Castroism," *Atlas*, II, no. 1, July 1961, 22-26.

Szulc, Tad. "New Era in Venezuela," *Foreign Policy Bulletin*, XXXVIII, no. 14, April 1, 1959, 109-11.

Uslar Pietri, Arturo. "Venezuela's Position Vis-à-Vis the United States," *Vital Speeches of the Day*, XXVI, no. 10, March 1, 1960, 295-99.

Villamizar, Marconi. "En Torno a Wolfgang," *Momento*, no. 334, 9 de diciembre 1962, 28-30, 33.

C. LATIN AMERICAN POLITICS

Aikman, Duncan. "New Political Leaders of Latin America," *United Nations World*, I, no. 4, May 1947, 37-38.

Alexander, Robert J. "The Latin American Aprista Parties," *Political Quarterly*, XX, no. 3, July-September 1949, 236-47.

Blanksten, George. "Political Groups in Latin America," *American Political Science Review*, LIII, no. 1, March 1959, 106-27.

Fitzgibbon, Russell H. "The Party Potpourri in Latin America," *Western Political Quarterly*, X, no. 1, March 1957, 3-22.

Gil, Federico G. "Responsible Parties in Latin America," *Journal of Politics*, XV, no. 3, August 1953, 333-48.

Gómez, Rosendo A. "Latin American Executives: Essence and Variations," *Journal of Inter-American Studies*, III, no. 1, January 1961, 81-95.

Silvert, Kalman H. "Political Change in Latin America," from The American Assembly, *The United States and Latin America*. New York: Columbia University Press, December 1959, 59-80.

Stokes, William Sylvane. "Violence as a Power Factor in Latin-American Politics," *Western Political Quarterly*, V, no. 3, September 1952, 445-68.

Tannenbaum, Frank. "The Political Dilemma in Latin America," *Foreign Affairs*, XXXVIII, no. 3, April 1960, 497-515.

## IV. SPEECHES

Betancourt, Rómulo. *Aniversario de la Revolución*. Caracas: Imprenta Nacional, 1946.

———. *Ante las Perspectivas de un Nuevo Año; Visión Realista en el Mensaje Presidencial*. Caracas: Imprenta Nacional, 1960.

———. *Discurso Radiado por el sr. Rómulo Betancourt, Presidente de la Junta Revolucionaria de Gobierno de los Estados Unidos de Venezuela el Día 30 de Octubre de 1945*. Caracas: Editorial Elite, 1945.

———. *El Presidente de la República ante el Congreso Nacional*. Caracas: Imprenta Nacional, 1960.

———. *Hour of Decision*. Caracas: Imprenta Nacional, 1961.

———. *Lo que el Dirigente Político Venezolano Rómulo Betancourt Dijo en la Inauguración del Sexto Congreso Socialista*. Santiago: Departamento de Publicaciones del Partido Socialista Chilena, 1940.

———. *Lo Sostiene el Pueblo*. Caracas: Imprenta Nacional, 1962.

———. *Mensaje del Día del Obrero Dirigido a la Nación en Nombre de la Junta Revolucionaria de Gobierno, por su Presidente, Ciudadano Rómulo Betancourt*. Caracas: Imprenta Nacional, 1947.

———. *Mensaje del Presidente ante el Congreso Nacional*. Caracas: Imprenta Nacional, 1961.

Betancourt, Rómulo. *Mensaje Especial Dirigido a la Nación con Motivo del Año Nuevo, en Nombre de la Junta Revolucionaria de Gobierno por su Presidente, 1948.* Caracas: Imprenta Nacional, 1948.

————. *IV Mensaje Presidencial (12 de marzo de 1962).* Caracas: Imprenta Nacional, 1962.

————. *On the Right Road Toward the Economic Recovery of the Country.* Caracas: Imprenta Nacional, 1960.

————. *Política Educacional; Conferencia y Discursos Pronunciados por Rómulo Betancourt durante el Ejercicio de sus Funciones de Presidente del Ejecutivo Colegiado.* Caracas: Imprenta Nacional, 1947.

————. *Se Reafirma la Fé en la Coalición.* Caracas: Imprenta Nacional, 1959.

————. *What Should the United States Do for Latin America?* Caracas: Imprenta Nacional, 1960.

————. *Will at the Service of the Nation.* Caracas: Imprenta Nacional, 1960.

Caldera, Rafael. *La Idea de Justicia Social Internacional y el Bloque Latinoamericano.* Caracas: Editorial Sucre, 1962.

Falcón Briceño, Marcos, *Cancilleres en Punta del Este— Posición de Venezuela.* Caracas: Imprenta Nacional, 1962.

————. *Voz de Venezuela en las Naciones Unidas.* Caracas: Imprenta Nacional, 1961.

Larrazábal, Carlos. *Bien Definida Posición.* Caracas: Imprenta Nacional, 1960.

Mayobre, José Antonio. *The Economic Realities of Latin America.* Caracas: Imprenta Nacional, 1960.

Pérez Jiménez, Marcos. *Discursos Pronunciados . . . con Motivo del Décimo Aniversario del 18 de Octubre de 1945.* Caracas: Oficina de Prensa, 1955.

Rodríguez, Valmore. *Discurso Radiado por el sr. Valmore Rodríguez, Encargado del Ministerio de Relaciones Interiores, el Día 1 de Diciembre de 1945 por los Micrófonos de la Radio Nacional, en Cadena con la Totalidad de las Emisoras Comerciales de la República.* Caracas: Editorial Elite, 1945.

Venezuela, Junta Revolucionaria de Gobierno. *Discursos de Rómulo Betancourt, Presidente de la Junta Revolucionaria de Gobierno y del Mayor Mario R. Vargas, Miembro*

de la misma Junta y Encargado del Ministerio de Com-
unicaciones, Pronunciados en los Estados Zulia y Falcón.
Caracas: Imprenta Nacional, 1946.

————. Jiras de Integración Nacional; Discursos de Rómulo
Betancourt, Presidente de la Junta Revolucionaria del
Gobierno y del Mayor Carlos Delgado Chalbaud, Miembro
de la Misma Junta y Encargado del Ministerio de Guerra
y Marina, en los Estados Yaracuy y Carabobo. Caracas:
Imprenta Nacional, 1946.

————. Mensaje de la Junta Revolucionaria de Gobierno,
Presentado por su Presidente, Ciudadano Rómulo Betan-
court, a la Asamblea Nacional Constituyente. Caracas:
Imprenta Nacional, 1947.

## V. PERIODICALS

### A. Party Publications

| | | |
|---|---|---|
| *A.D.* | 1958-64 | Acción Democrática<br>weekly |
| *A.D.* | 1962-63 | AD-ARS weekly |
| *Acción<br>Democrática* | 1942-48 | Acción Democrática<br>weekly |
| *Copei* | 1959-64 | COPEI weekly |
| *El Gráfico* | 1947-50 | COPEI |
| *El Popular* | 1936-37 | Communist (PRP) |
| *Informaciones<br>Venezolanas* | mid-50's | Occasional AD clandes-<br>tine bulletin |
| *Izquierdas* | 1937-39 | Occasional PDN clandes-<br>tine bulletin |
| *Jornada* | 1962-64 | CTV weekly |
| *Orve* | 1936-37 | ORVE weekly |
| *Semana* | 1962-63 | AVI semi-weekly |
| *UNR* | 1936 | UNR weekly |
| *URD* | 1961-63 | Occasional URD paper |
| *Venezuela<br>Democrática* | 1955-57 | Occasional AD clandes-<br>tine publication |

### B. Caracas Dailies

| | | |
|---|---|---|
| *Ahora* | 1936-37,<br>1941-45 | Pro-PDN and AD |

| *El Clarín* | 1959-64 | Pro-URD |
| *El Nacional* | 1943-64 | Independent |
| *El País* | 1944-48 | Pro-AD |
| *El Universal* | 1943-64 | Independent |
| *La Esfera* | 1937-41,<br>1958-64 | Independent,<br>conservative |
| *La República* | 1961-64 | Pro-AD |

C. MISCELLANEOUS

*Elite* (Caracas)  
*Gaceta Oficial* (Caracas)  
*Hispanic American Report*  
(Stanford)

*The New York Times*  
*Visión*  
*Washington Post & Times-*  
*Herald*

# Index

WIDENER UNIVERSITY
WOLFGRAM
LIBRARY
CHESTER, PA